Migration, Minorities and Citizenship

General Editors: Zig Layton-Henry, Professor of Politics, University of Warwick; and Danièle Joly, Professor, Director, Centre for Research in Ethnic Relations, University of Warwick

Titles include:

Muhammad Anwar, Patrick Roach and Ranjit Sondhi (*editors*)
FROM LEGISLATION TO INTEGRATION?
Race Relations in Britain

James A. Beckford, Danièle Joly and Farhad Khosrokhavar
MUSLIMS IN PRISON
Challenge and Change in Britain and France

Sophie Body-Gendrot and Marco Martiniello (*editors*)
MINORITIES IN EUROPEAN CITIES
The Dynamics of Social Integration and Social Exclusion at the
Neighbourhood Level

Malcolm Cross and Robert Moore (*editors*)
GLOBALIZATION AND THE NEW CITY
Migrants, Minorities and Urban Transformations in Comparative Perspective

Adrian Favell
PHILOSOPHIES OF INTEGRATION
Immigration and the Idea of Citizenship in France and Britain

Agata Górny and Paolo Ruspini (*editors*)
MIGRATION IN THE NEW EUROPE
East-West Revisited

James Hampshire
CITIZENSHIP AND BELONGING
Immigration and the Politics of Democratic Governance in Postwar Britain

Simon Holdaway and Anne-Marie Barron
RESIGNERS? THE EXPERIENCE OF BLACK AND ASIAN POLICE OFFICERS

Danièle Joly (*editor*)
GLOBAL CHANGES IN ASYLUM REGIMES
Closing Doors
HAVEN OR HELL?
Asylum Policies and Refugees in Europe

SCAPEGOATS AND SOCIAL ACTORS
The Exclusion and Integration of Minorities in Western and Eastern Europe

Christian Joppke and Ewa Morawska
TOWARD ASSIMILATION AND CITIZENSHIP
Immigrants in Liberal Nation-States

Atsushi Kondo (*editor*)
CITIZENSHIP IN A GLOBAL WORLD
Comparing Citizenship Rights for Aliens

Zig Layton-Henry and Czarina Wilpert (*editors*)
CHALLENGING RACISM IN BRITAIN AND GERMANY

Jørgen S. Nielsen
TOWARDS A EUROPEAN ISLAM

Pontus Odmalm
MIGRATION POLICIES AND POLITICAL PARTICIPATION
Inclusion or Intrusion in Western Europe?

Jan Rath (*editor*)
IMMIGRANT BUSINESSES
The Economic, Political and Social Environment

Peter Ratcliffe (*editor*)
THE POLITICS OF SOCIAL SCIENCE RESEARCH
'Race', Ethnicity and Social Change

Carl-Ulrik Schierup (*editor*)
SCRAMBLE FOR THE BALKANS
Nationalism, Globalism and the Political Economy of Reconstruction

Steven Vertovec and Ceri Peach (*editors*)
ISLAM IN EUROPE
The Politics of Religion and Community

Maarten Vink
LIMITS OF EUROPEAN CITIZENSHIP
European Integration and Domestic Immigration Policies

Östen Wahlbeck
KURDISH DIASPORAS
A Comparative Study of Kurdish Refugee Communities

John Wrench, Andrea Rea and Nouria Ouali (*editors*)
MIGRANTS, ETHNIC MINORITIES AND THE LABOUR MARKET
Integration and Exclusion in Europe

Migration, Minorities and Citizenship
Series Standing Order ISBN 1–4039–71047–9
(*outside North America only*)

You can receive future titles in this series as they are published by placing a standing order.
Please contact your bookseller or, in case of difficulty, write to us at the address below with your
name and address, the title of the series and the ISBN quoted above.

Customer Services Department, Macmillan Distribution Ltd, Houndmills, Basingstoke,
Hampshire RG21 6XS, England

Muslims in Prison

Challenge and Change in Britain and France

James A. Beckford
Professor of Sociology
University of Warwick, UK

Danièle Joly
Professor, Centre for Research in Ethnic Relations
University of Warwick, UK

and

Farhad Khosrokhavar
Professor, Ecole des Hautes Etudes en
Sciences Sociales, France

First published 2005 by
PALGRAVE MACMILLAN
Houndmills, Basingstoke, Hampshire RG21 6XS and
175 Fifth Avenue, New York, N. Y. 10010
Companies and representatives throughout the world

PALGRAVE MACMILLAN is the global academic imprint of the Palgrave
Macmillan division of St. Martin's Press, LLC and of Palgrave Macmillan Ltd.
Macmillan® is a registered trademark in the United States, United Kingdom
and other countries. Palgrave is a registered trademark in the European
Union and other countries.

ISBN-13: 978–1–4039–9831–6 hardback
ISBN-10: 1–4039–9831–0   hardback

This book is printed on paper suitable for recycling and made from fully
managed and sustained forest sources.

A catalogue record for this book is available from the British Library.

Library of Congress Cataloging-in-Publication Data
Beckford, James A.
    Muslims in prison : challenge and change in Britain and France / James
A. Beckford, Danièle Joly, Farhad Khosrokhavar.
        p. cm. – (Migration, minorities, and citizenship)
    Includes bibliographical references and index.
    ISBN 1–4039–9831–0 (cloth)
    1. Prisoners–Religious life–Great Britain. 2. Prisoners–Religious life–France.
3. Muslims–Great Britain. 4. Muslims–France. I. Joly, Danièle. II. Khosrokhavar,
Farhad. III. Title. IV. Series.

HV8865.B42 2005   2005046308
365'.66–dc22

10   9   8   7   6   5   4   3   2   1
14 13 12 11 10 09 08 07 06 05

Transferred to digital printing 2006

Contents

Acknowledgements

We could not have written this book without the help of many people and institutions. Some of them went to extraordinary lengths to make it possible for us to gather information and to gain access to prisons.

We wish to record our thanks to the Prison Service of England and Wales as well as to the Administration Pénitentiaire in France for granting us access to prisoners, prisons and prison staff. The assistance that we received from Madame Elisabeth Guigou, the Venerable William Noblett, Maqsood Ahmed, Moosa Gora, Nick Sanderson, Maureen Colledge and Michelle Crerar was particularly valuable. In addition, Professor Michel Wieviorka and Laurence Cirba were helpful to our project in many ways. The Governors and the Directors of prisons that we visited and where our fieldwork took place are also thanked for their co-operation and interest in our work. In addition, we are grateful to all the chaplains, Imams, prison officers and other prison staff who made time in their busy schedules to answer our questions and to talk at length about their experiences. In order to preserve their anonymity we shall not name any of them. But we are happy to record our thanks to Salah El-Hassan and to Bashir Ebrahim-Khan for their help in explaining some of the voluntary activities that form an important part of prison chaplaincy for Muslim prisoners in England and Wales. Other people who have earned our gratitude include Nihid Iqbal and Hisham Al-Zoubeir Hellyer. Finally, the financial support of the Economic and Social Research Council is gratefully acknowledged.

Most of the intensive fieldwork in prisons was carried out by Moussa Khedimellah, Muzammil Quraishi and Nikola Tietze. Their professionalism, persistence and perspicacity deserve a special vote of thanks. Above all, however, it is to the many Muslim prisoners who were willing to talk about their experiences with us and with our researchers that we owe our greatest debt of gratitude. They were a source of invaluable insights into prison life as seen through Muslim eyes. We can only hope that they will regard this book as a suitable return for the time and the trust that they invested in us.

Not all of the many people who have helped us will necessarily agree with our arguments, but our hope is that this book about the treatment of Muslim prisoners will at least draw attention to the progress that has been made and to the problems that persist. It is an important topic that deserves further investigation not only in Britain and France but also in other parts of the world.

James A. Beckford
Danièle Joly
Farhad Khosrokhavar

Abbreviations

ABH	Actual bodily harm
BNP	British National Party
BOV	Board of Visitors (now renamed Independent Monitoring Board)
CADIS	Centre d'Analyse et d'Intervention Sociologiques
CNA	Certified Normal Accommodation
CRE	Commission for Racial Equality
DOM-TOM	French Departements and Territories Overseas
EIHS	European Institute of Human Sciences
ESOL	English as a Second or Other Language
ESRC	Economic and Social Research Council
FIS	Front Islamique du Salut
GBH	Grievous bodily harm
GIA	Groupe Islamique Armé
HIV	Human Immunodeficiency Virus
HMIP	Her Majesty's Inspectorate of Prisons
HT	Hizb-ut-Tahrir
IESH	Institut européen des sciences humaines
IGAS	Inspection Générale des Affaires Sociales
IMB	Independent Monitoring Board
ISP	Inspection des Services Pénitentiaires
IT	Information technology
JAP	Juge de l'Application des Peines
LIDS	Local Inmate Data System
MDT	Mandatory Drug Testing
NACRO	National Association for the Care and Resettlement of Offenders
NCWMP	National Council for the Welfare of Muslim Prisoners
NOMS	National Offender Management System
NVQ	National Vocational Qualification
OLP	Organisation de Libération de la Palestine
OSG	Operational Support Grade
OU	Open University
PAG	Prisoner Administration Group
PSEW	Prison Service of England and Wales
PSO	Prison Service Order
REA	Race Equality Adviser
RRA	Race Relations Act
RESPECT	Minority Ethnic Staff Support Network
RESPOND	Racial Equality for Staff and Prisoners Programme

RRLO	Race Relations Liaison Officer
RRMT	Race Relations Management Team
SACRE	Standing Advisory Council on Religious Education
SOTP	Sex Offender Treatment Programme
SWIP	Shared Working in Prison
TOM	Territoire d'Outre-Mer
UOIE	Union des Organisations Islamiques d'Europe
UOIF	Union des Organisations Islamiques de France
VITA	Virtual Islamic and Traditional Arts
VP	Vulnerable Prisoner
YOI	Young Offender Institution
YOT	Youth Offending Team

1
Introduction: Aims, Access and Analysis

Aims

The research on which this book is based is an extension of inquiries that each of us has been conducting separately for many years. All three of us share interests in the 'fault lines' of French and British societies. We are all concerned with the inequalities and injustices that accompany social divisions along lines of class, 'race', ethnicity and religion. Our shared interests also include the positive attempts made by groups in civil society to contest and to combat inequalities and injustice. In this connection, Danièle Joly and Farhad Khosrokhavar have implemented an 'interventionist' method of not simply studying problematic social phenomena from a distance but also of intervening in the dynamics of conflict in order to steer the protagonists towards a better theoretical understanding of what is at stake in the conflict. They have employed this interventionist method in studies of young, disaffected and sometimes-violent members of minority ethnic groups in France and the UK. Both of these authors have conducted a great deal of research on Muslims in a variety of contexts. Religious minorities, including Muslims, have also figured prominently in Jim Beckford's research in France and the UK. His interests centre on the response of agencies of the state to religious change, especially the increase of religious diversity following large-scale migration to France and the UK from their former colonies after 1945. The findings of the project that he conducted with Sophie Gilliat on relations between the Church of England and 'other faiths' in prisons and hospitals are the starting point for the present work (Beckford and Gilliat, 1996, 1998).[1]

The central aim of our project[2] was to discover how Muslim prisoners are treated in the prisons of France and England and Wales.[3] Recognising that 'Muslim' is itself a complex and variable category, we set out to examine the ways in which this category was socially constructed and used in prisons. There was special interest in two dimensions of this question: the first was the extent to which inmates constructed their own identity as

1

Muslims, and the second was whether Muslim inmates were subjected to forms of unfair discrimination that were clearly associated with their religious identity. In order to avoid softening the focus on the dynamics of social relations in the closed environment of prisons, we chose to ignore the growing number of offenders either sentenced to forms of punishment in the community or released on licence.

A second focus for our research was to compare France with England and Wales. The geographical proximity of France and England conceals fundamental differences between their respective political regimes, criminal justice systems and religious histories. In particular, the combination of these political, legal and religious characteristics was thought likely to have a strong effect on the treatment of Muslim prisoners. This served as the project's working hypothesis.

It is not the first time that social scientists have tried to capture the differences and similarities between France and England and Wales, but this particular investigation is novel because it centres on issues of religion and ethnicity in the setting of prisons. This is an entirely new perspective. Our argument will be that, in view of the continuing growth of the population of Muslims resident in Western Europe and the Nordic countries at the beginning of the twenty-first century, public officials, politicians and religious leaders need to address a range of new issues. These issues concern the responsiveness of prison regulations, regimes and staff to the challenges that the increasing number of Muslim inmates presents to them. Attitudes and practices that are rooted in an era when very few inmates came from religious backgrounds other than Christian are now under pressure to adapt to changed circumstances.

In addition to being challenging to policy makers and prison officials, the treatment of Muslim prisoners is also a sensitive topic. This was apparent when we designed the project but it is even more sensitive now in the wake of so many incidents and allegations of Muslim involvement in international terrorism early in the twenty-first century. For this reason, among many others, we are grateful to the prisoners, prison officers, administrators and religious personnel who were willing to answer our questions, offer us hospitality and discuss our concerns. We were conscious of the fact that our inquiries were an intrusion into their conditions of life and work, but many of our informants responded with courtesy and curiosity. We can also understand why some inmates and prison officers (mainly in France) preferred not to talk to us.

We owe an enormous debt of gratitude to the three researchers who carried out most of the day-to-day investigations on our behalf. Muzammil Quraishi worked full-time in three British prisons over a period of 16 months. Nikola Tietze collected information in one of the prisons in France. And Moussa Khedimellah assisted Farhad Khosrokhavar with his fieldwork in two French prisons for men and women. These enthusiastic, resourceful and brave researchers displayed unfailing professionalism and intellectual acumen.

With the assistance of these three researchers we were able to conduct parallel investigations in France and England and Wales. Our original plan had been to concentrate the fieldwork in three men's prisons in each country. This was achieved in England and Wales, but it proved impossible to study in depth more than two French prisons for men. Although 14 inmates in a third prison agreed to talk to us, prison officials were reluctant to authorise further in-depth interviews. In addition, research was conducted in two women's prisons in each country. Similar numbers of interviews were conducted in the two prison systems, thereby making cross-national comparisons possible. As we shall explain later, however, the structural and cultural contexts of Muslims and prisons were so different in some respects that cross-national comparisons could be made only with major qualifications.

Rationale

We chose to investigate the treatment of Muslims in the prisons of France and England and Wales not simply because the findings would contribute towards the understanding of the differences and similarities between French and British institutions but also because prisons offer a uniquely important perspective on many of today's most pressing challenges. The second half of the twentieth century saw a steady rise in the prison population of many advanced industrial countries. Rates of recidivism kept pace with the rising prison population. Indicators of overcrowding, disorders, suicides, self-harm, boredom, illness and racism all pointed towards the existence of long-term, deep-seated problems in prisons, in the criminal justice systems that channelled the rising tide of prisoners, and in the societies that generated such high levels of criminal conduct and prison sentences. Not surprisingly, these problems have also been at the heart of political, criminological and philosophical debates.

We needed no excuse, then, for choosing to investigate prisons. Our particular reasons for doing this research also arose, however, from concern with wider issues about ethnicity, 'race' and religion as they have affected successive generations of international migrants and settlers in France and the UK. In this respect, Muslims were the people of greatest interest to us. This was partly because Muslims amounted to the second largest faith community in each country, as well as in Western Europe, and partly because they were over-represented in prisons. The fact that so-called Islamic extremism, fundamentalism, *intégrisme*, and terrorism have come to dominate the news headlines since September 2001 has merely confirmed our earlier belief that further research was already needed on Muslims in prison.

In addition, the decision to focus our research on the treatment of Muslims in prison was driven by the perception that the prison institution, as such, is especially important – albeit largely ignored – in studies of immigration and settlement. Why? Prisons, especially closed establishments, force prisoners from widely differing backgrounds to live in close proximity to one another. Admittedly, it is common for prisoners to learn ways of exercising a certain degree of choice about the fellow-inmates with whom they interact most frequently. But the fact remains that – at least in formal terms – prison officers and other staff control these interactions and therefore have the capacity to create unusual and unwanted patterns of mixing in cells, on landings, on wings, in workshops and classes, and in associational or recreational activities. In short, prisons are perhaps the least segregated institutions in the public sphere in the sense that prisoners, especially those serving short sentences, can be forced to mix on a daily basis and for many hours at a time with fellow inmates, prison officers and other staff with whom they share very little in terms of culture and religion. By contrast, studies of schools, voluntary organisations and residential areas have provided evidence of the rapidity with which minority ethnic and ethno-religious communities have sought to segregate themselves from others. This is much more difficult – though far from impossible – in prisons. Consequently, research on Muslims in prison offered us the possibility of studying the dynamics of inter-ethnic and inter-religious relations in circumstances that were unlikely to be conducive to high levels of communal segregation.

Finally, as we shall explain more fully in the next chapter, our interest in the treatment of Muslim prisoners also grew out of academic discussions and political debates about the respective merits of different strategies for minimising the damage inflicted on minorities by racism and ethnically biased opportunity structures. The two main strategies are, on the one hand, multiculturalism and, on the other, policies of equal rights for all individuals. The case of Muslim prisoners was ideal from this point of view because it allowed us to compare the French system of promoting the equal rights of all citizens of the Republic regardless of ethnicity or religion with the British tendency to favour the protection of minorities as a strategy for integrating them into a community of communities.

Access and fieldwork

The design of the project envisaged the appointment of two full-time researchers, one of whom would conduct fieldwork in British prisons while the other's fieldwork would be in French prisons. However, our initial inquiries convinced us that, rather than trying to recruit a British researcher who could re-locate to France for the duration of the project, it would be both desirable and necessary to work collaboratively with a number of French researchers. This decision quickly proved to be wise. This was partly because the French team, located at the Centre d'Analyse et d'Intervention Sociologiques (CADIS) in the Ecole des Hautes Etudes en Sciences Sociales, in Paris, already had extensive experience of researching Muslims in France. The decision also proved to be wise because the Director of CADIS, Michel Wieviorka, took only a few weeks to obtain permission for our research from the Minister of Justice. Moreover, the Minister expressed strong interest in the results of our research.

France

Although the Minister of Justice had given her enthusiastic support for our research, problems quickly developed with officials in two French prisons. In one of them (which might have been a fourth site for our research), administrative ploys were used to block our access. We had to wait for an unreasonable length of time, which amounted to a denial of entry into the prison. In the other one, we were obliged to wait for months before we obtained permission to go into the prison. We therefore had to be content with three prisons and to abandon our plans for work in an important establishment in Paris, which would have been a better replacement for one of the other three.

Prison A

This prison, built in the 1970s, was undergoing major repairs in 2001. It is located less than an hour's journey from Paris. But its main problem – aside from an acute problem of noisiness – is less about its physical structure than about the restrictions that it imposes on Muslim inmates. There is no Imam – and no readiness to recruit one. It is impossible for Muslims to lead a normal religious life here, and the level of general suspicion among staff towards any kind of Islamic ritual is strong.

There had been problems with Muslim 'fundamentalists' [*intégristes*] in the past when, in the absence of collective prayer, some inmates shouted from the windows or played a pre-recorded call to prayer, for which they were placed in the segregation unit [*le mitard*]. This is possibly one of the reasons why the prison administrators were reluctant to allow us to conduct fieldwork in their prison.

Prison A is supposed to have a capacity of 503 prisoners, including 56 places for women and 16 for young offenders, but in November 2001 the number of inmates had reached 791. The prison was holding 57 per cent more than its planned capacity. Foreign nationals amounted to 20 per cent of the total, with most of them coming from North Africa and Black Africa, more than half of whom were Muslims. During the first decade of the prison's existence the proportion of foreign prisoners was 15 per cent.

Data from 1999 indicate that the distribution of the prisoners according to age was as follows:

Under 16 years:	0.4%
16 to 18 years:	2%
18 to 25 years:	30%
25 to 40:	53%
40 to 60:	12%
60 to 70:	0.8%
Over 70:	1%

There has been a significant change in the categories of prisoners held in Prison A. Between 1980 and 1990, 60 per cent of the prisoners were on remand [*prévenus*], but by 1999 only 47.5 per cent of prisoners were on remand. There were no significant differences between 1989 and 1999 in the length of sentences served. In the latter years, the distribution of offences was as follows:

Larceny [*vol qualifié*]:	41%
Drugs offences:	22%
Other types of theft:	13%
Financial offences:	7%
Breach of immigration laws:	7%
Sexual violence:	7%
Murder:	3%

The final decade of the twentieth century saw a steady rise in the number of prisoners serving sentences for drugs and immigration offences.

The number of suicides increased from 1 in 1990 to 3 in 1999, whereas cases of self-harm remained more or less stable at between 40 and 50 per year. The sheer number of psychiatric cases among prisoners is a major problem for Prison A. This phenomenon is closely related to drug addiction and affects roughly 51 per cent of prisoners. This rate of addiction is 21 per cent higher than the national average for the prison population. It is not surprising, then, that 31 per cent of those who entered the prison had already consulted a psychiatrist; 50 per cent had been admitted at least once to a psychiatric hospital; and 16 per cent had made a suicide attempt.

The Muslim worshippers at Friday prayers in one week of November 2001 had an average age of 30 years, which is close to the average for Prison A, but the proportion of foreign nationals among them (43 per cent) was more than twice as high as the rate for the prison. The offences of which they had been accused or convicted included: 45 per cent for drugs offences, 21 per cent for theft, 17 per cent for sexual assaults, 7 per cent for murder, 7 per cent for illegal residence [*séjour illégal*] and 3 per cent for procurement [*proxénétisme*].

Prison B

The design of this prison, located roughly 100 miles from Paris, is based on the 'Panopticon' model of the nineteenth century, with a central tower and several wings radiating from it. With the advent of computers, the security staff who work in the centre of the star-shaped structure conduct their surveillance of the wings on computer screens. There are separate corridors for young offenders, women and vulnerable prisoners, including sex offenders.

Travel to the prison from the nearest town takes about 15 minutes by car. For many visitors, however, access is difficult because there is no direct bus service from the town to the prison.

The physical condition of this prison, built in 1906, is deplorable. The entire building is in a state of disrepair, and the cells have no modern sanitation: only what the French call a 'Turkish WC' – or hole in the ground – which is merely curtained off from the rest of the cell. Major repairs have been held in abeyance in many parts of the prison because it is due to be rebuilt at some point in the future. The problem is that the new prison will not be completed in the next few years. Meanwhile, inmates have to put up with a poor level of building maintenance. To make matters worse, overcrowding was acute in 2001–2002, and in the following year, the population increased by more than 10 per cent.

The entire building needs heavy investment in order to meet minimum safety and sanitary requirements. The noise level is incredibly high within the prison because of the heavy metal doors. Prisoners complain bitterly about the lack of minimal hygiene standards – particularly showers and toilets for the Muslims. Problems with the water supply and a lack of sufficient showers mean that inmates are limited to a maximum of three showers a week. The main worship place is also in a shabby state. The psychiatric ward is in a dismal place on the ground floor. The prison kitchen also presents a major problem because it is situated a long way from some of the cells. According to the person responsible for the kitchen, the food that has to be carried to the cells loses about 16 degrees of its heat on the way. Moreover, the building is so old and in contravention of health standards that the Head of Catering stopped preparing desserts in the kitchen. Instead, they are purchased outside the prison and served in pots.

The general atmosphere within the prison is depressing. Not only the prisoners but also the prison officers show signs of depression. The Director and his staff are lodged in a modern part, attached to the old prison. This part is in better shape, with enough light and fewer problems with sanitation.

In March 2001 Prison B was holding 724 prisoners, including 67 women and 17 young offenders. The occupancy rate was 151 per cent of the prison's 'normal' accommodation. Sentenced prisoners, amounting to 53 per cent of the total, were serving sentences averaging 3.5 months. Foreign nationals, most of them from North Africa and Black Africa, constituted 19.3 per cent of all prisoners.

Convictions were for the following offences, among others: theft 47 per cent, drugs offences 20 per cent, sex offences 7 per cent, visa problems 6 per cent, financial offences 6 per cent, and homicide 2 per cent.

The number of suicides in Prison B ranged between 6 in 1997 and 1 in 2000.

The participants in Friday prayers one day in November 2001, 43 per cent of whom were foreigners, had an average age of 30 years. Most of them, 83 per cent, were remand prisoners. The offences of which they had been either accused or convicted were as follows: drugs 45 per cent, theft 21 per cent, sex offences 17 per cent, murder 7 per cent, illegal residence 7 per cent, and procurement 3 per cent.

The women's section of Prison B

The women's section of Prison B is in relatively good shape. There are far fewer women inmates and they experience better services and better living conditions than their male counterparts. In July 2002, the number of female prisoners was 55. Young offenders amounted to 2 per cent of the total, while 8 per cent were 'high risk prisoners' (many from Basque separatist groups). Prisoners serving sentences shorter than one year were 21 per cent of all prisoners, while the sentences of 13 per cent were longer than one year, and 27 per cent were awaiting trial or sentencing.

Foreign nationals, coming from 51 different countries, constituted 63 per cent of the prison population, but only 5 per cent of them were from North Africa. By contrast, male prisoners from North Africa in Prison A represented 48 per cent of all foreign prisoners. On the other hand, the proportion of Muslim women among foreign prisoners is much lower than in the men's prison. The two most striking features of the foreign prisoners in this women's prison are the high number of Black Africans, amounting to about 14 per cent of the foreigners, and the rather high number of prisoners from some European countries. Spain has the highest number (19), probably because of the Basque separatist groups, followed by Romania.

Not only do women represent a much lower proportion of prisoners in France (only 3.5 per cent of the national prison population in July 2001), but their national origins and the structure of their offences also differ from those of male prisoners. Muslims, over-represented in the male population, are a minority in women's prisons. Their typical offences are different as well. Drugs offences amount to 32 per cent of cases, aggravated larceny [*vol aggravé*] and larceny as such represent 23 per cent, terrorism 8 per cent (mainly Basque in this case), immigration offences also 8 per cent, homicide 7 per cent, procurement 6 per cent, and homicide against minors 1 per cent. Thus, women are 50 per cent more likely than men to be sentenced for drugs offences but only half as likely to be convicted of theft.

Prison C

Prison C is one of the largest in Europe. It was built in the 1970s on a model of seven separate units (called *'tripales'*). Each one, including separate buildings for a health centre, young offenders and women, is under the authority of a Deputy Director. The distances between some buildings are considerable. Although the prison has been in operation for only three decades, the buildings seem to be in poor condition. Despite being much younger than Prison B, it still falls well short of the standards for a decent prison. For example, there is still a problem with showers, and many Muslims bitterly complained to us that they could not take a shower every day. The average entitlement is only three showers a week.

The individual cells are not as modern as one might expect of a 1970s building, but they look acceptable and the prisoners did not complain about the WC. Time is provided for daily exercise, and in general the inmates have much better living conditions than in Prison B.

Since Prison C consists of many buildings, Directors can move prisoners from one to another. Disruptive prisoners, for example, can be transferred to a different unit, one of which specialises in accommodating particularly difficult prisoners. Mobile phones are in frequent use between prison officers keeping track of prisoners in such a complex prison establishment.

There are now more than 5,000 inmates in Prison C, following an increase of 20 per cent in the last two years.

Local responses

In France, contrary to appearances, agreement reached with the highest authority (the Minister of Justice or the Garde des Sceaux), does not automatically guarantee access to prisons. It is necessary to go through the agency of an intermediary organisation (l'Administration pénitentiaire), albeit informally, to ease access to sensitive prisons. Even then, reluctant prison Directors can impose a veto on researchers entering 'their' prison. This happened in one case and lasted for some five months. In another case, the researcher had to convince the Director that he was 'secular' [*laïque*] in order to get access to the prison. On the whole, there was only one French prison in which the researchers were welcome. This was mainly due to the attitude of its Director, who happened to be 'liberal', open-minded and less suspicious about religious (particularly Islamic) matters than his counterparts in other prisons.

The French situation was entirely different from the British. Christian chaplains played no role in facilitating the research, and the researchers operated independently of them. The fact that the two male researchers were Muslims should also have strengthened the legitimacy of their work in the eyes of Muslim inmates. Yet, paradoxically, some of them voiced their suspicions about the researchers' 'real' motives and identities, even accusing them of being undercover agents of the security services.[4]

Gaining access to Muslim prisoners was not at all straightforward for many reasons. First, there are no official statistics available on ethnic and religious phenomena in France, and it is forbidden by law to ask for information about them. The Muslims themselves were suspicious and in many cases had difficulties understanding the nature of our inquiry. Some of the Muslim radicals did not appreciate our presence and refused to talk to us, suspecting us of belonging to the French secret police or even the Israeli Mossad. Others refused to talk because they had no time: they had to work and earn their living in prison or to take part in classes. Alternatively, they did not want to talk about themselves and their setbacks because these experiences were too painful. Last but not least, the prison authorities did not always welcome our presence. Some were anxious about our interpretation of religion (none of the researchers was French by birth) and at the same time they were worried that our report on the situation in prisons[5] might be too critical.

In order to persuade inmates to participate in our interviews, we had to make approaches at various levels. In one case, the Imam helped us by talking to the inmates and by facilitating our approach through meetings with some of them. In the second case, we were able to obtain the list of inmates who took part in collective prayers because the prison officers in charge of these gatherings were not obstructive (otherwise it would have been much harder to get them). In addition, the Director of this particular prison was well disposed towards our research. By contrast, the Imam was reluctant to cooperate with us throughout most of the fieldwork, and it was only at the very end that he agreed to be cooperative up to a point. In the third prison, the Director was initially opposed to our research on Muslims because he feared that we would be prejudiced against the official position of '*laïcité*'.[6] After discussion, however, he agreed in principle to our research – albeit with some reluctance. The procedure that was agreed with him was that we sent an open letter to the Muslim inmates explaining the aim of our research and asking them to let us know – by means of a letter to the administrators – whether they would consent to be interviewed. We received 14 acceptances, as mentioned earlier, and we subsequently conducted this number of interviews. In order to avoid putting strain on religious susceptibilities, the letter sent to the prisoners mentioned their 'religious practice' but not explicitly 'Islam'.

Getting into prisons on a daily basis depended on the rules governing each establishment. In this respect, too, conditions varied from one prison to the other. In Prison A, we conducted our 14 interviews in one week. Prison officials already knew the researcher, Nikola Tietze, because she had taken part in other academic research in this prison – in collaboration with the judiciary. In Prison B, we had the support of the Director, and on the whole (except when the prison officers were on strike) our access to prison was unproblematic. Inside the prison, the problem was to find prison officers who would agree to call the prisoners, sometimes making many phone calls to locate them. There were many cases in which the prisoners could not be found easily because they were in education classes (they followed lectures in various subjects), in the prison hospital, in the gymnasium or on the way from one of these places to another. This was a recurrent difficulty in all of the prisons. It took up a large part of our time. Sometimes, the prisoners were not available at all if, for example, they could not leave classes or other activities.

Another problem was finding a suitable time to meet them because, while one of them was taking a rest, the others might be in the hospital or somewhere else so that it was far from easy to get the timing right. Taking into account that in some cases many phone calls had to be made, some prison officers were more willing to cooperate with us than others. A further problem was to find a room [*parloir*] where we could conduct the interviews. In Prison C, one of the largest in France, we obtained what we needed through the good offices of a person in the higher ranks of management who authorised a one-year pass for us. This allowed us to go to the prison on any day we wished without having to give justification. Since this prison was divided into many independent sub-prisons, however, we had to ask for permission to visit each of them. We obtained this permission through the cooperation of the same person, who was of North African origin and who somehow had a better understanding of the 'specific' case of North African prisoners, almost all of whom were of Muslim origin. The problem with Prison C was that the sub-prisons were all different, and some were more willing than others to help us. This was also the prison where some prison officers rejected us for various reasons, so we asked the well-disposed North African contact to help us tackle this problem discreetly.

Each prison treated our demands differently. In only one of them, where the Director was on our side, were we permitted to tape-record the interviews. This was forbidden in the other two establishments. The formal reason for this was that, as some prisoners were still awaiting trial or sentencing, there was a risk that the recorded interviews might be used for or against the prisoners.

We were unable to take part in any solemn religious occasions such as Eid or collective prayers on Fridays either because collective prayers did not take place – as in two out of the three prisons – or because religious festivals were not officially organised. Moreover, the Imam in the prison where collective prayers did actually take place did not want us to participate.

In some sub-prisons of Prison C we had access to a notice board that carried a register of inmates' names, so that we could identify the Muslim names. In addition, prison officers suggested to us the names of a few prisoners who might have been of interest to us.

Our problems did not end even when we had gained access to Muslim prisoners. We still had to justify our research to them, and this took – depending on the prisoners – between a few minutes and half an hour of discussion. In many cases, the prisoners refused to answer our questions and some even refused to come to the visiting room. There was some kind of communication among the prisoners about this. In one part of Prison B, for example, after interviews with some prisoners, we had difficulty getting in touch with the others because they systematically refused to talk to us. On one particular wing, they refused to talk to us throughout one entire day, and we had to abandon our plans for interviews on that wing. The 'bush telegraph' – *téléphone arabe* in French – that was in operation sometimes worked in our favour and sometimes against us.

After 11 September 2001, the situation became more difficult, and we had more trouble talking to Muslim prisoners. Admittedly, we added some questions about September 11th at the end of the interviews, and this might have aroused the suspicion of some inmates. But the reasons actually seemed to be more general: the atmosphere within the prison had become more tense, and the inmates had become more suspicious about our integrity and our impartiality as sociologists. It was as if they felt that someone who could come to the prison and ask people about Islam could not possibly be neutral towards them. This, in turn, was evidence of the negative atmosphere in the prison and of the strained relationship between inmates and prison authorities concerning Islam.

Suspicion is not at all unusual in prison. We had plenty of opportunities to witness it among the inmates as well as prison authorities. Of course, suspicion is the hallmark of social relations in a hermetically sealed setting or, in Goffman's (1990) terms, in any 'total institution'. Neutral attitudes are difficult to maintain. But we still believe that suspicion would be less prevalent in prison if there were some acknowledgement of inmates' rights. The denial of the rights that they consider to be fundamental aggravates their feelings of suspicion. That is why, even in 'total institutions', the level of suspicion varies according to the way in which inmates' problems are handled.[7]

The case of Muslims in French prisons illustrates this gradation of suspicion. Basic religious rights are more or less respected among Catholics and Protestants these days, and the long tradition of negotiating these rights has helped them to become institutionalised in a positive sense. In the case of Muslims, however, there is widespread misunderstanding and heavy mutual suspicion about the nature and extent of these rights.[8] Prison establishments are fearful that recognising that inmates have some rights might encourage them to make even more claims about their religion. The dominant tendency is, therefore, to draw a very tight line and to refuse any 'concession' to prisoners. This line, obviously, has little to do with the real meaning of *laïcité*. It merely reflects what might be called a mutual misunderstanding. The best way that prison administrators have found for dealing with the religious situation is to ignore it – until the time comes when prisoners show their radical Islamic leanings. This forces the administration to impose tighter controls and harsher punishment on those who disturb the internal *status quo* in prisons. But this does not prevent Muslim inmates from becoming more and more 'religiously inclined'. The influx of young people from the disadvantaged suburbs [*banlieues*] and the presence – statistically insignificant but anthropologically meaningful – of Islamic radicals have helped to bring about the 'revival of Islam' in prisons. The emergence of Islam – over the last decade – as one of the major religions in prisons and sometimes as even 'the' religion cannot be ignored any longer (Khosrokhavar, 2004). In many prisons, there is still a failure to acknowledge Islam.

Outside prison, however, a new dynamic has set in and the French state shows signs of a new attitude towards Islam. Political elites are more and more keen to find a way of relating Islam to public institutions. In contrast to a decade ago, these elites are increasingly willing to acknowledge the presence of Islam in France. They want Islamic institutions to group together and to show that they can speak to the state with a single voice in the major institutions of the Republic. But prisons, in contrast to the situation in England and Wales, are lagging far behind. In spite of the high number of Muslims in prison, there is no clear sign of any movement towards accepting this religion.

The suspiciousness shown by Muslim inmates was obvious when we tried to get in touch with them. Many were at best reluctant to answer our questions at the beginning of the interviews. We had to explain to them at length about the purpose of our research, its comparative nature (Islam in prison in France and England and Wales), its aims and its strictly intellectual nature. We had to argue – probably without much success – that we were not subservient to the French secret police. One of our researchers, a French PhD student of Algerian origin, was accused of being a 'token Muslim' [*Arabe de service*] who worked for the French intelligence in run-down suburbs.

Although we had official permission for our research and the support of a senior administrator, some people ignored us. Others, mainly those in charge of the *Greffe* or registry where prisoners' records are centralised, promised to help us but did nothing in spite of our repeated requests for statistics relating to religion as reflected in inmates' names.

Prison officers were generally not interested in our research; some were even ill at ease about it and unsure whether we should have been working on a topic that was so 'sensitive'. Some suspected us of being secret sympathisers with Muslims and willing to defend their views against those of the institution. The problem was that they also distanced themselves from the institutions where they worked. Some had rather cynical views, and this made them unsure as to how far they should talk to us about prisoners: wouldn't we inform the authorities about supposed breaches of discipline and their prejudice against Muslim prisoners? In a system where the rules are not always applied as such and where the feeling of insecurity towards the administrative apparatus is rather high, the best way to protect oneself is to avoid getting involved as far as possible and to work hard at remaining 'distant'. Muslims are nowadays a real problem for prison officers less for what they do than for what they represent: a threat to the *status quo* when young people from the poor suburbs began arriving in prison, when the so-called revival of Islam called in question the norms of *laïcité* and when radical Muslims ('Islamists') started appearing in French prisons in the first half of the 1990s.

In summary, the prisoners were more than suspicious, at least at the beginning. Some thought that we were working for the courts and, since some had not yet been tried or sentenced, they did not wish to reveal anything that could have been used against them. Some were anxious that we might try to identify their accomplices so that we could denounce them to the prosecutors. Some thought they could exploit us as intermediaries with the criminal justice system. For example, a Brazilian thought we might intervene on his behalf in order to improve his communication with his family; a *Beur* (slang for 'Arab') thought we might make it easier for him to get a Presidential Pardon (leniency is shown towards many categories of prisoners every five years when Presidential elections take place). A Kurdish Iraqi who was arrested while trying to cross the border to get to the UK thought that Khosrokhavar, as an Iranian, could help him to get a visa from the Islamic Republic of Iran so that French authorities would not regard him as an illegal immigrant. In many cases, our research function could not match the inmates' hopes and plans, and this was at the root of some of the misinterpretations and misunderstandings that were hard to overcome.

The interviews that we conducted with 158 inmates in French prisons usually lasted between one hour and one and a half hours. In three cases, they were conducted in dialectal Arabic because the prisoners had recently arrived from North Africa. In two cases the interviews were in crude Spanish because one of the informants was a Lebanese resident of a Latin American country, and the other was a Bolivian female convert to Islam. There was also an interview in Persian with a Kurd who wanted to seek political asylum in England but had been arrested in France. In addition, two interviews took place in English with a Pakistani inmate and a Black English-speaking African. In all other cases, French was the language of the interviews. Finally, 28 interviews were conducted with prison officers and administrators.

England and Wales

Meanwhile, the process of obtaining official permission for research in the prisons of England and Wales was much slower and more complicated. It took four months to receive a response from the Director General of the Prison Service of England and Wales and then to satisfy his officials that our project was feasible and sound. We could only speculate that one of the reasons why the project was considered to be unusually sensitive was that the findings of Beckford and Gilliat's (1998) study of relations between the Church of England and 'other faiths' in prisons had embarrassed the Prison Service Chaplaincy. Nevertheless, the protracted negotiations had the incidental advantage of allowing us to benefit from the practical and methodological advice of various Prison Service officials.

Having received 'in principle' permission for our project from relevant authorities near the top of the Prison Service we also needed to negotiate access to three particular prisons. The selection of these sites for fieldwork had to take account of numerous considerations including the number of Muslim inmates, their turnover rate, ease of access for the researcher, levels of security, and so on. Officials at Prison Service headquarters in London suggested three establishments that could meet our requirements. We accepted two of these suggestions and added a third of our own choice in order to widen the range of types of prisons in which we could assess the treatment of Muslims. It was only at a later stage of the project that we also negotiated access to two women's prisons and, finally, to three male establishments employing a full-time Muslim chaplain.

Prison 1

Prison 1 is a local prison built in the mid-nineteenth century located close to the centre of a city in the English Midlands. The prison serves two Crown Court centres and many Magistrates' Courts in its region. It houses adult male prisoners and had a Certified Normal Accommodation (CNA) of 734 at the time of our fieldwork.[9] The average prisoner population at any one time, commonly referred to as the 'Roll', in 2001 was registered as nearly 1,100 (Leech and Cheney, 2001). However, over the research period the roll averaged roughly 850 prisoners.

The official category of the prison is 'Male Local' and 'Training'. Regarding accommodation and facilities, the prison consists of six cell blocks and a Healthcare Centre. Various additions and renovations have been completed since 1985. At the time of the research, one wing housed convicted prisoners and served as an induction wing. A second wing housed convicted prisoners; a third wing housed remand prisoners; a fourth wing housed segregated prisoners and 'poor-copers'; and two further wings housed the 'long-term' workforce.

All cells are fitted with in-cell sink, hot and cold water, light switch, and night sanitation. Televisions are fitted in wings 5 and 6, where there are power points. Card phones are available on all landings. The prison operates various schemes including: Bail Information, Drug Counselling, Mandatory Drug Testing (MDT), Personal Officer Scheme, and Shared Working In Prison (SWIP). The Canteen is stocked with 150 lines and staffed by Operational Support Grade staff (OSGs). Four wings operate a pre-select menu system, while prisoners on the other wings are offered a multi-choice menu. *Halal* food is provided at every mealtime.

The education department runs classes in Information Technology (IT), numeracy, National Vocational Qualification (NVQ) catering, vocational courses and literacy for 50 weeks a year. The four full-time and part-time tutors are contracted from a nearby college of further education.

The Chaplaincy includes a full-time Anglican Chaplain, full-time Roman Catholic Chaplain, a part-time Methodist Chaplain and sessional chaplains, including an Imam. The Imam runs Arabic classes on Mondays, visits segregated Muslim prisoners on Wednesdays and leads congregational Muslim prayers on alternate Fridays. A substitute Imam leads prayers on alternate Fridays.

The prison also has gym and sports facilities and a library, which is open seven days a week. The library contains Urdu and Arabic literature. Inmates can apply for jobs in the kitchens, laundry, stores, textile shops, cleaning, and servery. The prison employs two full-time medical officers, one part-time medical officer – supported by two locums – and 31 healthcare staff including nurses. There are 30 in-patient beds, and a dentist who visits twice weekly. An optician and a chiropodist make weekly visits.

Prison 2

Prison 2 began as a Young Offender Institution (YOI) in the mid-1980s but soon became an adult Category C training prison. It is built on a former military base on the outskirts of a small village in the rural hinterland of London. It has an operational capacity of 745 prisoners housed in seven wings. Four wings are built in an identical block design, holding 112 prisoners in each block. Two further wings, holding 264 prisoners, are for prisoners on enhanced status and an annexe accommodates 36 prisoners in single cells. Prisoners in the annexe have their own cell keys and use communal sanitation. Two wings are 'drug-free' wings. All prisoners begin on standard regime and progress to other regimes if their behaviour and security status warrant an improvement in their living conditions.

All wings have bathing and showering facilities and all cells have sockets for televisions and radios, although prisoners on basic regime do not have electrical power sockets in their cells. The canteen is stocked with over 200 lines, and certain prisoners on the drug-free wings get limited access to shared kitchens where they can cook their own meals.

There is a purpose-built education centre and over 100 inmates enrolled on education courses. The workshops include metalwork, light assembly, and computer data entry. The employment rate for prisoners was higher than 90 per cent during the research period.

The prison has a segregation unit with 20 cells containing sanitation facilities, one unfurnished cell and two strip cells. There is no full-time medical officer available, nor do in-patient facilities exist. But the modern gymnasium is well equipped, and the prison has an outdoor sports fields and cricket facilities.

The Chaplaincy was in a state of flux during the research period. When the research began, late in 2001, a Free Church Assistant Chaplain was temporarily in charge of the chaplaincy because both the Anglican Chaplain and the Roman Catholic Chaplain had left their posts. There had been no Imam for more than six months but, as an emergency measure, a member of the Board of Visitors (BOV) had volunteered to act temporarily as Imam. A full-time Imam at the Assistant Chaplain grade and a full-time Anglican Chaplain were both appointed while the research was in progress. In addition, there were female part-time Methodist and Roman Catholic Assistants. Sikh, Buddhist, Jehovah's Witnesses and Salvation Army representatives visited for a few hours each month.

The Chaplaincy is housed in a modern purpose-built multi-faith centre where Muslims use a large multi-faith room for congregational prayers and for festivals. Islamic texts and religious artefacts are stored in a multi-purpose office, and standpipes are in place for ablutions in the foyer of the building.

Prison 3

Prison 3 is a High Security dispersal prison, which opened in the late 1980s on the site of a former military base in the North of England. The Prison now operates under the Directorate of High Security Prisons. The prison is also an assessment centre for the Sex Offender Treatment Programme (SOTP). It has a Certified Normal Accommodation (CNA) of 602 and a roll of 575. Regarding accommodation and facilities, the prison comprises seven wings and a segregation unit. The accommodation and functioning of the prison is divided between High Security prisoners (Main) and High Security vulnerable prisoners (VPs). All prisoners are category A or B, serving more than four years.

All cells are single occupancy and have integral sanitation and mains power. The prisoners have access to the following facilities: sentence planning, drug counselling, MDT, telephone Personal Identification Number (PIN) systems, Personal Officer Scheme, on-wing access to cookers, boilers, TV rooms and in-cell TV. In addition, the prison has a well-planned visitors' centre on the ground floor and operates a 'Father and Child' visit on the sports field once a month. The prison has a well-equipped gymnasium and facilities for soccer, volleyball, basketball, badminton and hockey.

The education provision, which has been contracted out to a local college of further education, includes classes in art, cookery, woodcraft, IT, craft design technology, business studies, creative writing, food technology, Open University (OU), foreign languages, basic skills (literacy and numeracy), English as a Second or Other Language (ESOL) and a Pre-Release course (Ready Steady Go). Workshops include bricklaying, plumbing, painting and decorating and kitchen work.

Regarding the healthcare facilities, the Prison's Senior Medical Officer is supported by a local General Practitioner, one Healthcare Principal Officer, two Healthcare Senior Officers and 14 Healthcare Officers. The Healthcare Centre has a 10-bed in-patient capacity and a surgery which opens Monday to Friday in the afternoon. There are weekly clinics for physiotherapy and radiography. A dentist and psychiatrist visit twice a week, while an optician, chiropractor and HIV/AIDS counsellors visit fortnightly. The catering staff have played a pioneering role in helping to standardise procedures for the preparation of food for Muslim prisoners (Botterhill and Gora, 2000).

The Chaplaincy comprises one full-time and two part-time Anglican Chaplains, one part-time Roman Catholic Chaplain, one part-time Methodist Chaplain, one part-time Imam and one part-time Pentecostal Chaplain. The prison is also visited by Jehovah's Witnesses, Buddhist, Hindu and Jewish representatives. The Imam runs Arabic classes on Wednesdays for VPs and on Friday afternoon for Main prisoners in addition to leading the Friday congregational prayers.

Women's prisons

We interviewed small numbers of chaplains, governors, inmates and a Muslim counsellor in two female establishments. The first, Prison 4, is a large, refurbished establishment close to the centre of a major city. Serving a large number of busy courts, it houses slightly more than 500 remand and sentenced prisoners, including many of their very young children. It has spacious gardens and is well equipped but has been at the centre of controversies in recent years about its state of cleanliness and the conditions in which prisoners give birth. Opportunities for work are few and the rate of turnover among prisoners is high.

The chaplaincy enjoys its own facilities, including a large Christian chapel in the prison grounds and a world faiths room, and is staffed by two full-time Anglican Chaplains, a full-time Roman Catholic female chaplain, a part-time Free Church Chaplain and several sessional chaplains. More than a dozen volunteers also worked in the chaplaincy. There was no Imam at the time of our visit, but a Muslim woman with professional experience as a teacher visited Muslim inmates for six hours a week for group discussion and personal counselling. She confirmed that the certification of *halal* food was authentic.

The second female establishment in our sample, Prison 5, is centred on an old manor house in a rural setting that was hurriedly converted into a women's prison and YOI in the mid-1990s in response to the growing number of women receiving custodial sentences at that time. Its nearly 200 inmates, only five of whom were registered as Muslims at the time of our visit, live either in the main house or in adjoining buildings. Gardening and horticultural work are available.

The chaplaincy consisted of a part-time Anglican Chaplain, a part-time Roman Catholic Chaplain and several sessional chaplains who spend a total of 73 hours a week in the prison. But the Muslim sister who had been visiting inmates for several years had not been replaced while she was on extended maternity leave. The small number of Muslim inmates met for one hour on Fridays but were unsure whether arrangements would be made for the celebration of Ramadan and Eid ul Fitr. The Head of Activities had been asked to make inquiries about appropriate arrangements with the Muslim Advisor to the Prison Service.

Local responses

Given that we wanted the researcher to spend large amounts of time, spread over three months, interacting with inmates, staff, administrators and volunteers in each of the English prisons, we expected that the negotiations for access would be difficult. Somewhat to our surprise, the authorities placed very few obstacles in our path. In fact, two of the Governing Governors were sufficiently interested in our research to ask many questions and to make available most of the facilities that we requested. The process of obtaining security clearance for the researcher who would be conducting most of the fieldwork was straightforward – albeit protracted in the case of the maximum-security establishment.

It is highly significant that Church of England chaplains were instrumental in helping to arrange meetings with governors and that governors were content to 'attach' our project to their chaplaincies. They seemed to take it for granted that Christian chaplains would be responsible for anything to do with religion. None of the governors or chaplains suggested that we should seek the approval of Muslim Visiting Ministers or of chaplaincy committees. This assumption that Christian chaplains take most of the responsibility for matters related to religion was confirmed at many points during the early stages of our research. Indeed, only one – Catholic – member of a chaplaincy team ever expressed any reluctance to co-operate with the researcher on the grounds that the project ought to be the responsibility of Muslims instead of Christians.

It was also clear in our three English prisons that, although some prison officers and Muslim inmates had little interest in our research, they voiced very few 'in principle' objections to discussing religion or Islam. In part, this was because the researcher had the opportunity to meet most of the

Muslim inmates at Friday prayers and to explain the project's aims and methods to them as a group. The fact that Muslim Visiting Ministers endorsed the researcher's work in each prison also helped to allay any potential misgivings. There was no overt indication that the inmates suspected the researcher of being an undercover agent of prison authorities or of the British government. On the contrary, some of them went to the other extreme of presuming that the researcher, as a fellow Muslim, would be an advocate for them in, for example, supporting their complaints or applications for parole.

The conduct of interviews and observation in English prison establishments was subject to many predictable and unpredictable obstacles and frustrations. In some cases, it was the concern with security that made it difficult to contact informants at agreed times. In other cases, failures of communication or unforeseeable contingencies were the problem. But we did not have the impression that prison officers or administrators deliberately set out to obstruct our research.

The fact is that governors of English prisons took it for granted that chaplains would take general responsibility for escorting researchers into their establishments and would make space for them in their chaplaincy centres. Indeed, this arrangement was certainly helpful and convenient but it also ran the risk of possibly giving inmates the impression that Christians had somehow sponsored our project. Such an impression would have been particularly understandable in Prison 1 where the Research Fellow spent his first week 'shadowing' the senior Anglican chaplain during his full round of daily duties. The Research Fellow was able to counterbalance this by explaining to Muslim inmates that he was an English- and Urdu-speaking Muslim, that the funding for the project came from the Economic and Social Research Council (ESRC), that it had the support of the Muslim Visiting Minister, and that its aims were strictly scholarly rather than religious. Nevertheless, in two of the three prisons where he conducted fieldwork the Research Fellow was dependent on members of the chaplaincy teams for escorting him into and out of the establishments. This process was cumbersome and time consuming for all concerned. Two incidents that occurred in Prison 1 highlighted the disadvantages of dependency on staff in the chaplaincy. On one occasion staff refused to respond to a request from the gate officer to meet the Research Fellow who, after waiting in the reception area for nearly one hour, had to abort his visit. On another occasion a member of the chaplaincy team refused to accompany the Research Fellow into the prison because she did not wish to leave the chaplaincy centre unsupervised. Again, the visit was aborted. The Research Fellow's dependency on chaplaincy staff to escort him in and out of the same prison was also the reason why he found himself locked in the chaplaincy centre for more than an hour on a day when no members of the chaplaincy team were available. Even the fire doors were locked.

If the Research Fellow's dependency on chaplaincy staff carried certain costs, there were also disadvantages associated with being too closely identified with the interests of Muslim inmates. He went to considerable lengths to play down the significance of his training and qualifications as a lawyer, for fear that some inmates might expect him to become their advocate. Whilst not concealing his active Muslim faith he also wanted to be seen by inmates as independent from their Visiting Ministers. As it happened, however, he sometimes found himself in situations that could have jeopardised his independence and strictly academic status. They occurred when Visiting Ministers either drew inmates' attention to his legal training as a means of soliciting their co-operation in the research or called for his help when translations of the Qur'an were needed during *jummah* prayers.

In the third British prison, however, the Research Fellow had the privilege and the responsibility of 'drawing keys' on each visit. This meant that, after training in security and personal safety matters, he was authorised to collect a set of keys at the entrance and to move about the prison's public areas without escort and without being dependent on the help of chaplains. The advantages of this freedom of manoeuvre more than outweighed the risk that inmates would identify him with prison staff and might even regard him as a target for attack. In any case, he did not carry keys that would have opened individual cells. This was also the only prison in which he was able to obtain permission to make tape recordings of his interviews with inmates, prison officers, chaplains, Visiting Ministers and administrative staff.

Informing Muslim inmates about the research project and inviting them to participate was relatively simple in English prisons. Again, the ease of communication was due in large part to two facts. On the one hand, chaplains and Visiting Ministers were willing to announce that the project was going to take place and to encourage inmates to co-operate with the researcher. On the other hand, weekly gatherings of Muslims for *jummah* prayers were a good opportunity for the Research Fellow to introduce himself, to explain the project, to answer questions and to ask inmates to volunteer for interviews. The Visiting Ministers were also helpful in showing their support for the research. Other gatherings at, for example, Arabic classes and Eid festivals presented further occasions on which the Research Fellow had access to a large proportion of Muslim inmates.

The sample of inmates for interview in the three English prisons was drawn randomly from lists of those who had volunteered after Friday prayers to be interviewed and from each prison's computerised list of inmates – the Local Inmate Data System (LIDS) – which identifies each inmate's religious affiliation. All interviewees gave their consent to be interviewed after receiving information about the scope of questions, the proposed outcomes of the research, and the undertaking to preserve informants' anonymity within the limitations imposed by considerations of security (Jupp, 1989; Jupp, Davies and Francis, 2000). Interviews, lasting on average about one hour, took place with 68 Muslim male inmates in a variety of settings but most often in offices and other rooms within chaplaincy centres. The questioning followed a prepared schedule but was flexible enough to pursue unexpected leads that appeared to be promising. English was the medium of communication in all but five cases in which inmates preferred to talk in Urdu or a mixture of Urdu and English. It was not uncommon for interviews to be suspended and re-started when prison officers called inmates away when such things as meals, head counts, sports activities and visits took place.

In addition, a further 67 interviews were conducted with governors, Race Relations officers, other prison officers, chaplains and kitchen supervisors in each prison. The Research Fellow took contemporaneous notes on these interviews in two British prisons, following a list of prepared questions but digressing into other subjects when appropriate.[10] In the third prison, interviews were tape recorded and transcribed for analysis. All notes and transcripts were subsequently coded for analysis in the Atlas-ti computer package.

The Research Fellow's field notes, composed during and after every day's visit to prisons, provided contextual detail and 'local colour' that also fed into the analysis of interview data. His observations covered everyday incidents, conversations and interactions on prison wings as well as in chaplaincy centres. He was in constant touch with prison officers at various grades. In addition, he was present during Ramadan in one prison where he also participated in Eid celebrations. Further information came from a meeting with leading Muslims in a large city mosque, a regional meeting of chaplains, and a seminar in Sweden on the treatment of Muslims in prison. Finally, Beckford visited three additional prisons and conducted lengthy telephone interviews with six of the 13 Imams who were working full-time as Muslim chaplains in the Spring of 2004.

The intention had been to ask Muslim inmates to compose a written record of their experiences in prison so that we would have a narrative account of their treatment. However, their response was so poor that we decided to abandon this part of our project design. We were probably too optimistic about the inmates' levels of literacy and command of written English, but they were also reluctant to take the risk of writing documents over which they would have no control. This was the only failure in our attempts to meet the project's objectives.

We collected information about female Muslim inmates in England and Wales in a different and less intense way. With the assistance of the Muslim Advisor to the Prison Service, we selected two establishments where the number of Muslim women was sufficiently high. Beckford and Joly then spent several hours talking informally to inmates, chaplains, a Visiting Minister, a governor and staff in these establishments and conducting group discussions about the treatment of Muslim women. Their contemporaneous notes form the basis of the observations about female Muslim inmates that are scattered through this book. It is clear that women prisoners' experience of practising Islam differs in many respects from that of men and that this should be the subject of separate research.

The final point to be made about the responses that our research received at the level of each prison establishment in both countries underlines the importance of the cross-national comparative perspective. The sharp contrasts between the prisons of France and England and Wales in terms of our project's reception among prison staff and Muslim inmates are indicative of a much broader pattern of differences. The project was greeted with extensive suspicion in France but generally welcomed in England and Wales as evidence of a concern to enhance policies of equal opportunity and respect for diversity. These differences are not accidental or cosmetic. They go to the heart of differences between the two countries in terms of (a) the place accorded to religion in public institutions (b) the priority accorded to policies and practices that foster religious and ethnic diversity, and (c) conceptions of citizenship and civil society. Later chapters will analyse these differences in detail.

Law and criminal justice systems

France and the UK have substantially different systems of civil and criminal law despite the fact that, as member states of the EU, both countries must harmonise their laws with the European Convention on Human Rights and other international agreements. The French legal system broadly follows the Roman Law tradition of 'right' or civil law, whereas English and Scottish law derives mainly from the Common Law tradition. These differences have serious implications for the institutions and practices of criminal justice, including prisons.

French laws are arranged in the form of codes or authoritative sets of clauses governed by consistent legal principles. The definition of rights is central to this system. Judges are trained from the beginning of their careers to interpret these codes. In England and Wales, on the other hand, common law represents (a) an accumulation of precedents established by the decisions of courts of law and (b) parliamentary statutes. The assessment of rights is only part of a broader concern with a relatively pragmatic search for remedies for wrongs or injuries. Most judges are appointed after they have had distinguished careers as barristers or, less commonly, solicitors.

The juridical framework for the administration of justice differs, therefore, between France and the UK. The frameworks have consequences for some key aspects of prisons. First and foremost, as shown in Table 1.1, French courts hand down a smaller proportion of custodial sentences than do their counterparts in England and Wales. Moreover, the average length of sentence is shorter in France than in England and Wales, according to Table 1.2. As a result, the incarceration rate per 100,000 of population was 85 in France and 139 in England and Wales in 2001.

Second, questions relating to the planning of prisoners' sentences in French prisons are dealt with by specially appointed judges, the *Juges de l'Application des Peines* (JAP) (judges attached to prisons who advise directors on the treatment of inmates and who make decisions about home leave and parole). They also receive sentenced prisoners' written requests and complaints about matters under their jurisdiction. Advice is available

Table 1.1 Prison populations by type of custody, France and England & Wales, mid-2002

	France §		England & Wales †	
	Number	%	Number	%
Remand	18,469	32.75	12,792	18.27
Sentenced	37,916	67.24	57,222	81.72
Total	56,385	99.99	70,014	99.99

Sources:
§ *Chiffres-clés de la justice*. Direction de l'Administration générale et de l'Équipement. October 2002. Online at: www.justice.gouv.fr/chiffres/penit02.htm.
† Average population in custody in 2002. Adapted from *Prison Statistics, England and Wales 2002*. National Statistics. Cm 5996. Table 1.1. Online at: http://www.official-documents.co.uk/document/cm59/5996/5996.pdf.

Table 1.2 Length of prison sentence, all offences, France and England & Wales, mid-2002

	France § %	England & Wales † %
Less than 1 year	33.9	13.6
1–3 years	21.3	
1–4 years		38.2
3–5 years	9.3	
4 years or more		48.2
5 years or more	35.5	
Total	100	100

Sources:
§ *Chiffres-clés de la justice*. Direction de l'Administration générale et de l'Équipement. October 2002. Online at: www.justice.gouv.fr/chiffres/penit02.htm.
† Adapted from *Prison Statistics, England and Wales 2002*. National Statistics. Cm 5996. Table 1.6. Online at: http://www.official-documents.co.uk/document/cm59/5996/5996.pdf.

to these judges from the *Commission d'Application des Peines* (a small committee advising the *Juge de l'Application des Peines*) at the level of each establishment. Some of their decisions can be overturned by the *Procureur de la République* (State Prosecutor) and challenged by inmates. Remand prisoners' issues remain subject to the decisions of the *Juges d'Instruction* (Investigating Magistrates) investigating their cases.

The situation in England and Wales is strikingly different in so far as judges have virtually no involvement in sentence planning and other matters concerning the conditions in which prisoners serve their sentences. Instead, questions of parole, remission, visiting rights, complaints and discipline are a matter for governors and/or statutory bodies such as Independent Monitoring Boards (IMB), the Parole Board and the Prison Ombudsman. Nevertheless, in exceptional circumstances, prisoners can seek judicial review of administrative actions.

It is significant for our research that grievance procedures in both France and England and Wales are mainly responsive to the complaints lodged by individual prisoners about their particular cases. In neither country is there machinery for receiving, let alone investigating, collective complaints or 'class actions'. It is unlikely, therefore, that Muslim inmates, as a collectivity, could succeed in having a complaint about, say, anti-Islamic discrimination investigated. Moreover, it is not clear how far the outcome of a successful complaint lodged by any individual Muslim inmate about, for example, the freedom to practise Islam, would necessarily redound to the benefit of his or her co-religionists in prison. Grievance procedures in both countries apply exclusively to the complaints lodged by individuals (Vagg, 1994).

It is worth adding that the systems of prison inspection also differ between the two countries. Since 1979, Her Majesty's Inspectorate of Prisons (HMIP) for England and Wales[11] has functioned as an independent agency for monitoring and investigating all aspects of prison life mainly on the basis of scheduled and unscheduled inspections. Successive Chief Inspectors have also made detailed recommendations to the Home Office about numerous issues. In addition, HMIP has conducted thematic reviews of issues affecting women in prison, the health care of prisoners, young prisoners, suicide, unsentenced prisoners, and Close Supervision Centres.

In the period August 2001 to August 2002, HMIP, consisting of 28 inspectors, two part-time inspectors and 16 support staff, carried out inspections of 62 prisons and immigration centres. In the same period the inspectorate published 64 inspection reports and thematic reviews. A central concern of most recent reports has been the question of how to ensure that prisons are 'healthy'. A healthy prison is described as 'one where prisoners are safe, are treated with respect, have sufficient access to purposeful activity, and are prepared for resettlement' (HM Chief Inspector of Prisons, 2002: 11). It is clear from inspection reports as well as from public statements made by Sir David Ramsbotham, who was Chief Inspector of Prisons in England and

Wales from 1995 until 2001, that he considered religion as a contribution towards the health of prisons. Moreover, inspection reports have consistently commended 'multi-faith' arrangements in prison chaplaincies.

By comparison, the inspection system in France is less independent than in England and Wales and less well resourced. The *Inspection des Services Pénitentiaires* (ISP) is a department of the *Administration Pénitentiaire* (the French Prison Service) and shares its responsibility for inspecting prisons with the *Inspection Générale des Affaires Sociales* (IGAS), which is concerned with the health of prisoners and the hygiene of prisons. The inspection work falls into two broad categories. One category is for routine monitoring of administrative procedures and resources; the other is for investigations into occasional incidents such as escapes or serious disturbances. In addition, inspectors produce studies of thematic issues and policies. The number of reports published each year is similar to that of the much larger HMIP team in England and Wales, but many of the French reports and studies are produced on the basis of very brief inspections conducted by only one or two inspectors (Vagg, 1991: 159).

As we shall show in Chapter 5, the question of 'race relations' in the prisons of England and Wales has also been the subject of several official investigations, including most recently the long awaited reports produced by the Commission for Racial Equality (CRE, 2003a, 2003b) and an internal report on the same subject (Race Equality Race Advisor, 2000).

The prison populations

The *size* of the prison population in France reached a peak of about 55,000 in 1996 then declined steadily to 49,718 in July 2001 before rising to 56,385 in mid-2002 and 60,963 by mid-2003. Most of the decline had been due to a reduction in the number of prisoners on remand. The prison population in England and Wales, which had been increasing steadily since the 1980s, reached 70,014 in 2002 (see Table 1.1). It has subsequently continued rising, however, and was at roughly 74,000 by the end of 2003.[12] These differences between the two countries in the size of the inmate population are not reflected directly, however, in their respective numbers of prison establishments. France had 185 establishments in 2003, whereas England and Wales had only 140. Nevertheless, high density of cell occupancy is a feature of prisons in both countries (see Table 1.3); and by June 2002 England and Wales had the highest rate of imprisonment in Europe, 137 per 100,000 of population, compared with 87 per 100,000 in France.

In view of the difficulty of establishing equivalence between the two countries' definitions of criminal *offences*, we will not attempt to make direct comparisons between the patterns of offending behaviour for which inmates have been sentenced to prison. Tables 1.4 and 1.5 merely report the official statistics.

Table 1.3 Rate of occupancy per 100 prison places and rate of imprisonment per 100,000 of population, France and England & Wales, 2002

	Prison population	Rate of occupancy per 100 places	Rate of imprisonment per 100,000 population
England & Wales			
31 August 2002	71,324	111	137
France	53,463	112	87

Source: *Prison Statistics England and Wales 2002*. National Statistics Cm 5996. Table 1.19. Online at: http://www.official-documents.co.uk/document/cm59/5996/5996.pdf

Table 1.4 Sentenced prisoners by offence group, France, 2003

	%
Simple and qualified larceny	20.3
Rape and other sexual offences	22.2
Drugs offences	12.7
Murder	9.0
Assault and battery	15.5
Embezzlement, receiving and forgery	6.3
Manslaughter	4.9
Immigration offences	2.1
Other	7.1
Total	100

Source: *Chiffres-clés de la Justice. L'Administration pénitentiaire.* 1 avril 2003.

Table 1.5 Adult sentenced prisoners by type of offence, England & Wales June 30 2002

	Number	%
Violence against the person	11,668	21.6
Rape	2,918	5.4
Other sexual offences	2,365	4.4
Burglary	8922	16.5
Robbery	7,197	13.3
Theft and handling	4,282	7.9
Fraud and forgery	917	1.7
Drugs offences	8,724	16.2
Other offences	5,941	11.0
Offences not recorded	1,002	1.9
Fine default	31	0.05
Total	53,967	99.95

Source: Adapted from *Prison Statistics, England and Wales 2002*. National Statistics Cm 5996. Table 1.5. Online at: http://www.official-documents.co.uk/document/cm59/5996/5996.pdf.

Further differences between the two prison systems and their respective frameworks of criminal justice become apparent when they are compared in terms of the *types of custody* in which inmates are held. Table 1.1 shows that French prisons held a significantly higher proportion of prisoners on remand in 2002 (33%) than in England and Wales (18%). The average number of days spent on remand in France in 2002 was about 115 days,[13] compared with 43 days in England and Wales[14] Moreover, the percentage of prisoners in France serving sentences of less than one year (34%) is more than twice as high as in England and Wales (14%) (see Table 1.2).

Taking into account the slight differences between France and England and Wales in terms of their respective definitions of age groups, Tables 1.6 and 1.7 show that the *age profile* of sentenced prisoners displays two main differences. On the one hand, people under the age of 25 are over-represented in both prison systems, but the extent of over-representation is marginally less severe in France. The index of over-representation for prisoners under the age of 25 in England and Wales is 2.66, and 2.14 for prisoners in France. On the other hand, French prisons hold 7.4 per cent more prisoners above the age of 40 than do their British counterparts.

Women represented 3.73 per cent of the French prison population in 2003 and 6 per cent of prisoners in England and Wales.[15] The rate of female incarceration has been rising steadily in the UK since 1968 and is mainly associated with increases in the number of offences relating to drugs. In

Table 1.6   Sentenced prisoners by age, France 2003 and England & Wales 2002

France § 1 April 2003		England & Wales † 30 June 2002	
Age	Total 50,963 %	Age	Total 57,306 %
Under 18	1.4	15–17	3.6
18–21	9.0	18–20	10.7
21–25	17.6	21–24	18.1
25–30	18.5	25–29	19.0
30–40	26.1	30–39	28.7
40–50	16.2	40–49	12.3
50–60	8.0	50–59	5.2
60 and over	3.1	60 and over	2.4
Total	100	Total	100

Sources:
§ *Chiffres-clés de la Justice. L'Administration pénitentiaire.* 1 avril 2003.
† *Prison Statistics, England and Wales 2002.* National Statistics. Cm 5996. Table 1.9. Online at: http://www.official-documents.co.uk/document/cm59/5996/5996.pdf.

Table 1.7 A comparison of age groups in the general population and in prisons, England & Wales and France

	England & Wales		France			
Age	% Population †† 2001	% Prisons † 2002	Age	% Population §§ 1999	Age	% Prisons § 2003
0–14	18.88		0–14	17.85		
15–24	12.18	32.4	15–24	13.06	Under 25	28.0
25–29	6.60	19.0	25–29	7.13	25–30	18.5
30–39	15.52	28.7	30–39	14.56	30–40	26.1
40–49	13.35	12.3	40–49	14.46	40–50	16.2
50–59	12.59	5.2	50–59	11.49	50–60	8.0
60 +	20.86	2.4	60 +	21.32	60 +	3.1
	99.98	100		100		100

Sources:
†† *Census 2001*, England and Wales.
† *Prison Statistics, England and Wales 2002*. National Statistics. Cm 5996. Table 1.9. Online at: http://www.official-documents.co.uk/document/cm59/5996/5996.pdf.
§ *Chiffres-clés de la justice, l'administration pénitentiaire*. 1 avril 2003.
§§ INSEE *Recensement de la population* 1999. Online at: http://www.recensement.insee.fr/FR/ST_ANA/F2/POPALLPOP1APOP1A1F2FR.html.

fact, 40 per cent of female prisoners in England and Wales were serving sentences in 2002 for drugs offences, whereas the proportion for male prisoners was only 16 per cent. Foreign nationals constitute about two thirds of all female inmates in English prisons.

Ethnicity is a notoriously slippery concept. The French prison service seems to take no official account of prisoners' ethnicity – only their nationality and that of their parents – but in England and Wales it is an important dimension of monitoring, practice and the daily experience of inmates. Table 1.8 shows how the prison population is distributed across the categories of ethnicity employed by the Prison Service. However, these figures need to be qualified in two ways. First, Muslims are distributed unevenly across minority ethnic categories – but perhaps not as unevenly as their public image would suggest, as is evident in Table 1.9. Women from South Asian backgrounds are particularly under-represented. Second, prisoners who are usually resident in the UK should be distinguished from others. If nationality is used as an approximate indicator of this distinction, Table 1.10 shows that, among foreign nationals, Whites represent 26 per cent, Blacks 50 per cent, South Asians 7 per cent, and Chinese and other ethnic groups 17 per cent. Furthermore, if female foreign nationals are analysed separately, then the Whites among them amount to 17 per cent,

Table 1.8   Prison population by ethnicity, England and Wales, 30 June 2002

	Number	**%**
White	54,985	77
Black	11,023	15
South Asian	2,197	3
Chinese and other	2,948	4
Unrecorded	63	–
Total	71,218	99

Source: Adapted from *Prison Statistics, England and Wales 2002*. National Statistics. Cm 5996.
Table 6.1. Online at: http://www.official-documents.co.uk/document/cm59/5996/5996.pdf.

Table 1.9   Gender and ethnicity of Muslim prisoners, England and Wales, June 30, 2002

	Male	**%**	**Female**	**%**	**Total**	**%**
White	652	12.1	23	20	675	12.28
Black	1,772	33	45	39.1	1,817	33
South Asian	1,580	29.3	16	13.9	1,596	29
Chinese and other	1,371	25.5	32	13.9	1,403	25.5
Unrecorded	4		–		4	–
Total	5,379	100	115	100.8	5,494	99.78

Source: adapted from *Prison Statistics, England and Wales 2002*. National Statistics. Cm 5996.
Table 7.4. Online at: http://www.official-documents.co.uk/document/cm59/5996/5996.pdf.

Table 1.10   The ethnic groups of foreign nationals in prison, compared with general population of England and Wales

	All prisoners 2002 §	**%**	**Male**	**%**	**Female**	**%**	**Population England & Wales 2001 †**
White	2,007	26	1,853	27.11	153	17.3	91.3
Black	3,871	50.14	3,242	47.43	628	71.04	2.2
South Asian	555	7.2	539	7.88	16	1.80	3.9
Chinese and other	1,283	16.62	1,196	17.50	87	9.84	1.3
Mixed	–	–	–	–	–	–	1.2
Unrecorded	4	–	4	0.1	–	–	–
Total	7,719	99.96	6,834	99.92	884	99.88	99.9

Sources:
§ *Prison Statistics England and Wales 2002*. National Statistics. Cm 5996. Table 6.3. Online at: http://www.official-documents.co.uk/document/cm59/5996/5996.pdf.
† Census of England & Wales, 2001.

the Blacks to 71 per cent, the South Asians to 1.8 per cent, and the Chinese and other ethnic groups to 10 per cent. In other words, the inmate population of foreign nationals contains an important difference between men and women. The pattern of the offences for which they have been sentenced to custody also displays significant differences, with 83.5 per cent of female foreign nationals being convicted for drugs offences (compared with 28 per cent of British female prisoners and 48.5 per cent of male foreign nationals).

Whereas French citizens whose fathers were born in North Africa represent 5.8 per cent of the population of France, their representation in the prison population is five times higher (30 per cent). Those whose mothers were born in North Africa constitute 22.2 per cent of the prison population but only 5.5 per cent of the French population. In both cases, prisoners with North African parents (mother or father or both) constitute a much larger proportion of prison inmates than of French society. These data appear to confirm the widely held view that the proportion of Muslims in prison is much higher than their proportion in French society.

The assumption that *Maghrébins* (people of North African origins) are the only Muslims in France is clearly wrong, but in view of the lack of official data on Muslims in France and the high proportion of people from North African background in the Muslim population of France, the figures for *Maghrébins* can serve as a reliable indicator of the over-representation of Muslims in French prisons. Furthermore, these statistics confirm the reports of prison authorities and especially of prison officers that the percentage of Muslims is high in prisons.

It would be wrong, however, to infer from these data that 'Islam' as such – or at least Muslim origin – is the sole cause of this over-representation. French prison statistics show that social class is also an important factor in imprisonment. People whose fathers are from the working class constitute a much higher proportion of prisoners than do the children of higher executives. Whereas prisoners whose fathers were executives constitute 6.6 per cent of the prison population, they represent 7.9 per cent of 'ordinary families' in France. This means that there are proportionally fewer people from the middle and upper middle classes in prisons than in society at large. The difference would probably be even greater if sexual offences (child abuse as well as sexual offences against women) were not taken so seriously nowadays in comparison to the past. Some 47.2 per cent of prisoners have fathers from the working classes, whereas only 32.4 per cent of the French population comes from this class background.[16] In other words, to be from the lower classes significantly increases the probability of going to prison. The class dimension of imprisonment, in spite of the recent criminalisation of child abuse, sexual harassment and financial offences (of which many people from the middle and upper classes are convicted) remains a prominent fact.

Still, the percentage of Muslims in French prisons is significantly higher than would be expected if the class origin of the parents is taken into account among people whose parents were from North Africa. Other factors, such as living in disadvantaged suburbs (Marpsat and Laurent, 1997) and social prejudice against North African immigrants – as well as the operation of criminal networks in these *banlieues* – help to raise the proportion of people from North African backgrounds in prisons. The NACRO report (2000: 3) on 'Race and prisons' in England and Wales also confirmed the view that the over-representation of Black and minority ethnic groups in the prison population reflects systematic disadvantages associated with 'unemployment, poverty, homelessness and poor education' which are, in turn, compounded by racial discrimination.

The question of the *religious* identity of prisoners is much more easily answered for England where, in the absence of a constitutional separation of religion and the state, there is no legal obstacle to the collection of official statistics about religion. On the contrary, the prison system has been collecting quite detailed data on the religion of its inmates for many years. They used to be collected by Christian chaplains on one particular day each year, but from 1999 religious affiliations have been recorded on each prison's Local Inmate Data System (LIDS) and supplied to Prison Service headquarters. The result of this change is that most of the data are probably more robust, but the system does not have the capacity to keep track of changes in prisoners' religious registrations. The data are not a reliable source of evidence, therefore, about the number of conversions or 'switches' from one religious category to another.

At the point of reception into a prison establishment, all prisoners are given the opportunity to register membership of, or identification with, one of about 40 religious collectivities. But, as Table 1.11 makes clear, the number of prisoners who specify 'no religion' is now the second largest category. The 'no religion' category has also been growing more quickly than any of the other categories since the 1970s. It grew by 182 per cent between 1993 and 2001, thereby easily outstripping the rate of growth in the prison population. Nevertheless, six other features of this distribution of religious identification are equally interesting and relevant to our research.

First, Christians continue to be by far the largest category, with 58 per cent of the prison population. Anglicans, as the largest category of Christians, are more than twice as numerous as Roman Catholics – the next largest category. Other Christian groups are all quite small by comparison. The proportion of self-reported Christian inmates has been declining for several decades.

Second, the number of prisoners registered as Hindu or Sikh has been growing slowly for many years but remains at relatively modest levels and has barely kept pace with the expansion of the prison population. By con-

Table 1.11 Religious registrations of prisoners, June 30, 2002, compared to the religious identity of the population of England & Wales

Religious registrations of prisoners §		Number of prisoners	%	General population † %
Christian		**41,325**	**58**	**71.7**
	Anglican	25,754	36.16	
	Free Church	1,397	1.93	
	Roman Catholic	12,375	17.37	
	Other Christian	1,798	2.52	
Non-Christian	Buddhist	**7,227**	**10.14**	**5.5**
		672	0.94	0.3
	Hindu	271	0.38	1.1
	Jewish	179	0.25	0.5
	Muslim	5,495	7.71	3.0
	Sikh	442	0.62	0.6
	Other non-Christian	168	0.23	0.3
Non-recognised		222	0.31	–
No religion		22,435	31.50	14.8
Not recorded		10	0.01	7.7
Total		**71,219**	**99.96**	**99.7**

Sources:
§ Adapted from *Prison Statistics, England and Wales 2002*. National Statistics. Cm 5996. Table 7.1. Online at: http://www.official-documents.co.uk/document/cm59/5996/5996.pdf.
† *Census of England and Wales 2001*.

trast, the Buddhists grew by 174 per cent between 1993 and 2001, admittedly beginning from a very small base. Only the Muslims represent a significant *and* growing proportion of inmates. For, although they constitute only 8 per cent of prisoners, they represent 77 per cent of all religious registrations other than Christian. Only the 'no religion' and Buddhist categories have faster rates of growth, since Muslims grew by 140 per cent between 1993 and 2001 – a period when the prison population expanded by no more than 58 per cent. Over the same period, the number of Jewish prisoners declined by 24 per cent.

Third, the pattern of religious registrations in the prisons of England and Wales shows some significant differences from the pattern of religious identity in the general population. As Table 1.11 indicates, the population of England and Wales, as reflected in answers to the optional question 'What is your religion?' in the 2001 Census, is significantly more Christian (71.7%), less Muslim (3.0%) and less likely to have no religion (14.8%)

than are prison inmates. In this respect, as in many others, prisoners are not representative of the general population of the country in which they are detained.

Fourth, female prisoners are less likely to have no religion (28%) than their male counterparts (31%) and more likely to be Christian (70%). Only 3 per cent of female prisoners are Muslim. The likelihood of having a religious registration increases with age for both male and female prisoners. Among 15–17-year-old prisoners, 59 per cent have no religion, whereas the percentage of prisoners aged 60 and over with no religion is only 15 per cent.

Fifth, the relationship between religion and ethnic groups among inmates is relatively clear. Table 1.12 shows that White inmates are predominantly Christian (63%) and more likely than other ethnic groups to have no religion (34%). The majority of Black inmates are Christian (54%), but 27 per cent of them report that they have no religion, and 16 per cent are Muslim. South Asian inmates are most likely to be Muslims (73%), with only 3 per cent of them choosing the 'no religion' category. Muslim was also the religious identity chosen by the largest percentage of Chinese and other Asian inmates (48%). Moreover, the Muslim category displays the highest degree of ethnic diversity.

According to Table 1.9, additional diversity within the Muslim category arises from gender differences. On the one hand, the proportion of White women among Muslims is close to being twice as large as the proportion of White men among Muslims. On the other hand, the proportion of Pakistani Muslim men was nearly twice as large as that of Pakistani Muslim women in 2001.[17] These data all underline the fact that the prisons of England and Wales are extremely diverse in terms of inmates' self-reported religious affiliation and that the association between religion, non-religion and ethnic group is strong in the case of most inmates.

Table 1.12   Prisoners' religious registrations according to ethnic group, England and Wales, 30 June 2002

	Christian %	Muslim %	No religion %	Other %	Total %
White	62.94	1.22	34.28	1.66	100
Black	53.53	16.48	27.00	2.99	100
South Asian	3.36	72.59	3.18	20.87	100
Chinese & other	23.88	47.59	17.50	11.03	100

Source: Adapted from *Prison Statistics, England and Wales 2001*. National Statistics. Cm 5996. Table 7.3. Online at: http://www.official-documents.co.uk/document/cm59/5996/5996.pdf.

Finally, the association between religion and sentence length is complicated, particularly if age and type of offence are also taken into account. In addition, given the small number of prisoners with certain combinations of religious affiliation and sentence length, it would be unwise to place too much significance on Table 1.13. Nevertheless, there are some interesting departures from the pattern of sentences being served by the entire prison population. For example, 42 per cent of Buddhist prisoners were serving sentences longer than ten years in 2001, whereas 12 per cent of all prisoners (and only 9 per cent of those with no religion) were serving such long sentences. At the other end of the scale, only 5 per cent of Buddhists were serving sentences of fewer than 12 months, but 20 per cent of all prisoners and 26 per cent of prisoners with no religion fell into this category.

The distribution of sentence lengths by religion has two peaks which, for all prisoners with a religious affiliation except Buddhists, fall into the categories of 1.5 to 3 years and 5 to 10 years. The two peaks in the distribution of Buddhist prisoners' sentences fall in the categories of 5 to 10 years and 'life'. Again, the sharpest contrast is with prisoners who register as 'no religion', for their sentences fall predominantly into the categories of fewer than 6 months and 1.5 to 3 years.

Table 1.13   Percentage of sentenced prisoners by religion and sentence length, England and Wales September 1999

	Total	<6 mths	6–12 mths	1–1.5 years	1.5–3 years	3–4 years	4–5 years	5–10 years	>10 years	Life	Total %
All	52,393	13	7	7	21	13	9	17	4	8	99
Christian	32,058	10	6	6	18	11	10	22	5	11	99
Buddhist	252	1	4	4	9	11	6	22	11	32	100
Hindu	199	8	9	9	25	13	7	17	5	9	102
Jewish	168	8	4	6	18	10	10	17	11	15	99
Muslim	3,317	8	4	5	17	12	11	24	10	8	99
Sikh	325	11	6	6	25	9	10	12	5	16	99
Others	74	9	4	4	14	14	3	22	7	23	100
Non-recognised	128	5	4	4	20	16	15	27	6	5	101
No religion	15,868	16	10	9	23	13	8	13	3	6	101

Source: adapted from F. Guessous, N. Hooper and U. Moorthy 2000.

Structure of the book

The research teams in each country analysed their own interviews, fieldwork observations and documentary evidence in the first instance, producing draft analyses of agreed themes. The writers also exchanged their respective drafts before discussing ways of integrating them into a unified text. After further reflection and discussion, Jim Beckford revised the text and introduced a uniform style of presentation. Nevertheless, the book tries to avoid 'flattening out' the significant differences between the materials gathered in each country. In fact, our aim has been to retain as much 'local colour' as possible and only to insist on points in common between the two countries when fully warranted. This is why the treatment of some issues takes up different amounts of space for each country.

The book's conceptual and theoretical framework is explained in Chapter 2. The key notions are 'race', ethnicity and religion, but the argument insists that their use has tended to evolve in sharply different ways on both sides of the English Channel. While official statistics, researchers and politicians in Britain make extensive use of these concepts in their attempts to understand and to respond to immigration and settlement patterns, this is less common in France. Nevertheless, questions about the identity and life chances of Muslims – particularly young Muslims from disadvantaged backgrounds – have attracted great interest in both countries. This is why the issue of how Muslims are categorised in prisons is a focus not only of this chapter but also of the entire book. The chapter concludes with a discussion of philosophical arguments about the academic and political significance of competing discourses about minorities, communities and multiculturalism. The prisons of France and England and Wales are the location for practical application of these different discourses.

Chapter 3 takes the discussion from a conceptual to an empirical level of analysis. It presents the main features of the political, social and religious backgrounds in France and England and Wales against which the research on Muslim prisoners was conducted. The most salient features of the British context relate to church-state relations, the distinctiveness of the Muslim communities, the problems of racism and Islamophobia, the challenge of Islamic extremism and the wide range of difficulties associated with prisons. Consideration of the background in France is dominated by the term *laïcité* – a form of secular Republicanism that pervades state schools and other public institutions. It shapes not only the perception of France's large Muslim minority but also official policies and strategies for responding to the country's ethno-religious diversity. However, the chapter argues that *laïcité* is applied ambiguously in French prisons and that, in conjunction with other aspects of the prison service, it gives rise to special problems for Muslim prisoners. The significance of the book's focus on the treatment of Muslim prisoners therefore differs between France and Britain.

The magnitude of some of the contrasts between the French and British strategies for treating Muslim prisoners begins to become clear in Chapter 4. It begins by showing how extensive the provision of religious facilities for prisoners has been in British prisons for more than a century. But it is also apparent that adjustment was slow at first to the steadily growing number of Muslim inmates since the 1970s. Nevertheless, recent and rapid changes in chaplaincy arrangements have facilitated – and possibly helped to re-shape – the practice of Islam in British prisons as part of wider campaigns to combat racism and to promote the value of 'diversity'. By contrast, the practice of Islam in French prisons is constrained partly by the general weakness of provisions for all religious and pastoral care and partly by the exclusion or marginalisation of the relatively few Imams who are allowed to visit prisoners. As a result, levels of dissatisfaction and alienation are high among Muslim prisoners and, in the absence of Imams, they have many opportunities to cultivate 'extremist' views.

Given that the majority of Muslim prisoners are from visible minority ethnic communities and that many of them are foreign nationals, Chapter 5 asks how far their treatment provides evidence of discrimination against them based on 'race' or ethnicity. Again, the response of British laws and prison policies has centred on identifying and protecting clearly demarcated minorities including Muslims. Nevertheless, Muslim prisoners allege that they are still victims of racial discrimination, although prison officers deny that blatant racism is common. Muslim prisoners in French prisons also allege that prison officers routinely treat them in a racist fashion and that Islam is frequently targeted for special attacks. In the absence of policies and administrative frameworks for protecting Muslim and ethnic minorities as such, prisoners have very little faith in the available procedures for investigating complaints about racism. The persistent accusations of anti-Muslim racism in the prisons of both countries call into question the responses of their respective prison systems.

Chapter 6 explores the day-to-day experiences of Muslim prisoners with special emphasis on the extent to which life in prison shapes their self-identity as Muslims. In the case of England and Wales, the influence of the Prison Service's official categorisation of prisoners in terms of ethnicity and religion cuts across their own forms of self-categorisation. Sensitivities are strong about respect for copies of the Qur'an, *halal* food, physical cleanliness and modesty. There are also revealing divisions among Muslim prisoners along lines of nationality, ethnicity, language, politics and views of religious extremism. In France, the paradigms of universalism and *laïcité* prohibit the recognition of any ethnic or religious minorities in the public domain. However, prejudice against North Africans and Muslims dominates the general context of prisons. Muslim inmates, in turn, have developed a strong sense of their group identity as the young men from the *banlieues* (rough suburbs); and they turn to their own interpretation of

Islam either for guidance and solace from their plight or as a reversal of the stigma that they suffer in the shape of radical Islam.

The central point of Chapter 7 is that the work of Muslim Imams or chaplains has a major effect on prisoners' self-identification as Muslims, on their patterns of religious practice and on the attitudes of prison staff towards Islam. The prisons of England and Wales have progressively created space for sessional and full-time Imams in pre-existing chaplaincy teams, although questions still persist about the extent to which they are fully integrated into all functions. Moreover, Muslim prisoners express strong appreciation for most Imams; the presence of full-time Imams in a growing number of prisons is beginning to influence the operation of not only chaplaincies but also programmes for fostering diversity and challenging offending behaviour. The situation in France is sharply different because the number of Imams visiting prisons is small in relation to the number of Muslim inmates and because French prisons have never housed strong chaplaincy facilities. As a result, many Muslim prisoners find it difficult to fulfil their basic religious obligations in matters of diet, cleanliness and prayer; they deny that their religion is respected; and some warm towards the politico-religious messages on offer from 'radical' inmates who assume informal positions of leadership.

The Conclusions draw together the many strands of the contrast that the book makes between the treatment of Muslims in the prisons of France and England and Wales. It situates the contrast in the context of political, legal, historical and religious factors that have shaped each country's perception of minorities and each country's response in terms of policies, strategies and practice. The chapter's recommendations take account of these differences but also insist on the necessity to re-think some aspects of the current situation. The final argument is that since the Muslim population in Europe is large and growing – inside and outside prisons – it is important to find ways of reconciling the right to difference with the right to equality.

The meaning of the many Arabic, French and Urdu terms that appear in the text is given in English in square brackets. The Glossary provides a listing of these terms and, in some cases, an expanded explanation of their meaning.

2
Conceptual Framework: Categorisation, Muslims and Captivity

Introduction

Prison is one of the state institutions that most clearly exercises coercion. In a way it is doubly coercive because it removes disorderly elements from wider society by force – and then organises a tightly controlled regime for these elements within prison. A number of assumptions underlie the prison environment, such as the need to hold inmates on tight reins since their background reveals a propensity to break rules and cause disruption. Although the prison institution as such is mostly accepted as legitimate by the rest of society, this is not necessarily the case for the majority of inmates. On the contrary, there is a tendency for them not to accept their situation. This is why prison authorities see the need to govern through the enforcement of discipline.

Prisons are widely thought to pursue a double mission. Firstly, they aim to ensure security by removing serious deviants from the rest of society and keeping them separated. This also includes making sure that security and order prevail within prisons. As noted by the then Director General of the Prison Service of England and Wales: 'Our principal responsibility has to be to ensure that our prisons are, first of all, secure and secondly, safe, both for staff and for prisoners.' (Leech and Cheney, 2001: 556). Secondly, prisons are expected to prepare inmates for their release into society. During their time in prison inmates are supposed to learn respect for norms, rules of conduct and morals so that they can become law-abiding citizens. Prisons categorise inmates in this process of re-socialisation, regardless of the actual impact that they have on reforming inmates' thought and conduct. Indeed, the capacity of the prison institution to deliver on these two objectives has been seriously challenged on the grounds that they are incompatible with each other and that prisons exercise surveillance and punishment as part of the state's regime for controlling its citizens (Foucault, 1975). Either way, prisons are bound by a number of legal instruments, directives and guide-lines so that certain rights are established for the inmates – albeit more limited rights than those enjoyed by people outside. For example, Rule 42 of the 'Standard Minimum Rules for the Treatment of Prisoners' specifies that:

> So far as practicable, every prisoner shall be allowed to satisfy the needs of his religious life by attending the services provided in the institution and having in his possession the books of religious observance and instruction of his denomination. (quoted in Coyle, 2002: 48)

Despite these points about the centrality of categorisation processes to all prison regimes, this chapter will begin to explore some of the differences between prisons in England and Wales and France with regard to their treatment of Muslim inmates. The first section reviews the main components of social scientific thinking in the UK about 'race' and ethnicity and religion. The second section focuses on the categorisation of Muslims in British and French prisons.

Categorisation, self-definition: ethnicity and religion

Prisoners are uprooted from their social environment and confined in a new environment that is not of their choosing: the minutest details of their everyday life are regulated and imposed. Their social networks and their status are dislocated, and their group identification challenged. As noted by Le Caisne (2000), inmates undergo a process of de-socialisation and a process of re-socialisation. They are removed from their social networks, affiliations and social characteristics such as family, group, community or job; in some respects, they lose their group identification and personal identity. The prison setting may even damage their capacity for humanity and sociability. Nevertheless, some prisoners manage to re-create patterns of meaning and value, a new group identification within the institution, and new modes of social interaction and organisation.

According to Le Caisne (2000: 78, 79), inmates are under pressure to forge a new common identity, i.e. to share specific moral values, which may seem opposed to those of ordinary citizens; they must recover a form of social identity as protection against the impact of the degradation, mortification, profanation and mutilation which may be the fate of people confined in total institutions (Goffman, 1990). Finally, they must re-create their personal identity. Being forced to live in close proximity to other inmates in prison – and the promiscuity that can result – makes it all the more necessary to distinguish oneself from 'the other', as argued by Levi-Strauss (1997). Yet, the characteristics of inmates and their circumstances do not easily give rise to group solidarity and collective action from which a sense of belonging and identification may arise. Individualism may prevail in the sense that each will look after his own interest first and foremost.

On the other hand, in the case of 'Muslim activists' in French prisons there is a sense of collective identity, which sometimes goes in the direction of group action such as illegal collective prayers for Muslims in the courtyards or a collective refusal to return to their cells in the case of Basque political prisoners.

This process takes place within the spatial confines of the prison and in the context of the strict rules and regulations enforced by the prison staff. In other words, the balance between constraint and choice is strongly tilted in favour of constraint. Re-socialisation in prison takes place, if at all, mostly on the institution's own terms and according to the categories that it imposes. There are few areas in which there is group protest against this imposition, particularly in the case of the so-called radical Muslims: they find justification for their views ('the Western world is against us') by provoking officials, by trying to raise their importance in the eyes of Muslim inmates and by playing the role of 'intermediary' between the prison administration and other Muslims, therefore obtaining some recognition from officials. Incidentally, the same holds for the Basque and Corsican activists held in French prisons – albeit for different reasons. The parallels are also quite strong with Republican and Loyalist prisoners in Northern Ireland.

The process of self-definition, which happens in interaction with categorisation processes that occur before, but particularly during, incarceration, is strictly limited. The capacity of inmates to formulate and reformulate their group identification is subject to the numerous conditions and constraints of prison life, although the latter ultimately do not determine outcomes.

Some of the questions asked about Muslim inmates in prison can thus be answered in terms of the dialectical relationship between institutional categorisation and self-definition, which in turn reflects the interaction between structure (the prison institution) and actors (Muslim inmates). It also involves prison staff and other interested parties such as chaplains, educationalists, healthcare workers, and so on. The inmates with whom we are concerned display ethnic and religious characteristics that were shaped by processes of categorisation and self-definition in British and French society before they were sentenced to prison. This is why we need to situate our analysis in the context of debates about ethnicity and ethnic groups, although this is not the place to review all issues pertaining to ethnicity. In any case, many of them have already been clarified, particularly in Jenkins (1997). What particularly interests us here is the interaction between categorisation and self-definition.

We need to bear in mind a number of important considerations. The boundaries and markers that play a significant role in the formulation of ethnic identification (Barth, 1969; Wallman, 1986) are elaborated in interaction between the potential ethnic group and the majority population. Moreover, the mobilisation of ethnic identifiers is not necessary or automatic but is situational and socially constructed, involving social structures and social organisation (Barth, 1969). In other words, ethnic identifiers change according to context and related interests. Ethnic identity is expressed in the course of social interaction and collective action as well as internalised in personal identification (Jenkins, 1997).

Finally, it is important to remember that a relation of power is involved so that we are not examining the meeting of two groups on equal terms. However, this does not imply that the dominant group is simply able to impose its categorisation on the other. The less powerful group, in this instance the potential ethnic or religious group, can muster some response to categorisation. The group's identification is indeed linked to resources on which it draws in order to resist categorisation. As Jenkins (1997: 23) puts it, the relation of power 'relates to the capacity of one group successfully to impose its categories of ascription upon another set of people, and to the resources which the categorised collectivity can draw upon to resist'. It cannot be assumed that the dominant group totally defines the relationship or predicts and controls the outcome of the interaction (Modood, 1992). The meeting of the two collectivities and its outcome are never what either of them is striving towards (Archer, 1995); acceptance, alienation and resistance are components of the categorised group's self-identification in any given set of circumstances. Ethnicity cannot be regarded as the inherent property of a group or purely the expression of its aspirations. Nor is it primordial despite the fact that primary socialisation in the family may inculcate a number of cultural practices. These practices *per se* do not account for the constitution and consciousness of a group involved in collective action (Joly, 2001). What constitutes ethnicity is a cultural emergent property resulting from specific social and historical circumstances (Carter, 2000).

Religion frequently appears in the list of potential markers of ethnicity; it may even sometimes amount to its principal marker, as in Northern Ireland where its significance clearly derives from specific historical and social circumstances. Each of the three paradigms that will be elaborated below regarding populations of Muslim background in the UK (race relations, ethnicity and community, and religion) has taken account of the rising salience of Islam. However, it is not merely the case that one paradigm totally eliminated what preceded it; each paradigm supersedes, but overlaps with, earlier ones as a kind of palimpsest, with old ones appearing in filigree under the new one. Their trace survives in laws, institutions, policies, practices, culture and claims. There may be some lag in the progress of paradigms and various sectors of prisons and the inmate population may articulate them differently. This is one of the dimensions to be unpacked. Nevertheless, it cannot be disputed that Muslims and Islam have become part of British society in a way that contrasts sharply with the integration of Muslims into French society (Joly, 1995).

Our hypothesis is that the situation in prisons both corroborates this finding and heralds a greater institutionalisation of Islam in British society in future. This is not necessarily the case in other societies such as France, since the cultural and structural emergent properties surrounding ethnicity and religion differ markedly in Britain and France – although both of them harbour a substantial population of Muslim origin. Islam operates on a different scale and in different ways in French prisons, as we shall emphasise at various points in this and subsequent chapters.

'Race', ethnicity and religion: emerging identities in the UK

As a precondition of understanding the treatment of Muslims in the prisons of England and Wales, we need to set out the frameworks of ideas within which minorities of immigrant origin have been understood in the UK. Three levels of analysis need to be borne in mind when considering these theoretical frameworks:

- The minorities themselves with regard to their structural incorporation within the majority society and their own modes of social organisation
- The majority society's categorisation of these minorities as it underpins the policies directed towards them and the accompanying discourses
- Social science as it conceptualises them and their interaction with majority society.

The following three frameworks of ideas or theoretical approaches depict Muslims and their interaction with the rest of British society in terms of 'race relations', ethnic communities and religion.

The race relations approach

Immigrants who arrived in Britain soon after the Second World War were incorporated within the framework of what has been called the 'race relations' paradigm. This was a distinctive feature of the situation in the United Kingdom at that particular time, but it was to be superseded by a focus on ethnicity.

The structural position of these immigrants derived from the fact that they met the needs of an expanding economy and filled the jobs that the native population had left vacant. In this way, they tended to occupy low-wage, precarious and relatively undesirable positions towards the bottom ranks of the labour market. They were also disadvantaged in terms of the housing market and in terms of their access to the benefits of the Welfare State (Daniel, 1968; Smith, 1974; Brown, 1984). They settled mainly in industrial towns where their labour was needed and took up residence in the more derelict areas as they were *de facto* excluded from social housing. This contributed to their geographical concentration in what came to be called twilight zones. It also meant that they occupied substandard housing and were disadvantaged educationally (Rex, 1988, p. 17). Several studies commissioned by the government documented the multiple disadvantages from which these immigrants suffered despite their formal entitlement to the whole gamut of social and political rights since they were British citizens as soon as they took up residence in Britain (by virtue of the 1948 Nationality and Commonwealth Act). It would not be an exaggeration to talk of the 'differential social incorporation' of these immigrants who were 'excluded as workers from participation in the normal benefits of the welfare state in such areas as employment, housing and education' (Rex, 1988: 29–30).

Cultural emergent properties that stress 'racial' differences result from a combination of elements. These immigrants came mainly from the New Commonwealth: they were West Indians, Indians, Pakistanis, East African Asians and Bangladeshis. This meant that they were visibly different from autochthonous Britons (at the time), although there were no sound reasons why this difference was bound to assume any social or political significance. A number of processes explain why it did. One factor was that they were former colonial subjects from the 'new colonies', that is, they did not originate from the old colonies of settlement such as Australia or New Zealand, which were mostly populated by people of British or European origin who had gained their independence long ago. The new colonies had become independent after the Second World War and had until then been governed on the basis of a clear gulf at every level of society – economic, political, social and cultural – between a small group of colonial rulers (white Britons) and colonised people. Prejudice and racism also characterised the British colonies as in other colonial contexts (Memmi, 1972). However, the main factor that promoted the 'race relations' paradigm came from the United States and exercised a predominant influence on British politics and culture (for complex reasons which cannot be examined here). In brief, the concentration of 'visible' minorities in disadvantaged areas was deemed to correspond to US black 'ghettos'. For example, the Notting Hill riots of 1968 evoked fears of events paralleling 'race riots' in the United States; and the notion of a black and white divide was readily borrowed as policies emulated those implemented in the United States to deal with the issue (Layton-Henry, 1984).

Policies and legislation played an important role in the construction of the race relations paradigm. After a period of assimilationist policies, the British government developed a set of policies that addressed the 'social disadvantage' and 'urban deprivation' of immigrants from the New Commonwealth such as section 11 of the 1966 Local Government Act, the 1968 Urban Programme and the 1977 Policy for the Inner Cities (Candappa and Joly, 1994). These policies were meant to redress the manifest discrimination and social disadvantage that 'non-white' groups suffered, as evidenced by indicators of deprivation well documented by social scientists. Smith (1974: 321) notes that 'the links between membership of a racial minority group and each particular form of deprivation are exceedingly strong'.

Meanwhile, successive Immigration Acts (1962, 1968 and 1971) increased restrictions on immigrants from the New Commonwealth, eventually subjecting British passport holders from the Commonwealth to immigration regulations if they did not have a parent or grandparent born in the UK. Only 'patrials' were granted the right of abode. This introduced immigration controls based on colour/racial distinctions (Miles and Phizacklea, 1984). Even legislation that was intended to favour immigrants stressed the 'race' dimension. The notion of discrimination based on racial distinctions was reinforced on the public agenda as it was explicitly enshrined in legislation against discrimination on 'racial grounds', meaning any of the following: 'colour, race, nationality or ethnic or national origin' (Race Relations Act 1976, Chapter 74: 2). Earlier Race Relations Acts (1965, 1968) culminated in the 1976 Race Relations Act that not only outlawed direct and indirect discrimination but also established the Commission for Racial Equality. The latter was empowered to investigate cases of racial discrimination and conducted a large number of investigations (Layton-Henry, 1984). It was assumed that all non-white minorities suffered from disadvantages that set them apart from 'white' groups, because of discrimination and racism.

Some of the immigrants, responding to those policies and the perceived racism in society, had organised themselves to challenge discrimination and mobilised on the basis of blackness, so that 'black' became a political term used as self-identification by anti-racist activists of immigrant origin (Lloyd, 1998). They also formed black sections in trade unions and in political parties and campaigns. Some of those groups seemed to make an attempt to create a particular form of consciousness and unity out of the experience of racism (Modood, 1994). This mode of mobilisation was also largely inspired by earlier movements in the USA (such as Black Power and the Black Muslims).

Social scientists conceptualised all these developments in terms of a 'race relations' paradigm. Some set out to demonstrate the overlap between 'colour' on the one hand and 'class' on the other. This amounted to the claim that issues of power, status and stratification had led those groups to be excluded from access to resources and had relegated them to an 'underclass' (Rex and Moore, 1967), while others argued that contact and proximity would in time improve 'race relations' (Banton, 1967). An extensive literature appeared on this issue. The argument was that the formulation of race relations in Britain resulted from the emergent properties of a labour shortage and the cultural emergent property of ideas about race, colour and Britishness (Carter, 2000). For a time the race relations paradigm held sway despite being challenged (Miles, 1989); and immigrants from the New Commonwealth, including those from a Muslim background, had to fit into this racial categorisation. This was not, however, to remain their sole or permanent option.

Ethnic groups and communities

While the 'race relations' and 'ethnic communities' paradigms are interrelated they nonetheless represent two different stages of thinking. A combination of specific factors led to the conceptualisation of ethnic groups and communities. Although the phrase 'race relations' was widely used in legislation and the mass media, the minorities concerned were not addressed as racial groups for a variety of reasons – including the proven anti-scientific basis of 'race' theory and the negative connotation attached to the use made of it by extreme right-wing ideologists and political parties.

Immigrant minorities from distinctive backgrounds had regrouped in particular areas of British industrial cities as a consequence of several factors including the structure of housing and employment, chain migration, immigration laws and the whole process of settlement. Taking as an example migrants from the Indian subcontinent, chain migration brought together people from the same region and even from the same villages: Punjabis from Pakistan, Mirpuris from Azad Kashmir, Sylletis from Bangladesh, and Jullunderis from the Indian Punjab. When families were reunited, it became all the more necessary – and possible – to reconstitute social networks, associations and institutions establishing some kinds of communities. They acquired great salience and visibility in the areas in which the migrants were concentrated. 'Ethnic' shops lined the streets with tropical vegetables, clothing, jewellery, travel agents, banks and religious institutions (temples or mosques). Their cultural markers were clearly displayed, and their dense networks established each community's mode of social organisation. The different responses of these groups, as they interacted with the rest of British society, reflected their internal characteristics, divisions and modes of social organisation, as shown by the study of Mirpuris from Azad Kashmir and Jullunderis from the Indian Punjab (Modood, 1992). They participated in mainstream political parties and had strong relations with local authorities through their associations with a view to defending their material and cultural interests. Muslims were classified and organised along national/ethnic lines – Punjabis from Pakistan, Azad Kashmiris, Bangladeshis, East African Asians – and they formed distinct communities.

Policies began to promote the 'ethnic community' paradigm. These groups soon ceased to be perceived as undifferentiated racial groups, and it became clear to themselves and to the majority society that they were here to stay. The term 'immigrants' was replaced by that of 'ethnic minorities', which is still in use today. Here again, the US model of immigrants' integration as ethnic minority groups was influential. Differences between the groups were construed on the basis of 'ethnic' characteristics deriving from their place of origin, as described in monitoring exercises; and an ethnic question was introduced in the 1981 UK Census as well as in many public institutions.

Meanwhile, in the 1980s local authorities began to address the question of equal opportunities that had been stipulated by the Race Relations Act 1976 but had been left unheeded until it was driven home by the mobilisation of groups that were discriminated against, through their associations, their participation in political parties and their involvement in urban riots in the main industrial towns (in 1980, 1981 and 1985). Municipal authorities sought out interlocutors in the form of 'community leaders', along the lines of the former colonial system that had utilised local structures. Not unlike the situation of colonial self-rule, community leaders were sometimes 'appointed' from above as suited an institution in search of gatekeepers. Local authorities also set up an internal apparatus to deal with the issue, in the shape of race relations and equal opportunity committees or units that, in turn, organised forums bringing together representatives of ethnic communities. This was rendered necessary by directives issued in 1990 about the application of Article 11 of the Local Government Act 1966, which had emphasised the need to consult with communities and to provide posts for ethnic minority associations (Joly, 2001).

The 'ethnic' question in the 2001 Census and other monitoring exercises consolidated this trend, categorising people under a variety of labels which remained controversial: Black (including Black Caribbeans), Black African and Black other; South Asian (including Indians, Pakistanis, Bangladeshis, and so on). The realisation gradually dawned that membership of a minority community could invite discrimination on the basis of cultural attributes associated with an ethnic group (such as dress or dietary habits), and that this could be indicted under the 1976 Act.

This process reinforced the formation of communities and community associations since it made resources available for a number of community activities, such as the teaching of ethnic minority languages, organising activities for women or older people, and giving advice on a range of issues (Rex, Joly and Wilpert, 1987). It also imposed this model *de facto* on all the groups concerned since it came to constitute a gateway to resources. On the whole, groups took advantage of the opportunities offered to formalise and multiply their community networks where a basis for them already existed, thereby consolidating themselves. At the same time, this situation sometimes fostered rivalries within groups of the same origin and between groups. Groups that, for a variety of reasons, had not defined themselves as ethnic minorities created the format, without the content, of elaborate community associations in order to attract resources and defend their interests (Wahlbeck, 1999; Kelly, 2001). This policy ran the risk, however, of disempowering groups that opted for different modes of social organisation (Joly, 2001).

For social scientists interested in these minority groups, the ideas of ethnicity and ethnic groups dominated the scene. Multiculturalism became the official policy, and the ethnic minority community paradigm emerged from the conjunction of official policies, the minorities' own forms of organisation and social science. Social scientists focused their studies on ethnic groups, their characteristics and mobilisation. The discussion explored various dimensions of ethnic groups and ethnicity (Joly, 2001): primordial versus situational definitions (Barth, 1969); ethnic markers and the importance of boundaries (Wallman, 1986); the necessity of interaction with other groups as a *sine qua non* of ethnic consciousness; the ethnic group as Gemeinschaft or Gesellschaft, as a group for itself or in itself; the relationship between categorisation and self-definition (Jenkins, 1997); private/public ethnicity and ethnic mobilisation (Rex and Drury, 1994); ethnicity as a resource (Saifullah Khan, 1977); and its relation to integration and the question of transnational communities. Ethnicity and ethnic groups also became a key theme because it was fed by an extensive American literature on this question.

This paradigm had the merit of giving a real place to social actors, the ethnic minorities, who were thus considered not just as passive victims but also as agents mobilising to defend their interests (Rex and Drury, 1994). However, this paradigm ran the risk of taking ethnicity and ethnic groups as a taken-for-granted reality, both in the realm of social science and in British society itself. It was therefore criticised for reification. The shortcomings of an ethnicity approach have been exposed from a variety of viewpoints (Modood and Werbner, 1997; Baumann, 1999). Groups from countries with Muslim culture were identified as distinct groups only after the stages of 'race relations' and 'ethnic communities' had passed. Without entering into the complex debate over the nature of ethnic groups and their religious attributes, we shall now turn to their characterisation on the basis of religious markers, with special reference to Muslims.

Muslims

People with a Muslim culture of origin were initially subsumed under 'black' and subsequently 'Asian' categories (because the vast majority of them had come from the Indian subcontinent). Their treatment by institutions and social scientists did not identify them *per se* as Muslims (Joly and Nielsen, 1985). The Race Relations Act 1976, for instance, does not cover religious discrimination; and the 1991 UK Census did not include a question on religion. Muslims set up networks and institutions following the contours of ethnic/national and theological differences, forming several communities rather than a single Muslim community. But they were initially identified primarily by their ethnic characteristic according to their region of origin.

Muslims distinguished themselves from other Asians when they began to mobilise in the defence of specific Muslim interests. There are roughly 1.6 million Muslims in the UK according to the 2001 Census. This figure is based on answers to a voluntary question about religion. There are about 1,000 officially registered Muslim places of worship in Britain, in addition to numerous others based in private homes. Unquestionably, Muslims have taken concerted action to make a space for themselves in British society (Joly, 1995). They organised a number of associations that negotiated at first on the local level. They keenly participated in the Labour Party and local politics, bringing pressure to bear to further their interests in negotiations with municipalities and public institutions on issues such as cemeteries, planning permission for mosques and dietary requirements. Muslim associations came together to press for provisions that took their needs into account with an initial focus on education. For example, the Muslim Liaison Committee and Birmingham Local Education Authority held negotiations which led to 'Guidelines on meeting the religious and cultural needs of Muslim pupils' (Joly, 1995).

Muslims engaged with British society in multiple spheres, and their religious authorities even recommended this course of action. For instance, the Muslim Council of Britain stated that all Muslim citizens had a religious obligation to participate by voting in the national parliamentary election of 1997 (Joly and Imtiaz, 2002). Local action was extended on to the national level towards the end of the 1980s with the 1988 Education Reform Act and the Rushdie affair. A National Coordination Group of Muslim organisations came together with other religious minorities (such as Jews) to lobby against the 1988 Education Bill which stipulated that school assemblies had to adopt an unequivocally Christian character.

When Salman Rushdie published his *Satanic Verses* in 1988, protest developed amongst Muslims from the Indian subcontinent in the UK, long before Ayatollah Khomenei's Fatwa came into effect: demonstrations took place on 11 October 1988 in Birmingham and on 6 December 1988 in Bradford, whereas the Fatwa was not pronounced until 14 February 1989. A large number of Muslim organisations took part in the campaign including the Shar'ia Council, the Imams and Mosques Council, the Muslim Institute (London), the British Muslim Action Front, the Muslim Youth Cultural Society, the Muslim Youth Movement, Ahl and Hadith, the UK Islamic Mission, the Islamic Defence Council and the Federation of Sunni Mosques. Not only Muslim leaders but also grassroots Muslims and young people took part in the campaign. Protests challenged the Blasphemy Laws that apply only to the Christian religion – or more precisely, the doctrines of the Church of England. The structure of British society, especially the organic alliance of church and state, created a window of opportunity for Muslims in the sense that the compulsory teaching of religion in schools provided an opening through which they could pursue their broader interests.

At the level of policies, Muslims have made good progress in securing a number of provisions to cater for their needs in public institutions (Joly, 1995; Nielsen, 1999), and these provisions increasingly recognise Islam as a legitimate category (Samad, 1997). Small and significant modifications have been introduced to public life that take Islam into account: it is possible to swear on the Qur'an (rather than the Bible) in a court of law; and hospitals, prisons and local councils cater for Muslim dietary needs where there is a substantial Muslim population. Hospitals and local health authorities generally include Muslims in their consultative bodies to reflect the composition of local populations. The following arrangements are in place: local authorities have removed some of the obstacles to obtaining planning permission for building new mosques; plots of land have been granted in cemeteries for Muslim burials; and a representative of the Registry Office celebrates marriages in mosques. Prisons, which have a specific policy on religion and religious discrimination, have appointed Imams alongside Christian chaplains and made provision for other Muslim needs such as *halal* food and arrangements for Eid celebrations. A high-ranking national Muslim Advisor to the Prison Service was appointed in 1999. Advances have been made in the educational sphere, at first on a local level. Local Education Authorities and schools have taken on board many of the Muslim concerns in areas with a substantial Muslim population: assemblies, modesty dress code, *halal* meat or vegetarian meals, time and place for prayers, allowances for Islamic festivals, and sex education as part of other subjects.

In the political sphere, the active involvement of Muslims has increased their representation in local government: at the time of writing, Birmingham, for example, has 11 Muslim councillors out of 23 ethnic minority councillors and out of 117 councillors in total. A large proportion of the electorate consists of Muslims in constituencies such as Sparkbrook, Birmingham (27 per cent) or Bradford West (17 per cent). Two Muslim Members of Parliament and five members of the House of Lords are the only representatives of Muslims in the British Houses of Parliament.

Other gains are notable at the national level: Muslim and other religious minorities, lobbying on the 1988 Education Bill, forced an Amendment, as acknowledged by Kenneth Baker, the Secretary of State for Education, in a letter dated 20 July 1988 to Gullam Sarwar, the head of the Muslim Educational Trust. The Act also required that Local Education Authorities should set up a Standing Advisory Council on Religious Education (SACRE), an institution which had been pioneered in Birmingham with strong Muslim support. In the legal domain, on two occasions, the courts have forced Muslim husbands to comply with the contract which requires the payment of a dowry in case of divorce according to the Shar'iah (Shahnaz v. Riswan, 1965; Qureshi v. Qureshi, 1972). Changes in the interpretation of commercial law have also made possible schemes such as the Muslim

Mortgage and Islamic-run housing cooperatives; this is necessary because Islam forbids usury (Joly and Imtiaz, 2002).

Finally, the turning point of placing Islam on the public agenda was the Rushdie affair, with the main Christian figureheads extending their sympathy: the Archbishop of Canterbury (News Release, 3 March 1989), the Bishop of Birmingham (*Independent*, 22 February 1989), the Bishop of York (*The Times*, 1 March 1989) as well as the Chief Rabbi (*The Times*, 4 February 1989). It generated a national debate, with an unequivocal intervention by Roy Hattersley, a former Deputy Leader of the Labour Party, who said at the Birmingham Mosque on 2 April 1989, 'That Muslims are denied equal treatment under the law is a matter of undisputable fact...'. An exchange of correspondence took place between Muslim organisations and the Home Office. Muslims have definitely made a place for themselves in British society in a process which began at local level and then spread nationally (Nielsen, 1992).

Islam was equally firmly projected to the front of the national stage by its invigoration overseas, starting with the Islamic revolution in Iran in 1979 and the spread of Muslim political movements in other countries with a Muslim culture. Following the collapse of communist regimes in Eastern Europe, Muslim movements have acquired even greater prominence by being perceived as an international challenge to Western control. The 11 September 2001 events have exacerbated this perception worldwide and particularly in the UK because of Britain's close identification with the USA, as expressed in Tony Blair's speeches and policies. This was further emphasised through the war against Iraq in which Britain took part alongside the USA in 2003. In the UK these changes are reflected in the presence of a religious question in the 2001 Census and the introduction of policies taking on board specific Muslim needs in public institutions. One symbol of the official recognition of Islam is the fact that an Eid party is held annually at the House of Commons. The place of Islam was also symbolically enhanced by several statements by Prince Charles (Hewer, 1994) and by the Queen's Christmas speech to the Commonwealth expressing good wishes for Eid in 2000. The Prince of Wales is also patron of the Foundation for Architecture and the Building Arts, VITA (Visual Islamic and Traditional Arts).

Social scientists strongly advocated the need for a separate 'Muslim' category in the study of ethnic minority populations; and Muslims and Islam became an important area of investigation among scholars of ethnic relations (Modood and Werbner, 1997). The prevailing categorisation of Pakistani and Bangladeshi minorities as ethnic groups was at odds with their emerging self-definition as Muslims. Some organisations such as the Muslim Parliament put the case against a race relations or ethnicity approach on the grounds that they were denied self-definition and had allowed themselves to be defined in terms of 'colour, race, ethnic or national origin' because they had been pressurised to conform to the definition put forward in the Race Relations Act 1976 (Mohammed, 1992). In their view it had led to Muslims being divided and omitted as a substantial group. Meanwhile, resources had been directed to 'black' or 'Asian' needs whereas 'Muslim needs were ignored' (Mohammed, 1992).

Some social scientists have focused their research on the 'anti-Muslim' prejudice that led to the coining of a new word, 'Islamophobia', arguing that its consequences have been 'unfair discrimination against Muslim individuals and communities' (Commission on British Muslims and Islamophobia, 1997: 4). Other social scientists start from the vantage point of the Muslim population itself. According to Tariq Modood, for example, what is important is that a group should be able to define itself on the basis of its 'mode of being' as distinct from its 'mode of oppression' as it is best equipped to resist oppression by those 'dimensions of its being from which it derives its greatest collective psychological strength' (Modood, 1992: 55). However, one must remember that Muslims in the UK are in the main South Asian Muslims with their own specific branches of Islam and cultural characteristics (Joly, 1995); this was illustrated by their reaction to Rushdie's *Satanic Verses* which was not paralleled among other Muslim populations in Europe (Modood, 1990). This seems to refer to their self-definition which itself evolves through the interaction of the group with majority society. This self-definition is open to modification, so that it is possible for the same population to organise itself on an ethnic group basis and subsequently to emphasise its religious, Muslim characteristics.

Young Muslims and the identity debate

Young people of Muslim origin in the UK were not prominent in most of the activities outlined above. A minority of them joined the anti-racist movement, and only very few have been active in mainstream political parties – unlike their elders – while their participation in the urban riots of the 1980s was barely noticeable. Muslim associations themselves have been mostly led and supported by first-generation immigrants, although young Muslims born in Britain usually took part in cultural/religious gatherings (such as Eid celebrations) with their family. Young Muslims erupted onto the scene with the Rushdie affair, playing an active role in demonstrations and meetings. This gave them a first impetus, and one can now find Muslim associations in most colleges and universities with substantial numbers of Muslim students. The distinction between ethnicity and religion appears to be particularly relevant for young Muslims brought up in Britain. Their elders, while pressing for provisions for Muslims in the public sphere and setting up the internal structures for the practice of their religion, also maintained their traditions, language and customs. The religious institutions that they created are firmly steeped in their ethnic networks based on the country/region of origin. These institutions are now

being abandoned or challenged by younger Muslims, who seem to emphasise a distinction between religion and ethnicity. Many of the vocal ones
tend to distinguish their Islam from its cultural tenets, thereby opposing
their elders. Islam is used in diverse ways as a marker for a form of group
identification that is different from that of ethnic-based communities.
Some Muslim organisations themselves posit that the only distinguishing
feature of the children of immigrants (from Muslim background) that will
persist, as national and ethnic differences disappear, will be their religious
belief. Their strategy is thus to 'establish a Muslim identity as a means of
unity for the future' (Mohammed, 1992).

A number of studies have explored these new findings. Knott and
Khokher (1993) offered a typology of young Pakistani women as religiously
orientated, ethnically orientated, not ethnically orientated and not religiously orientated. In Jacobson's study (1997) young Pakistanis emphasised
the distinction between religion and ethnicity as sources of identity; they
also expressed their greater affinity with Islam than with ethnic characteristics. One criterion they stressed is the universalism of Islam against the
particularism of ethnicity. They perceived ethnicity as a matter of attachment to a set of traditions or customs that are non-religious in origin and
an attachment to a place of origin. Islam was perceived, by contrast, as a
global community with which they felt they could most easily identify.
The young Muslims in this instance even argued that the ethnic culture of
their parents was mistakenly believed to be Islamic but that it actually
betrayed the 'true' teaching of Islam (Jacobson, 1997: 241). It was also
noted that ethnic boundaries seemed permeable, while religious boundaries
were clear-cut and pervasive; and this, in the author's view, provided a
greater measure of security and a means of dealing with ambiguities and
contradictions in their social environment. Others have shown how Islam
was called upon to challenge parents and community leaders (Nielsen,
1999). Their positioning would thus be the result of their interaction with
the majority society and with their own family and or community.

Other studies specifically look at the mobilisation of young Muslims
during the Rushdie affair and its aftermath. Burlet and Reid (1998), for
example, attribute the actions of young Muslims in the Bradford disturbances of 1995 primarily to disadvantage and disempowerment: high
youth unemployment, inadequate educational provision, and no resources
or facilities. Another factor is that young people were ready to be mobilised
because of the manifest discrepancy between their expectations and their
experience. Anti-discrimination legislation and policies, combined with
multicultural and multi-faith programmes in schools and public institutions, had promised them full participation in society, equal opportunity
and equal respect. But their experience of disadvantage and unemployment
had dashed their hopes (Nielsen, 1997). Protests about Islam would
have carved for them a space of dignity (Lapeyronnie, 1993); it was also

suggested that Islam is the one criterion with which they most closely identified and which could mobilise them (Modood, 1990).

Events following the disturbances in Bradford in 1995 seem to uncover another layer of discrepancy, namely, the feeling among young Muslims that established, first-generation community leaders were exercising exclusive control over Muslim communities as they mustered negotiating rights with local authorities and access to resources (Burlet and Reid, 1998). In the particular case of Bradford's young Muslims, it appears that another dimension has to be taken into account to explain the violent actions they undertook in 1995 and again in July 2001: young men are said to have mobilised a particular Islamic code as a power resource against their elders, women and liberal Muslims as well as the white establishment (no-go areas); public and private violence and harassment are deployed to exercise control in the name of what they perceive as Muslim values (Macey, 1999). Women, on the other hand, call upon different interpretations of Muslim values to promote their position either by challenging parents (Nielsen, 1999) or young Muslim men.

Consequently, although religious markers appear to have gained in strength at the expense of other identity markers, this process is still in the making. It suggests that there are variations in the aspects of religion that are emphasised according to generation, gender, educational level and class (or degree of deprivation) (Kahani-Hopkins and Hopkins, 2002). Islam may also be used as a strategy to obtain resources, in the way that ethnicity was used previously, and this is particularly clear when Islam is incorporated *de facto* (although not legally) as a category of discrimination through the religious question in the UK Census. At any rate, one must be careful not to assume that all people from a Muslim cultural background conform to this model. Some, such as Kurdish refugees, do not recognise or organise themselves on a religious basis but on a political basis (Wahlbeck, 1999). Bosnians, who have also failed to mobilise on that basis, have encountered disagreements with their South Asian Muslim counterparts (Kelly, 2001). This model applies better to people from the Asian subcontinent. Yet, some groups within those communities might also prefer other patterns of identification – such as organisations for the Liberation of Azad Kashmir – which are more politically than religiously based.

The debate is not over and has been rekindled by renewed riots in the twenty-first century. During the spring and summer of 2001, a number of disturbances took place in the North West of England which involved young Asians, including many Muslims and other youths. Some local authorities such as Oldham and Burnley established local enquiries. The Home Secretary's response was to set up a Ministerial Group on Public Order and Community Cohesion. Several substantial reports were published which convey a general perception of segregation and alienation among young Asian Muslims; as one of them expressed it: 'I think that they think we don't belong here. They think only white people should live in England' (Burnley Task Force, 2001). The Muslim communities in those areas are generally portrayed as clearly segregated from white communities in such a way that 'the twain almost never met'. Moreover, young Muslims seem to suffer disproportionately from all the indicators of deprivation including education, employment and leisure opportunities. But one important element that compounded their disaffection was the feeling that they did not have a voice. They perceived a kind of collusion between the local authority and the leaders of their community (community elders from the first generation), and this disenfranchised them. The situation was exacerbated by a strong British National Party (BNP) presence which recurrently used 'Muslim' as a racist insult, emphasising the religious marker and, incidentally, thereby circumventing the 1976 Race Relations Act which does not apply to religion. In Oldham West and Royton, in particular, the BNP obtained 6,552 votes in the 2005 election.

In summary, then, New Commonwealth immigrants from a Muslim cultural background have undergone three successive modes of group identification since their arrival in the UK. They initially fitted into the framework of the 'race relations' paradigm; subsequently, they organised themselves and were redefined as 'ethnic minorities'; they currently differentiate themselves on the basis of their religion.

This process of group formation and identification results from a combination of factors that pertain to what Margaret Archer calls 'structural and cultural emergent properties' (Archer, 1995). In this instance, those emergent properties have to be examined with regard to both the reception society and the immigrant populations. The pattern of group formation emerges from the interaction between the two and its relation of power. Subsequently, social actors challenge this pattern in the search for a new form of group identification.

The categorisation of Muslims in France

In France, since ethnicity has never gained official recognition, the 'Muslim' paradigm did not have to fight against the 'ethnic' paradigm. But as ethnicity has always been treated with suspicion from the point of view of the universalist paradigm of French citizenship, the religious category of 'Muslim' has had problematic implications, including:

- the identification of Islam with a specific kind of 'particularism'
- the identification of Islam with an alternative political project (a 'non-republican', 'non-democratic' one)
- the identification of Islam with terrorism (Khosrokhavar, 1997).

It is symptomatic of the situation in France that, for a whole decade, the interpretation of Islam that prevailed was either in terms of political science (most of those working on its implications for French citizens were political scientists such as Gilles Kepel or Rémy Leveau) or in terms of critical abstract philosophy (for example, Mohamed Arkoun).

France has a problem when it comes to the recognition of communities. The only community that has legitimacy is supposed to be the national one. Still, in the face of real communities, the refusal to recognise them swings wildly between two extremes. At one pole, the assertion of the 'universalist', 'national' identity is effective in pitting the cultural traits of the majority against the minorities, which are denied recognition. In this case, 'ethnicity' or 'religiosity' are rejected as evidence of the 'un-patriotism' or 'un-Frenchness' of those who support these bases of identity. This means that minority communities are rejected in a 'communitarianist' fashion, with the majority community denying legitimacy to the minority communities in an 'ethnic' rather than 'ethical' way, as claimed by the universalist view. At the other pole, the assertion of the 'abstract' and 'universal' values of French citizenship renders those who uphold these ideas 'blind'. In this case, they attribute all the religious or ethnic features of the 'communities' to social disadvantages alone. According to this type of interpretation, ethnicity arises only where there is some kind of social injustice or oppression such as racism, economic exclusion, social inequality, or lack of equal opportunities for access to jobs.

In both of these extreme positions, 'Islamic particularism' is undermined on the left (because of the attribution of this particularism to social grounds) and discredited on the right (in tune with the 'un-frenchness' hypothesis). English society is a partially multicultural one in which the domination of some groups in religion (the Anglicans) or in culture (the White British) is implicitly justified, but in French society the explicit refusal of multiculturalism makes the *de facto* recognition of 'ethnic minorities' a case of 'bad faith'. This is because the culture of *laïcité* and universal citizenship works as a kind of 'cultural Unconscious' that constantly interferes with reality and denies it legitimacy. This fact is even more obvious in the case of many teachers (*enseignants*) in state schools (*écoles publiques*) where any headscarf or Islamic symbol is associated with offending against 'Frenchness' and genuine citizenship on account of the scarf's antiquated character, its radical political meaning or the manipulation of young girls (Gaspard and Khosrokhavar, 1995).

The French way of dealing with ethnicity and any form of 'particularism' prevents groups from expressing themselves – except in one of three different ways. The first form of self-expression is an entirely implicit way, which operates outside the public realm and allows the consequences of ethnicity to become visible only in urban settings. The so-called 'Chinese ethnic groups' or 'Portuguese' ones are an example of this tendency. These communities claim no official recognition but are active only through their 'ethnic business' or economic activities. They make no official claims in their name, but there are some geographical or urban implications of their existence as such. For instance, there are Chinese communities in the 13th *arrondissement* of Paris or in the vicinity of the Porte de Choisy and the Porte d'Ivry that are 'visible' in the form of their businesses and their ways of life. This visibility is purely *de facto*, however, and is not claimed as such by any 'representative' of Chinese people. They are simply present there in an objective and impersonal way.

The second form of self-expression is antagonistic, especially in its break away from the public sphere. This is the case with Corsican and Basque regionalism or with radical Islamism.

The third form of particularistic self-expression concerns the construction of communities which lack official recognition from the state but which still have to be dealt with when government agencies consider it urgent to do so. This is the case with the Tabligh and the Union des Organisations Islamiques de France (UOIF), for example. In both cases, a kind of religious community already exists, but the French authorities tend to recognise them in one way or another in order to prevent radical Muslims from attracting their members. For instance, both of these organisations were co-opted on to the so-called preparatory committee for the Muslim Council of France even before Muslims had had the opportunity to vote for them in 2003. Nicolas Sarkozy, who was then Minister of the Interior, said publicly that the co-optation was intended to push these organisations towards co-operation with others, thereby preventing them from becoming radicalised as a result of feeling rejected by public authorities. By prompting them to be co-operative, French authorities try to prevent them from being radicalised as well. The fact that they are communities is not officially recognised as such, but the way in which their members are taken into account makes it possible for the State to show some implicit, although problematic, recognition of their existence.

Typologies

Finally, two typologies of young Muslims go some way towards confirming our account of the differences between Britain and France in terms of the disadvantage and unrest experienced by their respective populations of Muslims.

Nielsen's (1997) typology of young Muslims in the UK is as follows:

1. The random retaliation option: Asian youth gangs with Islamic symbols and growth in youth activity on the margin of the law deriving from social marginalisation (it is posited that there are more gangs where there is more racism).

2. Collective isolation: quiet retrenchment within family and community concomitant with loyalty to community norms.
3. Limited participation: young people who are successful in higher and further education, active in the wider economy but who keep this area of activity separate from home and community.
4. High profile separation: young people involved in organised Muslim activities campaigning for social and political space and confirming their religion and cultural tradition.
5. High profile integration: developing new cultural ways of being Muslims while finding ways of a constructive participation in wider society, combining internal and external agendas.
6. Aggressive action: a programme of radical Islamic political action to change society towards an Islamic model (at least in propaganda if not in implementation).

Common to all is the fact that they separate tradition from perceived religious essentials against the old generation linked to village, region, and country of origin.

This typology of young Muslims in Britain shows some interesting similarities to, and differences from, that proposed for young Muslims in France by Farhad Khosrokhavar (2000) who identifies four types:

1. Individual Islam: adopted as a salvation from deprivation, marginalisation and discrimination. Faith gives a meaning and a dignity that are remote from the value given to socio-economic status.
2. Neo-community Islam: quietism, an ascetic mode of living and a retreat in the community of believers that turns marginalisation into a chosen virtue.
3. Radical Islam: the rejection of an impious Western society and support for violent action in the name of holy values. It is also a means of identifying with an international ideological movement.
4. Young women's Islam: affirmation of oneself *vis-à-vis* modern majority society and within the family, especially in relation to father and brothers.

Although the two typologies differ, they also suggest some comparable types: 'Collective isolation' (Nielsen) broadly corresponds to 'neo-community Islam' (Khosrokhavar), while 'aggressive action' (Nielsen) matches 'radical Islam' (Khosrokhavar). Khosrokhavar makes a special mention of Islam among young women whereas Nielsen does not, but his 'high profile integration' resembles the process described by Khosrokhavar: Islam constitutes newly developed affirmative resources *vis-à-vis* both the family and community elders. Several of these types are not obviously linked to the disturbances described above but might be relevant in a less evident manner. More research is needed on the metamorphosis of 'Islamicity' to ascertain its different shapes in the new Muslim paradigm.

The categorisation of Muslims in prison

The periodisation, presented earlier in this chapter, of the changing modes of identifying immigrant minorities and their descendants is necessarily a broad-brush sketch of complicated changes but it serves well as an historical context for our research into the treatment of Muslims in the prisons of France and England and Wales. One further detail should be added, however. The rapid growth in the number of Muslims living and being born in France and the UK coincided with a variety of social and cultural changes that contributed to the spread of new social movements and to greater sensitivity to cultural differences in many advanced industrial societies (Wieviorka, 2001). Although most British commentators on 'race' and ethnic relations have not attributed much significance to this coincidence or conjunction, it seems important to bear in mind that the 'ethnic revival' (Smith, 1981) was not confined to so-called immigrants. The last quarter of the twentieth century saw a growth of interest in many different expressions of cultural, and hence ethnic, identity – especially among young, middle class, liberal students and professionals. The diversification, if not fragmentation, of what had previously appeared to be fairly homogeneous cultures in France and the UK was part of the opportunity structure that facilitated mobilisation along lines other than social class and that stimulated awareness of new inequalities and injustices. The next task is to show how the changing modes of identification have given rise to important research questions.

It is important to clarify a few points before relating these general theoretical arguments to the specific case of Muslims in prison. First, we must make clear that the notion of identification involves *internal and external aspects*. That is, individual Muslims and groups can choose to identify themselves as such, but other agents and agencies can also choose to categorise people as Muslims. Identification is therefore a complex process of negotiation between the forces of self-identity and externally offered or imposed identity. In the terms employed by Jenkins (1997: 55):

> Social categorization – the identification of others as a collectivity – is no less a routine social process than the collective self-identification of the group. Whereas social groups define themselves, their name(s), their nature(s) and their boundary(ies), social categories are identified, defined and delineated by others. All collectivities can be characterized as, to some extent, defined, as thus socially constructed, in both ways. Each side of the dichotomy is implicated in the other and social identity is the outcome of a dialectical process of internal <u>and</u> external definition. (emphasis original)

Second, identification is *situational*. This means that self-identified Muslims and people who are externally categorised as Muslims do not necessarily attribute the same degree of salience to this form of identity in every situation. Indeed, they may not even enjoy the freedom to decide for themselves how far to give priority to their Muslim identity in some circumstances. It may be forced on them or they may be unexpectedly induced either to display or to conceal their Muslim self-identity.

Third, the notion of Muslim identity is, within limits, *variable* and far from binding on all people who could be categorised as Muslims. With the exception of some extreme circumstances, it is inaccurate to claim that Muslims constitute a single category, even in one country or region. Discourse about 'the Muslim community' or 'French Muslims' and 'British Muslims' might betray wishful thinking or inflated rhetoric, either for or against Muslims, but there is no basis for it in the findings of careful social scientific research. And there is no warrant for assuming that even those people who routinely and willingly identify themselves as Muslims all think, feel and act alike. The people categorised as Muslims are no different in this respect from those categorised as, for example, Jews, Christians or Sikhs.

Why Muslims? Why prisoners?

In the light of what we have identified as the potential problems involved in using the category of 'Muslim' in social scientific research, it may seem perverse or at least paradoxical for our research project to be narrowly and precisely focused on the treatment of Muslim prisoners. Is there not a danger that our project will lend respectability to, and reproduce, an outdated and unjustified form of categorisation? Does the project not imply that Muslims can be regarded as a homogeneous and unitary category in all circumstances?

In fact, the aim of our research was not to take the category of 'Muslim' for granted but, on the contrary, to examine the processes whereby it was *constructed and used* in the highly specific circumstances of prisons. (For this reason, we investigated only Muslims who had received custodial sentences. Muslims serving community sentences were excluded from our study because they were not exposed to the categorisation processes that operate in prisons.) We also investigated the variety of ways in which prisoners categorised as Muslims responded to the formal and informal identification of themselves as Muslims. There were at least four cogent reasons, therefore, for focusing our research on the treatment of Muslim prisoners:

(a) The main reason why our project was necessary is that the laws and administrative instruments governing the prisons of France and England and Wales make specific provisions for the religious and spiritual life of prisoners. The question of how well these provisions work in the case of

Muslim prisoners assumes great significance in the light of widespread concerns about Islamophobia (Commission on British Muslims and Islamophobia, 1997; 2004) and about religious discrimination in Britain (Weller *et al.*, 2001) and France (Khosrokhavar, 1997, 2000).

Unlike France, the UK sanctions group rights and differential, collective integration into the social fabric. Prisons are among the sites where religious group rights are in operation, albeit in an extreme situation. The project's findings will therefore contribute to social scientific understanding of the capacity of religion, in this case Islam, to act as a vehicle of integration into two societies that differ strongly in their respective modes of accommodating minorities.

(b) Research has clearly shown that the religious dimension of personal and collective identity is central to many people's lives and that Muslims living in France and the UK display relatively high levels of concern for their religion (Home Office, 2004). It makes good sense, therefore, to examine the role of Islam among Muslim prisoners. But certain features of religion as a marker of collective identity make our research project challenging for the following reasons.

Religion and ethnicity should not be confused with each other. The practice of religion usually, but not necessarily, involves reference to foundational texts that anchor its followers' views of their history and place in the world to a sacred narrative of real or mythical events. Theology rationalises religious identity to a degree that is rare in relation to ethnicity, although overlap between religious and ethnic identification is evident in the case of, for example, Shinto, Sikhism and Judaism. Rituals permit the expression of religion in strictly codified forms. Religion is also mediated in large part by formal organisations that seek to control its practice. Professional and lay leaders regulate religion at all levels. The constitutions and codes of law in many countries and in many international agreements attribute various rights and obligations to religious organisations. In short, the religious identity of individuals and collectivities is inseparable from this complex apparatus of texts, rituals, organisations, personnel and law.

It follows, then, that research into the treatment of prisoners categorised by their religion has to take proper account of this institutional framework. In this respect, the study of religious identification must be, to some extent, different from that of ethnic identification. It is also worth adding, however, that the religious, ethnic, cultural and national bases of identification are heavily imbricated in some circumstances. Our research, therefore, tried to tease out the extent and patterns of overlap.

(c) The fact that the legislation and administrative rules governing prisons in France and England and Wales require that provisions are made to cater for prisoners' religious needs was not in isolation a particularly strong justification for our research. A more cogent reason for wanting to know how Muslim prisoners are treated was that, since Christian chaplains have tended to play a dominant role in prison chaplaincy, it was important to discover how well chaplaincies have responded to the growing number of Muslim prisoners (Beckford and Gilliat, 1998).

(d) Our research was concerned not only with the day-to-day conditions of life for Muslim prisoners and visiting Imams but also with broader issues of discrimination, racism and equal opportunities. Given that the overwhelming majority of prison staff are white and are not Muslims, allegations that they are guilty of discrimination and racism against Muslim prisoners are not unexpected. The research therefore aimed to discover how far Muslim prisoners agreed with such allegations and how far they believed that their religion was the basis for the unfair treatment. Both the spontaneous and the reflective responses of Muslim prisoners who regarded themselves as the victims of unfair discrimination were examined for evidence of the capacity of Islam to serve as the basis for individual and/or collective resistance and protest. At the same time, prison staff were questioned about their perception of Muslim prisoners and about the use that they made of the category of 'Muslim'.

In short, our research was concerned with issues that go well beyond the internal, group identification of Muslim prisoners and the peaceful transaction of their ethnicity and religious belonging. Its focus was simultaneously on the structures of power and authority that constrain how Muslim prisoners were able to use ethnic and religious resources *and* on how they responded to these structures. The categorisations of Muslims that were implicit and explicit in the everyday working practices of prison staff and chaplaincy workers were an important component of the structures of power and authority.

Can group rights underpin a multicultural society?

What are the implications of our research findings for debates about multiculturalism? The fact that religious and ethnic minorities adopt collective strategies for promoting themselves may appear to be a hindrance to the development of a multicultural form of society. Indeed, it is questionable whether any society could ever be multicultural so long as it 'essentialised' differences. Gerd Baumann (1999: 13), for example, is critical of the UK's conflation of civil rights and communal rights, for the outcome is anything but even-handed in terms of the life-chances and treatment given to ethnic, cultural and religious minorities. His charge is that the British version of multiculturalism tends to favour various 'deals' between the state and minorities regarded as collective entities rather than as aggregates of individual citizens with rights equal to those of the majority of Britons. Thus,

The dominant idea of freedom [in the UK] is not an equality of all, but enough acceptable deals to satisfy each community in its own way. The fight for emancipation is not an individualist battle, as it is in America; it is community-based, and even collective outbursts can be neutralized as a sign that, after all, the team is sticking together – 'as it should' (Baumann, 1999: 47).

Our research examined the operation of this system of communal deals and, in particular, its effects on the opportunities for Muslim prisoners to practise Islam in England and Wales. At the same time, we analysed the contrasting case of Muslim prisoners in France where 'communal deals' are officially discouraged in favour of treating all citizens as equals and where the public sphere is supposed to be free from all religious influences.

According to Baumann (1999), the state of affairs in the UK is unlikely to provide a suitable basis for multiculturalism. His logic may be unassailable, but it is questionable whether his arguments take sufficient account of factors that are central to our particular research project on the situation of prisoners. Two considerations are especially relevant.

First, the logical objections to group or communal rights are just that – logical. They do not relate directly to the 'real' world. Social scientific research cannot begin from abstract principles of justice; it must analyse social situations as they are found or constructed. And the fact is that, for historical reasons, the distribution of power, prestige and authority between different religions and religious groups has never been equal in the UK and other countries. This is still the case in the prisons of England and Wales today (Beckford and Gilliat, 1998; Beckford, 1999). Consequently, the categorisation, self-identification and mobilisation of prisoners on the basis of ethnic and religious identity are, in part, a practical way of dealing with existing inequalities and injustices. It could be argued, then, that the salience of ideas about communal and collective rights is not the result of faulty logic or of misunderstanding: it is an appropriate response to the continuing existence of long-established inequalities and injustices. It could also be argued that the call for equal opportunities in relation to the practice of religion in prison is an echo of Michel Wieviorka's (2001: 61) plea for an approach that, instead of opposing culture and social justice, actually seeks to articulate them better.

It is characteristic of a predominantly Christian country such as the UK that the earliest arrangements for the practice of religion in prison did not differentiate between different faiths or factions. The entirely reasonable assumption was that virtually all prisoners were at least nominally Christian. In this sense, the right to practise religion may even have appeared to be universal and equal. Special arrangements had been made for Jewish prisoners early in the twentieth century, but it was only when the number of prisoners from Muslim, Hindu and Sikh backgrounds began to grow slowly in the 1970s that some prison chaplains raised questions about the provision of religious and spiritual care to prisoners from faiths other than Christianity. Nevertheless, the issue was rarely framed in terms of equal rights for all faiths. Instead, it took the typically British form of such questions as 'What special provisions can be made for other faiths without fundamentally revising the assumption that chaplaincy belongs in the hands of the majority?'. It was a pragmatic response and it reflected a large measure of sympathy and goodwill towards minority religions. Yet, it also expressed the taken-for-granted view that the best outcome would be the creation of separate, special provision for 'other faith' prisoners. There was never any political will or religious impulse to re-organise prison chaplaincy on an equal rights or multicultural basis. And there was resistance in some places to ideas about sharing any responsibility for chaplaincy with representatives of other faiths (Beckford and Gilliat, 1998). It is against this historical background that the treatment of Muslim prisoners today must be located for the purposes of sociological analysis. The salience of ideas about communal and collective rights is not the result of faulty logic or of misunderstanding: it accurately confirms the continuing existence of long-established inequalities.

Second, as we stated at the beginning of this chapter, prisons are one of the sites where the state's power to coerce its citizens and other residents of its territory is beyond doubt. Discussion of how religious and ethnic minorities are treated in prisons must take the reality of coercion fully into account. It would be misleading, therefore, to give the impression that a new, egalitarian basis for multiculturalism could be established merely on the basis of arguments about logic and moral principles. When it comes to the treatment of prisoners, the discussion is not necessarily about their *choice* of identity: it is primarily about their navigation of the rigid structures, procedures and categories that ultimately govern so much of prison life. The highest ideals of tolerance and equality have to be mediated by overriding concern with security, punishment, efficiency and austerity.

Conclusion

In the special circumstances of prison, then, religion can assume a degree of significance that is found in very few areas of late modern societies. Prisoners have many different reasons for participating in shared religious activities, and it is well known that relatively few prisoners could be described as having been regular participants in organised religion before their incarceration. Given the availability of facilities and opportunities for collective religious activities, in a context where the range of other permissible activities is drastically reduced in comparison with life outside prison, it is not difficult to understand the attractions of identifying with other prisoners partly on the basis of shared religious identification. Other considerations, such as the psychological, physical, existential and spiritual difficulties experienced by many prisoners, may also give rise to levels of religious consciousness and practice that are higher than for comparable people outside prison. None of this is surprising or new, but it needs to be stated as part of the rationale for conducting sociological research into the treatment of Muslim prisoners. Our focus on religion as a form of collective identification *in prison* is necessary because it throws light on individual and collective strategies for responding to an extreme situation where religion, as mediated by chaplains and volunteers, is available either as a statutory or a conventional entitlement.

In short, we are fully aware that our research runs the risk of seeming to essentialise, reify, rigidify, standardise and sensationalise notions of ethnic and religious identity in the UK, but we are careful to guard against these problems. We also contend (*pace* Baumann, 1999) that, in view of the particular circumstances of life in the prisons of England and Wales, it would actually be irresponsible to overlook the potential of ethnicity and religion to serve as crucial markers of collective identity and as a potential basis for mobilisation.

The situation in the prisons of France is more complicated because of the high degree of variability between prisons in relation to the recognition of ethnic and religious differences. Much depends on how each prison Director interprets *laïcité*. The fact that Islam is not yet 'organised' on an institutional basis that accords with French principles governing relations between religions and the Republic only increases the variability. By comparison, Protestants and Jews have 'consistories' that speak for their communities – and are consulted by agencies of the state – on matters of public interest. This enables them to negotiate with the state on controversial issues. Many attempts to create a comparable body for Muslims have failed in the past. The most recent attempt, in 2002–2003, gave birth to the regional and national assemblies of the French Council of the Muslim Religion [*Conseil Français du Culte Musulman*], but the Council has not yet made much of an impact on such controversial issues as the wearing of Islamic head scarves in state schools or the training of Imams in higher education institutions. If it manages to overcome internal strife, the Council could eventually find itself in a position to influence the perception and treatment of Muslims in, for example, prisons, state schools, the armed services and public hospitals. At present, however, Bernard Stasi's (2003) Commission on Laïcité is setting the pace by proposing fresh legislation that will prohibit proselytism and the wearing of '*ostensible*' religious symbols in public institutions.

In the absence of a Muslim consistory, institutions of the French Republic have tended to base their treatment of Muslims on the personal preferences of their Directors rather than on any policies of multiculturalism. This leads to arbitrariness as well as variability. As we shall show in later chapters, French prisons vary widely in the extent to which they provide *halal* food and appoint Imams to work with prisoners. Only the fear of 'Islamic radicalism' appears to be persuading a growing number of Directors to appoint Imams who, they hope, can intervene to curtail the influence of radically minded Muslim prisoners. This development does not arise from any kind of multicultural impulse or concern with equality. It is merely a belated response to the perception that the threat of disorder or serious disaffection among Muslim prisoners might be handled by a better recognition of their religious needs.

Chapters 3 and 4 will analyse the arrangements that exist in the prisons of France and England and Wales for the practice of Islam. Chapter 5 will then examine the ways in which religion interacts with ethnicity and 'race' in prisons. The focus of Chapter 6 will be on processes of self-categorisation and identification among Muslim inmates as well as on the complexities of their identities and strategies for responding to prison circumstances. Our analysis in Chapter 7 of the role played by Imams or Muslim chaplains in prison will demonstrate the crucial character of their capacity to intercede on behalf of prisoners with prison authorities. All these chapters will make the case for focusing our research on the treatment of prisoners with particular ethno-religious identities.

3
Research Contexts

The previous two chapters have shown that, although social processes of categorisation appear to be universal in prison, the outcomes are necessarily different in the prisons of France and England and Wales. This is partly because of differences between the countries' systems of law and criminal justice and partly because of differences between their respective modes of accommodating religious and ethnic minorities. This chapter will take the analysis one step further by examining the differential salience of questions about Muslim prisoners in the two countries. It will examine a wide range of contexts that bring issues about Islam and prisons to the fore in particular – and distinctive – ways. Beginning with England and Wales, the argument will attribute special significance to the history of church-state relations and the role of the Church of England as a 'broker' for other faiths in the public realm. The second half of the chapter will examine how the French Republic's constitutional doctrines of *laïcité* have influenced the treatment of Muslim prisoners. It will also emphasise the consequences for the treatment of Muslims that can be traced back to France's colonial ventures in Africa and the perception that is widespread in many sections of French society that Muslims are associated with political extremism, if not terrorism.

The research context in England and Wales

The treatment of Muslims in prison is not the kind of topic that has often been newsworthy or high on the agenda of British politicians. Nor is it located in a clearly demarcated field of academic research. In fact, there have been few investigations of this topic in England and Wales. By comparison, interest in the incarceration of Muslims has been much higher in the USA – mainly because of controversies surrounding the conditions in which 'Black Muslims' or members of the separatist movement, the Nation of Islam, have been imprisoned. These controversies have given rise to numerous court cases and a substantial literature in legal studies. No echoes of these legal questions have been heard in the UK, although a small number of prisoners in England and Wales have associated with the Nation of Islam. In short, the reasons for conducting an intensive study of the treatment of Muslim prisoners may not be immediately self-evident.

Nevertheless, questions about the treatment of Muslims in prison have taken progressively clearer shape in recent years. The questions take many different forms and they emerge from a variety of contexts. Each context generates its own formulation of the issues that concern the conditions in which Muslims are incarcerated. No single context is more influential than the others. It is the conjunction of these different contexts that makes the research timely and important.

State and Church

In the absence of a written constitution in the UK there is a general assumption that freedom of religion nevertheless exists. In fact, the Human Rights Act 1998 incorporates the European Convention on Human Rights into English and Scottish law, so the protection of religious freedom now has some substance in law. But leading representatives of the mainstream Christian churches, which fulfil certain public functions in relation to education and the solemnisation of marriages, negotiated a partial opt-out from certain clauses of the Act. As a result, it would not be an offence under the terms of the Act for clergy in these churches to refuse to marry a homosexual couple or to appoint an atheist as head teacher in a church school. In other words, the British state accepts that churches fulfilling public functions may have values and doctrines that would probably make certain actions incompatible with legislation designed to outlaw unfair discrimination. Only the main religious traditions in Britain enjoy this concession because they are the only religious bodies that regularly fulfil public functions on behalf of the state.

The legal scholar, Anthony Bradney (1993: 158), argues that the idea of religious freedom in Britain rests on the assumption that the country is homogeneous in religious terms.

> It speaks of a country where all are essentially the same, where there are 'our traditions' which unify 'us' and divide 'us' from other nations. 'We' know there is religious freedom because 'we' can follow our religion (which 'we' take lightly) and if others are different they are different in no significant way. If the religious beliefs of others vary in any important manner, altering the way in which they view the family or children or education or whatever, then this indicates that their beliefs take them outside the magic circle of acceptable standards; this, in itself, justifying their different treatment.

The Church of England, in particular, has been enjoying privileges and responsibilities that derive from its status as 'established in law' since the sixteenth century. Other churches are nowadays 'tolerated' in the sense of being implicitly permitted to function in Britain without explicit legal or constitutional legitimation. As Bryan Wilson (1995: 101) has pointed out, however, tolerance is a much weaker form of protection than a legal guarantee of religious freedom.

The growth of religious diversity since the 1950s, especially in England, has helped to re-open debates about the 'establishment' of the Church of England and about the advantages that mainstream Christian churches enjoy in public life. This is not to deny that tensions – as well as schemes for co-operation – have long existed between the Church of England, the Free Churches and the Roman Catholic Church: it is merely to observe that the increase in the number of Buddhists, Hindus, Muslims and Sikhs in Britain has moved questions about equal opportunities in religion higher up the public agenda. The issue of the individual citizen's 'right' to hold religious beliefs is not really at stake. But issues about the public recognition of the main faith traditions have come to the surface of political life – aided, no doubt, by the linkage that exists in some cases between religion and ethnicity. These issues are particularly acute in prisons for a variety of reasons that will be examined later. The issues flow from the fact that certain Christian organisations have enjoyed either *de jure* or *de facto* privileges in their relation with prison authorities. The minority faith communities insist that they should also benefit from the same opportunities for public recognition, respect and resources. In fact, the British government currently supports and encourages all faith communities to engage with the processes of public policy making (O'Beirne, 2004).

Muslims in Britain

Estimates of the number of Muslims resident in England and Wales have varied between about one million and two million. The 2001 Census puts the figure at roughly 1.6 million or 3 per cent of the population. Most British Muslims are either migrants to the UK from Pakistan, India, Bangladesh and East Africa or descendants of these migrants. With the exception of asylum seekers and refugees from the former Yugoslavia, Somalia, Afghanistan, Iraq and some parts of the former Soviet Union, relatively few Muslims have been permitted to enter the UK for the purpose of settlement since the 1980s. Nevertheless, the Muslim population of England and Wales is increasing because its birth rate is higher than the national average. This is to be expected in view of the relatively large proportion of British Muslims who are young. In addition, Britain has perhaps as many as 10,000 white and African Caribbean converts to Islam.

The geographical distribution of Muslims is not even in England and Wales. Most of them live in the major conurbations and cities of England, with dense concentrations in parts of the North West, the Midlands and London. Nevertheless, the fact that the number of mosques, Muslim organisations and *halal* food businesses continues to increase in many other parts of the country suggests that a process of internal re-distribution is beginning to take place. Those British-born Muslims who have completed their education in England and Wales are also beginning to develop careers and businesses outside the boundaries of the predominantly manual and service occupations. This is not to deny that Muslims face a wide range of obstacles and forms of discrimination in the employment sphere but it also emphasises that differentiation is taking place. A small minority of British Muslims have already achieved high levels of prosperity and material security, while the majority still struggle to achieve parity with their white compatriots.

As legislation and administrative practice in England and Wales place so much emphasis on monitoring and penalising the 'racial' or 'ethnic' basis of unfair discrimination, it is difficult to identify the separate effect of religious factors (Lindley, 2002). Nevertheless, the Employment Equality Regulations, which came into effect in December 2003, make it an offence to discriminate unfairly on religious groups in the field of employment; and health, educational and military institutions go to some lengths to foster equal respect for all religions and cultures. Despite the lack of official statistics on religious discrimination, there are numerous grounds on which British Muslims can claim, with justification, that their position tends to be inferior to that of other sections of British society. Their sense of relative deprivation and injustice is particularly strong in relation to housing, education, employment, policing, and generalised discrimination (Weller, Feldman and Purdam, 2001; Commission on British Muslims and Islamophobia, 2001; Anwar and Bakhsh, 2003).

Turning points in the development of a sense of marginalisation and social exclusion among British Muslims include the 'Rushdie affair' in 1988, the mounting hostility towards asylum seekers beginning in the 1990s, the large-scale disturbances in Oldham, Burnley and Bradford in the Summer of 2001, and the aftermath of Al-Qaeda's attacks on aircraft and buildings in the USA on 11 September 2001. This aftermath includes the introduction of new anti-terrorist legislation, the Anti-terrorism Crime and Security Act 2001, and the detention in custody – without charge or trial – of about 12 foreign nationals suspected of involvement in terrorism linked to radical currents in Islam. Moreover, 30 per cent of respondents to an ICM opinion survey conducted by telephone interviews with a sample of 500 British Muslims (generated by a two-stage process of random sampling and 'snowball' sampling) in November 2001 reported that hostility or abuse had been directed against them or a member of their family as a result of the events in America on September 11th.[1] According to a second survey of 500 adult Muslims conducted in March 2004 by ICM Research, 33 per cent of respondents reported that they or members of their family had experienced hostility or abuse from non-Muslims because of their religion.[2] Similarly, a survey of a representative sample of 1,890 electors throughout Britain in November 2002 found that 84 per cent of respondents agreed with the statement that 'Britain's non-Muslims have tended to be more suspicious of Britain's Muslims since 11 September last year'.[3] Nevertheless, the same percentage of respondents thought that 'it is possible for Britain's Muslims and people of other faiths to live peacefully together at close quarters'; and 69 per cent believed that 'Islam is mainly a peaceful religion; terrorists comprise only a tiny fraction'.

English law affords limited protection to Muslims, as a religious category of people who believe that they are the targets of deliberate violence and discrimination. In some circumstances, the Race Relations Act 1976, the Race Relations Amendment Act 2000 and the Human Rights Act 1998 offer remedies against discrimination on grounds of 'race'. In addition, the race relations policy of the Prison Service makes it an offence to discriminate unfairly on grounds of religion in prisons. However, it is debatable whether these legal provisions, valuable though they are, can act as an effective deterrent against personal violence or institutional discrimination. Moreover, the anti-Islamic, anti-Muslim and anti-Asian machinations of movements and parties on the extreme right wing of British politics show no signs of declining in strength or frequency in the early twenty-first century. On the contrary, extremist ideologues are now targeting Muslims directly in the former mill towns of Lancashire and Yorkshire, thereby provoking serious anxiety, unrest and, on occasion, violence among young Muslims in particular. No doubt, these considerations weighed on the minds of the 51 per cent of respondents to an opinion poll commissioned by the BBC in 2001 who agreed with the statement that Britain was a 'racist society' (ICM poll for BBC News).

Public opinion about Muslims in Britain has not been studied in depth, but the results of an opinion survey conducted into Islamophobia in July 2001 showed that only 22 per cent of respondents, drawn from a representative sample of British adults, would oppose the conversion of a relative to Islam. Nevertheless, exactly the same percentage of respondents claimed that Muslim beliefs condoned terrorism. It is regrettably inevitable that the mass media tend to give much higher priority to news items or features about extremism, terrorism and the most controversial Muslim leaders than to coverage of moderate or liberal tendencies among ordinary Muslims. Yet, a series of documentary programmes on BBC television in July 2001 clearly attempted to portray a better-balanced image of Muslims in Britain. A daily series of Channel 4 television programmes about the preparations for the pilgrimage to Mecca in 2003 also emphasised the diversity of Muslims and their concern with peace.

Increase of Muslims in prison

The fact that the number of Muslims, male and female, serving prison sentences in England and Wales has nearly trebled since 1991 from 1,959 to 5,865 in 2003 – whereas the total prison population has grown by about one third in the same period – gives rise to many concerns. Muslim prisoners have increased as a proportion of the prison population from 4.49 per cent in 1991 to 8.05 per cent in 2003. They have also become more diverse in terms of their national origins and reasons for being in the UK. For example, civil war in Somalia and the former Yugoslavia, genocide in Central Africa, warfare in Afghanistan and Iraq and economic hardship in parts of Central and Eastern Europe have all raised the numbers of Muslim asylum seekers, refugees and other actual and would-be migrants to the UK in recent years. Inevitably, some of these foreign nationals have ended up in prison, thereby adding to the diversity of the Muslim inmate population. In fact, foreigners amounted to 24 per cent of all South Asian sentenced prisoners and 31 per cent of all Black sentenced prisoners in 2003.

In addition to being diverse in terms of their nationality, Muslim prisoners come from a wide variety of ethnic backgrounds. In fact, the ethnic background of Muslims in the general population is sharply different from that of Muslims in prison. For example, roughly one third of prisoners registered as Muslims in England and Wales are Black, whereas the 2001 Census showed that only 2.2 per cent of the general population was Black. People who identified themselves as of 'Chinese or other' ethnic identity in the Census amounted to only 1.3 per cent of the population, but this category accounted for 26 per cent of Muslim prisoners. The proportion of Muslim prisoners who are white is 12 per cent, whereas white people constituted 91 per cent of the population according to the 2001 Census.

Again, ethnically South Asian Muslims constitute only 29 per cent of all Muslims in prison, whereas people of South Asian descent amount to 74 per cent of all Muslims in the UK.[4] The stereotypical image of the Muslim prisoner as of South Asian or British-Asian origin is therefore misleading. Claims about the over-representation of this stereotypical Muslim prisoner in the prisons of England and Wales should be scrutinised carefully (see also FitzGerald and Marshall, 1996: 144). There is certainly an over-representation of Muslims in the inmate population, but many of them are foreign nationals and/or from backgrounds other than South Asian.

It was not part of this project's remit to investigate the reasons for the increases in the absolute and proportional number of Muslims in prison. It is evident, however, that the Prison Service of England and Wales (PSEW) has faced a significant change in the religious composition of the people whom it is required to hold securely and safely. The training of prison staff, the design of diets, the configuration of chapels and chaplaincy centres, and the appointment of Visiting Ministers of 'other faiths' (called 'sessional chaplains' since 2003) have all undergone changes intended to accommodate a growing proportion of prisoners from religious back-grounds other than Christian.

In addition, the research that Beckford and Gilliat (1998) conducted into the politics of prison chaplaincy in the mid-1990s had identified problematic issues that have subsequently been addressed by the PSEW. These changes have had a particularly significant impact on the provision of facilities and opportunities for Muslims to practise their religion in prison. First, the recently retired Chief Inspector of Prisons, Sir David Ramsbotham, emphasised the contribution that appropriate facilities for religious practice could make towards his vision of 'a healthy prison'. Some of his reports commended attempts to respond positively to the growth of religious diversity among inmates. He also spoke in approving terms, at a meeting organised in October 1999 by the Islamic Cultural Centre in London, of the efforts being made by Muslim groups to improve the oppor-tunities for Muslim inmates to honour their religious obligations. Second, the Chaplain General of the PSEW who took up his appointment in the summer of 2001, the Ven. William Noblett, had previously established the chaplaincy at HMP Full Sutton on a thoroughly multi-faith basis. His policies and practice had set new standards for co-operation between chaplains and Visiting Ministers. There was a clear expectation that his appointment to a position of leadership at the Prison Service headquarters would herald major advances in the recognition that Muslims, as well as the followers of other faiths outside the Christian category, should be better integrated into prison chaplaincy at all levels. Third, the creation and filling in 1999 of a new post of Muslim Advisor to the PSEW was also evidence that the Prison Service intended to give more voice to Muslim opinion and to establish a more satisfactory basis on which Imams could be selected, trained, inducted and remunerated for their services as Visiting Ministers, sessional chaplains[5] – or, more radically, as full-time Muslim chaplains.

Voluntary organisations for the welfare of Muslim prisoners

The history of links between the PSEW and representatives of Islam in the UK is lengthy, but formal co-operation did not begin until the early 1980s. For most of the 1980s and 1990s the Islamic Cultural Centre, based at the London Central Mosque, took the responsibility of looking after the interests of most Muslim inmates.[6] One senior administrator, Bashir Ebrahim-Khan, acted as the main point of reference for questions about the religious, cultural, social and dietary needs of inmates. In his capacity as Prison Affairs Co-ordinator, he negotiated with governors of prisons as well as with staff at Prison Service headquarters about such things as the nomi-nation of Muslim Visiting Ministers, the authentication of *halal* food, the precise timing of the beginning and end of Ramadan and the availability of copies of the Qur'an and religious artefacts. In addition, Mr Ebrahim-Khan was the representative of Muslim communities in various formal and informal consultations conducted by the Prison Service Chaplaincy. Along with leading representatives of other faith communities he campaigned for changes in the resources, facilities and status accorded to inmates who belonged to religions other than Christianity. Indeed, he was one of the compilers of a radical plan for the overhaul of the Prison Service Chaplaincy that was presented to the Secretary of State at the Home Office in a meeting at the House of Commons in March 1996.[7] He also organised in October 1999 a one-day conference at the Islamic Cultural Centre on the topic of 'Religious provisions in HM Prisons – the Muslim needs'. The principal speaker, Sir David Ramsbotham, who was HM Chief Inspector of Prisons at the time, lent his support to the proposal for a better co-ordination of efforts to improve the provision of religious and spiritual support for Muslim inmates.

High on the list of Mr Ebrahim-Khan's priorities were two particular issues. First, he sought an improvement in the ways in which Muslim Visiting Ministers were appointed, trained and reimbursed for their services and expenses. There were wide variations between prison establishments in terms of, for example, their promptness in seeking replacements for Visiting Ministers who resigned, their willingness to appoint temporary substitutes for Visiting Ministers who were ill or on long-term leave, and their policy with regard to entrusting Visiting Ministers with prison keys. Second, he argued as early as 1992 for the creation of a new salaried post of Muslim Advisor to the Prison Service. The proposal was that such an Advisor, with the status of an Assistant Chaplain General, would assume responsibility for the recruitment, training and working conditions of Muslim Visiting Ministers as well as for the day-to-day issues affecting the religious obligations of Muslim inmates.

Ironically, the Islamic Cultural Centre's success in pressing for the appointment of a Muslim Advisor to the Prison Service heralded the loss of its position as the body mainly responsible for nominating Muslim Visiting Ministers. The Prison Service re-allocated this function to a new organisation, the National Council for the Welfare of Muslim Prisoners (NCWMP), which was supported by the Iqra Trust, an independent, charitable organisation with expertise in Islamic education and programmes of educational outreach in the UK and the USA. The NCWMP, formed in 1999, represented a number of prominent national Muslim organisations and became the agency most directly involved in looking after the interests of Muslim inmates and Visiting Ministers. The Iqra Trust's earliest initiatives in this field, around 1996, included the organisation of a seminar about the training of Visiting Ministers, which was attended by the Assistant Chaplain General with responsibility for 'other faiths'. Two similar meetings took place in 1997 on the training of Visiting Ministers and the special needs of Muslim inmates during Ramadan and its associated festivals. A further seminar of this type was held in 1998 and then a major conference was organised in conjunction with the Training Services division of the Prison Service in 1999. In other words, there was a history of successful collaboration between the Iqra Trust and the Prison Service, including the Prison Service Chaplaincy, before the first Muslim Advisor took up his post in the summer of 1999.

According to Yousif al-Khoei (2001), one of the leading supporters of the NCWMP, the National Council's work of visiting prisons and inspecting the quality of religious life from the Muslim inmates' point of view was complementary to that of the Muslim Advisor. It is easy to see, with the benefit of hindsight, however, that relations between the NCWMP and the Muslim Advisor might not always be smooth. For, despite significant levels of agreement and fruitful co-operation between them on the general principles concerning the need for better training for Muslim Visiting Ministers and the appointment of full-time Imams in some prisons, there were also 'boundary disputes' and disagreements about political strategies. None of this is surprising. The NCWMP and the Muslim Advisor assumed their respective responsibilities at roughly the same time and neither of them had the unqualified backing of all the many Muslim organisations and leading representatives of Islam in the UK. As a result, the NCWMP and the Muslim Advisor could not always agree on the best way of mobilising support for the work in prisons.

In a sense, the NCWMP and the Muslim Advisor were also competing with each other for the support and patronage of powerful Muslim interest groups including the Muslim Council of Britain and the handful of Muslims who had reached the highest echelons of parliament and of political parties. Moreover, the Muslim Advisor, as a civil servant, was accountable to senior managers in the Prison Service and was therefore subject to a certain amount of indirect political constraint. Some of the issues with which he dealt on a virtually daily basis were politically sensitive. For example, the furore that surrounded the so-called Shoe Bomber, Richard Reid, threatened to be highly damaging to the interests of Muslim inmates and Visiting Ministers. Reid was convicted of attempting to use explosives concealed in his shoes to blow up an airliner *en route* from Paris to Miami in December 2001. Some journalists and programme makers claimed that he had converted to Islam in prison whilst serving sentences in the early 1990s and that, by implication, English prisons were a breeding ground for Islamic extremism. Another potentially destructive controversy developed in the wake of the attacks by Muslim extremists on New York and the Pentagon on 11 September 2001. Again, there were allegations that Muslim Visiting Ministers had fermented dissidence in prisons by preaching radical forms of Islam. Press reports claimed that two Visiting Ministers had been suspended from duties on suspicion of circulating 'inflammatory anti-American literature' (*Guardian*, 29 December 2001) to Muslim inmates.

One of them was reinstated after an investigation; the other's suspension turned out to be unconnected to extremism (*Muslim News*, 3 January 2002).

The first occupant of the Muslim Advisor post resigned at the end of 2002 to take up a senior post concerned with faith communities elsewhere in the Civil Service and was replaced on a temporary basis by an experienced Muslim chaplain who spent two days a week at chaplaincy headquarters. The division of labour between the NCWMP and the Muslim Advisor is, as a result, even less clear. The Advisor has taken over many of the tasks previously performed by Mr Ebrahim-Khan and has invested much of his time preparing for, and overseeing, the appointment of the first generation of full-time Muslim chaplains in prison. Meanwhile, the NCWMP retains its function as the body that both nominates Muslims as sessional chaplains and offers some training and support. It also participates in the Chaplaincy Council, the new consultative body that replaced the Chaplain General's Consultation in 2003. But it has become more difficult for its staff to gain security clearance for the purpose of inspecting the facilities for Muslim inmates and it has had no involvement in the appointment of any full-time chaplains. The crucial question is, therefore, whether the appointment of a Muslim Advisor and the progressive increase in the number of full-time Muslim chaplains in prison will eventually weaken the direct involvement of Muslim voluntary organisations such as the Iqra Trust, the Muslim Council of Britain and the NCWMP, in the monitoring and guidance of the Prison Service's treatment of Muslim inmates. By the middle of 2004, it was clear that the full-time Muslim chaplains were making very little use of the NCWMP. In fact, some of them were quite critical of its alleged failure to deliver services or Islamic literature to prisoners.

Ethnicity

Muslims in England and Wales, whether in prison or not, constitute not only a religious minority but also an ethnic minority. This means that most of the 1.6 million Muslims who voluntarily answered a question about their religion by categorising themselves as such in the 2001 Census of the UK's population come from social, national and cultural backgrounds different from those of the majority of Britons. They were either born in countries such as Bangladesh, India or Pakistan or raised in the UK by parents who had originally come from these countries. Roughly 60 per cent of today's British Muslims were born in the UK, but their families and communities are still likely to observe social and cultural norms that are different in some respects from those shared by the majority in Britain. Moreover, the collective and individual identities of most British Muslims retain varying degrees of association with South Asian ways of life – remembered, adapted or invented. This means that Muslims in the prisons of England and Wales have access to distinctive notions of such things as morality, loyalty, solidarity, shame, cleanliness and propriety. They are not 'ruled' in any deterministic sense by these notions, and British ways of life have influenced their outlooks. Nonetheless, many British Muslims still honour and reproduce distinctive patterns of thought, feeling and action that reflect the ethnic origins of their parents and grandparents. The treatment of Muslim prisoners gives rise, therefore, to questions about the extent to which prisons magnify, challenge or repress ethnic distinctiveness.

Racism in a post-colonial setting

An investigation into Muslim inmates also helps to explain the continuing, but changing, nature of relations between Britain – as the former colonial power in most of South Asia – and its former colonial subjects and their descendants who are now resident in the UK. Indeed, prisons – as symbols and instantiations of the power of the state – could be considered as sites where the tensions and grudges of a post-colonial order would be at their most severe. Racism, in the sense of prejudice and discrimination aimed at people defined by their skin colour and other phenotypical characteristics, could also be expected to flourish in settings like prisons where the routines of official categorisation and discipline are backed by the threat and the reality of legitimate physical coercion. Since the vast majority of British Muslims are distinctive in terms of their ethnicity and physical appearance, then, the treatment that they receive in prisons – and their own patterns of action – can throw valuable light on the interplay of religion, ethnicity and 'race' in the aftermath of colonialism. Social class and gender are further dimensions of the post-colonial context that have a bearing on the way in which Muslim inmates experience custodial sentences. Many of these issues come to a head in perceptions, discussions and denials of racism. In view of the evidence that the criminal justice system is racially biased, directly and indirectly, against black and Asian minorities, the question of whether British Muslims receive equal treatment assumes added significance.

Islamophobia

Allegations that British Muslims were the victims of Islamophobia began to surface in the late 1980s at roughly the same time as some commentators started to argue that racism was no longer a matter of biological differences but was assuming a new form based on cultural differences. This was part of a political strategy to keep the categories of 'black' and 'Asians' separate in order to reflect more faithfully their different experiences of racism in Britain. Researchers have subsequently assembled more arguments in support of the claim that hostility to Islam and to Muslims has increased significantly in recent years. Meanwhile, evidence has also come to light of a growing willingness of British Muslims to identify themselves as

'Muslims' first and foremost in many situations – in preference to identification as, for example, 'Asians', 'Pakistanis' or 'Bangladeshis'. The British public first became aware of this movement towards the assertion of distinctively Muslim interests and identities in the course of the controversies that enveloped Salman Rushdie's novel *The Satanic Verses* in 1988, the hostility that it evoked among Muslims and the *fatwah* issued by Ayatollah Khomeini. Just over a decade later there was additional evidence of the salience attaching to 'Muslim' identity in the civil disturbances that broke out in various cities of Northern England, beginning in Oldham in May 2001 and continuing in Bradford in July 2001. It is no accident that political movements on the extreme right wing of British politics now target 'Muslims' as well as 'Asians', thereby helping to reinforce the very identity that these movements seek to undermine.

Islam and extremism

The context in which our research on Muslims in prison was conducted changed dramatically on 11 September 2001 when Al-Qaeda terrorists launched a series of co-ordinated attacks on targets in the USA. The loss of several thousand lives aboard hijacked aircraft and on the ground in New York City, Washington, DC and Pennsylvania has done more than any other event to suggest associations between extremist Islamic beliefs and serious criminal conduct. The UN-backed military campaign against the Taliban regime in Aghanistan, attacks on American embassies and a warship in Yemen, the widely publicised murder of an American journalist in Pakistan, the arrest and conviction of a Muslim convert for planning to blow up an aircraft with explosives concealed in his shoes, and the bombing of a nightclub patronised by Western tourists on the Indonesian island of Bali have also confirmed the suspicions of many observers that extremist currents in Islamic thinking are only the most visible symptoms of a deeper incompatibility between Islam and modern Western democracies, cultures and economies. Since many people suspected of being associated with these incidents – as well as a growing number of Muslims convicted of involvement in them – are currently held in prison in various countries, the topic of Muslims in prison has become eminently newsworthy. Particularly controversial is the fact that some of the Muslims charged with criminal offences are believed to have converted or reverted to Islam during previous spells in prison. Journalists therefore raise questions about the likelihood that prisons have become 'breeding grounds' of Islamic militancy. It seems unlikely that we would have received permission to conduct our research if we had applied for permission soon after 11 September 2001.

Prison problems

It would be a serious mistake to assume that the topic of Muslims in prison was timely simply because of links between Islamic extremism and acts of terrorism. Another aspect of the context for our research is equally important: that is, the well-publicised problems faced by the PSEW. Even before the rate of increase in the prison population began to accelerate sharply in the early 1990s, prisons were often in the news for reasons that had nothing to do with Muslims. There have been many allegations of, and inquiries into, such things as overcrowding, lack of time permitted for association with other prisoners, lax security, racism, brutality, high rates of suicide, poor nutrition, inadequate health care, inhumane treatment of female prisoners giving birth, and the failure to prevent illegal drugs from circulating among inmates. An extensive programme of building new prisons, refurbishing existing facilities and entering into contracts with private companies for the management of some prisons has reduced the possibility of a breakdown in the PSEW. Programmes of staff training and a rigorous regime of internal and independent inspections have also alleviated some of the worst problems. But the growing size of the prison population and the continuing failure to deal effectively with deep-seated problems and inadequate funding ensure that the state of prisons reappears from time to time high on the public agenda. By 2002, the incarceration rate for England and Wales had reached 139 per 100,000 of the population. This was the highest rate in Western Europe. At the same time, the Prison Service reported that it had failed to achieve six of its 15 'key performance indicators', thereby acknowledging that the system was operating in a far from satisfactory manner. Any consideration of the treatment of Muslims in prison must, therefore, take this context into account.

The conjunction of these nine contexts helps to show why the treatment of Muslims in prison requires careful, methodical investigation. The topic has become more urgent and more sensitive as the project has proceeded. But we are fortunate that none of the unforeseen and unforeseeable contingencies created insuperable obstacles. On the contrary, prison officers and governors seem to have become more aware of the project's significance in the light of the events at home and abroad that have made the combination of Muslims and prisons more newsworthy and challenging.

The research context in France

The most salient feature of the relation between religion and society in France is the set of secular, republican values and institutions known as '*laïcité*'. It was forged during and after the French Revolution and even more specifically during the Third Republic after 1871. The principal result was a law separating state and church in 1905 that still governs the relationship between the state and religion in France today (see Poulat, 1987; Boepflug, Dunand and Willaime, 1996; Baubérot, 1997, 2000; Willaime, 2004).

Laïcité

Laïcité, or republican secularism, contrary to appearances, has many shades of meaning. Historically, at least three of these meanings have been operative during different periods of the French Republic. One meaning sets religion and the state in an antagonistic and mutually exclusive relationship; another makes no concession to religion in institutional terms but, in practice, it shows flexibility towards religious rights; and the third meaning interprets *laïcité* as a kind of neutral or agnostic attitude of the powers-that-be towards religion. It holds that all faiths are supposed to be on a par, and the state recognises many of them if they respect public order, pluralism and the exclusion of religion from the institutions of the Republic – especially state-run schools. On the other hand, as Jean-Paul Willaime (2004: 296, 330–33) emphasises, the degree of actual – as distinct from ideological or legal – separation of church and state is open to various interpretations. For example, the public culture of France has remained predominantly Catholic; the French state's centralised and hierarchical structures seem to be modelled on those of the early modern Catholic Church; the Republic still finances extensive religious activities in the Alsace-Moselle region as well as in some overseas territories; state funds go towards the cost of maintaining church buildings forming part of the national cultural heritage. *Laïcité* is therefore nothing if not elusive, ambiguous and still potentially contentious. Further observations on its impact on religion in French prisons will appear later in this chapter as well as in Chapter 5 in connection with the 2003 Stasi report's revival of hard-line *laïcité* and in Chapter 7 where its implications for the recruitment of Muslim chaplains will be discussed.

Historically, the Catholic Church was opposed to *laïcité* but progressively (and particularly since Vatican II), it came to make compromises; the old animosity against the French Republic has given way to a new attitude which appreciates the neutrality of the state and finds comfort in the autonomy of the Catholic Church, and of Christian churches in general, from the state.

Given the background of French *laïcité*, it is not surprising that chaplaincy is a relatively modest aspect of the prison system in France. There is only one official at the prison service headquarters with responsibility for chaplaincy provision across the entire system. In addition, Regional Directors decide, in conjunction with prefectural officials, whether to accept or reject proposals that come from directors of individual prisons for the appointment and payment of chaplains. In effect, then, directors enjoy qualified discretion about the resources allocated to religious, spiritual and pastoral care of prisoners.

Nevertheless, according to Thiébaud (2000), the criminal law Code specifies that prisoners should be informed, on arrival in prison, of the opportunity to meet a representative of their religion and to attend religious services (Art. D 436). Other articles in the Code state that prisoners must be able to meet their religious, moral or spiritual obligations (Art. D 432), to write to their chaplains in confidence (Art. D 438), to keep religious artefacts and books (Art. D 439) and to talk to chaplains in privacy, even when they are in punishment cells (Art. D 437).

The number of unpaid and remunerated chaplains in post in January 2001 was 635,[8] of whom only 45 (7 per cent) received payment for full-time work and 249 (39 per cent) for part-time work. The remaining 341, or 54 per cent of the total, served as voluntary chaplains. In addition, 190 voluntary chaplaincy auxiliaries helped chaplains with their group work. Roman Catholic chaplains amounted to 47 per cent of all chaplains; Protestants 34 per cent; Jews 10 per cent; and Muslims 6 per cent. Other chaplains included three from Orthodox Churches and two Buddhists.

The proportions of chaplains paid by the prison service vary by faith community. Thus, 57 per cent of Catholic chaplains, 32 per cent of Protestant chaplains, 48 per cent of Jewish chaplains, and 50 per cent of Muslim chaplains received payments. The total budget for chaplains in 2000 was 2 million French francs.

The end of the 'war between the two Frances' (Poulat, 1987) and the relatively peaceful relationship between the Republic and the Church in recent decades have given rise to a new malaise: the tension that used to galvanise French society into two antagonistic parts has disappeared. This tension gave meaning to politics by structuring the basis on which public order was built in a society deeply marked by conflict-ridden social relations following the French Revolution (Gauchet, 1998). However, this declining tension between state and religion does not apply to controversial new religious movements – widely vilified in official discourse as 'cultic excesses' [*dérives sectaires*] – and, more importantly, Islam. As a newcomer to French society on a massive scale, Islam faces many problems in the French public sphere. Three sets of problems can be identified:

(a) Islam is mainly the religion of North Africans or of their offspring; Turks, although economically excluded to the same extent as young people from North African origin, do not come from former French colonies and are not yet radicalised. Even after two generations or more, the *'Islam des banlieues'* ['Islam from the deprived suburbs'] still bears the painful marks of the colonial legacy and the painful decolonisation of Algeria in the early 1960s. A significant proportion of Muslims in France consists of Algerians or of people of Algerian descent (about 1.5 million) (Amiraux, 2002). The return of about one million French people from Algeria after independence gave rise to resentment on their part towards the Algerians who came to France to work in industry.

(b) In Algeria, radical Islamists have been nurturing anti-French feeling, among other things, which in turn has given further ammunition to the French extreme right in their struggle against Muslims or 'North Africans'.

(c) Islam is a religion that seems to represent a more radical challenge to *laïcité* and to the customary French separation between the public and private spheres than does any other religion. The dominant institutions of France are resistant to recognising any kind of community other than the national one. Islamic communities are perceived as a threat to the pattern of individual citizenship, which has shaped French history over the last two centuries. All these problems are aggravated by the current trend towards Islamic radicalism in the world. The trend includes the Iranian revolution (1979), the radicalisation of the FIS (Front Islamique du Salut) in Algeria after the refusal of the Algerian military rulers to recognise their right to govern the country in 1992 when they had obtained a majority in parliament, and the Al-Qaeda phenomenon, particularly after 11 September 2001.

Particular problems for Muslim prisoners

The French prison system, in comparison with its English counterpart, is distinctive for holding prisoners indicted for being members of 'associations of criminals involved in terrorism' [*Association de malfaiteurs en relation à une action terroriste*]. A few hundred of them were arrested in the 1990s, and the trend, after 11 September 2001, is towards more arrests, convictions and long prison sentences. They form a category of 'Muslims' that, until 2002, were not represented in English prisons at least on the same scale as in France.

Another distinctive feature of the French prison system is that many prisons that are close to the so-called *'banlieues'* (deprived suburbs), where many Muslims live, have a much higher proportion of Muslim inmates than elsewhere. According to prison officials, the proportion of Muslim inmates can be as high as 70 or 80 per cent. This is not the case in Britain (see the statistics in Beckford and Gilliat, 1998; Guessous, Hopper and Moorthy, 2000).

Yet, unlike the situation in the prisons of England and Wales, Islam is very weakly institutionalised in French prisons, partly because of *laïcité* but also because of the fear of having inmates claim rights that might be used against the *status quo* within the prison. Treating Islam on a par with Judaism or Christianity might produce other claims that would entail consequences that could not be controlled by the prisons, given the prevailing situation in most of them.

Independence of prison directors

In addition to these factors, another important feature of the French prison system is the extensive independence enjoyed by prisons in terms of how they interpret *laïcité* and put in place their own rules in line with the preferences of their directors. In one prison, for instance, we were denied access to prisoners because, as we were told afterwards, the Director, an elderly man awaiting retirement, was not looking for 'trouble'. Even though this explanation might be only partial, it is not entirely without grounds. The prison in question did not explicitly refuse us access, but it 'bureaucratised' our requests and repeatedly refused to approve them in the foreseeable future. In another prison, by contrast, the director was a 'liberal' who did everything he could to facilitate our research. In the third prison, one of the largest in Europe, we were denied entry to the prison for some time, in spite of the authorisation that we had received from the Minister of Justice and the prison administration. After a few months, however, and with the co-operation of one of the leading officials who happened to be of North African origin, we were given generous access to the prison to do our research.

The extensive autonomy of each prison director to interpret *laïcité* in his or her own way can be provocative to inmates who realise that the rules of the game are largely dictated by the prison administrators rather than by central regulations. This might seem to be contradictory to the French state system, which is well known for its Jacobin tradition and centralism. But the fact is that in the three prisons where we were able to conduct our research, as well as in the one where we were denied access, the personal preferences of the director and of the senior staff together with, of course, the history of the prison and its location, had a major effect on shaping the interpretation of *laïcité* and the rights of Muslims within each prison.

Statistical uncertainty

Another difference between the French and the English prison systems concerns statistics. In England, people admitted to prison are asked to declare their religious identity so that they can receive appropriate religious support, including their dietary requirements. In France, since the second half of the 1990s, it is illegal to ask someone to declare his or her religious faith, and there are no official data concerning the religious or ethnic identity of French people in general and of those in prison in particular. It follows from the lack of official data about ethnicity and religion in the French prison population that official commentary on these phenomena is virtually non-existent. For example, annual reports of the Prison Service's work make no references to ethnicity and only brief observations about religion such as the number of paid and unpaid chaplains, the budget for chaplaincy, and the duties prescribed for chaplains and their auxiliaries by the Penal Code sections D 432 to D 439. It also follows from official lack of attention to ethnicity and religion that researchers must remain silent about them. The result is that otherwise excellent analyses of the demographic evolution of the French prison population can take no account of changes in its ethnic or religious composition (see, for example, Tournier, 2000). It would also be unthinkable in France to conduct any official investigation along the lines of the National Prison Survey carried out in

1991 by the British Home Office (Walmsley, Howard and White, 1992). The findings of this research project were particularly helpful in facilitating comparison between prisoners in England and Wales and the general population in terms of ethnic composition.

The only statistical data which might give some clue as to the number of Muslims in French prisons are those which distinguish between nationalities. But this is of very limited help since it would fail to distinguish between French people of North African origin who happen to be Muslims and other French citizens. Another possible way of trying to identify Muslims is to count the number of inmates who fast at Ramadan. Officials in charge of prison kitchens know this number. But some Muslims do not fast at Ramadan (around 20 per cent, according to the Muslim chaplain of Prison B); some abandon their fast before the end of the month and others do not inform the kitchen staff of their fast and provide their own food. Notwithstanding these defects, the number of those who inform the kitchen that they are fasting can give us a sketchy idea about the number of Muslims in the prison.

The only information that is more or less certain to identify Muslim inmates is their name. But in some cases (in few cases as a matter of fact) Muslims have French names. This is because some families, in the 1970s and 1980s, thought that giving French names to their children might ease their integration into French society. This does not seriously undermine the claim that names are the best indicator of Muslim inmates in French prisons. Some converts have chosen Arabic names, but since their official name is French, they have to be identified as such in the prison. Prison staff who work in close contact with inmates can also have a clear idea of which ones are Muslim, although people on the same wing can have slightly different ideas about the number of Muslim prisoners. On the whole, the lack of statistical data on religion makes it difficult to be precise about the number of Muslims within the French prison system.

Official statistics on the number of Muslims or of people from any other religious or ethnic background in French prisons do not exist, but unofficial estimates suggest that the percentage of Muslims in prison is between 50 per cent and 60 per cent of the inmate population. Yet, Muslims constitute roughly 7 per cent of the population of France, assuming that they number somewhere between 4 and 5 million.[9] If it is indeed true that 50 per cent of the French prison population of 50,000 are Muslims, they are seven times over-represented. In some prisons – two out of the three we studied – the proportion of Muslims appeared to be even higher than 50 per cent. According to some Prison Officers who were directly in touch with the inmates, the rate on some wings is close to 70 or 80 per cent. In any case, if it is true that more than half of the prison population is Muslim (or of Muslim origin) and that the vast majority of prison officers know nothing about Islam, French prisons have failed to adapt to these major changes in the prison population.

The ambiguity of *laïcité*

Each prison seems to interpret *laïcité* to suit itself and to reflect its own history and social setting. The problems arising from the practice of Islam within prison that result in some tension with *laïcité* include:

- daily collective prayers
- prayer mats (it is forbidden to carry them in prison)
- meals during Ramadan
- *halal* meat on sale in prison shops
- the provision of *halal* meat from outside
- daily prayers and the practice of prison staff entering cells during prayers
- meeting the Imam (the Muslim minister)
- the provision of a compass (a metallic object that cannot be received by post or handed over in prison) for determining the direction of Mecca when making daily prayers
- the performance of religious obligations (mainly the daily prayers) during working hours in prison
- the provision of the Qur'an in prison libraries
- female Muslim inmates wearing headscarves.

French prison officials seem to have no explicit solutions to these problems. Many refuse to discuss them formally, hiding behind *laïcité* and the necessity of having a secular public sphere in prisons. But this creates many problems for which the lower level prison staff, the so-called '*surveillants*' (prison officers), who are in constant touch with the inmates have to work out compromises. When these problems become too difficult to tackle (as for instance when prisoners refuse to comply and refuse to leave their cells in protest against their predicament), higher-level managers intervene and impose punishments. This whole process is somehow hostage to the ambiguity of *laïcité*: if there are too many problems within any prison and the mass media get hold of them, senior managers may have to be sanctioned or removed by their superiors at national headquarters. Therefore, the main policy is to have prisons in which problems are solved in such a way that external authorities and, in particular journalists, are excluded.

This policy has its limits, however, and with many prisons filled with Muslims, the problem of new patterns of conduct within prison is becoming more and more salient. In a way, French *laïcité* has actually been based on a double standard: firmness in the declaration of principle but some degree of flexibility in its actual application. In the school system, for example, the principle of *laïcité* was firmly asserted against the Catholic Church, but chaplaincies were established in state schools (*Ecoles Publiques*). In the same fashion, the day for the weekly holidays was chosen to be the same as the Catholic one, Sunday, although some radical proponents of *laïcité* had suggested a different day of the week, Wednesdays in particular. From its very beginning, *laïcité* has been characterised by intransigence at the level of principles, and flexibility in practice (Baubérot, 2000).

The capacity of *laïcité* for adaptation without conceding any notable change in its principles came under strain in the last quarter of the twentieth century. The advent of Islam, the policy of decentralisation, the end of the National economy, and the yielding of French regulations to European ones have generated a 'defensive *laïcité*'. Its protagonists tend to refuse compromise and to insist rigidly on the rules of the French system in schools, prisons and the public sector in general. The outcome is a refusal to accept cultural diversity and the display of any religious symbols (especially Islamic ones) in the public sphere. France is probably the only western country that can exclude any girls wearing a headscarf from its state schools for no reason other than *laïcité* (although the reasons given usually include allegations of Islamic proselytism and the girls' refusal to take part in sporting activities, especially swimming).[10] A new law enacted in 2004 prohibits the wearing of headscarves as well as all other '*ostensible*' symbols of religion in state schools. In prisons, Islam tends to be treated as 'non-existent' since prisons are public institutions and therefore compelled to follow the public rules of *laïcité*. But reality imposes the need for some flexibility: how to tackle the problem of food, how to cope with prayers and religious radicalisation?

The last problem is common to many European countries, but an aggressive interpretation of *laïcité* in the French case due to the cultural crisis within French society and the refusal to recognise some Muslim principles considered contrary to *laïcité* make the situation more tense than in many other European countries. The failure to recognise that any community, other than the Nation, stands between the individual and the State places some of the most vulnerable people in difficult situations. That is why those Algerian groups, who do not really amount to a community, pose the most 'communitarian' threat to the French state. They do not form a community in contradistinction to the so-called 'Chinese' or the Portuguese or Turks. The 'communitarianism' of North African young people, particularly those who are economically excluded, socially stigmatised and confined to the disadvantaged suburbs, arises from the fact that they do not receive sufficient economic support from the State[11] and they cannot count on any community assistance (the Algerians are the least socially organised people among the North Africans in France). 'Islamisation' in disadvantaged French suburbs operates as much as a religion substituting for non-existent communities, and that is why this process is most widespread in the *banlieues*. By becoming active Muslims, these socially disaffected people are seeking some form of community that could compensate for the lack of any social group capable of giving them a sense of dignity and identity within a society where they count for very little. But since any visible community in France is regarded with suspicion and as a potential threat to national identity, Islamisation meets with hostility. This hostility has increased because of the actions of radical Muslims in the Southern Mediterranean region and because of the historical links between France and Algeria.

Elsewhere in Europe, Muslim communities are tolerated (not without some difficulties), but in France every girl who wears a headscarf is likely to be immediately identified as *'intégriste'* or ' fundamentalist ' and culturally excluded from society. In the same way, real communities in France (such as the Turkish or the Portuguese) strive to keep out of public sight and to remain hidden in order to avoid being demonised. The paradox of the French situation is that where real communities exist, they have no public visibility; and where 'communitarian' visibility is highest, there is a lack of community except in a symbolic sense. On the other hand, since public visibility is denied to communities, whenever a potential community begins to look for legitimacy (like the newly constituted Islamic communities), they are forced into some kind of radicalisation because they are automatically treated as 'fundamentalist' or 'extremist'. The basic requirements for a peaceful community are sometimes denied to them in the name of a regressive *laïcité* that is inflexible and unwilling to extend any kind of tolerance towards solidarity groups.

Cases in point include the issue of headscarves in women's prisons, collective prayer or even *halal* food for Muslims. These cases are treated by most of the prison authorities as something that goes against *laïcité* and, therefore, as illegal. To wear a headscarf outside cells in prison is regarded as incompatible with *laïcité* by prison managers; permission for Friday prayers is refused; Muslim ministers are not recruited for fear of radicalism and fundamentalism. A change of policy on the recruitment of Imams in prisons began in 2004 when the director of one of our sample of prisons – one of the largest in Europe – appointed six Imams. But this remains a local exception to the large gap that exists in most French prisons between the need for Imams and their availability. In turn, all of this pushes Muslim inmates towards more radical and more rebellious attitudes *vis-à-vis* a management that denies them the basic right to practise their religion (which, incidentally, is formally recognised by the laws of *laïcité* that provide for religious freedom). In brief, in the present circumstances, there is a dialectical relationship between fear of Islam and inflexibility on the part of prison authorities. In return, this dialectic exacerbates rebelliousness among the prisoners who are constantly tempted to defy the authorities for not recognising their right to practise their religion. Prison staff, in return, have to deal with hostile acts on the part of the inmates.

Throughout the Western world Islam represents a new challenge whose multiple social and cultural dimensions are yet to be understood, tackled and somehow translated into the terms used in democratic traditions. But in France, Islam is even more of a challenge to society because the public sphere is defined in a way that radicalises the part of the Muslim population that feels more stigmatised than in many other European countries.

A comparison between France and England, in so far as prison rules and tolerance thresholds for Muslims are concerned, provides a clear example of these problems. In British prisons, it is acknowledged that Muslim inmates have the right to *halal* food as a condition of complying with their religious obligations. This right is not recognised as such in France. Greater or lesser degrees of tolerance exist towards it in different prisons. The minimal requirement is met that an alternative food is available when pork is on the menu. But there is no recognition of the right to appropriate food on religious grounds, neither for Islam nor for Judaism. In the prisons of England and Wales, the right to collective prayers is also recognised. In practice, there is no such provision in France. Friday collective prayer took place in only one out of the three prisons that we studied; and this was due in part to the director's favourable attitude towards religious matters and his open interpretation of *laïcité*, which contrasts with the rigidity that we found in the other prisons.

The *hijab* is accepted in the prisons of England and Wales, whereas in France it is simply prohibited except in cells. For the director of the women's section of Prison B, the question of the veil was handled like this: 'The rule is that they can wear it in their cells but not when moving about the prison or during classes or sport or walking time. The rule of *laïcité* is: no veil'.

The director seems to be unaware of the fact that the *hijab* is mainly intended to be worn in the public sphere and that, in the private sphere, it is useless, at least among wives, husbands and children. *Laïcité* is applied in a way that leaves no room for manoeuvre to Muslim women who believe in hiding their hair in the name of a religious tenet. Most European countries accord this tolerance to Muslim women and permit them to wear a *hijab* in accordance with their religious conviction.

Islam as such is a problem for *laïcité*, as an Assistant Director of Prison C acknowledged:

> The question of Islam is complicated [*délicat*] for us. We have many problems with the GIA prisoners [Groupe Islamique Armé, a military branch of the FIS, Front Islamique du Salut, after the Algerian Military refused to accept its parliamentary majority in the early 1990s] who provoke us [*font de la provocation*]. I would say: it is not a religion (in their case): it is politics. The other people who are a problem to us are the converts. They are very visible, with large beards, and they are very demanding [*très exigeants*]. For some time, we have been having problems with the (Islamic) call to prayer. We have had to put some people in the segregation unit [*mitard*]. But then, some people called for prayer from the windows. I should say that we are in difficulty with Islam and even religion in general. Prison is a *laïque* establishment. Everyone should be considered the same, yet one should make distinctions as well. In principle, we shouldn't take into account the prisoners' religion. That is a job for religious Ministers. But we have to manage the meals, for instance. When they enter the prison, we ask the prisoners whether they eat pork or not. These are questions about religion, but we don't dare to ask whether someone is a Muslim or not.

This is where the ambiguity of *laïcité* in religious matters becomes clear: in a way, the public sphere should be totally religion-blind but in fact it has to accept some compromise. Willingness to compromise seems to be very weak, however, as a result of internal as well as external factors such as the fear of radical Islamic groups such as the GIA and Al-Qaeda, the extremist movements in many parts of the Islamic world, and the defensive attitude of many people who are sceptical towards the new world in the making, especially towards a world where French ideals of universalism in non-religious terms are being challenged. All these factors lend a defensive and conservative tinge to the ideal of *laïcité* which is increasingly defined in a restrictive way. Instead of moving in the direction of recognising open communities as a way of fighting closed ones, defensive *laïcité* looks with suspicion on all attempts at new religious or communitarian phenomena. Social and cultural diversification is denied for the sake of a mythically homogeneous nationhood that refuses to acknowledge the existence of minority groups as a way of defending universality.

The only practical way that the French prison system has found to cope with the problem of Islam is to recruit prison officers from North African backgrounds who have a much better understanding than do the other officers of the cultural needs of Muslim inmates. For example, the Assistant Director of Prison C believed that the problem of the Muslim prisoners could be partially solved by appointing new staff from the 'DOM-TOM' [*Départements d'outre-mer*] or overseas French territories and from the families of former immigrants:

> Things used to be different. Officers recruited to the public service came from working class backgrounds most of the time – for instance, former miners. There were many Polish people. Now, it's beginning to look different. It'll change the relations between management and Muslim prisoners.

This solution to the problem of relations between prison managers and Muslim prisoners is satisfactory in many respects but it still does not solve the major problem of accepting Islam as a fully-fledged religion – which is the religion of the majority in some prisons – in many French prison establishments and of getting prisons to adjust to this fact.

The major problem in French prisons is to see how *laïcité*, as it is interpreted and applied by management, is received, re-worked and re-interpreted by prisoners. For our purposes there are roughly three types of prisoners:

(i)   Foreigners with no real experience of French culture (for instance, illegal immigrants, some of whom wanted to cross the Channel to get to Britain, some who were arrested as they passed through France in transit and some who were arrested in another country and handed

over to the French police on the basis of mutual extradition treaties).
Many of them do not speak French or speak it only in a rudimentary
fashion.

(ii) Foreigners from former French colonies in North Africa or Black
Africa. They include people from the Maghreb who came to France to
work illegally without necessarily having close relatives there.
But there are also others whose brothers and sisters are French
citizens but who, for various reasons, do not have French citizenship
themselves.

(iii) French citizens of African origin (Black as well as North African), who
are second- or third-generation immigrants. Most of them live in the
disadvantaged suburbs or *banlieues*.

The understanding that prisoners have of *laïcité* does not necessarily reflect
their cultural background, their social origin or their age. They display
many types of attitude towards *laïcité*, its rejection or its internalisation.
As we shall see from the interviews analysed in later chapters, the cultural
differences between the last two categories are not great. They have very
similar patterns of living in France, and their possession or non-possession
of French citizenship does not make a big difference to their subjective
feelings towards their situation. The major difference between the two
categories is that the foreigners are denied many rights that are accorded to
French citizens. On religious matters, the two groups are similar in their
reactions to *laïcité*, in their attitudes towards the French prison system and
in their understanding of Islam and its obligations. This does not mean
that they all behave in the same way. On the contrary, but their ideas
about Islam and their attitudes towards prison authorities at large and
French society in general depend on factors other than their nationality as
such. For all the guarantees that French citizenship offers to prisoners,
those from a North African background tend to feel that they are 'Arabs'
mainly because they are looked upon and stigmatised as such. That is why
our analysis does not make a distinction between French citizens of North
African descent – as well as some from Black African backgrounds – and the
North Africans who have lived in France for a long time.

Another problem is that in many cases even those who react against
French *laïcité* and reject it can find that they are directly influenced by it. It
is impossible to understand their views of religion and their relation to
themselves as well as to their other 'brothers in religion' without taking
account of how they internalise *laïcité* (in a positive or negative sense). This
is why their views of religion are not merely concepts or external notions
to be treated as superficial embellishments. Even when their attitude
towards the French rules regarding religion is derogatory, North African
prisoners still tend to act in a specific way which is culture bound in a
double sense: it is affected by the cultural inheritance from their Maghrebin

parents; and it reflects the French culture that they internalised mainly through school and daily life.

In any case, those prisoners – and they are the absolute majority in the prisons that we studied – who are French of Maghrebin descent or North Africans who share a similar culture, have a religious view of reality that does not seem to depend significantly on whether or not they have French citizenship. This is particularly true of those whom many French socio-logists and journalists call the 'young people from the disadvantaged suburbs' [*les jeunes des banlieues*].

Conclusion

Although our research was focused in both France and England and Wales on the apparently clear-cut topic of how each country treated Muslims in prison, this chapter has argued that the topic carries widely different significance in the two settings. In fact, questions about Muslim prisoners arise in sharply different forms. Discourse about them is also patterned differently. Our argument is that these differences are far from accidental. They are actually conditioned – though not determined – by complex sets of factors that, in turn, have been shaped by centuries of tension, struggle and compromise between the forces of religion and politics. The perception and treatment of Muslim prisoners are heavily affected, therefore, by the societal context in which they occur. The next chapter will analyse in detail the institutional policies and practices that have been implemented as a response to the increase in the number of Muslims in the prisons of France and England and Wales in the last few decades. Again, our evidence indicates that these policies and practices conform to the logic of each country's mode of accommodating religious and ethnic minorities.

4
The Practice of Islam in Prison

Introduction

The question of how Muslim prisoners are treated in the prisons of France and England and Wales has a different salience and resonance in each country. The question acquires its significance from the contexts of colonial and post-colonial history, legal systems, political cultures and debates about terrorism. Public discourse about Muslims in prison also follows the contours of these contexts. These high-level considerations are not, however, the only factors that influence the practice of Islam in prisons. This chapter will show that the everyday operation of prisons also exerts a strong influence on the conditions in which Muslim prisoners are able to practise their faith. The chapter begins with the historical development of policies regarding Muslims in the prisons of England and Wales. The implementation of these policies will also be shown to have passed through many evolutions, evoking various responses from prison staff and inmates alike. Particular attention will be paid to perceptions of change concerning the provision of facilities and resources specifically for Muslims. Moreover, the question will be raised of whether these policies and provisions are leading towards an institutionalisation of Islam in prisons.

The second half of the chapter analyses the institutional framework within which Muslims in French prisons seek recognition of the legitimacy of their claims for particular facilities and resources. The argument will be that prison staff have recourse – often inconsistently – to the principles of *laïcité* in justifying their practices when it comes to questions of diet, hygiene and fasting. The resentment that this creates among Muslim prisoners is aggravated by the fact that opportunities for collective prayer and for individual meetings with Imams are scarce in French prisons. As a result, French prisons give rise to highly individualised expressions of Islam and to a context in which 'extremists' have virtually free rein to influence other Muslim inmates.

Chaplains and 'other faiths' in the prisons of England and Wales

In the absence of a separation of Church and the State in the UK, religion still occupies a place in the British public sphere. This is apparent in, for example, the legal requirement that state schools should begin the day with an act of collective worship, the existence of publicly funded chaplaincies in the military, healthcare institutions and the emergency services, and the presence of the Church of England's most senior bishops in the House of Lords. The public visibility of religion is even more manifest in prisons because of the historical role that it has played in the development of the very idea of prisons as places for penitence and rehabilitation as well as punishment. 'The great Victorian prisons were designed to have religion at their core [..]. They were designed on a philosophical basis of Christianity and Utilitarianism, as factories of virtue' (Potter, 1991 quoted in Beckford and Gilliat, 1998). The importance accorded to religion was reinforced by the Prison Act 1952 which treats the chaplain as one of the statutorily specified posts in any prison: 'Every prison shall have a governor, a chaplain and prison officers, a medical officer and such other officers as necessary'. This statutory requirement has gone a long way towards conferring a degree of authority and stability on the position of chaplains, as acknowledged on many occasions by HM Chief Inspectors of Prisons.

Prison chaplains were key figures in British prisons throughout the nineteenth and twentieth centuries. They were in charge of carrying out not only religious duties but also a welfare and pastoral function. As of 1999, the chaplain's multifarious responsibilities, as stated in the Prison Rules,[1] include the following, in addition to conducting religious services:

Special duties of chaplains and prison ministers
14. – (1) The chaplain or a prison minister of a prison shall –
(a) interview every prisoner of his denomination individually soon after the prisoner's reception into that prison and shortly before his release; and
(b) if no other arrangements are made, read the burial service at the funeral of any prisoner of his denomination who dies in that prison.
(2) The chaplain shall visit daily all prisoners belonging to the Church of England who are sick, under restraint or undergoing cellular confinement; and a prison minister shall do the same, as far as he reasonably can, for prisoners of his denomination.
(3) The chaplain shall visit any prisoner not of the Church of England who is sick, under restraint or undergoing cellular confinement, and is not regularly visited by a minister of his denomination, if the prisoner is willing.

Regular visits by ministers of religion
15. – (1) The chaplain shall visit the prisoners belonging to the Church of England.
(2) A prison minister shall visit the prisoners of his denomination as regularly as he reasonably can.
(3) Where a prisoner belongs to a denomination for which no prison minister has been appointed, the governor shall do what he reasonably can, if so requested by the prisoner, to arrange for him to be visited regularly by a minister of that denomination.

Although the Prison Act 1952, which is still the operative legislation, required that every chaplain had to be a 'clergyman' of the Church of England, the 'Notes for the guidance of Visiting Ministers of religion appointed under the Prison Act 1952' eventually acknowledged that Roman Catholic priests and Methodist ministers could also perform the role. In addition, the number of female chaplains has increased substantially since the early 1990s.

A further provision of the Prison Act 1952, which has effectively under-pinned the role of chaplains, is the requirement that 'a full list of prison-ers registered in each faith must be sent out to, or communicated as agreed in writing with the individual minister, to the related Chaplain or Minister weekly, or at intervals agreed between the individual minister and the establishment'.[2] This apparently simple requirement means that each prison must keep records of the religious identity reported by each prisoner; it must also allow prisoners to change their religious registration from time to time; and it must instruct prison officers to ensure that prisoners are permitted to attend the religious activities to which they are entitled. All these practical measures provide chaplains with an institu-tional 'guarantee' that they will have access to prisoners who declare a religious identity. Indeed, chaplains have statutory responsibilities for contacting, on a daily basis, all prisoners at the time of arrival in prison, all prisoners in healthcare centres, and all prisoners undergoing punish-ment for infringements of prison rules. Again, this illustrates the point that chaplaincy is not just a voluntary complement to the normal round of activities in the prisons of England and Wales but is actually 'built into' their very structures and routines.

The salience of the Christian religion in the prisons of England and Wales created an opening for the members of faith communities other than Christianity in the last quarter of the twentieth century. To begin with, it was Christian chaplains who took most of the initiatives to invite volunteers and, eventually, Visiting Ministers to go into prisons for the purpose of conducting religious services or holding classes. In time, leading representatives of, for example, Buddhists, Jews, Hindus, Muslims and Sikhs assumed some of the responsibility for finding suitable people to serve as

Visiting Ministers and for offering them some training. The Chaplain General of the Prison Service of England and Wales (PSEW) formally entrusted general oversight of these developments to one of his Assistant Chaplains General in 1982 with the title of Chaplain Adviser for Ethnic and Minority Faiths. In addition, biannual meetings of the Chaplain General's Standing Consultation on Religion in Prison, which included leading representatives of other faiths, began to take place in 1992. But until the late 1990s, facilities for the practice of other faiths were still mediated by the Christian chaplains, who were in a position to act as 'brokers' partly because of their wider role as mentioned above (Beckford and Gilliat, 1998). This specific responsibility was made clear at national level:

An Assistant Chaplain General has special responsibilities for contact with representatives of other faiths and deals with enquiries about any aspect of religious practice in Prison Service establishments, including non-Christian religions and contact with visiting ministers.[3]

Nevertheless, feelings of dissatisfaction with this brokerage ran high among the representatives of some minority faith communities who sought to be more independent in their relations with the Prison Service. They insisted in particular on the need to avoid dependence on the goodwill of Christian chaplains. 'Dependence on the discretion of individual chaplains, governors and Prison Officers' was given as a reason for Muslims' scepticism about progress towards addressing the issue of religious diversity in prisons according to the Commission on British Muslims and Islamophobia (2001: 16). The main problem remained 'structural inequality'.

It is interesting to note, in passing, that the first Chaplain General's Adviser on Other Faiths unsuccessfully challenged the first version of the PSEW's 'Race Relations Policy Statement' for failing to cover religion, but subsequent modifications of the statement led to the incorporation of religion into the policy. This is an example of the fact that official thinking about 'race relations' in prisons was – and remains – in some respects in advance of anti-discrimination legislation in general. No doubt, the pressure brought to bear upon the PSEW by members of the Chaplain General's Standing Consultation on Religion did much to promote these changes. These representatives kept the Prison Service well informed about the day-to-day complaints from prisoners and Visiting Ministers about the obstacles that allegedly prevented them from practising their religious obligations properly. Nevertheless, it is worth noting that the *policy* was to eliminate discrimination on the grounds of religion:

The Prison Service is committed to racial equality. Improper discrimination on the basis of colour, race, nationality, ethnic or national origins, or religion is unacceptable, as is any racially abusive or insulting language or behaviour on the part of any member of staff, prisoner or visitor, and neither will be tolerated.[4]

It is also greatly to the credit of some members of the Chaplain General's department that the first edition of a *Directory and Guide on Religious Practices in HM Prisons* appeared as early as 1988. This comprehensive compilation of information about the beliefs, practices and religious obligations of Christianity and a selection of faiths, which is now in its third edition, has attracted favourable comment at home and abroad, especially now that it is based on information supplied by minority faith communities themselves. The *Prison Service Order on Religion*[5] is a more recent example of carefully documented procedures and requirements for meeting the Prison Service's standards on religion. The Prison Service's catering manuals also show considerable sensitivity to the need for diets that conform to religious requirements. And, according to the *Prison Service Order on Race Relations*, 'professionalism demands that staff are sensitive to the importance attached to the religious faith and to symbols or items of special religious significance for some prisoners'.[6]

The *implementation* of the policy left much to be desired, however, in the opinion of the most critical representatives of the Buddhist, Muslim and Sikh faiths in the mid-1990s. They complained forcefully about the systematic inequalities in the provisions made for Christian and other-than-Christian prisoners.[7] These inequalities called in question the assurances given in documents, such as the *Prison Handbook*, that prisoners enjoyed equal rights to attend religious services, to be exempted from work at times of prayers or major religious festivals, to receive religiously appropriate food, and to attend religious meetings even when segregated from other prisoners for disciplinary reasons.

The situation began to change substantially in the late 1990s, however, leading to a clearer recognition of the needs of inmates from 'other faiths' and the setting up of structures that were no longer under the direct or exclusive control of Christian chaplains. For example, after 1998, the Chaplain General's Consultation with other faiths, the Standing Consultation on Religion in Prison, was replaced by an Advisory Group on Religion in Prisons, which did not come under the remit of the Chaplain General's office. The Group was chaired by the PSEW's Director of Regimes and comprised representatives of those minority faiths with significant numbers of adherents in prison: Buddhist, Hindu, Jewish, Mormon, Muslim, Pentecostal and Sikh – together with the Chaplain General, members of the Chaplaincy headquarters team, a governing governor and members of the Prisoner Administration Group (PAG). In other words, liaison with minority faith communities ceased to be the sole responsibility of the Chaplain General's office. Instead, it became a responsibility shared with senior Civil Servants in the PSEW who were not ministers of religion. Some of them had professional responsibility for aspects of the Prison Service's programmes of 'racial' and ethnic equality.

At roughly the same time, a Working Group, chaired by the Head of the Prisoner Administration Group, drew together the representatives of various faith communities for the purpose of designing a new system that would allow the Prison Service to consult faith communities in a more open and even-handed fashion. The Advisory Group and the Working Group eventually made way in May 2003 for an entirely new body – the Chaplaincy Council. It consists of one chaplain from the headquarters group, the Muslim Adviser and representatives of the main faith communities who all carry the title of 'Prison Service Faith Adviser'. Some of these representatives also function as 'Faith Advisers to the Prison Service' or 'Religious Consultative Services'. In other words, they have hands-on responsibility for ensuring that appropriate religious and pastoral services are provided for prisoners who belong to their particular faith. The Council meets six times a year, with the Chaplain General chairing four meetings, and the Director of Resettlement chairing the other two. Its function is no longer simply to facilitate consultation but is also to guide and advise the Prison Service Chaplaincy, to aid the development of new policies, and to discuss topics of mutual concern. As an example of the Chaplaincy Council's new function, the Chaplain General explained that:

> The Chaplaincy Statement of Purpose, which is just about to be revised, will go through the Council for revisions. We don't want the Chaplaincy Statement going out that hasn't got the endorsement of the Council; and they are for us an extremely important body, frankly. I see those as being at the heart of decision making for the Chaplaincy (interview at Prison Service Headquarters, 13 May 2003).

The first fruits of the new spirit of multi-faith co-operation include, on the one hand, holding in 2003 the first ever national conference for 450 chaplains of all faith traditions and, on the other, a Faith Week at Prison Service headquarters, to which representatives of the major faiths made presentations for the benefit of staff involved in developing policies concerning equality and diversity.

This series of changes in the mechanisms for representation and consultation occurred roughly in parallel with two other significant changes. The first was the appointment of a full-time Muslim Adviser to the PSEW in September 1999. Extensive lobbying over many years by various Muslim organisations and influential individuals, led by the Islamic Cultural Centre at London Central Mosque, persuaded the Prison Service in 1998 to create a post of Muslim Adviser. The initial plan to appoint a part-time Adviser on secondment from a Muslim organisation at virtually no cost to the Prison Service was revised after protests from Muslim organisations. The advertised post was a full-time position in the Chaplain General's department, renewable after the first two years. The job description included much more than advising and consulting. It also entailed representing Muslims on the Advisory Group on Religions (and eventually the new Chaplaincy Council), liaising with other faith groups, contributing to training programmes, visiting Imams and serving as a link between Muslim communities and the Prison Service. The first post-holder, Maqsood Ahmed, became the highest-ranking Muslim Civil Servant in the UK. His contract was renewed after the first two years, and he eventually resigned to join the Faith Communities section of the Race Equality Unit in the Home Office early in 2003.

The second major change was the appointment of the Reverend William Noblett as Chaplain General in July 2001. He had not only acquired many years of experience of prison chaplaincy but had also pioneered 'multi-faith' forms of chaplaincy. This had not always made him popular with the previous chaplaincy headquarters team but it made him eminently suitable as Chaplain General because the terms and conditions of his appointment specified, for the first time, that the appointee would be expected to implement multi-faith forms of chaplaincy throughout the prison system of England and Wales. The Muslim Adviser had not only supported the policy of multi-faith chaplaincy in prisons but had advised the Prison Service to implement such a policy. Again, this is evidence that Prison Service policy was oriented towards improving the opportunities that inmates from minority faith backgrounds would have for the practice of their religion in prison.

It would be entirely reasonable to assume that the coexistence of a full-time Muslim Adviser to the Prison Service, a Chaplain General committed to the ideals of multi-faith forms of chaplaincy, and an inclusive Chaplaincy Council would be able to resolve most of the long-standing tensions in prison chaplaincy in England and Wales. Indeed, huge strides were made towards the integration of 'other faiths' into the processes of policy making and the operation of inclusive chaplaincy teams at the level of individual prison establishments. Muslims in particular benefited from the availability of a Muslim Adviser who could offer advice to Visiting Ministers and prison administrators, seek to improve the conditions in which Friday prayers were conducted, and investigate the authenticity of supposedly *halal* food. Moreover, he was able to exercise an unprecedented degree of supervision over the training and recruitment of Visiting Ministers. This involved complex negotiations with a range of Muslim organisations outside the Prison Service. Shortly before he left his position he had also succeeded in securing the employment of Imams as full-time assistant chaplains in about ten establishments.

In spite of these achievements, some difficulties have persisted. For example, at least one representative of a different minority faith community complained that funding for Muslims was increasing substantially at a time when resources for other communities remained meagre. Another problem was that there were also powerful tensions between the main actors in and around chaplaincy headquarters. Rivalry between different Sunni Muslim organisations had preceded the appointment of a Muslim Adviser, and this rivalry has hardly abated. In addition, there was tension between the Adviser and some Muslim organisations because of uncertainty about their respective areas of responsibility. Finally, the Adviser's relations with the Chaplain General were not without difficulty at times because the Adviser sensed that efforts were being made to restore the chaplaincy headquarters' control over the non-Christian faiths. A particular cause of friction was the Chaplain General's leading role in the new Chaplaincy Council. From the Chaplain General's point of view, it was consistent with the principles of an inclusive, multi-faith chaplaincy that it should be responsible for the interests of all faith communities.[8] But the Muslim Adviser suspected that it might be seen as a retrograde step in the direction of re-asserting Christian control over the entire chaplaincy service. He was also dissatisfied with the level of financial, administrative and clerical support for his work at chaplaincy headquarters, feeling that his position might have been better supported in the Prisoner Administration Group than in the Chaplain General's department.

Indeed, the Muslim Adviser's opinions were consistent with his reluctance to be considered as yet one more Assistant Chaplain General. His preference was for a role focused on 'race' equality and diversity as well as religion – and with an appropriate level of clerical and administrative support for an official who had to deal with all the 140 establishments in England and Wales. He would probably have felt more at ease if he had not been required to fit into a structure designed to accommodate representatives of Christian churches and to have to justify everything to an Anglican Chaplain General. A more acceptable arrangement might have placed chaplaincy under the control of a non-denominational Director supported by a team of Advisers representing the major faith communities.

As we argued in Chapter 3, it is ironic that, while the Muslim Adviser was experiencing some tension with chaplaincy headquarters, his relations with the National Council for the Welfare of Muslim Prisoners (NCWMP) were also difficult at times because he was seen to make some decisions without always consulting the Council fully. Here we see evidence of a problem that was highly likely to have occurred as a result of, on the one hand, appointing the NCWMP as the Religious Consultative Service for Muslims and, on the other hand, appointing a full-time Muslim Adviser. The fact that these two appointments occurred at almost the same time probably aggravated the difficulty. For example, the *Prison Service Order on Religion* specifies that staff who need to resolve an outstanding question concerning Muslim prisoners must first contact the Muslim Adviser and that he will, as appropriate, contact the NCWMP.[9] This dual circuit of communication was a recipe for misunderstanding. Indeed, relations between the Adviser and the NCWMP deteriorated to the point where each considered the other as obstructive. The National Council felt particularly aggrieved that the Prison Service had prevented its representatives from continuing to conduct their prison visits to all but one prison in London. The level of funding from the Prison Service for the NCWMP also made it hard for the Council to meet the Muslim Adviser's high expectations for its administrative efficiency and political effectiveness. Finally, the Adviser felt let down that the Muslim community at large in Britain failed to take much interest in the plight of Muslim prisoners or the needs of released Muslim prisoners.

The first full-time Muslim chaplains took up their positions as Assistant Chaplains after the completion of our fieldwork in 2003, so we were not able to take account of their work *in situ*. It would have been ideal from our point of view to assess the response of other staff and of Muslim prisoners to these unprecedented appointments, but we were at least able to talk to six full-time Muslim chaplains at length about their initial experiences of professional work in prison chaplaincy. Their views are reported in Chapter 7.

Full-time Muslim chaplains are expected to carry out the full range of tasks previously reserved for Christian chaplains, including the statutory duties. More specifically, their job description requires them to conduct Friday prayers, to organise Eid celebrations, to run Islamic education classes, and to offer religious and spiritual support to prisoners, visitors and staff. At the same time, they are expected to take a full part in the administration work of chaplaincies including the preparation of advice to governors, budgets, reports, business plans and training programmes. It is also a requirement that Muslim chaplains should undergo mandatory training and share some of the responsibility for facilitating the religious and pastoral activities for prisoners who are not Muslims. In effect, such chaplains would have a status very similar to that of 'institutional' or 'generic' chaplains in American prisons.

In short, the administrative and organisational framework governing the practice of Islam in the prisons of England and Wales has changed rapidly since the late 1990s. The almost simultaneous advent of the NCWMP, the Muslim Adviser and a Chaplain General committed to multi-faith principles – and, more recently, of full-time Muslim chaplains – has helped to resolve some long-standing problems and has generated some fresh tensions. Further changes are also planned as part of a strategy for reducing the power of the Chaplaincy headquarters by devolving authority to Area Chaplains and by opening up the role of Co-ordinating Chaplain in establishments to chaplains from all major faiths. All these changes, actual or planned, also create some fresh challenges that arise, ironically, from the implementation of multi-faith principles and practices. The next section will show that a shortfall still exists between policies and practice in some areas of prison chaplaincy.

Implementation of policies on the practice of Islam in prison

As we have outlined above, the PSEW has gradually put in place over the past few decades a large number of policies and initiatives designed to facilitate the practice of Islam – and other minority faiths in Britain – in prisons. The current framework of rules and practices permits a wide range of activities by prisoners, chaplains, visitors and voluntary organisations. Yet, as we shall argue in this section, the fact that the PSEW not only permits but also resources these activities leads to some ironic results. Nevertheless, by comparison with the inmates of French prisons, Muslim inmates in England and Wales enjoy significantly more numerous opportunities to fulfil their religious obligations and even to enhance their understanding of Islam. No doubt, 'practising' Muslims exert an influence on 'backsliders' to become more aware of their religious obligations, but we found no evidence of undue pressure to do so. The situation of Muslims in French prisons will be considered in the last main section of this chapter.

Perceptions of change

The situation regarding Muslims in English and Welsh prisons has undergone substantial changes in recent years. Many prison officers and governors, as well as prisoners, remarked on the contrast between the situation of only a few years ago and the current state of affairs. The issues that were problematic in the past took various forms and included practical arrangements, physical facilities and attitudes. The Head of Regimes and Resettlement Programmes at Prison 3, for example, put it like this:

> Two and a half years ago the Muslims were an isolated and forgotten group; they were not part of the Chaplaincy team as such; Ramadan was problematic; the Eid feast meant food was brought in, and this was not always easy to facilitate.

In another establishment, collective prayers used to take place on a Monday rather than a Friday as required by the Qur'an. There was no space for collective worship, and one officer recalled how 'all the Muslims had to cram into a single room at the end of a wing, and this was only a few years ago' (Prison 1, C Wing). The temporary Imam in Prison 2 described the lack of resources as follows: 'When I arrived here the inmates didn't have any books, didn't have any prayer mats, didn't have any magazines; there were no resources available'. At the time of his interview, this particular Imam doubted whether the situation had actually improved very much since his arrival in the prison. Although this was a minority view among our informants, the Imam in Prison 1 actually took an even more pessimistic view of change: 'The pace is very slow, and many a time the Chaplain says "Here we have two tracks: one is dead slow, the other is dead". We are on the dead track rather than the dead slow'.

Those Muslim inmates who had been in the prison system for several years tended to be more insistent that improvements had taken place in their opportunities for religious practice. Further evidence of improvements in the opportunities available to Muslim inmates – and members of other faith communities – for the practice of their religion can be found in the annual reports of HM Chief Inspector of Prisons throughout the 1990s.

Moreover, the judgement of the first Muslim Adviser to the Prison Service was categorical about recent changes. He could see evidence of progress on a number of fronts but he was also fully aware that the number of problems to be solved was still daunting. This view finds an echo in the opinion of the General Secretary of the NCWMP as far as the quality of *halal* food is concerned. He voiced reservations about the reality of improvements in other aspects of the treatment of Muslim inmates, but progress had clearly taken place in confirming the authenticity of food labelled as *halal* in many, but not all, establishments. The General Secretary also claimed that progress had been made since the late 1990s in increasing the number of hours for which Imams were paid to visit some prisons.

In short, few of our informants denied that opportunities for Muslim inmates to practise their faith in prison had improved significantly over the past few years. As we argued earlier, three developments contributed strongly to the perception of improvement. The first was the appointment in September 1999 of a full-time Muslim Adviser to the Prison Service. The second was the arrival of a new Chaplain General of the Prison Service Chaplaincy in July 2001 who was committed to the ideal of multi-faith patterns of work. And the third was the work of the NCWMP.

Persisting dissatisfaction

In spite of these developments, however, there are grounds for thinking that arrangements for the practice of Islam in the prisons of England and Wales still give rise to a wide range of complaints and dissatisfaction. We shall begin by summarising the dissatisfaction voiced by prison staff and Visiting Ministers. Subsequently, the complaints of Muslim prisoners will be outlined. Some of these complaints will be examined at greater length in subsequent chapters.

Resources

Beginning with questions of resources, we heard of very few establishments in which responsibility for the chaplaincy budget lay with anyone except the senior Anglican chaplain. Even where Muslims and other minority faiths had some representation on chaplaincy committees, we learned that it was common practice for the Anglican chaplains to make decisions about the distribution of financial resources. Indeed, the exceptions were rare enough to attract attention, as when the Head of Regimes and Resettlement in Prison 3 reported that the Anglican chaplain had deliberately re-distributed the chaplaincy budget in proportion to the number of inmates from each of the major faith communities. But the senior Anglican chaplain at Prison 1, who was well aware of the problem, did not think that he was in a position to make such adjustments because the overall budget for the chaplaincy was being reduced by 10 per cent annually. Consequently, there had been long-term friction with the Muslim Visiting Minister over payment for the additional hours that the Minister wanted to spend with the inmates in Arabic classes and pastoral counselling. The Deputy Anglican chaplain and the Methodist Minister in this prison did not believe that Muslim prisoners were treated unfairly. Nevertheless, the Muslim Visiting Minister had a long list of allegations about unfair treatment, including his exclusion from management of the chaplaincy and the inequitable distribution of the budget. It is interesting that the Catholic chaplain in this prison also expressed the wish to be more directly involved in budgetary decisions.

The Acting Assistant Chaplain at Prison 2 was also critical of the chaplaincy budget, especially as it was expected to meet the religious needs of inmates from 17 different faith groups. This highlights the fact that efforts to improve facilities for the practice of minority faiths, even in establishments where support for multi-faith chaplaincy was strong, intensified competition for limited resources. In fact, resistance to proposals for appointing full-time Imams in prison came mostly from Christian chaplains who objected to the corresponding reduction of their own resources. In the context of shrinking budgets for chaplaincies, competition between different faith groups was seen as a zero-sum game. It is therefore significant that it was only at Prison 3, where the Anglican chaplain regarded the chaplaincy budget as 'generous', that tension between faith groups over financial resources seemed not to be an issue.

Prejudice and discrimination

Regardless of whether chaplaincy budgets are actually distributed fairly, many of the inmates whom we interviewed were convinced that, as Muslims, they were the victims of prejudice in prison. It was not uncommon for them to claim that they were sometimes obstructed from attending Friday prayers. This was felt to be an important issue because it allegedly reflected a discrepancy between the treatment of Christian and Muslim prisoners regarding access to their respective forms of collective worship. The practice in prisons, including Prison 1, was automatically to permit all registered Christians to attend Sunday services unless they were serving a punishment, whereas Muslims had to apply in writing to have their name placed on a list before each Friday. The 'list system' frequently gave rise to delays that meant that some Muslim inmates failed to arrive at Friday prayers on time – if at all. Much confusion and dissatisfaction centred on the fact that some inmates failed to get their name on the list or applied too late and resented feeling that they were the victims of discrimination. Inmates frequently complained about this issue. Eventually the list system was abolished in Prison 1 and replaced by a more satisfactory arrangement, as explained by the governing Governor:

> Now, I know that when we first came here there were a lot of challenges about the routine in getting Muslim prisoners to be able to attend the services they wanted to; and the systems which were in place weren't the most helpful. It seemed that a Muslim prisoner had to go the extra mile to get to a service whereas the Christian prisoners, the way was a lot clearer. I think they had to make a written application, when we first came, to go to the service, whereas the Christian prisoners were using their cell bells to indicate and then they were unlocked. And neither method was suitable, you see. Now we tackled that quite vigorously to the point now where each wing has a list of Muslim prisoners who are located on that wing, and at the time of the service there is an officer designated to go around and ask them all if they want to go, so that is a small improvement that we have made.

In another prison a formula of coloured cards was adopted. On the other hand, this kind of progress is uneven. One of the women's prisons that we visited had a very haphazard way of dealing with Friday prayers which often did not permit Muslim women's participation. The reason given was that there were too few of them to warrant the complications involved. Another women's prison, by comparison, showed much greater flexibility by permitting the Muslim 'assistant' to go around the prison collecting Muslim women for their Friday gathering.

Facilities and religious artefacts

The lack of a clean and suitable prayer room for Muslims has long been a bone of contention in many prisons but had been dealt with – up to a point – in a variety of ways in all the prisons we visited. The chapel was the most common location for Friday prayers, although in the women's prisons a visitors' room was used as only a small number of inmates needed to be accommodated. The most far-reaching scheme involved converting part of the Christian chapel into a multi-faith area that could accommodate the growing number of Muslim inmates. In the words of the Anglican chaplain:

We are looking to convert the organ area as a loft conversion to provide a soundproof room which will be used largely by the Muslims since they represent about one eighth of the total prison population. So now, all Muslims, barring those on segregation wings or on 'discipline' should be able to attend prayers.

It is worth noting that the Substitute Christian Chaplain in this particular establishment voiced strongly critical views about this scheme:

Personally, I feel very offended and I feel nobody is listening to the Christians, because the chapel is sacred and consecrated; and nobody had deconsecrated it. I am against multi-faith. I do not believe in multi-faith and I feel it is sacrilegious. Nobody listens to us... We have been encroached upon.

The Roman Catholic chaplain also criticised multi-faith approaches as 'cotton wool' and lacking integrity. He was strongly opposed to the removal of statues and icons to accommodate Muslims and other faith groups in Christian chapels.

Even in establishments where the sharing of formerly 'Christian space' with Muslim inmates was no longer a problem, the question of finding an area for their ablutions in the vicinity of prayer rooms was far from resolved. Such areas were not always available or were impractical. For instance, ablution facilities in Prison 2 were so inadequate that they invariably led to a great deal of splashing of surroundings and inmates. As a result, both staff and Muslim prisoners were frustrated because the former had to clean the mess on the floor and the latter were drenched.

There is one issue on which there seems to be quasi-unanimity among staff and prisoners and for which training has undoubtedly had beneficial results, namely, the recognition that religious artefacts should be treated as 'sacred'. One officer mentioned that he had not initially been aware of their importance but was put right by the protests of inmates and the clarifications offered by colleagues; he subsequently paid attention to the necessary requirements:

Whilst doing a cell search I touched a Qur'an and I couldn't understand the prisoner being upset. I opened it and leafed through it. I went to a fellow officer and other inmates, and they explained it was sacred. And I spoke with the cleaners, and they explained it was sacred; and so to get around it I ask them to open it themselves (Prison 1, Prison Officer 1).

Training with regard to religious artefacts was mentioned several times in our interviews. In all the male establishments prison officers referred to sensitivity about religious artefacts. For example, 'All staff are advised about touching the Qur'an etc.; it never caused a problem; all staff are aware of it' (Prison 3, Prison Officer 7). 'Everybody is familiar with, or appears to be familiar with, the importance of the Qur'an and the importance of the prayer mat' (Prison 2, Prison Officer 4). This was corroborated by the vast majority of the prisoners who were interviewed, but there was also dissatisfaction with the procedures in a few cases. For example,

> I had a cell search. When you're away, I don't think they respect [the Qur'an]. I could tell it had been touched. My cellmate told me that the Officers had said, 'The Qur'an should be thrown away'. I was angry. I haven't had a chance to see that officer yet' (Prisoner 13 in Prison 1).

Another complaint was that officers had left a copy of the Qur'an on the floor of a cell after conducting a search.

Cell accommodation

However, prison officers were not always so discreet towards prisoners who were saying their individual prayers. It was not uncommon for prison officers to interrupt inmates praying in their cells. Indeed, some inmates cited what they perceived as deliberate noise and interruption. But the greatest inconvenience to inmates in the course of their daily prayers stemmed from being 'padded up' with non-Muslims, although in some cases their requests to pad up with Muslims were granted. This caused some controversy among prison officers, who felt that it was 'open to abuse and against the spirit of social integration' (Prison 1, C Wing). It was not made clear in what way this could be abused. Moreover, concern about social integration sounds incongruous in view of the fact that inmates in the prison concerned spent around 23 hours in a cell for two, so that little effective integration would take place in any case. Nevertheless, this comment certainly reflects a wider debate on the inter-action between ethnic minorities and wider society. In the prison context it might signal anxiety that inmates could form strong groupings of their own choice. The policy of 'divide and rule' may be an integral part of control strategies. As for other prisoners, they apparently saw this padding up as an 'unfair privilege', accorded to Muslims.

The list of Muslim inmates' grievances goes on. Some claimed that they were not informed on arrival of the facilities to practise Islam, and very few were seen by the Imam at that stage. Prayer mats were not always available as an entitlement and were otherwise provided in Prison 1 by outside communities through the good offices of the Imam. Caps were sometimes tolerated for Friday prayers but not routinely in every day life for fear that they could develop into a symbol of collective identity and promote gang identity, thereby becoming 'a security issue' (Prison 1, Prison Officer 8).

Halal *food*

The Prison Service Catering Manual[10] supplies a lot of detail about the 'Mandatory requirements for the dietary provision of Muslims'. These include a choice of 'a *halal* diet or a vegetarian diet or a vegan diet or a seafood diet, e.g. fish, prawn and seafood products'. The Manual also stresses the need to avoid cross-contamination with *haram* (or impure) material throughout the processing and delivery cycle, including persons handling the food, utensils, etc. Moreover, during the period of Ramadan, Muslim prisoners are entitled to two meals in the night, one of which must be hot, even though the kitchen would be closed at that time. In addition it is made clear that 'these meals, together with other provision, must be funded by establishments'. In spite of these instructions, however, our evidence shows that prisons still struggle to meet the expectations of Muslim prisoners.

In fact, *halal* food was a highly controversial issue partly because of the wide discrepancy between prison officers' and inmates' perceptions of the issue. On the whole, staff members congratulated themselves on the progress made in providing *halal* meals. At some point it seemed that all the meat purchased in two of the prisons that we investigated was *halal*. But this practice was abandoned in one prison in favour of offering a choice of menus. In a different establishment, Prison 1, the Principal Officer in charge of catering seemed very satisfied with the menu on offer:

> From a Muslim inmate's point of view, the choice has improved and the quality's improved; and I'm happy. What I want is a varied diet, and all inmates of all ethnicities and religions can actually have a choice off that menu.

The intriguing thing is that indeed all meat seemed to have been bought from *halal* butchers. On the one hand, this was irregular and unacceptable from the point of view of some other religions. On the other hand, inmates continued to question the *halal* character of the meat. Even some prison officers were aware of this paradox: 'Meat is 90 per cent *halal*, but most don't know about it' (Prison 3, Prison Officer 10). In fact, the disagreement also arises from concerns about cross-contamination between utensils used in the preparation of *halal* and non-*halal* food and the separation of *halal* and *haram* foods in storage units. These concerns gave rise to extensive dissatisfaction and doubt about the authenticity of *halal* meals. Was the meat truly *halal* (one inmate claimed to have found blood in it)? And were *haram* and *halal* utensils kept separate when there was no Muslim in the kitchen to verify the whole procedure? There were also allegations that officers kept some of the food for themselves because it tasted better. One way of alleviating Muslim worries was to employ a Muslim cook or at least to have a Muslim inmate working in the kitchen. Employing an inmate on a regular basis was not so simple, however, because of the relatively high turnover rate of prisoners in some establishments, but this was planned in one of the prisons:

> Actually we have a Muslim inmate who is a number one in the kitchen, so at the moment it doesn't seem too bad because he informs them that it is *halal*: the proposal is that we will have a Muslim inmate in the kitchen who actually prepares the food for Eid, and that's sent up to the Chapel for the celebration (Prison 1, Principal Officer in charge of catering).

One single area of grievances and controversy in relation to food stands out from all the others, namely, arrangements for the practice of Ramadan. Inmates expressed strong feelings about the facilities for fasting and for celebrating Eid, while many of the staff found it difficult to cope with the whole matter. Ramadan was so badly organised in one of the prisons that inmates could not meet their religious obligations. We collected many reports of instances in which prison officers were alleged to have passively or even actively resisted implementing the agreed arrangements. Ramadan is a good example of the things that many staff found problematic because of the extra work involved and because the timing of prayers conflicted with their lunch hour. In one prison the governors had to escort Muslims to their Friday prayers when prison officers refused to do so.

The provision of meals at night while the kitchen was closed and the escorting of inmates to Friday *and* Eid prayers during Ramadan were fraught with potential problems. In the words of a prison officer in an establishment with a regime that generally respected the religious needs of Muslim inmates, 'On the wing Ramadan can be a right pain in the ass; it makes meal times a problem' (Prison 3, Prison Officer 5). In other places a simple practical issue could jeopardise the whole operation. One such issue was obtaining flasks for keeping food warm long after the kitchens had closed. According to the Imam in Prison 1, 'The problems with the flasks last year – the whole month passed, and they were looking where to get flasks and how to get flasks – red tape or bureaucracy, or lingering on of things'.

Nonetheless, one of the prisons succeeded in solving most problems relating to Ramadan. In Prison 3 a solution was found which suited everyone and could probably be extended to other establishments. For instance, the controversy about escorting prisoners to prayers at break time was resolved through a discussion with the Imam and an agreement to set prayer time before lunch. This was facilitated by the chaplaincy and by the governor's insistence on equal opportunity. As Prison Officer 2 at Prison 3 put it:

> It has become easier now because we have specific sunset times. The Imam is very helpful. We sat down three years ago and worked out a

programme to adjust the regime, and we set an example for other prisons. We taught staff that everyone is supposed to have equal treatment and the very fact that it's difficult doesn't mean that you shouldn't do it.

All the same, views may differ on the organisation of Ramadan in the same prison. For instance, what one officer in Prison 1 (Prison Officer 4) considered to be a difficulty, namely, getting all the Muslim inmates together, was not problematic from the Imam's point of view: 'I think in Ramadan we have no problem. They [Muslim inmates] are put on a landing, not on a wing. They are on the same wing, but they try to gather them all on one landing. It helps them to organise things'. Nevertheless, and despite assurances from the Prison Service Chaplaincy that Governors now understand the necessity of conformity to an agreed schedule for prayer times, problems still arise. According to the *Guardian* (31 January, 2004), for example, Muslim authorities had to make strenuous representations to HMP Belmarsh in South London about the need to permit prayers to take place on the Eid al-Adha festival marking the end of the annual pilgrimage to Mecca. The fact that the festival fell on a Sunday was the prison authorities' reason for planning to defer it until the following day in order to avoid clashing with Christian services.

One of the most surprising features of the concerns about Ramadan was the strong conviction of some prison officers that Muslim inmates should faithfully adhere to their Muslim duties. For example, prison officers often displayed unexpected vigilance about fasting. They frequently took it upon themselves to 'police' the fast (in two of the Prisons in this study). If they saw an inmate eating during the day – for example while receiving visitors – they removed his name from the list of inmates fasting. In other words, Ramadan and the practice of Islam appeared to be construed as a privilege rather than a right in the eyes of these prison officers. In fact, they acted as the 'moral police of the fast', to use the very term that they employed, although some of them realised that this made them unpopular: 'Policing the Ramadan – if we catch them breaking it we take them off it and we are seen as the bad guys' (Prison 1, Prison Officer 4). Other officers thought that fasting was a matter of conscience and that 'it is between them and their god' (Prison 2, Prison Officer 6). In fact, the Senior Officer in charge of visits and receptions at Prison 2 was proud of being able to state that Muslims presented no problems for staff and that 'Ramadan was not morally policed as it was in other prisons'.

General views

Prison officers and governors expressed a wide range of opinions about the practice of Islam in prison. On the positive side, two Imams and some prison officers expressed optimism. The Imam of the prison with most problems was hopeful: 'I think it's on a chance of improving. Although the pace is very slow, it is improving', while one governor had no hesitation in asserting that 'the Muslim population' presented him with 'no logistic or administrative concerns' (Governor 1, Prison 3). Moreover, the head of security in the same prison, even after the 11 September 2001, was satisfied that 'there were no outstanding concerns that security had regarding the Chaplaincy, Muslims or the Imam.' And a group of prison officers in Prison 1 suggested that Muslim prisoners behaved better than Christians in the chapel area.

Nonetheless, the negative side of the scale carries more weight where attitudes are concerned. Negative attitudes towards Muslims were not the prerogative of prison officers alone. In one establishment at least, there were clear signs that Christian chaplains did not wish to relinquish any of their control and privileges: 'regarding the future, I am fearful there will be less and less for the Christians and this will always keep unnecessary tensions' (Prison 1, Substitute Christian Chaplain). One Methodist chaplain in the same establishment made no secret of the fact that 'those who don't want to be Christian, I don't have time for them'. This off-the-cuff remark has to be contextualised. It is not by accident that this particular chaplain belonged to a chaplaincy team that had effectively marginalised the Imam and thus rendered this kind of standpoint acceptable. The Catholic chaplain in the same establishment was strongly opposed to removing statues of Christian saints from the chapel when Muslims held their Friday collective worship there. The senior chaplain himself revealed his irritation about the Imam: 'The Imam tends to think that whenever something is suggested, it can happen immediately – such as the increase in hours for the Arabic class.' Such an Imam may indeed sound unreasonably impatient, but this assessment has to be balanced by the fact that the very same Imam had waited 14 years before being permitted to carry keys in the prison. Buddhist and Hindu sessional chaplains in the same prison also referred to their 'long struggle' to obtain keys – finally granted only a few months previously – although at the time of interview they had still not received keys to the chaplaincy general office or toilets.

Animosity seeped through many of the prison officers' remarks. Several of them evidently resented having to provide facilities for the practice of Islam: 'I think Christianity should come first. I don't mean to be racist but don't see Dubai giving equal treatment to Christians'. (Prison 1, Prison Officer 4). Muslims' piety and their insistence on respecting their religious obligations were often interpreted as deliberate obstruction rather than as genuine acts of faith:

> I don't think religion comes into it at all. Many use it as an excuse. Muslims don't think to do ablution in their cells; they wait to get to chapel, and that affects the running of the chapel (Prison 1, Prison Officer 7).

Some officers were also suspicious of Muslims who spoke in foreign languages at prayer times.

Strictly speaking, it may well be a requirement to perform ablutions just before prayers as the journey from the cell to the prayer room could be considered as a risk to ritual purity. The policing of Ramadan could also be construed as a way of bullying Muslims and 'making them pay' for their beliefs.

The views of Muslim prisoners

Interviews with Muslim inmates revealed a different set of opinions about the conditions in which they practised their religion in prison. On balance, Muslim inmates acknowledged that improvements had taken place in the three male prisons that we studied. The high security prison where the Imam was fully integrated into the chaplaincy team generated the highest measure of satisfaction among inmates. They felt that they could obtain most of the facilities necessary for the practice of their religion; one of them even called it 'a good prison'. In the local prison, the Muslim inmates offered a catalogue of complaints about the past – including the recent past – but the situation appeared to be changing significantly during the period of our fieldwork. The third prison was more ambiguous in so far as its management and policies were overtly favourable to the provision of facilities for the practice of Islam, whereas the absence of an Imam for six months engendered repeated complaints from inmates. The lack of an Imam was evidently connected to discontent and to complaints about inadequate facilities. In the interim, a Muslim member of the Board of Visitors who had taken the post of part-time Visiting Minister made arrangements for Ramadan and a very successful Eid celebration.

Halal *food and Ramadan*

While Muslim prisoners raised a number of issues regarding the facilities for practising their religion, the most emotionally laden were questions about *halal* food and Ramadan. These issues appeared to constitute basic markers for what inmates considered to be 'a good Muslim'. In the first place, not every prison had *halal* meat and Ramadan facilities. Even in the prisons we investigated *halal* food remained controversial despite assurances from catering staff and some Imams that the food served was indeed *halal*. Nonetheless, a great deal of suspicion continued to surround it. For example, 'I don't trust it's *halal*. I eat it but begrudgingly' (Prison 1, Prisoner 3). There seemed to be an inherent distrust of whatever the staff said about the *halal* quality of the food. The inmates wanted it verified by a Muslim; the mere fact that non-Muslims served it introduced areas of uncertainty, as in 'I am not happy with the food, I doubt it is *halal*; a non-Muslim serves it' (Prison 1, Prisoner 4). The presence of blood in the meat was taken as a sure indicator that the animal had not been slaughtered in the mandatory *halal* fashion: 'Also there's a lot of blood in the chicken'

(Prison 3, Prisoner 7). 'I do not trust these people, can't be sure it's *halal*, I order chicken, I often see chicken that is bruised and has blood in it, I don't trust it' (Prison 3, Prisoner 11). Worse still, an accusation was levelled at non-Muslim staff for deliberately contaminating the food, thereby making it *haram*, by spitting in it. One inmate also claimed that his accusation that the meat was not *halal* had led to an apology from the staff:

> There was an incident on Ramadan, this Ramadan just gone, there was chicken Kiev, supposed to be chicken Kiev but it had a slice of pork in it instead of chicken. And, you know, I don't know how – but not only me there were other people on different wings given that as a chicken Kiev – I asked them twice as well just to confirm that; and they said it's a chicken Kiev, but I know chicken looks white and pork looks pink and you know why. But I opened the thing up and I see a pink slice, it's a slice, it's not like a breast, like a chicken breast, you know what I mean. I looked at that, I talked to the officers and they apologised and said, well, sorry (Prison 2, Prisoner 15).

The same prisoner was convinced that it was not just an error but a deliberate flouting of Muslim requirements: 'We are fasting, and then to do that it's a deliberate thing – just for the Muslims – that was a deliberate thing'. This incident was perceived as all the more serious as *halal* food takes on greater significance during Ramadan. Moreover, the entire affair had reinforced the prisoner's doubts about the *halal* quality of the food: 'A lot of things they say is *halal*, but I don't think so'.

Other complaints revolved around negligence and the deliberate or unwitting lack of appropriate attention accorded to the preparation of *halal* food. One common criticism was that utensils were mixed: 'We are told the food is *halal*, but it's prepared by non-Muslims and cooked using *haram* utensils' (Prison 1, Prisoner 5) – not always because of maliciousness but because of negligence. Being vigilant about food was regarded as the sign of a 'good Muslim': 'Every now and then they give me a ham sandwich; it's a recurring problem. I'm waiting for the outcome. Happened to another brother, they gave him a pizza with pork topping; you have to be vigilant, there's constant negligence. It's an ongoing thing' (Prison 3, Prisoner 15). Kitchen staff were also said to be negligent about hygiene standards: 'I don't even eat it. The chicken is not washed; they mix chicken and meat in the same place, it is all steamed. They use the same knives and everything when handling *halal* meat, they don't care. They are writing down it is *halal*; the whites don't even wash their hands' (Prison 2, Prisoner 10). In effect, inmates did not consider that non-Muslim staff were capable of paying due attention and respect for *halal* food. For instance, prisoners reported that, at best, staff failed to see the problem involved in topping up *halal* meat with other meat when they were running short of the former.

A few additional complaints related to the discrimination that the inmates claimed to suffer because vegetarian ice creams and cakes were not made available alongside ordinary ones. The only precaution that seemed to allay their fears was the permanent presence of a Muslim cook in the kitchen and, sometimes, guarantees given by the Imam. The Imam's word counted for a good deal more in the prison where he had been integrated into the chaplaincy team; he obviously gave the impression that he had some authority with officers and inmates.

Ramadan acquires a great deal of symbolic significance in prisons. As a matter of fact, more inmates adhere to Ramadan than pray regularly or respect other obligations. Dissatisfaction with Ramadan and Eid related mostly to the way in which they had been organised in the past. In the male prisons under study, most problems appeared to have been ironed out. There were still complaints about the food being served cold, inadequate flasks, and prisoners being omitted from the fasting list by mistake. The mention of Eid was met with broadly favourable comments about the food being tasty and *halal*; inmates felt confident about this in at least two of the prisons where Muslims had prepared it. With only a few exceptions, comments were guarded but satisfied: 'I am reasonably happy with Eid; it could not be faulted' (Prison 3, Prisoner 15). Others were much more enthusiastic: 'Eid celebrations? Yes, it was brilliant. The food we got that day was delicious, and it was all Muslim guys who go to prayer service who prepared all the food. And it was really good, I enjoyed it'. (Prison 2, Prisoner 30). Eid assumed particular significance because it is the main Muslim festival; it marks the end of Ramadan and it enables Muslim inmates to enjoy their gathering with a special treat of food. In one of the prisons, however, some inmates were sorry that not enough time had been provided for rejoicing and socialising after Eid prayers.

Miscellaneous

Muslim inmates were concerned about a number of other points of practice. The handling of religious artefacts did not give rise to a lot of concern, although past practice on the part of the staff was criticised. Only a few incidents of disrespectful treatment of artefacts were cited. For example, 'They did a cell search and asked me to wait outside. When I returned, my Qur'an was on the floor; all of my stuff was on the floor. I made a noise, but they blanked me out' (Prison 1, Prisoner 8). There was also sensitivity about sniffer dogs coming into contact with artefacts. It is all the more significant, then, that the vast majority of prisoners reported that prison officers treated religious artefacts appropriately.

Inmates also stressed the significance of what they regarded as good hygiene. They said that facilities for ritual ablutions and showering had improved; and in one particular prison, they were pleased with the installation of sinks in their cells. The high security prison in our sample had very welcome ablution facilities adjacent to the prayer room. Prisoners were at pains to explain that it was not good enough to wash before leaving their cell for the prayer room as they could become contaminated again on their way. The lack of prayer mats was also mentioned several times; in at least two of the prisons they were not provided although inmates had asked for them. In one case, a community association eventually provided them, but several prisoners were still left without. However, questions about prayer mats were not among the most contentious issues. Similarly, although inmates appreciated the opportunity to wear prayer caps and *shalwar-kameez* when they were permitted, the issue of 'Muslim' clothing did not arouse as much passion as did the issue of *halal* food and Ramadan. Nevertheless, there was sensitivity among inmates about the derision and disrespect that some prison officers and non-Muslims showed towards them: 'We can wear a hat when praying but not on the landing wings. Prison officers say "It's not a fancy dress party"' (Prison 1, Prisoner 1). And 'what I don't like is when you get a non-Muslim laughing at your hat' (Prison 1, Prisoner 10). Finally, Muslim inmates objected to the fact that some – but not all – prison officers interrupted them while they were praying: 'When I am praying in the cell, some officers just pick up the trays and don't disturb me; others specifically ask for it and disturb prayers' (Prison 1, Prisoner 2).

Prejudice

The general view of Muslim inmates was that the facilities provided for the practice of Islam were not as good as those offered to Christians. In the words of the Imam in Prison 1, 'Islam is always perceived as a threat to the establishment. Christians have their chapel, they have proper seats, seating capacity, there is a proper speaker, there is a proper, you know, sort of drape'. Perhaps fear of retribution made inmates reluctant to lodge complaints. Our data show that prison officers make a curious distinction between Christians and Muslims, for it would be unlikely for officers to conclude that a Christian who does not adhere faithfully to all the Christian rites is not a good Christian and thus should be prevented from attending services. But where Muslims are concerned, it was not unusual for prison officers to label them as 'plastic' Muslims because they were supposedly registered as such only for the food. Another common remark was that they attended Friday prayers purely for the purpose of chatting to their comrades. The categorisation of Muslim inmates by some prison officers clearly involves negative connotations and reveals their reluctance to recognise the identity and entitlements of Muslims. The structural framework makes it difficult for prison officers merely to deny facilities that are actually stipulated in policy documents. Instead, officers have adapted their practices and found new ways of obstructing the practice of Islam.

Further reasons that some Muslim prisoners gave for complaining about current facilities and opportunities include the perception that Muslims did not stand the same chance as Christians of obtaining 'red badge' or 'trusty' jobs. This was one of the areas where there was heavy overlap between allegations of religious and ethnic discrimination. Another perception of discrimination against Muslims related to their allegedly low success rate of applications for transfer to other prisons, for temporary release to attend the funerals of close relatives and the provision of professional interpreters for prisoners whose command of English was not adequate for formal purposes. This particular issue was a major cause of concern to the NCWMP because it became clear that some Muslims who were being detained for reasons to do with immigration were being held for long periods in harsh conditions. The fact that command of formal English was not widespread among them only aggravated their problems.

Does this amount to the institutionalisation of Islam?

Opportunities for the practice of Islam had been enhanced in all the prisons that we visited (except the female prisons), although some still lag behind. In Prison 3, institutionalisation was evidenced by the Imam's position and the attitude of different members of staff towards him. He was fully integrated into the chaplaincy team – which actually worked as an effective team. The Imam took part in chaplaincy meetings, worked in the Race Relations Management Team (RRMT), participated in decisions on the budget and submitted reports on prisoners. The staff expressed respect and consideration for him and regularly called upon him to discuss issues and resolve problems involving Muslim prisoners. He also enjoyed the authority to draw keys. He was definitely part and parcel of the establishment and on occasions had helped to control difficult inmates. This was perhaps the reason why some inmates voiced their disagreement with this Imam on a number of issues.

Developments at the national level are the strongest testimony to the institutionalisation of Islam in the prison service. Maqsood Ahmed was appointed as the Muslim Adviser to the Prison Service, and this position constituted a point of reference for prison staff. Several mentioned consulting him and gaining his support on a number of questions. The Adviser took part in the appointment of new Imams and checked on their credentials and suitability. He convened meetings of prison Imams and circulated a guidebook. His post, which carried status and authority, undoubtedly did more than merely symbolise the Prison Service's commitment to facilitating the practice of Islam: it also strengthened the presence of Islam in prison establishments in highly practical ways.

Another significant move at the national level was the appointment of William Noblett as the new Chaplain General in 2001. His predecessors had not sought the incorporation of minority faiths into chaplaincy on an equal footing with Christians, but Noblett had demonstrated the feasibility and the value of inclusive, multi-faith policies in his previous post. His experiences there served as a blueprint for the policies that he subsequently implemented throughout the Prison Service. Moreover, his appointment demonstrated a clear political will towards change in the Prison Chaplaincy.

A kind of homogenisation of Islam is taking place in the prisons of England and Wales. The Muslim Adviser and other prison authorities decide what is appropriate as Islamic practice and what is not. Even the prisoners are not entirely free to decide for themselves who is a Muslim; self-definition has to contend with institutional pressures. For instance, Ahmadiyas are not recognised as Muslims. Applicants for a chaplain's post must show their credentials and demonstrate that they conform to the Prison Service's norm. Both Imams and prisoners have to restrict their discourse and themes of discussion to what is deemed acceptable (*jihad*, for example, is out of bounds). Institutionalised Islam and Imams come to play a role similar to that of Christianity in the prison environment, with an emphasis on control, reform and resettlement. By officially recognising the Muslim community in prisons the Prison Service is making a contribution to social harmony, especially by endorsing established associations and leaders. To borrow Sophie Gilliat-Ray's term (2001), the Prison Service has encouraged Imams to work in prison in a way that 'approximates' to the dominant model of Christian chaplaincy.

It remains to be seen whether prisons will become sites where a gulf separates community leaders and young people, as can sometimes be observed in mainstream society (Burlet and Reid, 1998). An interesting dialectical interaction is taking place whereby Islam loses some of its autonomy when it succeeds in gaining a space for itself in the Prison Service; it is a classic phenomenon of recuperation. This is also when young Muslim inmates begin to question the Imam if they perceive him as a member of the establishment rather than as one of them. The interaction between Muslim self-definition and the official categorisation of Muslims in prison could become a source of conflict.

The place of Islam in French prisons

One significant factor determining the opportunities created for Islam in each of the French prisons studied is the director's opinion of religion. A 'liberal' director can allow a measure of tolerance that would be banned by one who was strict on matters of *laïcité*. In some prisons in the region of Alsace-Moselle, where a Concordat on relations between church and state is still in operation, *halal* meat is available to the entire prison, and this does not present a problem. In prison A, where the director is open-minded about religion, Friday prayers are celebrated collectively, and the Imam can make his voice heard. In Prison B, which is subdivided into seven semi-autonomous prisons (each with its own Deputy Director) as a result of its sheer size, the role of the director is nonetheless important. The fact that he was less than well disposed towards our research meant that it took us six months to obtain access.

According to the Director of Prison A, overcrowding was one of the main issues. This old and dilapidated prison was designed for fewer than 500 inmates, whereas it was actually holding about 700 inmates in March 2002. There was a serious shortage of prison officers, according to the Director:

> We have 700 prisoners here for only 418 places in an old building dating back to the beginning of the 20th century. Prison is more and more seen as a testimony to the misery of society [*la prison est de plus en plus vue comme la misère de la société*].

He noted two key points about Islam: the practice of Islam was on the increase, while it remained difficult to find moderate Imams:

> Islam makes headway here. We said to ourselves, 'It would be nice to have Imams to channel this need, but the Imams are often more excited than those they would channel'. All of this is difficult.

The problem of *laïcité* is widespread in French prisons. For example, in the women's prison which houses 270 women in a separate section of Prison C, a part-time Muslim chaplain was recently appointed. One characteristic of this prison is that it hosts Catholic nuns wearing a 'veil' who do voluntary work. They teach the prisoners English, manual work, computer science and similar subjects, although they are not attached to the Catholic chaplaincy.[11] The Director explained that nuns were allowed to wear their veil in the name of tradition, while Muslim women were denied this right in the name of *laïcité*. It is one of the paradoxical features of the situation for Muslims in France that tolerance can be extended towards Catholic nuns in the name of tradition but the same right is denied to Muslim women in the name of *laïcité*. Unlike the men's prisons where people of North African origin probably constitute more than half the total number of prisoners, female Muslim prisoners amount to between 10 and 15 per cent. On the whole, 60 per cent of prisoners in the women's prison are foreigners; and most of them are from Latin America and Sub-Saharan Africa. There are a few prisoners from the GIA (Groupe Islamique Armé), the radical Algerian organisation that carried out acts of terrorism in France in the 1990s.

The plight of Islam

Some prisoners are shocked by the situation of Islam in French prisons. Yussef, a 25-year-old Frenchman of North African origin, finds fault with the facilities available to Muslims, especially the state of the prayer room:

> Here, I am shocked by the prayer room [of Prison A]: it is small, it is not clean, and it is not a place fit to pray in. But the Imam is very good and really listens to the people.

Muslim inmates voice their bitterness when they compare Islam to other faiths (Catholicism, Protestantism and Judaism) which seem to enjoy a much more favourable position, as Amali, a 51-year-old Algerian, put it:

> There is an Imam, a priest and a pastor here. For the Christians, there is a Mass; the pastor and the vicar walk freely throughout the prison with keys; they go into cells. For the Imam, there is only Friday and Wednesday, the days of meeting with the prisoners.

In the opinion of prisoners, the fact that there are few Imams but a relatively large number of Christian or Jewish ministers is indicative of the inferior status attributed to Islam and to Arabs. Fathi, as a 24-year-old Frenchman of North African origin, for example, has no doubt about this sorry state of affairs:

> There is no respect for people of Arab origin. There are many Jewish Officers [the inverted slang word *feuj*, meaning Jew, is used]. ... For us, to have an Imam is so difficult. It is not right. I told many Arabs [*robeux*, inverted slang word for Arab, i.e. French people of North African origin] to write [to the prison administrators] in order to have Imams and *halal* meat.

His view is shared by another prisoner, Ali who is a 32-year-old Frenchman from a North African background:

> Islam, here, you have to work bloody hard (*ramer*)! You have racism. There are only 17 Imams in France for the prisons, among whom 11 are not official.[12] It is serious, since prisons are filled with Muslims. In this prison, there are five Christian ministers, two more for women and a rabbi. The Imam does the best he can... This gets on my nerves, it is bad! With all these [Muslim] people, we'll get our way [for the increase in the number of Imams].

When prisoners compare the situation of Islam in France with that of other countries, for instance the United States, it shows up their relative disadvantage even more sharply. Thus, according to Ihsan, a 42-year-old

Algerian, 'In American prisons, they very much respect people; there are Imams on Friday and everything, [not here]'.

Comparing the predicament of Islam to the situation of other faiths, Muslims acquire a sense of being racialised, made to feel inferior, and not taken seriously as members of a genuine religion. They sometimes seem paranoid about the reasons why prison is a humiliation for them. For example, Hassan, a 40-year-old Lebanese explained:

> I don't eat meat here; I buy tins of tuna fish in the canteen. We always have choices. Salads, vegetables, chips; it is quite enough. They put some powder in [Muslims'] meals; they put some powder [tranquilisers], and sometimes they add wine. Here we are in Europe, we are not at home. As Muslims, we don't have the same rights as the other religions. The rabbi brings whatever he wants to the Jews in the prison. As for us, we don't have the right to do it, I don't understand why. I work here in the prison, and it's the same for prayers. The dawn prayer (*sobh*), I don't miss it, I never miss any prayer except the afternoon one (*asr*). I do it in the kitchen [the prison kitchen]. The boss doesn't say anything. Nobody has the right to forbid me that. Some pray secretly, during the exercise hour. Not me: I pray normally, without hiding myself while we're on the walk. Why do young people [from the poor suburbs] hide themselves to pray? Brother B, who is a high security prisoner [DHR or *détenu à haut risque*] hides himself and is afraid that someone will think he is proselytising. There are many Muslims here from all nationalities. I met the Imam once, but he can't do anything, he is alone. It is not the same for Christians and Jews... The other religions have all the rights and we, Muslims, none! There are Muslim Prison Officers but they do nothing for us. They only think of themselves.

Some people, such as Nabil, think that 'Islam is forgotten'. He is a 31-year-old Algerian:

> I have been saying prayers since 1990–91. In Algeria, I did not pray regularly. I took refuge in religion to protect myself from the offenders I saw. It is the same in France; on top of that, I do the prayers. I wasn't steady in my religious practice because I was ignorant of my religion. I have decided never to stop my prayers again, to do them for life. This is the first time that I have been thrown in prison. I would like to have an Imam who would hold a collective celebration (*jama'a*) on Friday [he is in Prison B, where there is no collective prayer]. Muslims are forgotten here. The Muslim minister doesn't do enough for us. I haven't seen him, I haven't even written to him because I am discouraged by those who have written and had to wait three months. The others praise him but I am impatient and it is hard for me to write to him and wait three months.

The situation of Muslim inmates in Prison C is particularly unsatisfactory. Working on his own in a large prison, the Imam cannot meet prisoners individually. It takes some three months for prisoners to meet him once they have sent a letter to him. Many prisoners have difficulties writing letters. They do not admit it openly, but from the high number of those who do not send him a letter despite their eagerness to meet him, it seems likely that they find it difficult to write either in Arabic or French. The system discourages prisoners from meeting the Imam. Since they cannot write, he does not meet them; and this in turn reinforces their tendency not to get in touch with him. Of course, some prisoners do the writing on behalf of others, but not all have access to someone who is able to write in good French. That is why some write to him and wait, while others, such as the following prisoners, give up:

> It is hard to see the prison Imam. I wrote to him about it and I have seen him only once. Here in France nothing is done to guide us in religious matters. It is obscurantism here!
>
> I met the Imam twice. He gave me books, but we didn't find the time to talk. There were ten of us guys, and there was just enough time for each of us to ask a question... I am not scared to talk to Muslims [he uses the word 'Muslim' in French, taking it from the Arabic instead of using the French word 'Musulman'] or to talk to the 'bearded' brothers [the word '*barbu*' is usually used in a pejorative way to indicate '*intégriste*' Muslims in French]. I do it, unlike the French [who are usually frightened].

Some become bitter after sending the Imam many letters which remain unanswered. For example, a 24-year-old Moroccan, Younès, was angry: 'I have written to the Imam many times for a meeting and I have never received an answer'.

Other inmates do not show any particular interest in meeting the Imam, either because they know from others that he is not available or because they suspect him of complacency towards the French prison system that employs him – perhaps because they are not religiously minded or simply because they do not know how to write (but they do not admit it openly because they are ashamed of it). A typical example of this attitude came from Yacine, a Frenchman of Algerian descent, who said, 'Fridays I don't go to meet the Imam [in the Collective prayer, in Prison A]. I know that many take part in it. I am not interested in it'. The case of Nordine, a 47-year-old Algerian, is even clearer:

> I fast during Ramadan, but I don't pray. I drink a bit from time to time, and take some pot [hashish]. I don't apply religion [to my life]. I am not interested in meeting the Imam.

Some, like Sharif, do not meet the Imam but manage their religious life through lending and borrowing religious books from one another. As a 20-year-old Frenchman with a North African background, he explained that:

> I haven't met the Imam in here because I haven't written to him yet. In prison, many young people from the *cités* [housing estates] do not put their religion into practice but they have books on Islam and they swap them among themselves. Otherwise, I buy kosher meat in the canteen because there is no *halal* meat. In any case, since I've been putting Islam into practice, there has been a change [in my life].

Some build up their religious life independently with no reference to the Imam, following a winding path that is loosely related to the rhythm of their spells of imprisonment and freedom. According to Lakhdar, a 20-year-old Frenchman of North African origin:

> Everything will change; I hope to go for *halal* food. I stopped alcohol 16 months ago. I used to drink, especially before going to parties at night, but it didn't happen much. Alcohol is the *Shaytan* [the Devil]. Here, I haven't seen the Imam... With my prayers, things have changed. I talk better, I do things well, I think. Still, I have a long way to go, I still have defects; but it is much better than before.

For some others, who are foreigners and have received their religious education outside France, the Imam is not essential, since they know the rituals and the main aspects of Islam. A good case in point is Hussein, a 23-year-old Pakistani, who explained that, 'I haven't written to see the Imam of the prison but I read Arabic. From the age of five until ten I went to the Madrassa and I learned Arabic and the Qur'an'.

Some of the prisoners who are still anxiously waiting to see the Imam become emotional when thinking about their first meeting with him. Since prisoners know that they cannot meet him in private due to lack of time, there is more than a hint of fantasy in the way that Ali, a 24-year-old Moroccan, imagines the meeting:

> I have never seen the Imam, but if I meet him I know that I'll cry. I'm not in good shape [*je ne suis pas bien dans ma peau*]. And when he'll talk to me and make the *da'wa* [preach to me], he'll teach me many new things.

The prisoners who feel that they are in the throes of vice and sin may doubt whether the Imam is able to help them. They prefer to manage their life themselves and to strengthen their religious life by looking forward to a future free from sin. For example, Lamara, a 29-year-old Algerian, was quite explicit:

> I only eat *halal* food but I haven't seen the Imam. I haven't written to him, I don't see how he can help me. I prefer to solve my problems myself. Those who fornicate, it is very serious [a sin], they should be stoned in the same way as those who sell pot. And in my case, my real problem is not the prayers, it is the women, they are my soft spot [*mon péché mignon*]. I am not in the drugs business, theft or anything like that, I am against them. My problem is sex. *Zina* [fornication] – that is my problem! I used to do this at the beginning with French women when I was a student. Then, when I no longer had a visa, it has been with all women.

The reason why some prisoners do not get in touch with the Imam is that they have a religiosity of their own, perhaps of a hyper-individualised kind that does not need an institutional intermediary. In such cases, the Imam seems structurally unnecessary for the fulfilment of religious duties. This is the case with Wade, a 29-year-old Frenchman who is more concerned that Muslims are considered as terrorists in Europe than he is with meeting the Imam. He considers that the Imam is, at best, irrelevant from his point of view:

> I don't need him, I only need God... They don't like us here. The Europeans don't like us Muslims because they think that there is violence in our religion. They are afraid of bearded people, of bomb attacks [*attentats*]. They don't want to admit that Islam is a genuine religion. All these things are wrong, our religion is just and clear... I am a Muslim but I am not someone who plants bombs [*poseur de bombe*] or a terrorist. I am a good guy; I respect other religions, I am not here to harm other people.

Wade, like many others, has been deeply influenced by the secularisation of French society which marginalises religious institutions for the sake of an individualised form of religiosity.

Many prisoners ask for an Imam who could bring them solace, teach them the rudiments of Islam, solve their existential problems, and answer their questions about what is permitted (*halal*) and what is forbidden (*haram*), what is prescribed as necessary (*vajib*) and what is not. Most of them ask for an Imam to bring them closer to Islam in a society which has alienated them from it through non-religious education and a general suspicion towards religion, especially Islam. They need an Imam to show them the 'right path'. Young Muslims in the poor suburbs are particularly keen to understand a religion that their parents practised in a basic way without teaching them how to apply it in their daily life. They also want to feel it deeply in their innermost self. But on the other hand, people from the same background tend to be completely out of touch with any kind of 'collective' religion, and their personal religiosity is tainted with an individualism that does not sit comfortably with close community involvement. For them, Islam means a personal relation with the sacred and not a socialised form of practice through an Imam who is not so much a person in whom one can confide but the representative of a collective religion.

The prisoners' *'bricolage'*[13] of Islamic norms

Halal meat

The situation regarding *halal* meat varies from prison to prison. Every prison makes a minimal concession to Muslims and Jews to serve them an alternative meal when pork is on the menu. But some prisons in the Alsace-Moselle region of Eastern France where a Concordat is still in operation make *halal* meat available most of the time.[14] Elsewhere, however, the problem of *halal* meat is a highly contentious issue in prisons. The authorities generally refuse to provide *halal* meat, and this leads many prisoners either to give up eating meat or to prepare their own meals whenever possible.[15] Muslims complain that Christians and Jews can avail themselves of the kind of food they want by buying it in the prison canteen, but *halal* food is not usually on sale there.[16]

Some prison authorities argue that *halal* food cannot be provided because it would be incompatible with the principle of *laïcité*, but this is questionable. If it is assumed that no religious considerations should have a bearing on the meals for prison inmates, then pork would be served to everyone. But this is not the case. When ham or any pork product is served, a substitute dish is usually on offer to inmates. This amounts to an implicit breach of the *laïcité* principle because it acknowledges that Muslims (and to a smaller degree Jews, since there are very few of them in prison) have a different identity from the official non-religious one.

In reality, when it comes to *halal* meat, the French prison authorities refuse to consider it for reasons which are not necessarily linked to *laïcité*. Expediency could even be one of their motives since they do not wish to make their job more complicated, but they often justify their decision by reference to *laïcité*. Some think that giving in on the question of *halal* meat might give rise to other Muslim claims and set off a chain of demands that would challenge the status quo. Moreover, introducing an entitlement to *halal* food would create complications for the staff in prison kitchens.[17] *Laïcité* is sometimes used as a kind of scapegoat to avoid dealing properly with prisoners' claims for greater recognition of their identities, religious or otherwise.

There are different attitudes among prisoners in France towards *halal* food. Many declare that they do not eat meat at all. They claim that they eat eggs, vegetables, tinned food and fish whenever meat is on the menu. Some eat meat and justify it in terms garnered from the *Sayings of the Prophet* [*hadith*], according to which one must adapt to the land one lives in. Many ask for *halal* meat and declare that they need it in order to show respect for the Commands of God. It annoys them that prisons refuse to satisfy them on this issue. Others simply refuse to eat the meat and buy other food in the canteen (fish, and particularly tuna); some eat the kosher meat that is on sale in the canteen; and others simply eat vegetables, pasta and desserts. Muslim prisoners' comments on the food provided by prisons include the following:

> The food is not *halal*, so I don't eat it. I never touch it. Instead, I eat tuna. At the beginning, it was difficult. I did not work in the prison. Now, I have a job and I get 130 euros a month. So I can buy food in the canteen.
>
> No, it is not *halal*. I don't eat meat. For Christmas parcels, I receive a *halal* meal from the family. Otherwise, I eat pasta, tomato sauce and rice that we buy at the canteen and cook. I do not eat kosher food.

Although some Muslims choose to eat kosher meat sold in the canteen they would prefer *halal* meat. Nabil, a 31-year-old Algerian, sees the wider significance of his choice:

> The meat is not *halal* and I don't eat it. Sometimes I eat kosher food [bought in the canteen], like the Jews, but I prefer our own food [*halal*]. [The fact that you can find kosher food in the canteen but not *halal* food] is proof that the authorities look after the Jews but not us.

Even food such as fish is suspect in the view of some Muslims because they suspect that it contains wine. For example, Abdallah, a 30-year-old Frenchman, alleged that, 'Once, they served mackerel and I saw they had put white wine in it. I didn't eat it. I eat rice, eggs, canned sardines'. The reasons for being suspicious of prison food range from the fear that it is deliberately contaminated to the claim that it is simply inedible. A small selection includes:

> Here, the meat is not *halal*. In Nanterre, they have *halal* meat in the canteen... Here, they jab the meat [*piquent la viande*] and put tranquilisers into it. A prisoner who works in the kitchen told me.
>
> Here I only eat French fries [*frites*], this is the only thing that is edible in their meal [*gamelle*]. Look at it: impossible to eat it. Even a dog would eat better than us. The fish, the fries, the steaks, I eat them (I buy them

myself at the canteen), but the *'gamelle'*, no, they think we live in the 1930s! They wait until it blows up before they improve things.
The food here is rotten. Even cats don't eat it when we throw it to them through the gates. I buy tuna fish at the canteen and I cook it myself. Here, Muslims cook for themselves, or else they don't eat meat. I don't eat steaks. Sometimes I eat chicken, but it is like rubber, it is mean and rotten. Their paella dates back to 200 years before Christ! Some of the shrimps give you spots [*vous donnent le bouton*]. God protect us! [*la istar*, in Arabic]

Relatively few Muslims confess that they eat everything, including non-*halal* meat, and this is probably because this creates difficulties for their self-image. They rationalise their action by claiming that they really do not have a choice or that, in any case, the food tastes bad. Another strategy is to argue, like Mamadou, a 24-year-old from Mali, that, 'I eat the food even though it is not *halal*, because it is not forbidden to eat the food of the "People of the Book" [Christians and Jews]. I have no choice, so I eat'. There are several variations on this theme, some of which centre on vacillation or confusion. Habib, a 34-year-old Tunisian, is a good case in point:

I don't usually eat meat; it is not *halal*. Still some pray [as Muslims] and eat it. I was influenced by them sometimes. That's how the ones with beards [*barbus*] do it that way: they say that if you are in prison you have no choice and, therefore, can eat non-*halal* meat. The Malian who is working in the kitchen says you shouldn't eat meat unless you can cut it with your knife and check [that it is not pork]. I don't know who to listen to. I buy my food in the prison's canteen [*cantine*]. But the food is very bad [*naze*], it is of the lowest quality. I am scared by the look of the steak; the chicken does not look good.

Refusing to eat non-*halal* food is not necessarily driven by the observance of other religious duties, especially daily prayers. For example, a 25-year-old Algerian called Habib explained:

I am very religious but I am not a practising Muslim, I don't know how to do prayers. But I respect the Islamic law on food, I don't eat non-*halal* meat. All my family respects it, my brothers and sisters as well. My parents are practising Muslims, but not my brothers and sisters.

Mas'oud, a 23-year-old Frenchman, was equally honest about his non-religious reasons for rejecting prison meals:

I don't eat pork. Here their food is crap [*dégueulasse*]. Everything has the same taste. They freeze the food; then they thaw it out and put it in a pot and heat it up. It is not because of religion that I don't eat their food: nobody eats it! Recently someone found worms alive in their food, real living worms!

As mentioned before, the number of prisoners who report that they refuse to eat meat is very high. But the statistics collected from the kitchen of Prison B show that many Muslims eat non-*halal* meat although they claim not to do so. These figures can be partially attributed to the fact that Muslims might give their meat to non-Muslims, but the large discrepancy between what the Muslims say and the number of meat dishes served still shows that at least some Muslims do what they are not ready to acknowledge: they eat non-*halal* meat. Their self-image as good Muslims abiding by the laws of Islam is not necessarily affected by their occasional transgression of those laws.

Nevertheless, their level of frustration is high: they suspect that prisons despise them, refuse to acknowledge their rights as Muslims and, thus, humiliate them. Some prisoners see it as highly significant that there is kosher food but no *halal* food in the canteen. Some, showing paranoid tendencies, even think that the prisons are intent on 'de-islamising' them. The absence of *halal* meat in conjunction with other bans (like the ban on carrying prayer rugs or compasses to determine the direction of Mecca), the lack of Imams, the absence of Friday collective prayers in many prisons and so on, are all identified as part of the general stigma attaching to Muslims as such.

On the whole, *halal* food is an important issue, and many prisoners are probably malnourished as a result of their refusal to eat non-*halal* meat. Their diet is not balanced: some reported that they had not eaten meat for many years. They are not vegetarians, but their diet is not in keeping with this. The provision of *halal* meat in some prison canteens, especially in the Alsace-Moselle region of France, is a practice that could be adopted throughout the entire prison system.

By turning a blind eye to Muslim prisoners' claims for *halal* meat, prisons are aggravating their suspicions. This suspicion can turn to paranoid attitudes. For instance, one prison serves sausages that are made of chicken or non-pork red meat. But, since they look like sausages made of pork, many Muslims refuse to eat them, firmly believing that the prison is trying to make them become sinful Muslims by forcing them to eat pork. This suspicion is unfounded and the sausages are not made of pork. But the suspiciousness which underpins the relation between prisoners and prisons makes it very difficult for the latter to prove that the prisoners' complaints about the food that is served are groundless.

The same problem arises with the issue of so-called medicine in meals. Many prisoners claim that the institution puts drugs in their food so as to calm them down. They say that the food sometimes tastes different and that this is caused by the addition of these drugs which make people less aggressive and even dizzy. This is the kind of rumour which thrives in prison. Moreover, since French prisons contain Islamic radicals and many young people from poor suburbs who have a reputation for being arrogant and uncivil, it is believed that drugs could be a way of reducing their insubordination in order to make them comply with prison rules. Many of the Muslims whom we interviewed saw this as evidence of the treacherous nature of the prisons. Even some of the prisoners who worked in the kitchens were convinced that 'something' was being done although they had no opportunity to witness it. Those who were involved in food preparation sometimes thought that, if anything was added to the food, it was done before they prepared it. Consequently, in spite of a lack of evidence about the addition of drugs to the food, many prisoners – and in particular Muslims – thought that this was another stratagem on the part of prison administrators to neutralise them by reducing their vitality and by transforming them into subhuman beings. This false idea finds further credence among prisoners in the belief that doctors in prison 'easily' prescribe drugs to inmates. The fact that doctors allegedly do it without any fuss (contrary to the general attitude of prison officials towards prisoners' claims) is taken as further proof of the conscious and deliberate policy of the prison to subdue prisoners. The belief is that making prisoners lethargic under the influence of tranquilisers and psychotropic medicines would be a subtle way of weakening inmates. This would give prisons a way of avoiding the legitimate demands that prisoners would otherwise make on them.

The allegations that Muslim prisoners make about prison food must be compared to the accounts given by prison staff in charge of kitchens. In Prison B, for example, the Catering Officer emphasised the problems associated with special diets in a prison where 80 per cent of inmates are Muslims. He explained that about 14 diets had to be provided for medical reasons: gastric illnesses, dental problems, cholesterol, diabetes and so on. But the prison does not support diets for other reasons. There are also problems of temporary resistance to new food items:

At the beginning, there was no turkey ham [jambon de dinde]. Now, it is served on the menu. At the beginning, out of some 580 prisoners, only 20 took it. Now, there are 500!

The Catering Officer added that taste is another important aspect of the consumption or rejection of food, for 'If we serve fish without seasoning, 30 per cent of it won't be eaten. If it is a fish fried in breadcrumbs [pané], 100 per cent of it is eaten!'. The consumption of non-halal but tasty food is also high, contrary to the views of the Muslim prisoners, who constitute an absolute majority in Prison A. According to the Catering Director, 'The take-up rate for bœuf bourguignon is 85 per cent and 95 per cent for steaks.

But "rissolettes of veal" are less popular, eggs as well'. The rate of consumption of pork is also higher than the reports of Muslim prisoners imply – but only slightly. The theory that Muslims might give their share to their non-Muslim friends is plausible, since pork dishes are eaten by about 25 per cent of prisoners although Muslims amount to about 80 per cent of prisoners according to the director.

The inequality of treatment between Islam and Christianity becomes clear in relation to the food provided at times of religious festivals. According to the Catering Director of Prison B:

> There are no special meals for *Ramadan* festivities, but the prisoners can purchase their food at the canteen. For Christmas and the New Year there are special menus: a *'feuilleté de langoustine'* as the first course, a *'magret de canard'* as the main course, two vegetables, and a good cheese. I have a budget for the entire year and I cannot have special meals for *Ramadan*.

The Director cites budgetary restrictions – not *laïcité* – as a justification of his choices. This is not the case with some other staff who justify their practices on the grounds of *laïcité* and the fact that Christmas has become a *laïc* national holiday with an obsolete religious background.

Needless to say, Muslims in Prison B resent this deeply and feel humiliated by it. This aggravates their frustration in a prison where about eight out of ten inmates are Muslims and where the Eid al-Kabir[18] festival, at the end of Ramadan, is not recognised as being on a par with Christmas.

Ramadan and prayers

Ramadan is very important in prisons. Its symbolic significance outstrips that of daily prayers. Many Muslims, in or out of prison, who do not say their daily prayers are keen on respecting the fast of Ramadan. There are, as a matter of fact, many groups of people who practise Ramadan rituals in different ways. Many fast without doing the five daily prayers. They regret it, at least when they are asked to give their reasons for not doing the prayers. Many of the *'banlieusard'* youth from the poor suburbs are among this category. Many do not even know the prayers, but they are strongly concerned about fasting. Some do it for part of Ramadan; and some do not eat but drink occasionally, although not in public. On the whole, in prisons as well as in the so-called *banlieues*, fasting during Ramadan comes top of the list of what Muslims consider most characteristic of Islamic rituals.

The importance of Ramadan has been partially understood in Prison A where dates and some other festive foods are provided, or at least sold in the prison canteen. Nonetheless, hot food is not provided at the appropriate time. The Imam, who has the ear of the director, organised a feast at the end of Ramadan, as is usual among Muslims, and all the prisoners were invited. It gave many of them an opportunity to fraternise and to forget, for a while, the difficulties of imprisonment. Nevertheless, the prisoners had some complaints about the lack of *halal* meat, even in the canteen. The work schedule was not adjusted, and this made it hard for some prisoners to carry out their work as they normally did. Prisoners were allowed to receive a few kilos of food in parcels from their family or friends. In general, apart from some minor help and the authorisation of the feast at the end of Ramadan [*fitr*], nothing else was done – even in this particular prison which is the most favourably disposed towards Muslims in our sample. By contrast, Prison B, one of the largest in Europe, did not even provide the minor facilities that were available in Prison A. The Imam could not celebrate the festivities of the end of the holy month; there were no Friday collective prayers and there was no *halal* food even on this solemn occasion.

The issue of prayers contains at least three different aspects: individual prayers in cells, collective prayer in general (in theory, Muslims are supposed to pray collectively whenever they can) and collective prayer on Friday. Muslims who were not able to get together for collective prayers in two of the three prisons in our sample tried, nevertheless, to perform them in some ways in the larger Prison C. This is forbidden by prison authorities because it is a gathering and, as such, is not permitted under prison rules. In spite of this, prisoners did celebrate collective prayers under the arcade of the courtyard during the exercise hours. There, partially hidden by the columns, they could pray together in small groups, alternatively under the leadership of a convert and some 'Islamists'. The prison officers were aware of this. They disciplined a few of the participants, but they could not do it systematically for fear that prisoners might refuse to obey. This 'mild' disobedience usually takes a few forms such as refusing to return to cells after exercise, refusing to leave the courtyard, and committing minor attacks on prison officers.

As they wanted to celebrate collective prayers in the courtyard, the prisoners needed a prayer carpet. But it is forbidden to carry this small carpet around in a prison. Thus, they had to do it in breach of prison regulations. This might be sanctioned – and it sometimes was – but to no avail. The fact that Muslims did not have a room where they could celebrate collective prayers and the fact that they did not have an Imam who could lead the prayers, at least on Fridays, contributed to the para-doxical situation where the authorities had to 'tolerate' breaches of the rules. They also had to put up with the possibility that some of the radical Muslims who led these prayers might influence other Muslims. But the prison authorities continued to deny Muslims the religious facilities that might jeopardise the prison's habit of denying that Islam was a fully fledged religion. In this way, a balance was struck between some groups of

Muslim inmates and the authorities: the prisoners performed their religious prayers collectively while the prison officers closed their eyes to the celebrations. From time to time, there was some form of a crackdown, but this could not be implemented systematically. An *ad hoc* solution was to transfer prisoners from one semi-autonomous prison to another in order to break up the group's identity. But this ran the risk of spreading the practice to other prisons. In any case, some groups of Muslims did manage to conduct their collective prayers, sporadically, while the authorities coped with it more or less, alternating between prohibition and toleration. Muslims felt frustrated, all the more so as Sunday Mass was regularly celebrated for Christians.

On the whole, Muslim inmates expressed a general sense of frustration with prison authorities. They claimed that whenever facilities were requested for Muslims, the authorities refused to cooperate, while many of the very same facilities were provided for Christians and Jews. Muslims complained that the religious festivals for Christians and Jews were recognised and that Christians could receive parcels for Christmas, whereas this was not permitted for Muslims during the festival of the end of Ramadan. (Incidentally, Muslims could receive parcels at Christmas time but they argued that it was not their religious festival.) The resentment that Muslims expressed towards Christians and Jews increased when it came to religious gatherings. The general feeling of Muslim prisoners was that they were treated as second-rate citizens, their religion was unrecognised, and their customs were at best ignored.

According to most interviewees, Ramadan plays a very important role in their identity as Muslims – at least as much as (if not more than) daily prayers. For many of them the hallmark of being a Muslim is to respect the fast at Ramadan, to participate in it and to avoid eating pork. Many are ignorant about daily prayers in Arabic and therefore do not recite them. They have a twinge of conscience about this but still consider themselves Muslims. Many of them consider Ramadan to be a minimal sign of Muslimhood. Nevertheless, some who do not pray and do not fast in Ramadan still consider themselves as Muslims in their heart.

Muslim prisoners show wide variations in their observance of Ramadan and prayers and in the factors that shape their religiosity. There is great diversity in the way in which they recite prayers, fast during Ramadan or carry out their religious duties on time or with a delay. There are also variations in the extent to which the prison environment influences their faith (encouraging it for many, deterring it for some) and in the role of their fellow-inmates.

Most of the time, the dawn prayer [*sobh*] is the most difficult to perform in prison because of its timing. It may even be necessary to group some of the prayers together in prison in order to fit them into the schedule of events. For example, Abdallah, a 30-year-old Moroccan resident in Holland, explained, 'I am a believer. Outside prison, I prayed regularly. Here, in prison, I pray too. I do my five daily prayers but since I don't want to miss the exercise hours, I sometimes group some of my prayers together'. Similarly, Hussein, a 23-year-old Pakistani, said, 'I do the prayers but when I work [in prison], sometimes, I cannot do them on time. I don't dare ask the boss to allow me to do it, he is a Jew, but he is kind. I miss that'. Many other prisoners were keen to establish that they did their best to say their prayers whenever possible.

Some prisoners claimed that prayers could give added impetus to self-control and to overcoming one's physical and mental deficiencies. Prayers allegedly enhanced their self-confidence and promoted a feeling of well-being. At least, this was the experience reported by Abdel, a 33-year-old Algerian, who had begun praying regularly two months before the interview:

Prayer prevents [bad things], it makes you walk straight. If you pray, you never do wrong, you'll be straight. That is religion. I have chosen a delinquent way, I haven't won anything. That's why I have written to the Imam to try another way, the way of Islam... For the past two months, I have felt well; I feel in good form [*j'ai la pêche*] in my job [within the prison]. My boss told me "I can count on you"'.

For Sharif, a 20-year-old Frenchman of North African origins, living in accordance with religion means snapping out of offending behaviour and getting on to the right path, as it does for other young people from the *Cités* who 'take up religion' and, in so doing, break the vicious cycle of delinquency and '*galère*' [living in a hell on earth]. In his own words,

I used to pray from time to time. I went to the mosque and made the *dua* [the invocations]. I went with one of my friends whose father is a devout believer in Champigny. There, many young people from the *banlieues* take up religion and put Islam into practice. In this way, they get out of the '*galère*' [hell on earth]. But there is also juvenile delinquency because many young people from the *banlieues* are in a dump. They don't put their religion into practice although they don't forget it entirely, never. As for me, I thought about it for a long time. My parents advised me to do so, and one day I did it.

For many second- or third-generation people of North African descent who have had no serious Islamic upbringing, prison can be a good place to learn the basics of religion and to put it into practice with the help of other prisoners who come from North Africa or even Sub-Saharan Africa and who know much more about Islam. In this situation, the role of the Muslim chaplain is actually minimal, since he cannot help the Muslims, owing to his lack of time. Other prisoners, on the contrary, play a significant part in this process of 'islamisation'. For example, Ahsen, a 26-year-old Frenchman of Tunisian origin, told us, 'I have always prayed. Here, I do the daily prayers with a prison mate [*codétenu*] who is Tunisian. At the beginning, he did not pray, but now he prays with me'.

Djamal, a 40-year-old Frenchman of Algerian origin, is one of those who claim to have benefited from this: 'I am a Muslim; I learn the prayers with other Muslims. We take books, we learn Islam. They know what is inside the Qur'an. I did not practise before. I have never seen the Imam... I have nothing, no prayer carpet'. A variation on this theme was recounted by Amir, a 22-year-old Frenchman with an Algerian father and a Tunisian mother. Although he could not describe himself as a practising Muslim he added, 'Islam is still very close to my heart... There are practising prisoners who dedicate themselves to us and say, "I am here whenever you like [to help you]"'. What is distinctive about Amir's case is that he has decided not to accept these offers of help from fellow-Muslims.

Having a prison mate in the same cell can work to the benefit of the more and the less experienced practitioners of Islamic prayers. This was the experience of Ali, a 20-year-old Frenchman from a North African background who shared his cell with prisoners from Malaysia, Algeria and Tunisia. He reported that, 'We do prayers together; I have learned the way the Algerians do them. I know Arabic and the Qur'an and how to do prayers'. In fact, religious conversions do occur in prison, and the change to Islam can offer a way of reshaping one's outlook in a new way. A good example of this concerns a young Latin-American woman, Aysha, who regarded her conversion as the completion of a process that had begun some years previously in her own country:

> A girl, Zubeda, converted me to Islam here in prison, with four witnesses. She gave me a paper with names, and I chose Aysha. She was a black African. Now, I read the Qur'an [in Spanish] all night. I already know seven *surats* plus *Fatiha* by heart. I pray and I fast in Ramadan.

It does not necessarily follow, however, that practising Muslims – or members of any other faith community – are entirely devout in every aspect of their life. This was crystal clear in the case of a black 17-year-old man from Gabon:

> I am a Muslim, I pray in prison. Since it is not clean here in my cell, I do it outside. I fast during Ramadan as well... I eat rice, meat, dessert, except pork... I read the Qur'an, but I look at *Playboy* as well. I have an Arab girlfriend. I know it is *haram*, but I need it.

Many prisoners recognise that being imprisoned has actually helped them to begin praying or to take up prayers again after a long period of interruption.

Others claim that reciting their prayers in prison has opened up new vistas in their life. One in particular, Lakhdar, a 20-year-old Frenchman with a North African background, reported that he used to stammer and could now communicate much better since he began praying.

> In the past, I was in a jam [*j'étais coincé*]: my father used to beat me; the more he beat me, the less what he told me entered my head. Before this, I stammered and didn't talk to anyone. Since last year [in prison], with my prayers, things have changed. I talk better, I do things well, I think. I still have a long way to go, I still have defects, but it is much better than before.

For many of the prisoners who are multiple offenders, the constant back and forth between prison and home creates the kind of disorder and instability that they try to master through prayers. But from this perspective, praying is not so much a means to break the vicious cycle of crime, conviction, prison, release, re-offending, reconviction and prison again. It becomes a way of coping with this disorderly life which is punctuated by spells in prison and temporary spells out of it. Praying can help to give shape to their life inside or outside prison rather than a way of escaping imprisonment by moulding their life to stringent Islamic rules. In this way, it can be integrated into the vicissitudes of life without necessarily playing a major role in breaking a pattern of immoral or criminal conduct.

This can be so discouraging for prisoners that they resist it by not praying in prison. As a 24-year-old Moroccan, Ali could look back on his experience and recognise the pattern:

> I prayed when I was a child, but then I stopped. I went to the mosque every Friday. In France, I kept on doing it a bit, but it was very difficult. I got an 18 months' prison sentence and, in prison, I prayed all the 18 months! But once outside, I stopped praying. I told myself: 'It is utterly useless to pray to God in prison, when you are living in a hell on earth [*en galère*]; it's not fair and it doesn't make sense'. And now, I want to pray when I am in good shape, outside. This time I have stopped saying prayers in prison. I carry on with fasting during Ramadan. Even when I was praying, I carried on taking pot, alcohol and cigarettes. By the way, pork, I never touched that! I know full well that once I am outside, it'll be hard [to be a good Muslim].

One interpretation of postponing one's prayers is that one is not yet ready for a 'pure' Islamic life. Since prison is associated with impurity and religious laxity, some prisoners merely prepare themselves for a time when they can be impeccable Muslims and good citizens who will not do stupid things that spoil their lives. This interpretation, which is not uncommon among prisoners, can be seen as a way of refusing to abide by restrictive religious rules (such as the five daily prayers beginning before dawn and finishing in the evening) and of putting off obeying them to an indefinite future. This second attitude has the advantage of not closing off for ever the prospect of a serene and orderly life. It simply creates a contrast between the hopeless predicament of living in prison and the bright horizon of a promising future on the outside – when the released prisoner can have a religious life that will fill him with joy. Yaseen, a 31-year-old Algerian whose religiously devout parents had been heartbroken to visit him in prison, epitomised this approach:

> My room mate prays and he told me, 'It's useless to pray if you go and do the same stupid things [*conneries*] afterwards'. I'll pray when I'm in better shape, outside prison. For the time being, I'm enjoying my freedom not to pray! [said with a smile].

Some prisoners are so disillusioned with themselves and their sinful life that they feel too impure to pray. They cannot imagine moral improvement for themselves in the foreseeable future. Similarly, others worry about not being able to live up to the expectations of their religion, but at least fasting during Ramadan can provide a degree of reassurance. In a few cases, prisoners attribute their inability to obey the laws of Islam to the influence of the Devil [*Shaytan*].

Female Muslim inmates can face similar problems of anxiety about not fulfilling all their religious obligations, but the issue of wearing a headscarf or *hijab* adds a further complication. This is how Khadija, a 35-year-old French woman of Algerian origin, put it:

> I am a believer. I fast during Ramadan but I do not do prayers. In my family, my mother, my four brothers and my three sisters do prayers; and women do not go out without the *hijab*. But I do not practise. I used to do it before but here in prison, no. Here I cannot wear the *hijab*.

There was support from Sakina, a 25-year-old Tunisian woman, who confessed that, 'It is not easy to pray in prison. The *hijab* is forbidden. For prayers, you need a long dress; you have to wake up at dawn, it is hard'.

Male prisoners, in comparison, were more likely to argue that praying did not necessarily mean an ostentatious display of religion. And in the opinion of Baqir, a 40-year-old North African, religious fanaticism should certainly be avoided: 'I pray with my reading and my reflections. I pray in the night, in my cell. I do not need the call for prayers; these are acts of provocation or fanaticism [made by some prisoners]'.

Prisoners were quick to point out that, regardless of whether their practice of Islam was complete or partial, religious observance in prison was not always constant. There were ups and downs, periods when they became more religious – and times when they had doubts about religion. This was captured well by Mohsin, a 35-year-old Frenchman of Algerian origin, who admitted that, 'There are periods when practising Islam is important for me. But there are periods when I believe and others when I don't. There are also periods when I believe but I do not practise!'. Sometimes this depended on the encouragement or discouragement received from other prisoners. Some pray and fast during Ramadan, but they stop praying afterwards. For them, prayers during Ramadan make sense because they enable them to live a 'complete' Islamic month, but for the rest of the year they do not fulfil their religious duty.

The institution of collective Friday prayers is not well established in French prisons but once it starts to take place it becomes one of the defining features of Muslims from their own point view. Some, but not all, prisoners take part in it, but it certainly becomes a point of reference for them. In Prison A (the only one in our sample where there was a Friday prayer), prisoners referred to it as a significant Islamic phenomenon. The question of whether prisoners participate or not becomes important; and this is why some of them try to justify their absence. For example, a 32-year-old prisoner from the Ivory Coast who described himself as a believer and a practising Muslim explained that 'the Friday prayer is a good thing but unfortunately I can't take part in it because I am attending a training course'.

Some feel compelled to 'take up Islam' [*entrer dans l'islam*] after a long absence. The example of a Muslim who had been a criminal and had then, in some special circumstances (for instance, having a nightmare), come back to Islam becomes paradigmatic for prisoners. In this way, they take up their religion again and become diligent about their religious duties; prayers and Ramadan fasting become the most important things to them. This is what happened to Benamar, a 26-year-old Frenchman, who had been praying five times a day for the previous two years:

I was fed up [being in prison] and I had a 'flash'. As a child, I prayed but then I stopped for a long time and afterwards I went into alcoholic frenzies [*j'avais des délires d'alcool*] and hashish as well. A guy who was into vice, drugs and delinquency was able to put a stop to it [*s'en sortir*]. He stopped everything; he gave all his *haram* [illicit] money to the poor and got married. This bewildered me. Since then, he has become serious. Once he had a nightmare. He was the trigger mechanism for me. I entered Islam smoothly, I tried to get back into Islam. We talked about death, and this impressed me. I was on the dark side. Since I've been praying, it is much better: I am much less depressed, I am always happy. I take the good side of things.

For recidivists, the alternation between living in prison and in the outside world creates opportunities for revitalising their religious experiences and recovering Islam. Being part of Islam somehow counteracts the instability that goes with moving backwards and forwards between the world of freedom and the constraints of life in prison. This is how many prisoners come to renew their ties with Islam.

For those prisoners who do not pray or fast during Ramadan, the main symbol of being a Muslim is their refusal to eat non-*halal* meat. This kind of minimalist Islam exists in prison alongside the version in which fasting during Ramadan without performing prayers becomes the main characteristic of a Muslim. Younes, a 24-year-old Moroccan, exemplifies this pattern. He said, 'I don't know how to pray but I keep a *halal* diet; I don't eat non-*halal*. My parents are practising Muslims but not my brothers and sisters... I fully intend to pray one day, but, with all my problems it's not possible. Here I work and I earn 136 euros. I send 75 euros to my family. It's not clear how I can pray at the same time'. A more extreme case concerns Omar, a 40-year-old non-practising Muslim who is honest about the fact that the Palestinian question is the only thing that makes him feel like a Muslim.

Obstacles

One of the major obstacles to the practice of Islam in French prisons is the sense that prison persecutes prisoners for their religious faith. A 26-year-old Palestinian called Ryad explained:

> I have the faith. The policemen asked me: 'Do you like Bin Laden?'. And they made my life a misery in the prison of Fresnes. God protect us! Here, I pray five times a day, I fast during Ramadan as well. I began to pray four years ago.

Lotfi, a 41-year-old Tunisian, added, 'If you practise here, the prison authorities treat you like a terrorist'. A more generalised obstacle is that living in a cynical society where lack of modesty is widespread makes it difficult to be a devout Muslim. This point was made forcefully by Kamel, a 34-year-old Frenchman, who denied that it was straightforward to have faith while living in France

> ... with all those movies where they show arses and so on. In prison, it is worse. I am too demoralised to do anything. I am a drug addict, but no treatment centre has accepted me. I have nowhere to go, I have nothing to lose. I am a believer and I know people who have gone to Afghanistan; they could not stand this any more.

Furthermore, some prisoners find that being in a confined environment makes it difficult for them to pray regularly, if at all. In such cases, contrary to other instances where the existential problems of prison life give rise to religious practice, having grave anxieties is an obstacle to the observance of religious duties. The disturbing experience of being imprisoned disrupts old habits, particularly those associated with the management of time in the outside world. Saying daily prayers is one of those habits. The religious impurity [*najis*] of their cells aggravates their anxieties and concerns about life.

Even reading the Qur'an and other edifying Islamic books is difficult in prison either because they do not exist in the prison library or because the number of copies is too small, particularly in establishments where more than half the inmates are Muslims. A further problem is that some prisoners are unable to read such books because they are not available in their mother tongue.

Conclusion

In the prisons of England and Wales, the relatively privileged position of religion and chaplains opened a window of opportunity for Islam and 'other faiths' in the 1980s. The special responsibilities of Christian chaplains enabled them to operate a kind of brokerage on behalf of Muslim ministers and the practice of Islam in prison. This used to mean that individual chaplains had a decisive influence – positive or negative – on the fate of Islam in prison. However, the situation has been transformed in recent years by national policies and institutional mechanisms which have incorporated religion as a criterion of discrimination into the Prison Service Race Relations policy. The appointment of a Muslim Adviser to the Prison Service of England and Wales and of a Chaplain General favourable to a multi-faith approach has been matched by the appointment of at least 15 full-time Muslim chaplains since 2001.

In practice many measures have been taken to facilitate the exercise of Islam, to create spaces for collective prayers, to encourage greater respect for religious artefacts, to make *halal* food more available, and to make it easier for Muslim inmates to observe Ramadan. Prison officers and inmates both testify to the reality of these improvements. Nevertheless, a number of areas of dissatisfaction still persist in relation mainly to the authenticity of *halal* food and the opportunities for observing Ramadan, as well as the inmates' perception that some prison officers still have negative attitudes towards Islam. There is also some evidence of an ill-defined sense of dissatisfaction with the standardised, apolitical Islam which may be in the process of becoming institutionalised in British prisons.

The situation in French prisons stands in sharp contrast to developments in the Prison Service of England and Wales. Opportunities for the practice of Islam in French prisons are very limited or simply non-existent. The unavailability of *halal* food, the scarcity of Imams and the lack of facilities for collective prayers, for fasting during Ramadan and for the celebration of Eid festivals all make it extremely difficult to adhere to Muslim norms in most prisons. This situation may be better in those prisons where the director happens to be tolerant and open-minded about Islam. Contrary to the assumption that provisions for Muslim prisoners would be based on nationwide regulations and structures in a country as centralised as France, in reality much is left to generalised prejudice, to serendipity and to the personal discretion of directors. Altogether, this leads to highly varied patterns of individualised practices among Muslim prisoners alongside the more structured practice of radical Islamists. This fosters acute frustration among young inmates from Muslim backgrounds.

5
Islam, 'Race' Relations and Discrimination in Prison

Introduction

One of the constant themes of this book is the sharp difference between France and England and Wales in terms of how each country seeks to integrate its immigrants and successive generations of their descendants. France favours a model of republican citizenship with codes of law designed to offer equal rights and equal protection to all individuals regardless of ethnic, racial or religious background. Britain has moved some way towards incorporating elements of an individual rights-based notion of citizenship but is also wedded to the importance of communal identities. Consequently, the law and public institutions in England and Wales recognise the need to protect certain communities or to exempt them from otherwise universal requirements. Nowhere is this clearer than in the legislation regarding 'race relations'. In the circumstances, this chapter necessarily places a heavy emphasis on the legal and administrative framework of race relations and other aspects of what is now termed 'diversity' in the prisons of England and Wales. The absence of such a framework in France means that our analysis is necessarily limited to the experiences of racism reported by Muslim prisoners and discussed by prison staff.

The first part of the chapter reviews the history of responses to legislation regarding race relations in the Prison Service of England and Wales,[1] paying special attention to incidents that elicited public concern and to the effects of this history on the position of minority faith groups in prisons. The views of prison officers and of Muslim prisoners about the state of race relations in the prisons of England and Wales form the second part of the chapter. Finally, the chapter considers reports from Muslim prisoners in French prisons about their experiences of racist discrimination.

Racism and the implementation of race relations policies in England and Wales

One of the unintended consequences of the introduction of anti-racist legislation and norms in British society has turned out to be a heightened level of sensitivity to religious and ethnic diversity in prisons. Although religion was not included among the grounds for discrimination prohibited by the Race Relations Act 1976 (RRA) or, indeed, by subsequent legislation in England and Wales until the advent of the Anti-terrorism, Crime and Security Act 2001 – which amended the Crime and Disorder Act 1998 by introducing a new category of 'religiously aggravated' offences – the implementation of anti-racist policies in the prison sector has indirectly afforded considerable protection and official recognition to mainstream Christianity and minority religious faiths. In the first instance, this was because two such minorities, Jews and Sikhs, were defined as ethnic groups and, therefore, covered by the RRA's protection. Subsequently, the Prison Service encompassed a much wider range of faith communities in its own policy to prohibit unlawful discrimination.[2] Recent initiatives to protect 'diversity' in the Prison Service have also increased the degree of official acknowledgement of ethnic *and* religious differences. Furthermore, the Employment Equality Regulations which came into effect in December 2003 will probably be used to challenge some aspects of the Prison Service's practices for recruiting, remunerating and promoting staff from religious minorities.

Although prisons were the direct responsibility of the Home Office and therefore in the front line when the Race Relations Act 1976 was passed, there was 'considerable uncertainty regarding the extent to which the provisions of the 1976 Act apply within the prison system' (Genders and Player, 1989: 15). Moreover, the Prison Service had not had time to forge its own procedures for dealing with race relations before minority ethnic protests erupted in the early 1980s on the streets of inner cities in such major British urban centres as Bristol, London (Brixton and Southall), Birmingham (Handsworth), Liverpool (Toxteth) and Manchester (Moss Side).[3] The Scarman Report of 1981 into the disturbances in Brixton indicted the police for racism and made recommendations for remedying the situation. In the same year, the Prison Service issued its first instruction to Governors (Circular Instruction 28/81) about race relations and called for the creation of Race Relations Officers' posts. It alerted its staff to the fact that 'the potential sensitivity over race relations problems adds a new dimension to the professionalism required of the prison service' (quoted in McDermott, 1989: 216).

The implications for racism in the Prison Service became clear in 1983 in the case of John Alexander, a black prisoner of African-Caribbean origins. Southampton County Court determined that the Home Office had unlawfully discriminated against him by refusing his application for work in the kitchen at HMP Parkhurst. Bearing in mind that working in the kitchen was considered one of the better jobs – much sought after by inmates – adverse comments included in the reports accompanying Mr Alexander's application were likely to have damaged his prospects. In this instance both the initial assessment report and the induction report, which contributed heavily towards the adverse decision, displayed clear evidence of racist discrimination:

> He displays the usual traits associated with his ethnic background, being arrogant, suspicious of staff, anti-authority, devious and possessing a large chip on his shoulder which he will find very difficult to remove if he carries on the way he is doing (Assessment Report, quoted in Circular Instruction 56/1983).
>
> He has been described as a violent man with a very large chip on his shoulder which he will have great difficulty in removing. He shows the anti-authority arrogance that seems to be common in most coloured inmates (Induction Report, quoted in Circular Instruction 56/1983).

The court's judgement was a milestone in the Prison Service's belated response to the RRA. In addition, it shows that the progress of anti-discrimination policy was advanced through legal action on the part of a minority ethnic constituency and its advocates. The finding for Mr Alexander was bad publicity for the Prison Service and was directly responsible for a statement made by the Director General and Deputy Director General which drew attention 'to the absolute commitment of the prison department to a policy of racial equality and to the elimination of discrimination in all aspects of the work of the service' (Circular Instruction 56/1983, Addendum I). This statement unequivocally asserted 'the need to avoid racially offensive remarks and derogatory language in written reports on inmates' (Circular Instruction 56/1983, Addendum I). Moreover, the Circular insisted that Race Relations Liaison Officers (RRLOs) needed to be appointed from senior staff ranks thus lending them a more authoritative voice in prisons. Exactly 20 years later, the Formal Investigation into the Prison Service conducted by the Commission for Racial Equality (CRE 2003a, 2003b) repeated the same requirement that RRLOs should be senior officers. No doubt, the earlier response was partly a symbolic measure designed to demonstrate that the Prison Service was taking 'racial' issues seriously. But at least new procedures for recording the ethnic origin of prisoners were set in place in 1984 (Circular Instruction 25/1984), and the categories for recording ethnicity were subsequently amended to match those of the 1991 Census (HM Prison Service, 1997: Chapter 4: 2).

The Prison Service eventually issued a policy statement on race relations and circulated it for the attention of 'staff, inmates and members of the public' who dealt with the policy's practical implementation (Circular Instruction 32/1986). This happened in the wake of the riots – more severe and widespread than the 1981 disturbances – that raged through many British cities in 1985. The riots had a strong impact on British society, leading some major institutions to implement policies that had previously existed only on paper (Joly, 2001). The Prison Service followed up its policy statement with efforts to recruit more minority ethnic staff in 1990 and produced its first comprehensive document in 1991 – the *Race Relations Manual* (which superseded Circular Instructions 25/1981, 56/1983, 25/1984 and 39/1990). It also published a training book and pocket book for all prison staff. The *Manual* incorporates the following policy:

1. The Prison Department is committed absolutely to a policy of racial equality and to the elimination of discrimination in all aspects of the work of the Prison Service. It is opposed also to any display of racial prejudice, either by word or conduct by any member of the Service in his or her dealings with any other person.
2. All prisoners should be treated with humanity and respect. All prisoners should be treated impartially and without discrimination on grounds of colour, race or religion. Insulting, abusive or derogatory language towards prisoners will not be tolerated.
3. Race relations concern every member of the Prison Service. It is the responsibility of every member of staff to ensure that the Department's policy is carried out in relation to other members of staff as well as prisoners.
4. Members of minority religious groups have the same right to practise their faith as those of the majority faith. Wherever feasible in prison circumstances arrangements are made to give them the same practical opportunity to do so.
5. All inmates should have equal access to the facilities provided in the establishment including jobs. The distribution of inmates throughout the establishment and its facilities should as far as is practicable and sensible be broadly responsive to the ethnic mix of the establishment.
6. No particular racial group should be allowed to dominate any activity in the establishment to the unfair exclusion of others (HM Prison Service, 1991).

The *Manual* also includes definitions pertaining to race relations, a detailed description of policies, proposals for audits and action plans and a detailed list of staff responsibilities.

At this time of writing, the *Prison Service Order on Race Relations* (PSO 2800), first issued in 1997 in replacement of F2116 and revised in 2002, contains the most recent statement of the Prison Service's race relations policy:

> The Prison Service is committed to racial equality. Improper discrimination on the basis of colour, race, nationality, ethnic or national origins, or religion is unacceptable as is any racially abusive or insulting language or behaviour on the part of any member of staff, prisoner or visitor, and neither will be tolerated (HM Prison Service, 1997).

To some extent the Prison Service is in advance of other public authorities because it has already implemented the kind of policy that the Open Society Institute's report on Muslims in the UK recommended to the British Government: 'a positive duty for public authorities to eliminate unlawful religious discrimination in relation to their function and to promote equality of opportunity and good relations between persons of different religious belief' (Open Society Institute 2002: 440). Two elements are especially notable in the Prison Service statement. First, the policy explicitly prohibits 'racially abusive or insulting language' (a legacy of the Alexander case). Second, and more importantly for our investigation, the statement specifies that improper discrimination on the grounds of religion is unacceptable in prisons. Although the inclusion of religion was discussed during the preparation of the RRA 1976, it was not retained in the final version of the Act. The Prison Service justifies the inclusion of religion on the grounds that there is considerable overlap 'in the prison context' between ethnicity and religion. The other argument put forward is that religion is a 'practical race relations factor':

> Strictly speaking, religion is not a race relations issue [...] nevertheless, in the prison context the minority ethnic dimensions in Hinduism, Sikhism, Islam, Judaism and other faiths mean that religion is an important practical race relations factor (HM Prison Service, 1997: 5.6.1).

It is worth adding that this broad interpretation of ethnicity and race relations was also implemented by Her Majesty's Chief Inspector of Prisons in the late 1990s. Sir David Ramsbotham had to postpone long-standing plans for a thematic review of 'inequalities' in prisons while the Commission for Racial Equality was preparing its own investigation into racism in the Prison Service (HM Chief Inspector, 2000: 16–17). But the Chief Inspector's intention had been to inquire into all forms of inequality and discrimination against minorities under the rubric of 'racism'. His report describes 'minorities' in prisons as 'ethnic or cultural minorities, females, the elderly, the disabled and the mentally disordered'. His warrant for this approach was that 'race' in this context was not just a matter of black versus white but also included 'cultures' of soccer fans and of other bases for identity that had underlain various public disorders in Britain. This approach is congruent with the Prison Service's current focus on 'diversity' as a value to be cultivated in prisons. The first Muslim Adviser to the Prison Service also believed that issues of 'race' and religion could not be separated on a day-to-day basis. He wanted issues of diversity and equality to be treated in a holistic fashion, especially when it came to investigating complaints of unfair discrimination. Support for the idea of considering issues of 'race' and religion as inter-related comes from the Home Office study of prisoners' and prison officers' perceptions of 'race' and conflict (Edgar and Martin, 2004: 14). This survey of 273 male minority ethnic prisoners in four establishments found that the second most frequently cited area in which prisoners perceived that their treatment by prison officers had been racially biased was 'access to/practice of religion'.

Part Two of the Commission for Racial Equality's report on 'Racial equality in prisons' (CRE, 2003b) gives further support to the policy of linking religion and ethnicity or 'race'. The rationale for this linkage is that

> [G]iven that a number of very important aspects of a prisoner's life are determined by their religion (such as their food, and who they can turn to with trust to discuss private matters or get help with a letter to their family – the prison chaplain or imam, for example), a failure on the part of staff to respond positively to particular faiths can be damaging both to the immediate relationship between the establishment and the prisoner, and to any prospect of a prisoner developing well during their time in custody (CRE, 2003b: 84).

Again, pragmatism is characteristic of the CRE's insistence on treating discrimination on grounds of religion as evidence of racism in prisons. In particular, the report holds that, 'Failure to meet the faith needs of Muslims in prison therefore has a disproportionate impact on ethnic minority prisoners as opposed to white prisoners' (CRE, 2003b: 88).

Citing the House of Lords as its authority on the imbrication of ethnicity with religious and cultural differences as well as differences of race and colour, PSO 2800 (HM Prison Service, 1997: Chapter 2: 3) describes two particular characteristics as 'fundamental' to ethnic identity: 'a long shared history and a recognisable tradition', within which 'a common religion different from that of neighbouring groups' plays a role. This begs the question of why this argument applies only in prisons in England and Wales, and there have certainly been spirited attempts to secure legal prohibition of discrimination on the grounds of religion outside prisons – not least in the response to 'Islamophobia'. Academic research has also investigated 'religious discrimination' (Weller, Feldman and Purdam, 2001) and the feasibility of introducing legislation to make it unlawful (Hepple and Choudhury, 2001). Well-founded anxieties about Islamophobia (Commission on British Muslims and Islamophobia, 2001) failed to persuade legislators to include religion in the Race Relations (Amendment) Act 2000. Moreover, the hostility levelled at Muslims after the 11 September

2001 also revived discussions of the issue but failed to bring about a change in the law.

In other words, the Prison Service of England and Wales extends to religion the protection widely granted to ethnicity inside and outside prisons. No doubt, there are practical reasons, to do with security and good order, for doing so, but it chooses to stress that 'The Prison Service has long accepted its obligation to make provision for the practice of religion within establishments' (HM Prison Service, 1991. 6.5: 62). It is also committed to ensuring 'that the religious life of the prison community and of individual prisoners may be practised in freedom and dignity'. In other words, there is a happy coincidence between the moral duty to treat all inmates equally and the 'practical' risk involved in not doing so. In the 'heated' atmosphere of prisons, where some ethnic and religious minorities are over-represented, the risk of disruption or disorder would be high if only Sikhs and Jews were protected – by the RRA – against discrimination on the grounds of religion, while others, such as Muslims, enjoyed no such protection in law.

PSO 2800 lays down mandatory standards for handling legal obligations and prison service policy, management structures and performance assessment, ethnic monitoring, facilities and services, complaints and racial incidents, external contacts, and training and information. It accords pride of place to Race Relations Management Teams (RRMTs) and to ethnic monitoring, which must apply to accommodation, work, education/training, adjudication, temporary release, segregation and requests or complaints. The RRMT in every establishment is responsible for developing local race relations strategies as well as for monitoring performance in conformity with the national race relations policy. A clear indication of the RRMT's importance is the fact that it has to be chaired by the governing Governor or Deputy Governor; it generally includes the RRLO, a chaplain, representatives from different areas of each prison, probation and education, community representatives and, in some cases, a full-time or, more likely, a part-time chaplain belonging to a minority faith community (Leech and Cheney, 1999). In addition, a RRLO, appointed by the Governor, is in charge of promoting good race relations and dealing with day-to-day issues; he or she must also ensure that proper ethnic monitoring takes place, that staff are trained in race relations matters and that they keep a record of complaints. All these measures have considerably enhanced the profile of race relations in prisons and have underlined the importance of implementing correct structures and procedures.

The enhanced standing of minority faiths in prison has grown, in part, out of the increasing recognition that sensitive and robust handling of issues to do with ethnicity, 'race' and diversity are increasingly essential to healthy prisons. High-level discussion and monitoring of these issues are the remit of the Director General's Advisory Group on Race, which, since

1999, has included a full-time Race Equality Adviser and representatives from the CRE, NACRO and other prisoners' support groups. It is important to add that most of the reports produced by HM Chief Inspector of Prisons in England and Wales also contain careful scrutiny of the state of race relations in individual establishments and of the relative effectiveness of the many procedures for monitoring and for responding to complaints about 'racial incidents'. While reports since 2000 acknowledge that race relations issues have acquired a higher profile in prisons than previously, there are still grounds for criticising weaknesses. The Chief Inspector's annual report for 2001–2002 (HM Chief Inspector, 2002: 18), for example, is critical of the fact that staff responsible for race relations 'often lack the time, training or understanding' to tackle the issues effectively. Incidentally, this report also regrets that there is 'a great deal of confusion' in the Prison Service about the best way to cope with inmates who are foreign nationals 'who may or may not have specific language or religious needs' (p. 20). This illustrates the strength of commitment to policies and practices that take proper account of the full diversity of inmates' cultural background.

A fresh impetus for re-thinking race relations in the Prison Service came indirectly from the official inquiry conducted by Lord Macpherson (1999) into the way in which the Metropolitan Police handled the murder of a Black teenager, Stephen Lawrence in April 1993. The fact that such an inquiry took place is testimony to the determination of his parents and of minority ethnic groups who persisted with their challenges to racism in the police. The Macpherson Report (1999) identified the pernicious influence of institutional racism not only in the Metropolitan Police force but also in other British institutions. The Prison Service of England and Wales reacted, in part, by creating the RESPOND (Racial Equality for Staff and Prisoners) programme[4] and by appointing its first Race Equality Adviser (REA) in August 1999, who was to be responsible for taking forward the RESPOND programme and for leading the newly formed Diversity and Equality Group at headquarters. One of the programme's aims is to make the Prison Service more representative of the whole community and to ensure equal opportunity for prisoners and staff through the adoption of five key strategies at the level of local establishments:

- Confronting racial harassment and discrimination
- Ensuring fairness in recruitment, appraisal, promotion and selection
- Developing and supporting minority ethnic staff
- Ensuring equal opportunities for prisoners
- Recruiting minority ethnic staff.

This constitutes an ambitious programme and a major challenge to deep-rooted prejudices and ignorance but it stands a good chance of transforming race relations in prison if it achieves its goals. A further impetus for taking a more robust attitude towards anti-discrimination ideals was the enactment in 2000 of the Race Relations (Amendment) Act, which extended to all institutions delivering a public service the need to actively promote equal opportunities. In this sense, the amended Act was an advance on its predecessor in 1976, which had not applied unambiguously to prisons.

Another significant development in the Prison Service's strategic response to racism and other forms of ethnic and religious discrimination occurred in January 2001 with the launch of RESPECT, the Minority Ethnic Staff Support Network,[5] despite concerns that it might be a political movement. Its aim is to create support groups for minority ethnic members of staff in local establishments. Moreover, a whole section of the *Prisons Handbook* (Leech and Cheney, 1999: 344) deals with the reporting of racist incidents and quotes the Macpherson Report to define them as 'any incident which is perceived to be racist by the victim or any other person' thus removing any possible ambiguity. The burden of proof is removed from the purported victim. The *Handbook* also gives explicit examples of discrimination and unacceptable behaviour such as:

- jokes aimed at particular groups
- graffiti
- the use of inappropriate terms
- unfair treatment based on prejudices
- assumptions and stereotypical views
- denial of access to work, facilities etc., because they belong to a certain ethnic, national and religious group (Leech and Cheney, 1999: 344).

Such a plethora of anti-discrimination tools could indicate that the Prison Service enjoys exemplary race relations. It might mean, on the contrary, that racism is so deeply ingrained that it warrants vigorous intervention and/or that policies are repeatedly ignored so that they need to be strengthened by additional strategies. There is no doubt, however, that the Prison Service has been stung into action by some high-profile scandals involving allegations of racism, ethnic discrimination and a failure to protect inmates belonging to vulnerable minorities.

Some of the earliest research on this topic claimed that racial discrimination was intrinsic to the social organisation of the prisons of England and Wales in the 1980s (Genders and Player, 1989). McDermott's (1989: 219) survey of prisoners in four prisons in the English Midlands confirmed that 'nearly three out of five Blacks, half of Asians, and a third of whites' thought staff were racist and that levels of racism were higher in prisons with higher levels of security. Stereotyping seemed to be rampant, labelling

Black prisoners as 'not industrious, only interested in their bodies', while Asians were perceived as 'no trouble, work hard' (McDermott, 1989: 221). Prison staff showed a lack of understanding about discrimination, tending to attribute race relations problems to the attitudes of minorities and not to themselves. This view was confirmed in a recent study by NACRO (2000) which quotes a prison officer asserting, 'This prison does not have a race problem' whilst a white prisoner counters with, 'This prison is exceedingly racist among all staff. I have personally heard officers, workers, education and even chapel staff make racist comments' (NACRO, 2000: 15).

Research has also shown that it is not uncommon for prison staff to complain that minority ethnic prisoners exploit the system to obtain unjustified advantages while whites are missing out (McDermott, 1989; NACRO, 2000). What is left out of the equation is the relation of power between minorities and the white majority. For instance, inmates may hesitate to complain about race relations for fear of reprisals and sanctions such as the loss of enhanced status (Leech and Cheney, 1999: 345). One major problem identified by McDermott as long ago as 1989 concerning anti-discrimination policies is their lack of teeth: no accountability, no mechanisms for enforcement, no penalties under the disciplinary code, all of which led her to conclude that 'At its worst, the policy may be no more than a legal document with which the Home Office can defend itself against critics' (McDermott, 1989: 225).

Evidence of the persistence of serious failings in the Prison Service's responsiveness to issues of 'race' and diversity is all too clear in the findings of the long-awaited Formal Investigation conducted by the Commission for Racial Equality into HM Prison Service of England and Wales (CRE, 2003a, 2003b). Part 1 of the report, which appeared three years after the murder of a Young Offender at HM YOI Feltham, Zahid Mubarek, by his racist cellmate in March 2000 culminated in a 'finding of unlawful racial discrimination' contrary to section 1(1)(a) and sections 20 and 21 of the Race Relations Act 1976. In particular, the report found that the Prison Service

> had discriminated against prisoners in its care in that it failed to put in place an effective delivery of equivalent protection which comprehensively addressed the needs of prisoners to be safe from detrimental treatment by act or omission of other inmates on the grounds of their race and failed to implement a comprehensive equivalent protection policy by providing the following: appropriate deployment of staff, adequate training to staff, adequate systems for making and investigating complaints, and adequate monitoring of racially discriminatory activity in its prisons (CRE, 2003a: 172).

Since the murder of Zahid Mubarek, a number of significant developments have occurred. In addition to introducing the RESPOND and RESPECT programmes noted above, the Prison Service has also sought to combat racism by, for example, increasing the representation of minority ethnic staff from 2.9 per cent to 5 per cent of the workforce;[6] by stipulating that RRLOs must set aside at least eight hours per week for their duties relating to race relations; by requiring governors or deputy governors to take personal responsibility for leading race relations work; by prohibiting prison staff from belonging to racist organisations; by adding four new 'racially aggravated' offences to the Prison Discipline Manual; by publishing a Race Equality Scheme, as required by the Race Relations (Amendment) Act 2000; by setting up a Diversity and Equality Group at headquarters; by instituting new procedures for making complaints about racist behaviour; and by publishing in 2003 PSO 8010 on Equal Opportunities. In addition, the Home Office commissioned research into perceptions of 'race' and conflict in prisons (Edgar and Martin, 2004). These achievements are evidence of substantial progress, but it would be a mistake to forget that they are designed to address grievous failings in the system in the recent past.[7]

Indeed, evidence of serious problems and failings was plentiful in the report of an inquiry conducted by the Race Equality Advisor (2000) into race relations at HMP Brixton in May 2000. The report found that:

> Many minority ethnic prisoners spoke of harassment and discrimination by staff and their lack of confidence in the grievance procedures available to them. This is borne out by the number of complaints that are raised and not resolved. We found no evidence to suggest that any complaint was followed by a thorough investigation... It was relatively simple to reach the conclusion that the administration at Brixton was institutionally racist and that a small number of staff sustained and promoted overtly racist behaviour (Race Equality Advisor, 2003).

The high number of recommendations that the REA made for changes in policy and practice as well as for further investigation at HMP Brixton is itself evidence that the problem of race relations was indeed serious in this establishment. The Director General of the Prison Service of England and Wales admitted that it was institutionally racist.

HMP Brixton, along with HMP Parc and HMP YOI Feltham, was also one of the establishments where the Commission for Racial Equality (CRE, 2003a, 2003b) conducted a three-year long inquiry into racial equality in prisons before 2000. The inquiry was into 'HM Prison Service, with reference to the need to eliminate unlawful racial discrimination and the need to promote equality of opportunity and good relations between people of different racial groups' (CRE, 2003b: 210). The report identified unlawful discrimination in 14 different areas of prison life and made 17 findings of unlawful discrimination in specific incidents or circumstances. The report concludes by gathering all the areas of failure into two 'omnibus findings' (see Appendix A of the report). The investigation focused on numerous incidents of discrimination against Muslim prisoners that were deemed to be of a 'racial' nature because the vast majority of Muslim inmates in England and Wales came from Black and Asian backgrounds. The Prison Service was found to have discriminated against Muslims by, for example, intentionally limiting the number of hours that an Imam may attend on Muslim prisoners; failing to put in place a staffing complement that would enable Muslim prisoners to attend Friday prayers; failing to provide suitable prayer rooms or to provide facilities for pre-prayer ablutions; and failing to provide a Muslim prisoner with a *halal* diet. Particular acts of discrimination included requiring a Muslim prisoner to stand naked, in view of prison officers, for 15 minutes after a strip search and requiring a female Muslim visitor to lift her veil in order to identify herself.

The CRE report represents the most sustained argument for framing discrimination on grounds of religion as a matter of 'race' and of equal opportunities. The evidence that our own research also unearthed of the complex intersection between 'race', ethnicity and religion in the case of Muslim prisoners shows that this way of framing the issues is not widely shared by prison staff.

The views of prison officers about race relations and religion

In order to answer the question of how these developments in Prison Service policy and practice regarding race relations have affected Muslim prisoners we shall now turn to the data gathered through our empirical research in three male prisons and two female prisons of England and Wales. The proportion of minority ethnic staff in the entire system and their distribution across our research sites are among the factors to be taken into account. So, we begin with the fact that minority ethnic and Muslim staff are still relatively rare in the Prison Service. According to the Prison Service at 30 September 2002,[8] only 1.31 per cent of all prison staff had Asian ethnicity.[9] Some of them are from the Sikh, Hindu, Christian and other faith traditions, so the proportion of Muslims among prison staff is probably no higher than 1 per cent – allowing also for Muslims who are not from Asian backgrounds. The distribution of minority ethnic staff between establishments is uneven, however, reflecting the concentration of settlers from South Asia, East Africa and the Caribbean region in certain locations. This helps to explain why Prison 1 had 56 minority ethnic staff out of a total of 212 (26.4 per cent) at the time of our study, whereas Prison 3 had found it hard to recruit more than a handful of staff from black and ethnic minority groups.

Several prison officers noted that an effort had been made to appoint minority ethnic staff and that 'We try to keep an ethnic mix regarding employment' (Prison 1, Prison Officer 5). However, where Islam is concerned, it is not only a question of minority ethnic employment. Being of minority ethnic origin does not necessarily equip one to understand specific Muslim practices. In fact, there is a paucity of Muslim staff who could help to provide a better understanding of Muslim prisoners' needs. The Imam of Prison 1 stated unequivocally that 'there is not a single Muslim officer' in his establishment despite the fact that it had numerous Muslim inmates. In fact, his statement was wrong, but he felt that positive initiatives were necessary because the prison career did not seem to appeal to members of Muslim communities.

Indeed, the Governor of Prison 1 recognised that a Muslim cook would be an advantage among the kitchen staff and that 'if we had more Muslim officers they would have a better understanding, especially at times like Ramadan, which can raise all sorts of issues'. He also expressed the wish to reach out to Muslim populations in such a way that 'our advertising campaign reaches into those community groups'. He was thinking of asking for the Imam's help in this. Indeed, since the appointment of full-time Muslim chaplains in about 12 prisons, beginning at the end of 2001, various initiatives have been taken to improve relations between prisons and their local communities. One of the aims is to advertise staff vacancies in local mosques and to raise awareness of the desirability of recruiting more Muslim prison officers.

In another of our prisons the RRLO had been made specifically responsible for promoting the recruitment of minority ethnic staff and was trying to target their communities (Prison 3, RRLO). But it is still too early to assess whether more Muslims actually joined the prison staff as a result. While equal opportunities seemed to be making progress in terms of prison officers' employment, most minority ethnic members of the chaplaincy suffered *de facto* discrimination because they were classified at that time as 'visiting ministers', as signalled by a Buddhist chaplain at Prison 1 who said, 'Also part-time chaplains, like the Imam and myself, are effectively unprotected by employment law; we have no pension rights and limited security, so this has to be looked at'.

Race Relations *training* is mandatory under PSO 2800 although it does not specify precisely how much training is required. According to the Minister of State at the Home Office, a new package of 'diversity training' had been introduced by 2002 but he also recognised that 'more needs to be done' and that the Prison Service 'will continue developing the programme that is already in place'.[10] Training has the potential to influence attitudes and behaviour *vis-à-vis* minority ethnic inmates and thus represents an important issue. In the prisons in our sample, training had definitely been made available to the officers interviewed but, while some referred to regular training, others merely had a distant memory of the last training course that they had attended. For example, it was 'just basic initial training, a day course on religion five years ago' in the words of Officer 7 in

Prison 1. There is also conflicting evidence from staff in the same prison. For instance, Officer 7 in Prison 3 attended 'an annual course held in-house by the RRLO' and had been on 'a five-day residential course in RRMT at Newbold Revel'. Yet, the RRLO of the same prison admitted that he had received very little basic training. By contrast, Officers 5 and 6 in Prison 2 talked about their race relations training 'last week' within the framework of *weekly* training which covered various aspects of diversity.

One area in which substantial change seems to have taken place is that of the *language* that prison staff use when talking to, or about, prisoners. This is actually part of a wider effort to be more professional and more self-critical. It may involve subjecting personal feelings to professional discipline:

> Regarding racism, you can't change persons' personal views but can guide their professional views. If you have got racist views you are not going to change; but on the professional side, we have become more knowledgeable of the effects it has and the unfairness of it (Prison 2, Prison Officer 2).

In the same vein, prison officers recognise that they can no longer get away with this kind of racist behaviour, which used to be more common:

> See, even the comments are fairly rare because you cannot be overtly racist any more. It's illegal for a start, you can go to prison for it; it's a criminal offence. You can lose your job for it, certainly in the Prison Service. If you can prove that somebody's said something racist to you, they will lose their job, no ifs, no buts, no maybes. The bloody shame of that is that it's driven people underground; and, as you say, the racism is much more subtle and you can't say with any degree of certainty 'That was racist'. You can't do that any more. People, even blatant racists know, unless they're complete idiots, that you can't do that any more (Prison 2, Prison Officer 4).

Edgar and Martin's (2004) investigation also showed that acts of blatant racism were not common even among the 44 per cent of their sample of 105 minority ethnic prisoners who claimed to have been the victim of racial discrimination. Interviews with a subset of 73 of these prisoners elicited allegations of at least one incident of blatant racism by prison officers in the preceding six months from only 12 of them.

The other side of this particular coin is that many prison officers emphasise the sharp difference *between themselves and the prisoners*, who are not constrained, apparently, by the same scruples about racism. This may involve 'playing the race card':

> The colour of a man's skin or his faith is of no significance to me, obviously, [but] prisoners are prisoners. You hear prisoners call each other words that you know as well as I do, is against the law: Paki, nigger, wog – all that sort of stuff comes out, prisoner to prisoner (Prison 2, Prison Officer 4).
>
> We work with all multi-faith groups. Most of the racism comes from the other side: 'You are only saying this because I am black'. They abuse the race card (Prison 1, Prison Officer 3).
>
> But if you say 'no' to anything, they are likely to say you are racist. Now you have to be more selective in your words than when I started nine years ago (Prison 3, Prison Officer 1).
>
> Twice it's happened to me where a person's said: 'Ah that's because I am…' and I've said 'I'm sorry but I find that offensive when you know that is offensive because you've been treated the same as everybody else'; and when I've actually said that I find it offensive them saying that, they're the first to say 'Yeah, yeah, I'm sorry' (Prison 2, Prison Officer 5).

There can be no doubt, then, that prison officers have become more aware of the unacceptability of racist attitudes or language and of the penalties that can be imposed for breaching the rules. In the words of the Deputy Christian Chaplain in Prison 1, 'I am unaware of any specific racism on the part of any chaplain. I suppose the political climate is such that even if anybody did have such prejudices, these would not surface because nobody wants to lose their job'.

Nevertheless, some prison officers are still grappling with the issues of racist stereotyping that McDermott had identified in 1989. For example:

> I don't feel racism is a big problem but I still think it happens – but not blatant. Things have improved, officers have moved on. Regarding Black stereotypes, I think I have done this myself. In the chapel Blacks tend to be more boisterous, and I believe Blacks are like this; and I am also internalising the stereotype (Prison 1, Prison Officer 11).

'You get the odd bad apple' was the view of the RRLO on Prison 3 about evidence of persisting racism among prison officers. Many of them, in turn, echoed his judgement. Edgar and Martin's (2004: 16) view was that 'blatant racism was reported to us infrequently', although prisoners 'suggest that some officers felt they could behave in these ways openly'.

Another common move in prison officers' discourse about racism is to attribute it to misunderstood or outdated forms of *humour* rather than to deliberate offensiveness, as McDermott (1989) also observed in her study. Thus, 'I had a joke with some Asian lads huddled together in the showers. I said "What the fucking hell is this? Pakistan International?", but it was just joking around' (Prison 1, Prison Officer 1). Needless to say, minority ethnic prisoners do not always see the funny side of this kind of taunting. It is not surprising, then, that prison officers have learned to make their racist jokes in private. For example, 'There is no evidence of racism from officers to prisoners. There might be the odd joke but nothing serious' (Prison 3, Prison Officer 9). Other officers reported more than 'the odd joke', however:

> Regarding racism, yes there is – but nowhere near as much as people think or accuse. Between staff themselves they joke. Many times a day, there's an odd comment from staff to inmates. It's not very harmful and no harm is intended. Staff only talk about certain things between those who they can talk to and get away with. Racism as a whole is down in the prison since they clamped down on it. The race card is used and so they are treated better than whites for that reason (Prison 3, Prison Officer 1).

> Regarding racism, there is a lot of behind the scenes verbal racism and sexism. It's between staff and is never shown to inmates. Some would like to give the impression they are racist but it wouldn't manifest itself in the job. It shocked me because I was very aware of race relations training and harassment and it was shocking... There is no overt racism but there must be some underneath... It was in general conversation; the language used was quite shocking, but I haven't seen it transferred to inmates (Prison 3, Prison Officer 6).

As we shall show later, this particular prison officer was mistaken in thinking that inmates were not aware of his colleagues' verbal racism.

A closely related strategy is for prison officers to deny that racism is a 'real' problem in their prison but to admit only that some *individuals* are racists. Thus, for example:

> Racism has never been at a level where it is a problem. You can never change individuals. I don't see it, I don't think it's a problem. Sometimes you get officers and prisoners who are racist, but that's at an individual level (Prison 3, Prison Officer 10).

A variant on this strategy for deflecting accusations of racism is to say either that it is *endemic* or that it exists only in other establishments. The following prison officer managed to combine these two claims in a single, contradictory statement:

> Racist humour is obviously deemed inappropriate, but this is endemic in the Prison Service. Racist and sexist humour is there. But why is it that Black lads need to be shown respect? I can't think of any specific racist

incidents. We get quite a lot of younger staff; and in-bred racism has not come to [Prison 3], but if you go to Leeds or Durham you might get it. They use humour as a shield but it's not serious (Prison 3, Prison Officer 11).

This statement's juxtaposition of the officer's failure to understand why he needed to show respect to 'Black lads' and his inability to call any racist incidents to mind is alarming. Equally puzzling was the view of racism offered by two chaplains in Prison 1. The first was dismissive: 'I think racism is a red herring. People just like to hate one another. There are visible differences, and that's when the race card is played'. The second blamed the alleged victims: 'The vast majority of inmates say that there is minimal to zero explicit racism here',[11] adding that when prisoners made accusations of racism 'this is down to attitude rather than racism'.

Some prison officers also raised the further complication of *'reverse racism'* – or bending over backwards to appear non-racist for fear of being accused of discrimination: 'I think [prisoners] get slightly better treatment because of fear of racist incidents or discrimination being alleged' (Prison 3, Prison Officer 1). The temptation to use reverse racism was not confined to white prison officers, however. An Asian officer in Prison 1 reported that he had been the victim of racism from his fellow officers when he first joined the Prison Service and that he had experienced pressure from them to avoid showing favours towards Asian inmates. Meanwhile, a Black officer said, 'I feel I have to overcome fearing to favour blacks sometimes. Some officers think I am racist against white officers because I don't talk to them, but it's their personality' (Prison 1, Prison Officer 11).

The picture with regard to prison officers' categorisation and treatment of prisoners *as Muslims*, rather than as members of racial or ethnic groups, is rather different. This is partly because officers find it much more difficult to identify 'Muslims' than members of an ethnic or racial category such as 'Asians'. Indeed, it is common for prison officers to say that they find it impossible to know who the Muslim inmates are unless they go the length of consulting prisoners' records. But another reason why the religious categorisation of prisoners is less problematic than ethnic or racial categorisation is that training has helped to dispel ignorance about the practice of Islam; and very few of our informants objected in principle to facilitating that practice. Nor was it common for officers to admit to making even private jokes about Muslims as a religious category. On the contrary, they emphasised the importance of treating members of all faiths equally and of supporting the right of prisoners to practise their religion in prison. Nevertheless, some officers expressed reservations about two particular aspects of their work with Muslims. The first concerns the *amount* of work involved; and the second refers to suspicions about the authenticity of some Muslim prisoners' professed commitment to Islam.

The first reservation takes the form of a complaint that prison officers, who tend to regard their working conditions as already demanding, are expected to go to unusual lengths to make it possible for Muslim prisoners to fulfil their religious obligations such as attendance at Friday prayers or ritual ablutions before prayers. For example:

> [Officers] would see Ramadan as creating extra work; they would see various other things that we have to do to – not to appease Muslims – but to allow them to practise their faith within the guidelines that they should be able to, as creating work for them (Prison 2, Prison Officer 4).

This type of complaint refers mainly to the cumbersome arrangements that some establishments operate for collecting and escorting Muslims to Friday prayers and Eid celebrations at the end of Ramadan. Regardless of whether it involves assembling the prisoners whose names appear on a list or whether it involves a system whereby prisoners ring a bell if they wish to attend prayers, the prison officers have to implement special procedures. To make matters more difficult, Friday prayers in winter may coincide with officers' lunch break. This generates a degree of resentment in some officers, especially those who doubt whether comparable arrangements would be made for Christian inmates in predominantly Muslim countries. In some establishments, the Muslim chaplains who carry keys are able to assemble the prisoners themselves, but in other places the job falls to prison officers. It is noticeable that officers rarely complain about having to assemble Christian prisoners for visits to the chapel.

The second type of complaint that prison officers sometimes voice about Muslim inmates is that some of them *abuse* the 'privileges' that they enjoy to celebrate Ramadan and to eat *halal* food. A strong sense of moral indignation seems to drive some officers to police the practice of fasting during the month of Ramadan. Thus:

> Many Muslims, especially the younger ones, attend not to pray but to meet their mates and natter. It's not as though they are religious; they just want a natter. I can say this because some know the Arabic and the actions, whilst others are just watching and copying. And if they go every week they are just using it as an excuse to chat. If people chat at Christian service they are subtle; at Muslim service they are more obvious. I think the majority are praying and treating it as a religious service, but there are some trouble makers (Prison 1, Prison Officer 1).

A more serious accusation of abuse came from Officer 4 in Prison 2:

> If somebody's saying 'Right I'm off to the chapel' there's no problem with that. What we then find is that people go to the chapel as Muslims and they don't go to the chapel at all; they just congregate. It's Friday

afternoon, they've all got their cards, they've all had their canteen and now they've got collateral and they start exchanging and they start paying debts and they start accruing debts.

In some cases, prison officers have high expectations of prisoners' adherence to their faith. Thus:

If somebody comes to me and says 'I'm a Muslim', fine. By being a Muslim, I would expect them to behave in a Muslim way; I would expect him to do his prayers, I would expect him to deal with the Qur'an, I would expect him to fast during Ramadan etc., etc. Now, when somebody comes to me and says 'I'm a Muslim' so that he can get the different types of foods that Muslims look to; and when the time comes to fast and I see him going to have his breakfast, and I see him going to have his lunch, then see him going to have his evening meal in daylight, I see him eating or cooking during the day, then I'm obviously now beginning to question where the bloody hell he's coming from. Now, my father was a Muslim and if people from outside the faith are going to embrace it – and I've got no problem with that – then I expect them to embrace it the way it should be, not part-time. You can't be a part-time Muslim (Prison 2, Prison Officer 4).

In more robust terms, 'Ramadan can be a pain in the arse. Have to have them all in one place, policing the Ramadan. If we catch them breaking it we take them off it and we are seen as the bad guys' (Prison 1, Prison Officer 4). In this particular prison, an inmate who is observed eating or drinking during visits when he should be fasting loses the 'privilege' of being on the Ramadan list[12] and is forced to return to the normal diet.

The combination of sensitivities about 'race' and religion can be provocative, as in the following statement from Prison Officer 5 in Prison 2:

Sometimes – it's not so much with Asian Muslims – but the biggest problem is where people are using Islam as a weapon to get things. With the Afro-Caribbean prisoners we are accused of being racist, but they also add on faith because they can be quite vociferous. We know who is a regular attending Muslim. It's annoying because I used to think that they were hiding behind a barrier or flag of conversion... It was simply because of diet and they could use it as another weapon against the establishment as a fail-safe. The problem with a person using faith as an avenue to back up a complaint is that it misrepresents genuine Muslims in the prison estate.

It is significant that none of our interviews detected any sign that prison officers felt driven to withdraw the 'privilege' of attending chapel from any prisoners registered as Christians who were seen to fail to live up to the standards stated in, for example, the Sermon on the Mount. This type of 'informal partiality' (Edgar and Martin, 2004), as exercised by prison officers, is perceived by some Muslim prisoners as a form of racism. It exemplifies the officers' attempts to set boundaries as part of a wider strategy for controlling prisoners, but the latter can interpret it as discriminatory behaviour because they never see prison officers making judgements about 'good and bad' Christian prisoners.

The moral indignation that some officers expressed towards less-than-perfect Muslims seemed to arise from a fear that prisoners who were prepared to manipulate religion for their own advantage were *duping* them. This made it an issue of power relations. The concern about being duped is connected with a more general issue of uncertainty about who is 'really' Muslim among the inmates:

> We don't always know who the Muslim prisoners are because a lot of Afro-Caribbeans have taken up the Muslim faith, er, some with real purpose and some sort of whenever it suits them to have a particular food diet... If I feel that the individual is in any way trying to con me then I would go to see someone else who I know to be a Muslim and put the question 'This is the situation. Is this correct?' and if they say 'No' then I will ask the direct question of him 'Do you think this particular man is taking the piss? And is he trying to con me or take advantage and using his religion?' (Prison 2, Prison Officer 4).

Another criterion that this particular officer uses to determine whether a prisoner is truly Muslim is whether he speaks Arabic and knows the Qur'an. One of his colleagues relies on his knowledge of the first names that Muslims typically have, while the presence of a prayer mat in a cell is sufficient evidence in the eyes of a different colleague. By contrast, officers in Prison 1, with a more rapid throughput of prisoners, rely more heavily on the official list of Muslim inmates than on their own intuition or rule of thumb. Officers in Prison 3, a Category A establishment where the inmate population changes more slowly, find it relatively easy to remember who the Muslims are by observing the regular participants in Friday prayers.

In sum, our interviews with prison staff gave the clear impression that racist discrimination against prisoners from minority ethnic, racial or religious backgrounds had generally declined in frequency but was still a feature of some private conversations and casual encounters between prisoners and prison officers.[13] There was a strong feeling that racism was virtually inevitable in prisons but that relatively few officers were insufficiently professional to control its expression. The long-term effects of training programmes and monitoring exercises seemed to have fostered a new sensitivity among younger staff in particular towards the value of diversity. Nevertheless, accusations persisted that prisoners were likely to act in racist ways and that some members of minority ethnic groups 'played the race card' for their own benefit. The latter accusation could be interpreted as the very expression of prejudice.

The views of Muslim prisoners about ethnicity, religion and racism

The question that we want to raise now is whether the Muslim prisoners in England and Wales whom we interviewed shared the same opinions as prison staff. Or was their perception of race relations and of their treatment as an ethnic and/or religious minority significantly different? Other researchers have argued that the perceptions that minority ethnic prisoners have of 'race' relations are quite different from those of either their white counterparts or of prison officers (Burnett and Farrell, 1994; NACRO, 2000). The NACRO survey also found that Black prison officers had less positive opinions about the state of relations between prisoners and staff than did their white counterparts.

To begin with, several prisoners who had been in prison for long periods of time acknowledged that improvements had taken place. For example, 'The screws have changed, for the better (Prison 1, Prison Officer 2). A small number of prisoners simply responded 'no' when they were asked if prison officers had behaved in a racist manner towards them.

Some prisoners also reported that they had become aware that the sanctions against racism had increased and that prison officers had been disciplined for breaching the rules against, for example, racist language. According to two prisoners in Prison 3, 'Two and a half years ago an officer called me something like "dirty nigger"; the officer was transferred' (Prisoner 15); and 'Regarding racism, certain officers probably say things behind my back; one was sacked' (Prisoner 14). This may partly account for the confidence expressed by a prisoner in Prison 1 that 'There is no express racism, those days have gone' (Prisoner 7). Racist language is not the only area in which improvements were noted, however. Unfair discrimination had also declined in some of the practices relating to employment for inmates. Thus, 'two years ago an Asian guy wouldn't be on the job I'm on now' (Prison 1, Prisoner 19); and the Imam of Prison 2 admitted that 'I have to praise this prison... that the Governor has suspended even Governor Grade and other staff on questions that there has been racial discrimination'.

On the other hand, many prisoners agreed that racism had been forced into more subtle manifestations: 'See it in the face, they never say' (Prison 1, Prisoner 4); 'I know it's there. A lot of it is hidden under the carpet, but you can see it under the surface' (Prison 1, Prisoner 2); or 'It's all fucking racism, man. It's all racists. Screws racists. He talking to your face he friendly; but he's talking behind you he don't like us' (Prison 2, Prisoner

12). This suspicion of latent and indirect racism seems to be related to the fact that few of our informants were able to give eyewitness testimony to incidents of racial discrimination or abuse. We recorded many claims of racist discrimination from 25 per cent of interviewees. It was also common for prisoners to make statements along the lines of 'In my personal opinion the Asians are treated a different way, with disrespect, not taken seriously. I have heard this from others, and in my opinion it's true' (Prison 1, Prisoner 23). A prisoner who claimed to be able to 'sense' the racism in Prison 2 put an interesting twist on the theme of unseen but strongly suspected racism:

> No I haven't seen [any incident of racial discrimination]. I hear about it because people say, but obviously I haven't seen it. But the people who do say it most of them do have a problem anyway because everything happens to them; it seems to be racist for them. Some people claim it too much (Prison 2, Prisoner 16).

It is also noticeable that prisoners had a tendency to report more racist incidents in their previous prisons than in the establishments where we interviewed them.

Nonetheless, prisoners amply confirmed the view of prison officers that jokes and banter between them with a racist flavour are common currency in prisons – but still resented. For example, 'Prison officers have called me "Paki" quite a few times. He said "No gym for Pakis, no gym for Pakis, no association for Pakis, only whites". He joked, but I didn't take it as a joke' (Prison 1, Prisoner 10). Other prisoners 'gave as good as they got' in the exchanges of racist banter, with such gems as this from an Asian inmate: 'All the officers used to call me "corner shop" as a joke, and I used to say "fucking bacon butty" back to them' (Prison 2, Prisoner 10).

In spite of some convergence between the accounts, offered by prisoners and by prison officers alike, of improvements in race relations, there are still marked differences between them. The strength of feeling among some minority ethnic inmates that they are the victims of serious racism is inescapable in statements such as:

> I believe there is a racist element in prison. White people don't like people of different or other nationalities. A lot, the majority, are racist. Certain Black people are not seen working in the main stores, don't see them getting Cat-D. I have made enquiries. Blacks work on rubbish money and rubbish jobs, like in the kitchen (Prison 2, Prisoner 1).

Other inmates of the same prison reported, among various incidents, that 'I attempted to get parole. They told me to "fuck off" with no reason. I think it was because of me being Pakistani' (Prison 1, Prisoner 21); and

'The officer would swear at me "fuck off". There was a *gorah* next door, and he spoke to him very politely' (Prison 1, Prisoner 12). A Turkish Cypriot inmate even carried out his own empirical test whereby he arranged for a white prisoner and himself to submit the same application to a female prison officer. His was rejected; the white prisoner's was successful:

> I went to an officer – she was a woman. She said I was too late, and I said OK. I went back to my cell and asked a fellow English cellmate to fill in a false application and sent him to the prison officer; and she accepted it. So, I challenged her, and she denied prejudice. But it clearly was. They nick Muslims for silly things; they are much more stringent on Muslims and Blacks (Prison 3, Prisoner 17).

Discrimination may manifest itself in several ways. According to the Head of Regimes and Resettlement Programmes in Prison 3, statistics indicate that minority ethnic prisoners are less likely to be accepted on a resettlement programme and that if they were accepted they were more likely to be taken off it. Many of the prisoners in our samples certainly claimed to be the victims of persistent prejudice, often in the shape of refusals to grant applications for jobs, training or education courses.[14] This also included allegations that prison officers sometimes turned down prisoners' applications to attend Friday prayers or to obtain Islamic books and artefacts because of anti-Muslim prejudice. For example,

> It's been a sneaky discrimination. For example, I couldn't get Islamic tapes; have to go through authorised supplier for certain things that you want. I know why they delay them. I had it in [another prison], the attitude 'you're not getting anything; we don't like Pakis' (Prison 3, Prisoner 5).
> Prisoners, and in some cases officers, are prejudiced. There are some good officers here, yet it's a fact there is racism here. It's in the treatment, attitude and behaviour. You can feel it. Why are you being treated differently... when you know somebody has got these things quicker than you and you've been waiting three months, and another gets them much quicker? Of course, you think 'What is the difference?'. The only difference is religion and colour (Prison 3, Prisoner 8).

Although many prisoners acknowledged that overt racism and racist language were no longer levelled at them as in the past, they offered countless examples of more subtle cases of discrimination. For example, repeated requests to a Medical Officer for nicotine patches never succeeded, while 'a lot of English were getting them' (Prison 3, Prisoner 4). Another Asian prisoner was denied leave to attend his mother's funeral, whereas 'the whites get to go to the church and the funeral' (Prison 1, Prisoner 7); he apparently found out from a prison officer that leave had been denied because of the Bradford and Oldham riots. Allegations about discrimination referred to virtually everything, including music:

> On [one particular] wing there used to be a group of Black prisoners. Officers didn't like too many black guys on the wing. Some white guys play music loud, and the officers don't mind; some Black guys play reggae, and they tell us to turn it down. One Black guy was moved; they clocked him, they moved three or four Blacks (Prison 3, Prisoner 11).

Not all of our informants shared these ideas, but prisoners who denied that racism, prejudice and discrimination existed against Muslims were rare. It was actually more common for them merely to express a sense of resignation about the *inevitability* of the discrimination that they perceived. This was allied, in some cases, with a determination to 'keep their noses clean', simply to do their 'bird' and to be released at the least cost to their self-esteem. This may also be connected with the fact that only 29 per cent of the male prisoners in our samples said that they knew who their RRLO was.[15] Furthermore, a similar proportion of them denied receiving any information about race relations issues and procedures for dealing with them when they arrived at their prisons. It is not surprising, then, that very few of them said they had reported racist incidents or other episodes of discrimination to their RRLO, a Governor or the Board of Visitors.[16] The experience of those who reported doing so was mostly discouraging, although we must add that we have no way of checking the veracity of accounts, some of which are even more complicated than this one:

> I had a problem with some officers. One officer was picking on Black people. I got nicked for saying 'Don't talk to him because he covers up for others'. I was told I was telling other prisoners that staff were racist. I was adjudicated, and the RRLO and Principal Officer did not support me. I got the Ombudsman involved, and he investigated my complaint. So I have had a long history of problems, with falsified claims. I took them to court and have been successful; I got an adjudication quashed. They tried to fit me up a few months ago. I was working in the workshops ... They were fiddling the money. I got adjudicated for not working because I said I didn't want to work because it was fixed pay, and they charged me with inciting other prisoners not to work. I was falsely charged, and the adjudication was thrown out (Prison 3, Prisoner 14).

Allegations of failure to take complaints seriously typically took the form of: 'I put in a race complaint but I never got an answer' (Prison 2, Prisoner 17). Others assumed that complaints were simply discarded: 'They don't take it seriously; as soon as it's been reported it goes straight in the bin'

(Prison 2, Prisoner 20). Some statements referred to the risk of incurring a sanction rather than an impartial examination of a complaint: 'So, unless you want a transfer, don't complain. If you want a transfer, put in a race complaint' (Prison 3, Prisoner 1). It is little wonder, then, that the cynical conclusion for one prisoner was 'You can't complain in prison. I practise not complaining' (Prison 1, Prisoner 3).

We have already mentioned the 'reverse racism' expressed by some prison officers about the Prison Service's alleged readiness to make too many concessions to minorities. It is not surprising that no prisoners took this position. But this was certainly the view of a substitute chaplain in Prison 2 who believed that 'Christians find it harder than the Muslims, because the Government is supporting ethnic minorities rather than white groups'. Beckford and Gilliat (1998) reported similar resentment among a few Christian chaplains in the mid-1990s. By contrast, none of the three Imams whom we interviewed reported any evidence of 'reverse racism'. Without using the expression 'institutional racism' (Macpherson, 1999), two of them implied that they had been systematically disadvantaged and marginalised. Spalek and Wilson's (2001: 8) study of nine Imams made more serious allegations. They argued that 'anti-Muslim sentiment and overt racism may be a commonplace feature in a penal setting'. We shall return to this point in Chapter 7.

The timing of our research gave us the unexpected opportunity to investigate the impact that the September 11th, 2001 attacks on New York and the Pentagon might have had on the treatment of Muslim prisoners. Prisoners and prison officers alike noted that there had been a flurry of negative reactions in the immediate aftermath of the attacks, as though all Muslims were held responsible:

> After September 11th [prison officers] all changed. You could see the hurt inside them, and they wanted you to pay for it. Officers and prisoners would say 'you are all the same' (i.e. Muslims) (Prison 3, Prisoner 10).
> I was in Armley on September 11th. There were rude comments; screws started calling me 'Bin Laden' and stuff like that if I was walking by, and sarcastic comments like 'Bin Laden's going down' and 'they've just started bombing the place' (Prison 3, Prisoner 18).

The inmates were clear about the central role of the mass media in this backlash against Muslims:

> I believe it was the very negative media coverage which made [an officer] behave negatively with me. It was a very tense atmosphere. I said 'I'm Muslim and I'm on the Muslim side'. The officer was very shocked, even whites guys; everyone was. They were waiting for World War III (Prison 3, Prisoner 11).

Nevertheless, prisoners and prison staff seemed to agree that the initial reactions to events were short-lived and that no longer-term damage was done to relations between Muslim inmates and others in prison.

Racism in French prisons

Since the concept of 'minority' – racial, ethnic or religious – has little place in France's constitution or system of laws, the official apparatus for responding to racism and religious hatred is to invoke two general principles. The first is that all citizens of the Republic are equal in the eyes of the law and that, consequently, there is no need to take account of ethnic or religious differences in the public sphere. The emphasis is, rather, on preserving the unity and solidarity of the Republic, which should be 'one and indivisible'. The second principle is that the notion of 'discrimination' is adequate as a way of identifying all actions and structures that are deemed illegal because they treat their victims differently from other people in an arbitrary fashion. This combined emphasis on the positive value of equality and the negative value of discrimination has underpinned French legislation since the Law of 1 July 1972 which first made it illegal to discriminate unfairly in the offering of goods, services and employment. Racism and religious hatred can thereby be framed as instances of discrimination in French law and public administration. This not only obviates the need for special legislation for minorities but it also makes it difficult or unnecessary for organisations in the public sphere to collect information about 'race', ethnicity and religion. The principle of *laïcité* – or Republican secularism – as explained in Chapter 3, reinforces the idea that consideration of minorities as sources of particularist values, beliefs and identities, should be irrelevant in public life. Nevertheless, French law protects the right of all citizens to practise their religion in the sphere of private life.

The legislative and administrative framework for combating racism indirectly in France is extensive, including the first Article of the 1958 Constitution which holds that 'France ensures the equality before the law of all citizens, without distinction of origin, race or religion'. For example, the French legislative response in November 2001 to the EU's Directive on Equality of Treatment was the implementation of a new law that prohibits discrimination on various grounds including ethnicity, 'race' and religion. The Penal Code and other Codes also establish the scale of penalties for acts of discrimination, but France still lacks a central agency responsible for monitoring and investigating ethnic and religious discrimination. Moreover, the law does not accord any special rights to religious, ethnic or even linguistic minorities. Furthermore, the Stasi Commission on Laïcité[17] recommended in December 2003 that a new law should be introduced to prevent the *ostensible* display of religious symbols in state institutions such as schools, hospitals and social welfare offices. This law was enacted in

2004 and represents a further refusal by French authorities to acknowledge that some minorities might need to symbolise their religious identity in public life. Admittedly, the French Government established the *Haut Conseil à l'Intégration* and encouraged the creation in 2003 of national and regional French Councils of Muslims, but the role of these bodies is largely consultative and unlikely, therefore, to change the way in which the grievances of minorities are dealt with in courts of law and public institutions including prisons. The ideal is clearly to strengthen and to prioritise national unity by integrating all citizens and would-be citizens into the indivisible Republic without making 'concessions' to minorities' requests for special consideration of their cultural and social differences.

Debates about racism are extensive in France, particularly in response to the successes achieved by the Front National in local and national elections. But official statistics on 'race', ethnicity or religion are virtually non-existent, and this adds further fuel to alarmism and xenophobia in some sections of the population. To aggravate matters, the few statistics that are available relate mainly to foreign nationals, thereby feeding public anxiety about immigration. Since the overwhelming majority of the four or five million Muslims in France are undoubtedly of North African origins, including those born in France and holding French citizenship, it is difficult to obtain reliable estimates of the extent of illegal discrimination against Muslims. Nevertheless, an authoritative report on 'The situation of Muslims in France' (Amiraux, 2002: 80) asserted that France has 'a legacy of ambivalent attitudes toward Muslims among public authorities in particular, which feeds upon and reinforces a broader public contempt and mistrust toward Islam and hatred of Arabs in general, and North Africans in particular'. The same report summarises the findings of numerous public opinion surveys in France which document relatively high levels of racist and xenophobic attitudes, although levels of opposition to Islam appear to have declined between 1994 and the events following 11 September 2001.

In France, racism is mainly directed towards 'Arabs', that is, people who are predominantly of North African origin. Islam, as such, has progressively become a prominent object of racism. But since the 'headscarf affairs'[18] in the 1990s and again in 2003 as well as 'Islamic terrorism' in 1995, in which some young people from poor suburbs were involved in Algerian networks of the GIA (*Groupe Islamique Armé*), suspicion towards Islam has been growing.[19] We shall provide evidence for this at the end of this section. Nevertheless, racism, even when it is directed against Muslims, is directed mostly at 'Arabs'. The Turks and the Muslims from Black Africa are much less frequently the targets of this racism which associates Muslims either with terrorists or with 'fundamentalists'. In the prisons that we studied, the North African inhabitants of the so-called *Banlieues* (deprived suburbs) are identified as problem people. Even the prison officers, as well as the other people who deal with them in prisons, claim that they create problems with their aggressiveness and lack of respect for others. From the point of view of Muslim inmates, it is almost always the 'Arabs' who are victims of prison racism. That is why the study of racism against Muslims is primarily focused on discriminatory attitudes towards the *'jeunes des cités'* (young people from public housing estates).

Racism in French prisons has been the subject of very few official reports but it was discussed in a chapter on violence in prison in the report by Jean-Jacques Hyest and Guy-Pierre Cabanel (2001) on 'Combating racism and xenophobia: 2000'. This report, produced by the National Consultative Committee on Human Rights, distinguishes between violence among prisoners, racism directed by prisoners against prison officers and racism of officers against prisoners. Further distinctions are introduced between different types of violence between prisoners (for example, rape, racketeering and 'settling accounts') and violence by prison officers against prisoners which, according to the authors, is very rare. Nevertheless, disciplinary action for violence has been taken against 260 members of prison staff (who number 23,000 in total).

The report provides a detailed picture of the different types of prisoners and their specific problems as well as the shortcomings of prison administration in terms of lack of qualified staff, lack of space and the inadequacies of sanitation and other aspects of prison life. The report's 700 pages analyse the problem of the judges who work in prisons (many of them allegedly 'indifferent' to the plight of prisoners), the problematic working conditions in prison and the ways of improving them, the issues concerning mentally ill prisoners and those who suffer from life-threatening illness, the question of alternatives to short-term prison sentences, and the ineffectiveness of surveillance in prisons or cells. The report proposes short-term and long-term solutions for these problems and for the difficulties that arise in relations between prison administrators and the judiciary. The report tackles these and other problems meticulously, but, curiously, racism and its different concrete forms seem to be ignored. The racism directed towards 'Arabs', Islam, Jews or Black people virtually disappears from sight.

Nevertheless, our study shows that there are specific types of racism related to the ethnicity or the religion of prison inmates. The Hyest-Cabanel report, which is careful and informative in other respects, brushes aside or ignores the evidence of racism in prisons. This failure is mainly due to the fact that the dominant institutional culture in France is 'blind' to any specific type of racism directed towards 'particularistic' outlooks. There is more and more recognition of anti-Semitism but this is the only officially recognised 'particularistic' racist phenomenon. The other forms of racism – many of which amount to Islamophobia or racism towards minorities – are simply ignored. The data that we collected in interviews reveal a huge gap between the real world of the prison in terms of racism and the impression created by the report. Our data call into question the way in which racism is handled in prisons, since the prisoners' real experiences and feelings are totally ignored in the name of *laïcité* and a particular model of citizenship.

The more recent Stasi (2003) report, which attracted much more publicity not only in France but also in other parts of the world, considered racism and xenophobia in the context of the principle of *laïcité*. The report of Bernard Stasi's '*Commission de réflexion sur l'application du principe de laïcité dans la République*' gave some space to the problems of racism and xeno-phobia by, for example, noting that acts of open hostility towards Muslims:

> ... which can go as far as desecrating graves and physical violence... are expressions of a kind of hatred towards Islam. This racism against Muslims is taking over from the previously well documented acts of racism against North Africans. In the eyes of some people, people of foreign origin, be they North African or Turkish, are treated as having nothing but a religious identity, finessing all the other dimensions of their cultural belonging. To this mixture is added an assimilation between Islam and political-religious radicalism, thereby forgetting that the majority of Muslims have a faith and a system of belief that are entirely compatible with the laws of the Republic (3.3.2.2, trans. J.A.B.).

One short paragraph in the Stasi report refers to prisons as follows:

> In prisons, each prisoner must be able to take advantage of spiritual help. Freedom of religion, in accordance with the law of 1905, is given special protection there: religious practices are taken into account as far as possible, and the presence of paid and officially recognised chap-lains plays a non-negligible role. The Commission is worried about the pressures, if not acts of proselytism, brought to bear as much on prison-ers as on their families, and considers it essential to prevent shared spaces from being appropriated by communities. It would like to see Muslim chaplains recruited (4.2.2.4, trans. J.A.B.).

'Communalism' seems to be the Commission's main anxiety. The fact that French prisons have so few Muslim chaplains or ministers is a secondary consideration. Although the number of Catholic prisoners is probably lower than that of Muslims in many prisons nowadays, there are still about 500 Catholic prison chaplains and fewer than 70 Muslim chaplains.

Some prison officers in France have also been the victims of racism in wider society. One of them explained that he had only entered the Prison Service because racist attitudes had prevented him from entering the legal profession despite the fact that his qualifications were adequate. He reasoned that his chances of being accepted for the Prison Service would at least be higher because entry was by means of a formal, anonymised competition. Yet, as one of only a handful of foreign members of staff, he had experienced institutional racism in prisons in the form of latent doubts about his capacity to do his work properly. The Muslim chaplain in Prison C also claimed that he had suffered from racism from his colleagues and other staff.

Nevertheless, very few prison officers, regardless of their ethnicity or religion, expressed explicitly racist sentiments about Muslim inmates. Instead, they gave the impression that racism was something that only 'inferior' people used towards their 'superiors'. Their own preference was, therefore, to talk about the 'insults' and 'incivility' directed towards them by young Muslims from the disadvantaged *banlieues*. The word 'racism' was rarely used, but the sentiments came close to conveying 'ethnicised' prejudice, especially against the unruly *banlieusards*. The complaint voiced by one of the Heads of Security, for example, was that,

> We've got practically nothing but Arabs here. There's no respect for authority any more, be it for their fathers or elder brothers... These 'Lascars' have got nothing but insults in their mouths. I'm sorry, but the *Robeux* [inverted slang for 'Arabs'] are OK when they're on their own, but it starts as soon as they get in a group. When there are four or five of them they change radically. What do we hear at night time? Insults and arguments... they call prison officers 'son of a bitch, arsehole, bastard, dirty race, fucker', and it's very hard to put up with this day and night. Some are good guys, but you can't trust them.

He added that these young *banlieusards* are always looking for a chance to disobey orders and to be confrontational.

French prisoners' experience of racism

Leaving aside the four exceptional cases that we shall examine next, all the prisoners talked about racism both in French society at large towards foreigners in general and North Africans in particular (regardless of whether they were French citizens or not) *and* in prisons, including racism from the prison officers towards prisoners and racism among the inmates themselves.

In the first exceptional case, a 33-year-old prisoner from the Ivory Coast did not deny the existence of racism but did not believe that there was anything specific about racism in prison. He said 'No, it is like outside, I don't think there is any racism [different from outside]'. Amali, another prisoner who had reached university level in his studies during frequent periods in prison, did not think that racism was peculiar to prison and that it was between individuals as such:

> Racism is not related to the prison but to the individuals. Here, in Prison A, it is not an explicit politics, it is not proven [*avéré*] or obvious

[*flagrant*]; but racism exists. It depends on the cultural level of the foreigners. Racism begins with bad mutual understanding, which results in aggressiveness and conflicts.

As a 51-year-old Algerian, Amali was not typical of Muslim inmates. Others have a kind of simplified Marxist view of racism. Yacine, a 32-year-old French prisoner of Algerian descent, reasoned that 'Racism is rather between rich and poor, otherwise there isn't any really [in Prison A]'. But for Habib, racism is the product of the insolent attitude of the 'Arabs' from the poor suburbs who overstep the mark and behave in a disrespectful way towards prison officers. Racism is, from his point of view, the fully understandable consequence of arrogance on the part of the inhabitants of the poor housing estates, although, in his words, they don't bother the others if nobody bothers them. Habib had not experienced racism as such himself, although he was sure that it existed in the prison:

> I don't say [racism] doesn't exist but I haven't personally experienced it. Here, there's no doubt that it exists among the officers. Many of them say 'hello' to me. But there are 'young' people [youths from the poor suburbs] who go too far. Young people feel hatred and they express it; they reap what they sow. But if they are not 'pissed off' [*on les fait pas chier*], they do not piss off the others [*ils ne font pas chier les autres*]. But some 'young' people overstep the mark. Now, racism exists in society but it is not serious; the hatred goes on. Here, there are many different people; there are many nationalities, even though the Arabs or the Blacks are those who have the major problems.

These four prisoners, as a result of some peculiar feature of their own situation, were not as sensitive to racism as was the large majority of the prisoners who denounced it. One of them, Amali, was acknowledged in prison as an intellectual with university degrees (he was in charge of the prison library); Yacine had a 'diplomatic' frame of mind, as he said himself, and suffered much more from maltreatment as such than from being locked up in prison; the third one, M.P., was a Black prisoner from the Ivory Coast and had probably suffered as much from racism outside prison as inside. He did not deny that racism existed inside prison; he only said that it was no different from the world outside. Habib was on good terms with the officers who greeted him in the cells, and the picture that he painted of racism showed that it was the interaction between the officers and the people from the *banlieues* that gave rise to it. According to him, this was because the latter were not respectful, and the former 'pissed them off' [*les font chier*].

The other prisoners, when mentioning racism, referred to concrete experiences that they had had with the law (judges or other actors in the criminal justice hierarchy), with police, with the prison system (prison officers) and with other prisoners. With regard to the law and prison officers, the experience of racism was placed in context: prisoners talked about injustice, the difference between Arabs and non-Arabs and the differential treatment of people by the law according to their ethnic category. At the same time they talked about their own impatience and sometimes their own reaction against it that only increased their chances of receiving a heavier sentence because of their own attitude. According to Kamel, a Frenchman of North African descent,

> I have often been thrown into prison and I know the legal system very well; and I am quick to get worked up about [*je pète vite les plombs*] those people who wear uniforms, their way of speaking and so on. I cannot stand them. One of them, a shit prison officer [*un surveillant de merde*] told me for example: 'Stand up, who do you think you are, you dirty *bougnoule* [an offensive word for 'Arab']?'. They made my life a misery. They told me: 'dirty *bicot* [another insulting word for 'Arab'], filthy race, go back to your own country'. This is it; this is what they said to me. It is racism; this is what I was told in the police station in Roubaix. I got furious with this racist policeman. There was an Arab policeman [that is, of North African origin] who was there, and I told him what had happened. He told me to calm down; he knew that it was true; I calmed down. If a police officer or a prison officer is 'cool', I am 'cool'.

The last case is that of Nordine, who thought that the main problem was that the young people from the *banlieues* were aggressive and created tension within the prison. He claimed that 'There is no racism. We respect [prison officers] but the young generations [from the *banlieues*] don't show respect like before. They have a fight for nothing, for a yes or no'.

Contrary to the first group of prisoners, Nabil, a 31-year-old Algerian, thought that there was a specific form of racism in prison:

> I didn't think that there was racism before being put in jail. But since then, ah, yes! Something serious happened to me at the beginning. Here, in prison, I was ill one morning. I got up with 4 grammes of sugar in my blood due to my glycaemia. I really was in bad shape because of my diabetes, and it is normal to become nervous when this happens. I called the officer because I badly needed an injection at 8 o'clock, and the officer didn't show up before 9 o'clock; and for the whole time I was banging more and more violently on the door. He told me that he was late because of exercise time. I told him that my health was more important than that. I shouted and waved my hands; I didn't understand what was happening then... I found myself surrounded by ten officers, they shouted like crazy people. This is the injustice. They put

handcuffs on me, and once I was handcuffed, one of the officers punched me in the neck. I shouted: 'Why are you doing this?' He told me: 'For what you did outside prison'. The Senior Officer held him back because he was trying to beat me more; and I was handcuffed, facing the wall and all naked. I had the '*hachouma*' (the dishonour) of being naked like that, and this Officer was 2 metres tall. For this, I got two days of segregation [*mitard*]; the doctor got me out. If this Officer apologises, I'll forgive him; but if he doesn't, he'll pay heavily on the Day of Reckoning [*le jour du Jugement dernier*]. There are not many prison officers like him – so mean.

Not all prisoners experienced racism from prison officers. There were good and bad officers, from the viewpoint of the prisoners. There were those who were helpful and those who refused to understand the situation of the prisoners. In any case, the presence of 'Arab' prison officers made it more difficult for the others to act in a blatantly racist way. Incidentally, the increase in the number of prison officers with North African backgrounds is not the result of an official policy to promote 'diversity', as in British prisons, but is a *de facto* outcome of their difficulty in finding other employment.

Some detected racism among the judges. For example, Abdellah, a 30-year-old Moroccan resident from the Netherlands reported that,

The Consulate of the Netherlands had come and visited me; they couldn't do anything for me at the level of Justice but they helped me with the papers, to get a translator, to inform my parents. They came once every month... I have been living in Holland for 20 years, and in Holland there are many laws favourable to liberty. I wanted a translator who spoke Dutch when I was in police custody [*en garde à vue*]. I wanted a Dutch interpreter because I speak this language better than Arabic, but I finally agreed to speak Arabic to show my good faith to the police, and they brought me a North African who didn't speak Dutch. But during the court case, I had a Dutch interpreter, and the Judge said: 'Why did you agree to speak Arabic in police custody and now you want to speak Dutch?'. This was racism. Why did he ask me this kind of question? This was a disturbed mind and racism. The first time, I spoke Arabic to solve the police problems. This is France! Racism has developed within the law, and there is no law for us. The law doesn't respect us, and we are tempted not to respect it. Even the police do not behave properly. They intentionally distort what we say. I didn't sign up to anything during my police custody but even then, it has some value according to them and in this respect, it is different from Holland: if you don't sign, it has no value. Here, justice is missing. It is racism in this country. I got two years imprisonment without any evidence! I really hate them!

Racism in this case arose from the feeling of extreme injustice due to the differences in legal norms between the Netherlands and France. But an additional consideration is that Abdellah was from Morocco, and he suspected that the French authorities were discriminating against him because of his North African origins. But cases like this are not very common. Most of the cases of racism are related not to Islam but to the fact that North Africans are 'Arabs' and the fact that they live in the poor suburbs.

Racism is lived through daily experiences in prison. Those who are from the *banlieues* accuse prison officers of racism. The others, mostly from the Maghreb or other former French colonies in Africa, find fault with the behaviour of people in the public housing estates and the way in which prison officers respond to their defiance. According to a 34-year-old Algerian, Abdelhakim,

> In Building 4 there are plenty of drug addicts; the prison officers are tough but they are not racists. Although, sometimes it looks like it. For instance, for the last two months, I have been asking to go to the hairdresser but nobody had called me yet. Isn't that racism? The prison officers are not even-handed in their conduct: if one of them is angry with a prisoner, all the prisoners are treated like him. There are bad prisoners as well, and the prison officers are fed up.
>
> Young people from the poor suburbs [*les jeunes des banlieues*] are proud; they feel abandoned by the rest; they cultivate a hatred [of society]; and they respect no one. They are violent because they have always known difficult situations. I talk to them myself about respect, and they understand a bit. They should be taken care of; otherwise, it is going to end badly... One should talk to these 'youth' and provide them with jobs. They are forgotten by other French people. They went to school here, they have their life here and they have no job: it is racism. It is hard to go upwards in French society, as an Arab it is hard; you cannot do it even if you have qualifications. There are, of course, a few exceptions to the rule.

Racism, according to Abdelhakim, has social roots in the 'hatred' nourished by young men from the poor suburbs towards the rest of society whom they accuse of racism and of being disrespectful towards them and of racism, as much in their daily encounter with other Frenchmen as in the job market from which they are excluded, even if they have the necessary qualifications. Abdelhakim extends this set of ideas to the situation of the prison where, according to him, the disrespect that these young men display makes prison officers aggressive towards all prisoners. Aït Faska, a 28-year-old Moroccan, is another prisoner who also thought that racism in the job market was stigmatising to 'Arabs', even if they held qualifications and had a high level of competence:

> It's the same for young people in the districts [*quartiers*, another name for poor suburbs]: they are jobless. Even in the job market, there is racism. When you see [Arab] engineers without a job, it is not an encouragement to study.

For Mehdi, as well, the problem of racism was not a one-sided one: it could not be attributed solely to the prejudice of French people towards Arabs but was also attributable to the bad behaviour of '*Robeux*' [the inverted slang word for Arabs]. As a 22-year-old Frenchman of North African origin, he believed that 'Racism exists... but Arabs show off too much. There are problems with the *Robeux*... I do stupid things [*je fais des conneries*], and they lead to problems for me; and on top of that, I know that it makes racism a bit worse'. This shows recognition of the close relation between racism and the unlawful actions of some 'Arabs'.

On the whole, a large number of North Africans realise that racism is not a one-way problem but is a consequence of the antagonistic interaction between prison officers and people from the *banlieues*. For many people, even from the so-called *cités* [housing estates], racism is not a simplistic problem that is due to a one-sided fault on the part of prisons but is one in which the reciprocal action of two groups ends up most of the time in tension and violence.

Some North African inmates believe, however, that racism is the result of an unwarranted generalisation on the part of French people of the misconduct of a few Arabs to all of them. Thus, Abdelrahman, a 24-year-old Moroccan, argued that 'Racism exists in the legal system. But there is also racism towards all Arabs. They are hated because one of them stole a car. The majority of French people are not like that, but there are some like that'.

For some of the prisoners, who are neither from the poor suburbs nor from North Africa, racism exists not only in the derogatory language used by prison officers *vis-à-vis* inmates but also among the inmates themselves. It is often Muslims who separate prisoners when they fight each other; they are the 'bearded ones' who are respected by the others and can curtail violence among the inmates. According to Hassan, a 40-year-old Lebanese, 'Racism... also exists between prisoners; but this is handled by ourselves. If there are brawls, most of the time those who pray and are bearded intervene and separate the two sides and prevent violence'.

The role of the devout Muslims is essential here. They intervene as prominent members of an implicit community and they are recognised not only by the prisoners but also by the prison officers, who ask for their help when tension arises among people of Muslim origin in prisons. For example, the Muslim minister of Prison B (which is the one in which Abdelrahman is imprisoned) says that he is the one who intervenes in cases of dispute among the prisoners. The reality is more complex: he plays a role, and in competition with him, other 'Muslims', the 'bearded ones', play a part as mediators between Muslims.

There are different opinions about racism between prisoners. One, already mentioned many times, takes note of the racism between inmates. But there is another one which is based on the idea of segregation between groups and the management of relations among them according to the rules of ethnicity. It is true that in those prisons where the majority of inmates are Muslims, the two groups – Muslims and Non-Muslims (most of whom are French) – do not mix together. This entails some specific problems, including the difficulty that might arise if a prisoner from one group is placed in the other group's section.

This was explained as follows by Yassine, a 31-year-old Algerian:

> Racism doesn't exist here because we don't mix; that's it, and it is better for all. Once they put a French guy [*petit Français*] with the Arabs... He was in his corner all the time, he was afraid of everyone. He was called Germain. He used to tremble with fear. We went and talked to him, I pitied him, he was afraid... After that, he didn't want to leave us, we get on so well.

This observation was made in informal meetings about prisons in Southern France and in Lyon where prisoners were loosely separated into ethnic groups. The fact of their 'not mixing', as Yassine put it, is contrary to the spirit of French citizenship, but the harsh laws of reality rule in prisons – not the ideal of a totally homogeneous society that underlay the utopia revered by the forefathers of the French Republic. For many prisoners, racism is rooted in their sense of injustice about the sentences that judges hand down to them and the disdainful attitude of the police and prison officers towards them. Fathi, a 24-year-old French citizen of North African origin, spoke for many others when he protested:

> I got four months in prison. There is injustice or racism in this sentence. The Judge issued a two months sentence, and once I arrived here I was told by them to sign up for four months... All the prison officers are *klebs* (dogs), two or three have some understanding, and the others are all racists.

A complex judicial system that delivers prison sentences that the prisoner does not understand – along with the suspicion that there is hatred towards 'Arabs' – breeds this attitude of total rejection on the part of a Frenchman who sees injustice (not about the conviction itself in this case) in the mysterious doubling of his sentence (from two months to four) in prison.

Ex-offenders remember the police (someone who has a file is a suspect in all the cases where some crime is involved in the neighbourhood, and the police automatically look for clues) and prosecuting authorities (they examine his file and his statements for evidence of his involvement) as constant threats to their peace of life even if they have given up criminality and are striving to become respectable citizens. On top of that, being an Arab *vis-à-vis* those prison officers who vote for the Front National (the French extreme right-wing political party) makes life much more difficult for prisoners, some of whom are sufficiently paranoid to exaggerate the number of such officers working in prisons. More generally, the lack of an independent agency within French prisons to which cases of racial discrimination could be referred leaves prison officers totally free to act in a racist way towards the prisoners, according to Youssef, a 25-year-old Frenchman from a North African background. This is one of the flaws of the French prison system in comparison to the British one where a Race Relations Officer is trained to receive prisoners' complaints and to bring them to the attention of higher authorities. Youssef's description of racism ties together several things: the political loyalties of prison officers who are defined as racist if they vote for the Front National (the two attitudes are not necessarily closely related); the fact that prisoners have no rights within the prison system; and the fact that repeat offenders are suspect in the eyes of the police and the criminal justice system, which makes any return to being a law-abiding citizen even more difficult. This complex web of different systems is centred on what Youssef calls 'racism'. He refers to only one aspect of racism in the strict sense of the term, namely, the attitudes of prejudiced prison officers towards 'Arab' prisoners. The other ingredients affect the life of all prisoners, regardless of their ethnic origin. Youssef explains racism as follows:

Racism exists here, in prison. There are prison officers from the Front National. You should see them searching [*fouille*] in cells... Many things happen in this prison. A prisoner who had only two months to serve before his release gets two extra months for disciplinary reasons and commits suicide. Is that logical?... In any case, a prisoner is never right. We have two-speed justice. Us, they assassinate us. I know that I have a heavy file but I have never used firearms, and the inspectors know it full well... Once, I had stopped everything and I was doing well. They [police and criminal justice] made me miserable, and I fell back into crime.

Being unjustly sentenced to prison terms and finding himself exposed to racism within prison, in a dual relationship where Muslim prisoners and prison officers are prejudiced against each other, is Allal's bitter summing up of his situation. As a 23-year-old French citizen of North African descent, he complains:

> I am here but I haven't done anything wrong, this stresses me out. In my family, no one has ever had any problem with the law. But the French and the Muslims, there is racism on both sides. Prison officers deliberately cut off the water supply to upset me [when I'm taking a shower]... If they want a reaction from me, they'll get it. They shouldn't cry then!

Another 26-year-old French citizen with North African origins, Benamar, claimed that there was a dual system of law – one for the Arabs, the other for non-Arab citizens: 'In France Human Rights don't exist. If you are French or Arab, you are not judged the same way; racism enters into it. We want to defend ourselves, but we can't'.

Recent events, especially the attacks in the USA on 11 September 2001, have created a new situation that favours a new type of racism in which Islam and Arabness are blended into a stereotype of the fanatical Muslim and Arab terrorist. Thus, according to Ryad, a 26-year-old Palestinian:

> The policemen asked me: 'Do you like Bin Laden?'. And they made my life a misery in Fresnes prison. This is intolerable. I said that I did my prayers, and their reply was, 'Then you are for Bin Laden!' and this has made my situation worse... This is racism... Here, *machallah* [thank God], there is solidarity among Muslims; they help each other, they have confidence among them.

The same person, bitter about the neglect of his health problems, found fault with the prison officers and the doctors who ignored him most of the time. More generally, prisoners with psychiatric problems can find themselves in difficult situations. They can harm themselves and become seriously disturbed if not taken care of. Since prisons have problems of overcrowding, particularly in their hospital wings, many inmates complained about the lack of health care. They saw racism in the fact that they were not treated seriously. Here again, racism and injustice went hand in hand in the prisoners' interpretation of their lot in the prison system. For example, a 26-year-old Palestinian called Ryad claimed that,

> Seventy-five per cent of the prison officers are racist here. Outside, in the police, I would say 100 per cent of them, from what I saw. Here, in prison, prison officers have insulted me many times or hit me. Look at my scars [he shows his arms and neck]. They take advantage of the fact that I don't speak French [well] and I cannot defend myself. I wrote many letters to change my cell, and they sent me to Fresnes prison

because my shoulder had been dislocated [*déboîtement de mon épaule*] and I wanted to go to Fresnes to be looked after. I thought Fresnes was better because it is more authoritarian but there is more respect towards us. I wrote from there for a blood test but I never received an answer. I told them, 'We are not pigs or dogs'. They closed the door in my face. I have become nervous since coming into prison; I have no news from my family. They made me nervous, I took a chair and I banged it against the wall. Twelve prison officers came to calm me down. I saw them coming, I took a razor blade and cut myself [*je me suis lacéré*]. They took me to the hospital, and I told the doctor there that I had written to him three times in order to get to Fresnes for my shoulder. They changed my cell with difficulty. The chief prison officer told me to calm down, he is a good guy. But a prison officer said to him: 'Let him die'. By the way, he doesn't know that I am ready to die. Adam's son dies if God wills it. I'll die if this is my destiny, and death doesn't scare me. It is something which is in store for all of us... My health problem continued. I had toothache due to a bad filling [*plombage*] which wasn't treated. For two months, I have been writing for a visit to the dentist to have this tooth taken out. If you don't have a residency card or a citizen's one, you don't exist for them here in prison. It is racism and a serious injustice. This shouldn't happen, but God sees them acting in this way.

Another common complaint about racism towards Islam and Black Africans was voiced by Mamadou, a 24-year-old from Mali, who was clear that,

There's a lot of [racism] here. It's true of 90 per cent of the prison officers and the police. The day of the police search [*perquisition*], the police officers walked over my mattress, they threw the Holy Qur'an on the ground; perhaps they didn't know what they were doing but they used racist words like 'Why don't you stay in your own country in Africa?'. While I was in police custody [*garde à vue*], they didn't give me anything to eat. It is different from Africa where parents bring food to their sons for each meal. The police officers told me, 'Go back to your own country'.

Lack of respect towards the Qur'an and trampling on the mattress, as well as the racist words, show ethnic racism and religious racism side by side. Another form of racism, related to disrespect for Islam, was often mentioned by the prisoners in connection with prison officers interrupting daily prayers. As Mamadou put it:

[Racism] exists. My cellmate was praying in the cell, a prison officer came and stopped him from praying, he didn't wait until the end of the prayer. I held him back and prevented him from disturbing my mate any more. It is serious. It is the same outside. Racism exists in society because we are of Arab descent. The people look at us like people from the moon. In public transport, the way they talk to us, in school or other places. I try, for my part, to be polite all the time and to keep quiet without being too visible. Le Pen's case is serious... It is true that some young people break things. But people confuse violence and delinquency. Some people steal to survive. I understand these people; they're living in a hell on earth [*ils sont en galère*]. It's hard to live through the '*galère*' especially if you've been a failure in school and you don't have a job. Many young people like me are in this situation, especially North African Muslims.

Mamadou's account of racism began with a prison officer disturbing a Muslim prisoner's daily prayer. But then the 'Arab' equation was introduced along with the social causes of the high rate of delinquency among young people from poor suburbs and the rationale for their criminality which is rooted in the '*galère*', that is, the combination of low educational level, unemployment and the social stigma attached to young people. In this way, prejudice against Islam, criminality among the inhabitants of the *banlieues* and racism go hand in hand. In fact, Mamadou made a remarkable sociological analysis of the predicament of the population of the *banlieues* who are subject to social prejudice and, at the same time, help to perpetuate it in a vicious circle.

Jean-Marie Le Pen's success in the first round of the French presidential elections in 2002 is a symptom of deep-seated racism in France in the opinion of some North Africans, including Lotfi, a 31-year-old Moroccan, who was adamant that racism existed in prison:

It even exists between us Arabs. There is racism towards us by the prison officers and racism among the prisoners. I personally get along with all people, but in French society, it is true as well, racism really exists. Look at the FN [the Front National, a party on the extreme right wing]. If Le Pen becomes President of the Republic, I'll go back home, I'll leave everything here and I'll leave France. In Morocco, people are poor, but it is a thousand times better than here with Le Pen.

For people who are half-French and half-North African, the problem of identity overlaps with the rejection of the Arabs by the French and of the French by the Arabs. For example, when we asked Karim, a 22-year-old Frenchman of Algerian descent, whether there was any racism in prison, he laughed and added,

Is there? Of course, there is! There are racist prison officers. They said, 'Fuck off [*ferme ta gueule*], bougnoule!'. I threatened to lodge a complaint, I got four days in the punishment cell [*mitard*]. The older prison officers are friendlier. Now, when there is racism, I do not react. Since I am half-Arab half-French, I get problems on both sides. I have had this problem in Algeria too, and I don't go there any more. With my surname, which is French, it is easier in France; but with my first name, which is Arab, I get racist problems.

There is racism not only in prison, according to Karim, but also in French society at large. Prison, in this sense, is a mirror of society. How can people defend themselves against it? Nothing can be done except to accept it and not react to it. Otherwise, there will be punishment, and Karim got four days in the disciplinary cell. Allal, who is a 23-year-old Frenchman of North African descent, encountered the same kind of problem because of his dual Arab and French identity, neither of which was recognised by people on the North or the South side of the Mediterranean:

They should change the nasty prison officers because they get revenge on us with their insults, injustices. I have been beaten by police officers in a police station, and while they were hitting me, they said, 'You little Arab, how do you like this? Get back to your own country!'. And in prison, the first week, the first month, it is hard. We have no visits room [*parloir*], no money order [from the family]. They make our lives a misery, they hold back our letters, we can say nothing, we can do nothing. Me, a little Moroccan shit [*moi, petite crotte marocaine*], I can't do anything. There are racists both here and there. In Morocco, they criticise me. There is hypocrisy. We are like a table tennis ball, and France and Morocco play with us. In Morocco, there are jokes about us, they treat us like Frenchmen; and I, I treat them as Moroccans; sometimes, they laugh – they don't take it in a bad way – but sometimes it is more serious.

Our findings show that racism, in addition to being a force in society in general, is also active in recruitment policies and the workplace. For example, the racist dichotomy between the French and the Arabs finds a direct application in the two different ways in which prison officers were said to behave towards each group. When the groups were combined, prison officers were more flexible; but with groups of 'Arabs' alone they became intransigent. Lamara, a 29-year-old Algerian, testified that,

There is racism here. In 1995, I felt it in my work: North African people were rejected. Myself I physically look different, and the French tell me, 'You are not an Arab, you are a Kabyle'. The French are racist. In prison, there is a lot of racism from the prison officers. There are two or three of them and I don't talk to them any more. They don't even hide it. But most of the time, there is an underhand racism, even though there are Black or Arab prison officers... When there are French people with us, prison officers accept everything; but if they are with a group of Arabs, they refuse everything such as shower time. Even the leading officers are racist. One of them was insulted and treated as racist, and the prisoner got 15 days in the disciplinary cell.

Lamara made this distinction between covert and open racism because he could sense the differences between the ways of dealing with Arab and French inmates in the prison. This suspicion of creeping racism can develop into paranoia whereby every attitude of prison officers is interpreted in an obsessively comparative way. This widens the gulf between the Self (the Arab) who is supposed to be persecuted by the racism of prison officers and the Others (the French) who are favoured by the officers.

It is important to emphasise that racism applies not only to foreigners or North Africans but also to French people of North African descent who are stigmatised as only 'French on paper' [*Français sur le papier*], an expression attributed to Le Pen, the head of the Extreme right-wing Front National who denies that such people have any genuine 'Frenchness'. The expression has subsequently been used by the 'Arabs' themselves in order to denounce racism and the hostile attitude of French people towards them. For Kamel, if an Arab commits a crime, people treat the particular case as a general one that is allegedly applicable to all Arabs, whereas a Frenchman who commits an offence is regarded as an individual and not necessarily as a representative of a collective category. As a 34-year-old Frenchman, Kamel put this as follows:

Racism exists towards North Africans. I myself have French nationality. I am 'French on paper', but it doesn't do any good. We, French people of North African descent, are respectful [of others], we work on showing respect [towards the others]. There are good French people who are not racists, but these are a minority. If a Frenchman does something illegal [*une connerie*], no one talks about it; they don't say that all French people commit crimes. But when it is us [the Arabs], they generalise, they say, 'They are all like that'. The attitude should be the same for everyone, be it Pierre, Mohammed or Ali.

A member of Tabligh, Aït Faska, a 28-year-old Moroccan who wore a beard and carried a *siwak*,[20] shared the same view of stigmatisation. He believed that racism prevented him from finding a job and from going to Morocco to look for a wife. Others gave the feeling of being stigmatised as a reason for admiring those whom normal people hate, such as Osama Bin Laden. For example, Omar, a 40-year-old Frenchman of Algerian descent said:

There is a lot of racism in relation to jobs for people who have no qualifications. I am in prison for armed robbery [*braquage*]. I have no project for the future, I am 'done with' [*grillé*] in France. I could end up anywhere, in *habss* [an Arabic word for prison] for something I haven't done, and this is not acceptable. Is this justice? For me, someone like Bin Laden is a great man. Jihad is first of all an effort on oneself, and he has done it. He is the only one to have defied the West. Every day we are being anaesthetised by words, but on the ground, things happen differently. For me the injustice against Muslims is unbearable. Bush, as someone who is anti-Arab, doesn't deserve any pity – just as he hasn't had any pity for us. He should be judged with Sharon in an International Tribunal, but who would dare to do it these days?

In Omar's case, the sense of injustice and humiliation was compensated for by the heroic figure of Bin Laden who was seen as someone who had dealt with Western arrogance and defied it on its own terms. Omar's daily humiliations were projected on to the mythical figure of Bin Laden who was supposedly taking revenge for the racism that the 'Arabs' were having to endure in France on a daily basis.

According to Fitzgerald and Marshall (1996: 156), 'French discourse is at least as likely to problematise North Africans in terms of religion rather than colour and to bracket them – as "Muslims" – with Turks in Germany'. Yet, our findings about prisons in France indicate that Islam is becoming a main focus of racial discrimination. In fact, specifically religious racism was not frequently mentioned in the interviews, although many Muslim inmates complained about the disrespect shown by prison officers towards the prisoners performing daily prayers in their cell. Indeed, a 42-year-old Algerian prisoner deliberately called this racism and identified it as intended to prevent the celebration of prayers.

Racism exists here. There is a discrimination against the practice of Islam because I have seen many North Africans in Les Baumettes prison, and these are not usually stupid people. They prevent them from practising their religion. But they will never succeed in doing this because Islam is a transcendent religion! The danger is that violence will become a legitimate means of voicing your opinion. Some members of the Muslim community have been radicalised. Here, in prison, the Jews can bring in the food they want for Shabat. They even have kosher products in the prison shop [but Muslims have no *halal* food and do not receive it for their celebration of Eid al-Kabir].

For the Muslim chaplain in Prison B, racism was the result of the different ways in which Islam and other religions were handled in prison. 'Racism exists here. Myself, when I first came here, I got to know it: they didn't give me the key to the cells, unlike the Christian ministers and the rabbi. The lack of *halal* meat, and at Christmas, the presents for the Christians while the Muslims receive nothing on their holy day, Eid al-Kabir.' In a society with equal opportunities, where hierarchy can at best be based on competence or some other explicit criteria, the prison authorities' lack of even-handedness towards Islam amounts to racism; the harsh sentences handed down by judges is racism; the perceptible discrimination that prison officers make between 'Arabs' and other inmates is also racism. Many of the complaints that prisoners make to prison officers or judges about racism might not qualify as racism in a narrow sense of the term. But the suspicion of unjust treatment and the strong belief that Muslims are stigmatised increases the subjective feeling of racism to which many North African prisoners are subject in prisons. The accusation of racism becomes, in the last analysis, a way of expressing one's anger or one's dissatisfaction towards the authorities. But the suspicion of stigma is ironically even stronger among some 'Arabs' because they can see that non-Arabs may justify their racism by pointing to the violence perpetrated by young people from the *banlieues* and to the supposed lack of respect they show towards others, particularly prison officers.

The long list of racisms has acquired a new item: racism towards Islam, as reported by some of our interviewees and confirmed by an Open Society report which claims that in France 'racist violence clearly often has a religious dimension, most usually associated with anti-Semitism or anti-Arabism' (Amiraux, 2002: 110). Since this religion is growing as an expression of the way in which dominated groups in French society, particularly in the poor suburbs, choose to spell out the culture of the dominated and the excluded, Islam is gaining ground in French prisons. Two decades ago 'religious racism' in French prisons was either non-existent or simply covered up as much by prison officers as by Muslim prisoners themselves. Nowadays, however, racism against Islam (or 'Islamophobia') is gaining the upper hand in the mass media and in the institutions such as prisons where Muslims are well represented. In prisons, Islam can be considered as the religion of 'Arabs' (although French people of Turkish origin and French Blacks are not Arabs) and as the religion of 'terrorists'. As such, Islam creates fear and elicits repressive attitudes among the authorities.

Conclusion

Although our sample of three prisons in England and Wales does not include any establishments with a bad reputation for racism these days, our investigations still uncovered extensive evidence of two things. First, many Muslim prisoners made allegations of racist discrimination against them by prison officers. The allegations often combined elements of 'race', ethnicity and religion. By comparison, allegations of racist discrimination by other prisoners against Muslims were much less frequent. Second, prison officers displayed a variety of responses to allegations of racism, but none of them denied that it was a fact of prison life. Other prison staff, including chaplains, also considered that racism was real but they were less likely than officers to rationalise it.

The rationalisations of racism that we encountered took at least four different forms. Some officers described themselves as 'colour blind' in the sense of deliberately not taking note of prisoners' skin colour and, by implication, of their ethnic or religious background. This often went hand in hand with a claim that the behaviour of *other* staff and prisoners was shaped by considerations of 'race'. A second form of rationalisation held that racial inequalities and discrimination were merely a part of 'human nature' and were therefore inevitable. By implication, then, prisons were not significantly different from other areas of social life and did not require special intervention. Third, racism was framed variously as a relic of the past, a form of joking behaviour or just a matter of 'a few bad apples'. The intended effect of each 'frame' was apparently to suggest that the importance of racism tended to be exaggerated. The fourth form of rationalisation – which amounted to a way of 'blaming the victim' – was to interpret allegations of racism as evidence that prisoners were 'playing the race card'. Even when this particular rationalisation accompanied an admission that racist discrimination was a reality in prisons, the emphasis tended to fall on the intimation that its significance was often exaggerated.

None of these four forms of rationalisation is unique to prisons: they actually have a long history in many areas of human life. But they have a special significance in the context of prisons precisely because the Prison Service of England and Wales, as we explained at the beginning of this chapter, has gone to considerable lengths to combat racism. One way of interpreting our findings about the persistence of allegations of racism and of the prison officers' rationalised responses to the allegations is, of course, to see in them signs that anti-racist policies and regulations have at least moderated the virulence of racism. It takes mostly mild forms in our sample of prisons and is more subtle than it used to be. Nevertheless, a former Director General of the Prison Service and its own Race Equality Advisor have both admitted that the Service is 'institutionally racist'; a former Chief Inspector of Prisons and the Commission for Racial Equality have concluded that a culture of racism still infects certain establishments; and research has continued to unearth reliable evidence of racially biased behaviour (Burnett and Farrell, 1994; NACRO, 2000; CRE, 2003a, 2003b; Edgar and Martin, 2004) in the prisons of England and Wales.

An alternative way of interpreting our findings is to see them as evidence that the implementation of the Prison Service's policies and procedures to combat racism, as expressions of the 'new managerialism' in public services (Law, 1996), has been relatively successful but has also tended to give higher priority to bureaucratic procedures than to anti-racist strategies. Moreover, these procedures could be described as 'ethnic managerialism' (Law, 1999) in so far as they aim to monitor and to remedy degrees of inequality among ethnic categories of prisoners without necessarily tackling head-on the beliefs, structures and practices that generate it. Certainly, the Prison Service has put in place an impressive array of policies, regulations, initiatives, structures, personnel, training programmes, manuals, complaints and investigatory procedures, accounting operations and monitoring devices. Governors are expected to implement the entire array and to produce evidence that the system works effectively at the level of each establishment. Evidence of the professional competence of staff to follow the required procedures carries special importance. But the mammoth nature of the apparatus may be counter-productive either if it masks a failure to get rid of racist staff and to discipline racist prisoners or if it discourages staff and prisoners alike from having faith in the system's effectiveness. Both eventualities foster cynicism.

Nevertheless, the Prison Service of England and Wales is officially committed to the defence of 'diversity' and 'race equality'. Now that the more violent and blatant acts of racism have been explicitly outlawed, Muslim prisoners' grievances tend to be mainly about 'relative deprivation'. That is, when they compare themselves with prisoners from other ethnic and religious groups they may decide that they are being unfairly disadvantaged. This explains why so many grievances concern failed applications to obtain, for example, access to Friday prayers, *halal* food or visits. Muslim prisoners claim that their applications are unsuccessful more frequently than are comparable applications made by white and/or Christian inmates. The irony in all this is that, as the Prison Service tries to make more facilities and services available to minorities, so the latter's expectations rise. Their sense of deprivation is therefore relative to rising standards of service *and* rising expectations. A similar situation arises in the state education sector. Since the British state has long funded schools identified with Christianity and Judaism, Muslims understandably campaigned for state funding of schools identified with Islam – on grounds of equality. The campaign indeed resulted in the creation of Muslim schools within the system of state-funded education.

The situation is different in French prisons partly because of the higher density of Muslim prisoners and the still painful memories of the war of independence in Algeria in the 1950s but also partly because, in the absence of positive schemes for defending diversity for its own sake, there is a much stronger sense of social exclusion among Muslims. Admittedly, the official insistence on the notion that all prisoners have equal rights offers a degree of legal protection against unlawful discrimination. But the policy of not collecting statistics of ethnic or religious differences – to say nothing of monitoring the distribution of disadvantages and inequalities by ethnicity – undermines any political will to challenge racism. As a result, gross forms of racial discrimination against Muslims are reported more frequently in French prisons than in British prisons, and the French machinery for combating racism appears weak compared with its British equivalent.

The question that needs to be asked in France is why the racism that is all too real in prisons was so systematically overlooked in such a serious and thorough investigation as the Hyest-Cabanel report (2001). The reason is not bad faith or a conspiracy of silence. The reason lies, rather, in the cultural norms dominating the entire constitutional and institutional framework of French society: they simply ignore what racism means, in concrete terms, because they refuse to take into account the real data, the reality of French society for the sake of preserving an ideal bequeathed by the French Enlightenment and implemented in the French Revolution as well as the Third Republic. France is a *de facto* multicultural – or, at least, ethnically and religiously diverse – society which deliberately chooses to ignore this fact in the name of the ideal of the cultural homogeneity that characterised it until the 1970s.

Public policies in France are also grounded in the philosophical assumption that rationalism is the key to universal truths and that the public sphere must, therefore, be closed to particularist values associated with faith communities representing only a fraction of the nation. Prisons, as institutions of the state which offer no choice of 'membership', have to manage the tension between universalism and particularism on a daily basis. They struggle to find ways of permitting the expression of cultural, ethnic or religious identities without appearing to compromise universalist ideals and the state's stance of neutrality. As a result, the very notion of 'minority' finds very little protection in French law. Instead, the notion of universal rights and obligations, as defined by the state, holds pride of place in both law and the practice of public institutions. The implementation of these supposedly universal principles in prisons, where the majority of inmates come from 'unrecognised' minorities, runs the risk of breeding strong feelings of injustice, exclusion and alienation. The sad irony is that the prisoners' accusations of racist discrimination cannot be taken seriously in a system that does not recognise the reality of minorities. The fact that accusations of racism in French prisons increasingly involve discrimination on the grounds of religion only aggravates matters. This is because the long-term effect of *laïcité* has been to foster the view that religion can only function legitimately in private life and that, for the sake of the unity of the Republic, it must be kept out of the public sphere. Furthermore, the fact that the religion in question is Islam – many of whose believers regard it as a complete way of life – adds fuel to the fire by raising the spectre not just of particularism but also of fanaticism and fundamentalism, that is, the very negation of universalistic rationalism.

6
Categorisation and Self-definition Among Muslim Prisoners

Introduction

The main themes of Chapter 5 underlined the fact that discrimination based on notions of 'race', ethnicity and religion is common in British and French prisons. Forms of discrimination are also inter-related in complex ways that reflect each country's history, legal provisions and religious composition. The effect in both cases is similar, however, in the sense that prison officers and Muslim prisoners alike perceive that considerations of 'race', ethnicity and religion shape the way in which prisoners are treated. Nevertheless, there are major contrasts between the officers and the prisoners in terms of the reasons that they give for this differential treatment. The contrast between France and England and Wales is also sharp in respect of the extent to which differential treatment is officially encouraged or discouraged. Respect for 'diversity' is a value that guides both the principles and the practice that prisons in England and Wales are supposed to follow in their treatment of minorities. In French prisons, by contrast, principles and practice are expected to be guided more by the value of 'equality' in the sense of uniform treatment of all prisoners regardless of ethnic or religious differences.

In the light of these fundamental contrasts between the recognition accorded to ethnic and religious diversity in the prisons of France and England and Wales, the question arises of how far these differences affect the way in which Muslim prisoners think about and make use of, their own identity. In particular, we wanted to know how Muslim prisoners responded to the variable opportunities that their prisons afforded to them for the cultivation and expression of identities drawing on ethnic, racial and religious resources. In fact, the term 'identification' is preferable to 'identity' for our purposes because it conveys the active, contingent and situational character of the processes whereby prisoners work out and experience their similarities with, and affinities to, other people. No less important is the capacity of identification processes to mark out differences as well as similarities.

186

The main aim of this chapter is to bring to light the processes through which Muslim prisoners identify themselves in ethnic and religious terms. The emphasis will necessarily be on the prisoners' self-definition, but this has to be placed in the context of two aspects of their categorisation by prison authorities: the particular prisons where they live and the nature of the national prison system in which they are detained. Special attention will be paid to the extent to which Islam operates as a basis for the identification and self-identification of Muslim prisoners and how far this translates into a basis for their sociability and solidarity in France and England and Wales.

England and Wales

While many people outside prison have access to dense social networks of friends, associates, neighbours, relatives, fellow-students or workmates, the situation in prisons is different to some extent. Admittedly, variations between prisons are wide, but in general they all impose limitations on the range of people with whom prisoners can mix. Phenotypical characteristics, diet, language and religious practice are therefore more likely to serve as a basis for identification in the confined spaces of prison than outside. Moreover, since 'race relations' enjoy the backing of mandatory policies, procedures and personnel to curb discrimination on grounds of ethnicity and religion, as we argued in Chapter 2, prisoners can hardly fail to be aware of the significance that they have for prison life. And, as we showed in Chapter 3, facilities for the practice of Islam in British prisons have improved in recent years. At the same time, Chapters 4 and 5 provided evidence of the prejudicial racial and religious stereotypes that some prison officers continue to exercise in their daily interaction with prisoners. In view of the official and unofficial attention paid to 'race' and religion in prisons, then, it is not at all surprising that prisoners from minority ethnic and/or religious backgrounds experience a process of self-identification and group identification in which 'race' and religion assume greater salience than in wider society.

Before prison

Our starting point is the finding that only 20 per cent of the male Muslim prisoners in our samples reported any active involvement in Muslim activities outside prison. The level for female prisoners was lower still. Some men, such as Prisoner 12 in Prison 1, acknowledged that members of their family had been devout but that they had been inactive themselves: 'No, I was a very bad Muslim on the out. I used to sell drugs and defraud people... My mum prays five times a day... my father was not that much religious, he used to work. My brothers and sisters pray when they can'. It was not uncommon for prisoners to say 'When I am out I am not religious, just Ramadan and Fridays' (Prison 1, Prisoner 22). Another frequent report was that prisoners had attended mosques regularly during childhood or before migrating to the UK but had drifted away from Muslim activities in their late teenage years. For example, Prisoner 16 in Prison 2 claimed,

> When I was younger I was going [to the mosque], I was about 10. I was going to the mosque to learn my prayers and everything. I done it up to my *saparah* [Qur'anic recital] and then suddenly I stopped going and I couldn't really focus on the Qur'an or anything, and that's it. And once you stop you start forgetting slowly everything.

The Imam in Prison 1 confirmed that most of the Muslim prisoners came from 'families where their commitment or knowledge of Islam is minimum'.

Moreover, our informants rarely described their links with local Muslim communities outside prison as close. Some stressed that they knew many Muslims 'on the out' and that 'Muslims stick together' (Prison 1, Prisoner 2). But even those who regularly attended prayers did not seem to have strong links with communities associated with mosques.

Others said that the shame associated with being a convicted criminal prevented them from maintaining links with Muslim communities. For example, 'I'm the only bad fish in my family. My family are very respectable. No support from the community; I am the talk of the community. I am gossip' (Prison 1, Prisoner 5). This was echoed by Prisoner 15 in Prison 2:

> As you may be aware in our culture, we have problems, especially when someone goes to jail. It doesn't matter what you've done or not done, once you're found guilty and you go to prison, the community criticises that and they try and put you and your family down. They make it look bad. I mean, my father was a very educated man, he was a head teacher in a high school in Bangladesh and very respectable. Now, because I am in here, people sort of look at me and my family differently, think that, you know, his father was like this and he's in prison, you know what kind of family is that, but they don't really want to see the real thing, what really happened.

When we asked Muslim prisoners about their friendships before they entered prison, it was apparent that, although a minority had chosen their friends exclusively among fellow-Muslims, it had been much more common for them to be friendly with people from a range – albeit narrow – of ethnic and religious backgrounds. Friendship with 'Asians', not necessarily Muslims, was common, but about one quarter mentioned 'whites' as well.

The finding that many of our informants felt that they had learned more about Islam in prison than outside makes sense when placed in the context of their relatively weak involvement in Muslim activities and Muslim communities. Some of them, of course, had acquired the basics of their faith during childhood but they had abandoned regular prayer during their teenage years and early adulthood. And, although a small minority denied that Islam meant anything to them, many prisoners said that it was in prison that their interest in Islam had been stimulated for the first time or rekindled. For example, 'What I have learned is from reading, stuff I should've been told when younger... Most of my knowledge [of Islam] is from being in prison' (Prison 1, Prisoner 14). A more elaborate account of what Prisoner 16 in Prison 2 had learned about specific practices related:

When I was younger I never even knew how to pray. In prison when I started coming in first, I started practising my religion. I didn't know how to do two *rakat* [prostrations] *namaaz* or four *rakat namaaz*. I was just doing two *rakaat* every time and I kept doing it like that. I didn't even know what *dua* [recitation] to read on the praying and I was just doing 'Allhumdillah' and eventually in prison every time I came in I kept on practising and it seemed to, every time I do something, I just seem to learn more and more; and now I know all my prayers for my *namaaz* and know when to do how many *rakat*.

An inmate in the same prison made an interesting observation about the different aspects of Islam that are learned in the home environment and in prison:

I think I've got more understanding about Islam, because when you grow up in a Muslim family you go through the stage of going to the mosque. They do teach you how to read it, but they don't teach you how to understand it. They teach you how to read Arabic. You know, they teach you the basics, but when you come inside prison I find that you start listening to cassettes and read more books and you educate yourself really because you learn things that you never knew before; and it broadens your mind a bit more.

Only two of our informants explicitly denied that they had learned more about Islam in prison than 'on the out'. One of them explained that 'I'm very cautious of getting too deep into it when in prison, I've seen many that become Sufis, and the minute they're out they lose it all. At the end of the day, it's just for myself, something will be part of me' (Prison 3, Prisoner 7). Nor did the others all claim that the experience of prison had produced a major change in their attitude towards Islam, but there was no doubt that being free from certain distractions and simply having the time to think had boosted many prisoners' increasing interest in their religion. In the words of a white convert to Islam, 'I've been given the opportunity to sit and read and to practise' (Prison 3, Prisoner 6).

In short, the picture that most of our informants painted of their life before entering prison did not give pride of place to the practice of Islam, to Islamic knowledge or to active involvement in Muslim community affairs. Their choice of friends also suggested that their life had not been lived exclusively in Muslim circles. On the contrary – and with some exceptions – they gave the impression that it was in prison that the practice of Islam had assumed greater importance for them and that their relations with fellow-Muslims had been strengthened. Their performance of individual and congregational prayers, their reading of the Qur'an and other Islamic texts and their attempts to avoid pollution from unclean or illicit [*haram*] food or conduct had all increased in prison, thereby sharpening their sense of identity as Muslims. The remainder of this section will try to establish the factors that had a bearing on these changes.

Prison conditions and categorisation

To begin with, we need to remember that prisons in England and Wales are subject to a large number of rules, regulations and administrative procedures intended to monitor the ethnic and religious composition of the prison population, to detect and punish unfair discrimination and to produce equality of opportunity. Leaving aside for the moment all questions of the effectiveness of these devices, prisoners are aware that ethnic and religious issues enjoy a degree of importance that is considerably higher than in any institution 'on the out'. They also know that these issues are sensitive. Indeed, 'playing the race card' – or mischievously seeking advantage on spurious grounds related to 'race' – is a strategy that depends on having this knowledge. Similarly, it might be thought that prison staff could use the statistics of ethnicity and religion in order to generate change. As Officer 10 in Prison 1 acknowledged, however, it is not enough to know the statistics – someone also needs to act on them:

> I pointed out that there were hardly any Asian prisoner cleaners and I managed to get them more jobs. About two years ago I worked out the job allocation; it transpired that Asians weren't getting the jobs. This has changed now, I personally pushed this issue.

Yet, whereas it is established that ethnic statistics are meant to ensure equal opportunity, ethnic markers are taken into account only selectively by prison authorities. For instance, a number of documents are translated into foreign languages, and foreign language books are supplied in prison libraries. But only a few measures generally cater for the cultural habits and diets of prisoners from minority ethnic groups: curries may be provided, but Caribbean food is not much in evidence despite the relatively high number of prisoners of Caribbean origin. This did not escape the notice of Officer 4 in Prison 2:

> We have a large Afro-Caribbean population, for example, yet we don't have a large Afro-Caribbean choice of food. I mean I know that's difficult but when you're operating an establishment that has something like 40 per cent Afro-Caribbean, then you really should be thinking of supplying yams and sweet potatoes and one thing and another.

There are exceptions to this: in one of the female prisons that we visited, Jamaica's national day is celebrated in collaboration with the embassy, and a Spanish Mass is conducted for the benefit of Spanish-speaking inmates. The Imam in Prison 1 also noted that the regulations which stipulate a certain diet for ethnic minorities were not applied satisfactorily:

> Muslim inmates have double punishment. One, they are serving their sentence, and the other because they are not having food that they are used to. And I think the law does, there is a PSO or something, which says that their habitual diet or the diet they are used to, because it's not cooked properly, so obviously the end result is, although it may be *halal*, but it's not appropriate for them.

From the standpoint of many Asian prisoners, however, ethnicity does prevail where diets are concerned; for instance, food intended for Muslims is not assessed only in relation to its *halal* quality. It is also challenged if it fails to meet the standards for an adequate curry. It was a catering officer in Prison 1 who pointed this out: 'One of the curry days when a certain officer is on he puts too much turmeric in which makes the curry bitter'.

Curry thus figured on the menus of the prisons that we investigated; it incarnated 'ethnic' food *par excellence*. It could be argued, however, that curries are simply part of the typical British diet these days, since they have been shown to be the most commonly eaten dish in Britain. This is so much the case that non-Asian officers and inmates often compete for the curry dishes on the menu in some establishments. The boundaries between ethnicities are therefore porous and movable in prisons where people from widely different backgrounds are forced to live in close proximity to each other.

In fact, prison staff often collapse the 'Asian' and 'Muslim' categories into each other, as testified by the practice of showing so-called 'Muslim' films that African-Caribbean Muslim prisoners complain about because they cannot understand the Hindi or Urdu languages in which the films were made. According to Officer 4 in Prison 2,

> A lot of the English guys or the non-Muslims will complain about the film, including some of the Afro-Caribbeans who are supposed to be

Muslims but who obviously don't speak the language so they don't...
they can't relate to it.

This is part of the wider problem that prison staff have of not being able to
distinguish easily between Muslim and non-Muslim Asians. Officers
reported variously to us, 'Can't distinguish them' (Officer 8, Prison 1) and
'Wouldn't have a clue' (Prison 3, Prison Officer 8). However, officers can
generally find out who the Muslims are in a variety of ways: if they escort
them to prayers or when they find the Qur'an in their cells; officers who
have worked abroad in Muslim countries claim that they can identify
Muslims by their names. Among Asians themselves the differentiation is
clear; an Asian officer went so far as to claim that he could easily spot the
Muslim inmates by their 'facial expression and mannerism nine out of ten
times' (Prison 1, Prison Officer 10). But the same officer readily fell back on
a broad Asian category/identification when talking about his treatment of
prisoners:

> I tend to look after the Asians better than the whites though [...] when
> I first started, there were hardly any provisions for any Asians, let alone
> the Muslims. They had the basic session for the Sikhs and Muslims and
> Hindus; now there are more Asian officers, so the Asian inmates, they've
> someone they can talk to if they wish to.

Some establishments where prisoners have to share cells permit Muslim
inmates to 'pad up with' fellow Muslims. All our informants in Prison 1, for
example, expressed a preference for this arrangement, and it clearly serves
as a public expression of identification on the basis of religion and/or
ethnicity. The policy does not meet with universal approval, however,
among prison staff. For, whereas many prisoners saw it as a practice that
not only confirmed their Muslim identity but also protected it against
various threats, some prison officers and governors regarded the practice
as an unhealthy form of 'ghettoisation'. For example, the Substitute
Christian Chaplain in Prison 1 was generally in favour of allowing Muslims
to 'pad up', but at the same time he wished to avoid 'segregated wings'. He
confirmed that 'the most common complaint I receive from Muslims is
regarding wishing to be "padded up" with a fellow-Muslim'. By contrast,
when a group of three prison officers in the same prison had a discussion
with the researcher, they expressed concern about 'padding up' because it
was open to abuse and was contrary to 'the spirit of integration'. They also
considered that it was an unfair privilege for Muslim inmates. Moreover,
there was a suspicion among some prisoners that officers used the prospect
of permission to 'pad up' as a device for manipulating them.

The two main advantages for Muslim prisoners were that 'padding up'
helped to foster solidarity with like-minded people and reduced the likelihood of disputes with non-Muslim cellmates who might, deliberately or

otherwise, offend Muslim or – more accurately – cultural sensibilities about, for example, nudity, sexually explicit posters or photographs, pork-based snacks and the use of in-cell toilets. In the words of a Muslim who had to share with a non-Muslim, 'Would prefer Muslim. I'm with a white lad, and he's fucking dirty. Manners are dirty, smell of food, way they talk. They smell, vulgar. End up having a fight. Had a shit and didn't wash his hands' (Prison 1, Prisoner 23). Another Muslim prisoner in the same establishment alleged that 'Gorahs piss everywhere. They have dirty pictures, disgusting smells' (Prison 1, Prisoner 4). Noise was a further cause of dissatisfaction – in shared and single cells – as in the case of Prisoner 18 in Prison 1:

> [Non-Muslims] used to turn up the radio or TV high when I was praying. I used to put ear plugs in because there was no point in complaining to officers because they were two-man cells, and I didn't want to cause any friction. In Wakefield I had my own cell and I used to put up a notice on my door so I wouldn't be disturbed when praying. I also didn't like the smell of pork.
>
> When I came I was padded up with my cousin, which was OK. Now I'm with a non-Muslim and I explained that he can't keep walking past me whilst I was praying. Once I explained, he was OK (Prison 1, Prisoner 16).

Conversely, some Muslims were concerned that they might annoy non-Muslim cellmates with their early morning prayers: 'I'm with a non-Muslim who doesn't like me praying in the morning, so I don't do it' (Prison 1, Prisoner 12). In some other cases, Muslims sharing a cell also felt less exposed to the risk of attacks. Others complained that their requests to 'pad up' had been ignored or rejected. For example, 'Pad mate is suicidal; and because he causes problems for officers I get ignored. I've put in requests to be with a Muslim but they don't pay any attention to it' (Prison 1, Prisoner 20). A prisoner who had lived in shared cells in a previous prison recalled phoning his solicitor and warning him that 'the screws better put me in a cell with a Muslim' (Prison 3, Prisoner 5). A more positive reason for 'padding up' with fellow-Muslims was given by Prisoner 2 in the same establishment: 'All stick together. Older ones teach you how to change your life. The Governor helped us, got us to share pads'.

Ethnic categorisation is most apparent in the stereotypes that prison staff deploy. For example, Asians are perceived as more docile, while Black prisoners are said to be quarrelsome and aggressive. According to the Lifer Governor at Prison 3, Asians tend 'not to be a problem'. These attributes are usually identified by prison staff independently of inmates' religion, but as Officer 9 in Prison 3 pointed out, the intersection of ethnicity and religion can give rise to confusion:

> For most of the Asian Muslims it doesn't cause an issue, the only time is with Black prisoners who have converted; sometimes they invent things

and think it's because they are Black. If they challenge me I say 'prove it'.

This is the prevailing view except in one instance when a prison officer found that Muslims were noisier than Christians during their collective prayers. The stereotype of Asians as quieter might be undergoing modification, however, as explained by Officer 3 in Prison 1:

> We very frequently hear, 'We don't speak English'; on a regular basis they use this as a tool, regarding discipline. Over the years they [Asians] have been more conformist as a group, but it is not necessarily the case now. They used to be more servile; there is more resistance than in the past; it's across the board but it shows more with ethnics.

Some Muslim prisoners were no less willing than officers to deploy demeaning ethnic stereotypes when trying to locate the boundaries between Asian and white inmates. For example, Prisoner 4 in Prison 1 claimed that Muslims needed money for phone cards because 'we love our families too much. *Gorahs* spend it on drugs and they don't have phone cards'.

Multi-layered group identification

While many prison officers were content to use all-inclusive categories such as 'ethnics' or 'Asians', our research unearthed plenty of evidence that Muslim prisoners and other, non-Muslim Asians also have ways of identifying themselves more carefully according to sub-categories which may act as the basis for conflicts. For example, there was a fight in Prison 3 between rival groups of Muslims who took different sides in relation to the issue of Kashmir. Another line of division among Asian inmates followed the contours of regional and tribal loyalties in Pakistan. For example, a prisoner who described himself as a 'Mohajir Pathan' who had been brought up in Karachi, said that he could not get on with Mirpuris, despite being a Pakistani Muslim like them: 'In prison Pakistanis hang out together, and amongst them the majority are Mirpuri. I can't get along with Mirpuris, so there is a split between attitudes, not ethnicity, but I can't get on with them' (Prison 3, Prisoner 18).

Furthermore, the processes of identification among Muslim prisoners are multi-layered and based on a variety of criteria. The two main criteria that they use are ethnic and religious. Statements about their self-identification rarely stressed the Muslim aspect on its own but sometimes gave it priority: 'First Muslim, Kashmiri or Pakistani second' (Prison 1, Prisoner 6); or 'Muslim, then possibly Bangladeshi' (Prison 2, Prisoner 15). On rare occasions the term 'Muslim' was left out altogether, as in the case of the inmate who unhesitatingly declared that what made him was being

'Jamaican' (Prison 3, Prisoner 14). While 'Muslim' figured as a regular identifier for prisoners, they generally qualified it with an ethnic marker. For example: 'Kurdish Muslim' (Prison 3, Prisoner 4); 'Muslim. Lahori-Pakistani' (Prison 3, Prisoner 16).

Contrary to some reports of changing patterns of self-identification among young Muslims in the UK (Modood, 2000), we encountered very few Muslim prisoners who would freely choose to describe themselves as 'British Muslims', although many had been brought up in Britain. Indeed, several explicitly rejected this possibility: 'I am Sunni Pathan. Even though I was born here I don't feel British. People judge you on the colour of your skin' (Prison 1, Prisoner 8). If national identification was generally rejected by Muslim inmates they often seemed keen to affirm their local identification and attachment to the area where they had grown up – sometimes in conjunction with their country or region of origin.

More seriously, there was also friction in one establishment between Asian Muslims and prisoners who were described by Prisoner 15 in Prison 2 as 'African Jamaican people'. He claimed that 'a lot of these people' abused Ramadan 'just so they could take drugs or whatever'. Another of his complaints was that the same prisoners acted badly in Friday prayers:

> They are talking, they are sitting in the back row while everybody else is praying. You can't hear the Imam, with his prayers, you can't hear the lecture, all sorts of things. But nothing has been done about that. I've had a word with the Imam as well, and he said 'Well, if somebody wants to be a Muslim I can't stop them'. But they just come there to distract people and that wasn't right, because they destroyed our time, as a peace loving time for an hour or two for us, and that was affected badly as well.

Another Muslim in the same prison was critical of the Imam for 'spending most of his time converting Black Muslims' who allegedly had little understanding or appreciation of Islam (Prison 2, Prisoner 20). In his own words,

> Most of the guys that are coming to Muslim service don't actually know a word of Islam, they don't know the first *kalma* [prayer], they don't even know the meanings. All right, they turn them into Muslims, they call themselves Muslim; but when it comes to the faith, they don't even have a clue about it... They haven't got a clue what they're saying to people. One person stands up, they all stand up. I mean, they should at least have evening classes or Muslim classes where they could at least come and practise Islam, read it in Arabic or English or whatever.

These critical comments reinforce the argument that the quality of Imams working in prisons is of crucial importance. In the words of the General Secretary of the NCWMP, prisoners

> ... wake up to the fact that they're Muslim; and they start to search and read. And they ask a lot of questions; they want to ask many questions about the faith, about what is a 'must' and what isn't a 'must' and what is recommended. And their first point of contact is the Imam. If the Imam is not equipped to deal with this... (interview, London 26th June, 2003).

Indeed, it was not uncommon for prisoners to complain about the ignorance of Muslims who had never learned the correct procedure for prayers.

> They need educating about what to do when someone is praying, not to come before them, not to talk in front of them. This all goes on here, and that is why I am upset and haven't been going to Friday prayers for two to three weeks. I said to another Muslim there that my prayers are being broken by others stepping in front of me (Prison 2, Prisoner 19).

This particular prisoner also criticised his fellow-Muslim inmates for being 'very bad. I have seen some that eat pork, and they swear all the time... A lot are on drugs, and I don't keep relations with people involved in drugs'. But the most comprehensive doubt about the fraternal solidarity of Muslim prisoners was voiced by Prisoner 3 in Prison 2, a Turk, who admitted:

> To be honest with you, all right, they're Muslims, but most of the guys are Muslims when they want to be – just that they come and pray and they think it's all about that. Just because they are saying *As-Salaam-Alaikum*, that makes them Muslim. Most of the guys are like that, you know what I mean, all they do is come and pray. But being Muslim is not just about praying or saying *As-Salaam Alaikum*. I mean, when we were in Muslim prayer services, the Imam always advises us, you know, how Muslims should be and prepares you. To be honest, I think he is doing a good job... And most of the guys over there are like, 'Yeah, we all believe in this, we all believe in that, we agree with what the Imam says'. But that is just in there... When you're in the mosque, everyone's like 'Brother' and this and that, but when you get out, when you step out of that mosque, it's a different story. Everyone is for themselves, not all the guys, but some guys.

Age divisions were also a sensitive issue for a few Muslim inmates such as Prisoner 10 in Prison 1, for whom 'Younger ones are terrible. Younger Muslims don't make any sense. Older Muslims are OK. Younger ones are trouble makers and try to abuse the system. The younger generation are into drugs'. There was support for this opinion among prison officers as well. Generational friction led to violence in the case of Prisoner 12 in Prison 2 who had shared a cell with a Muslim, but:

> I wanted to hit him, because he used to smoke drugs behind my back, and when I came back in the cell I smelled it. I told him once, because he was younger, I said he should stop using drugs. 'I sell drugs; I can also use them'. 'But if you use them in this cell I will throw you out. I won't let anyone smoke'. I said 'It's OK, for you don't have any children or family to care for; if we have a search they will nick us both'. I wish to go home, I want to live a clean life.

In short, Muslim prisoners, as a category, are far from being homogeneous or uncritical of one another. Divisions among them follow the contours of nationality, language, skin colour, age and morality. In turn, these differences reinforce some prisoners' sense of what 'real' or 'true' Muslims are like.

In spite of the fault lines and tensions that fracture the category of 'Muslims', however, our research uncovered extensive evidence of mutual support and co-operation among the majority of Muslim inmates. In fact, the combination of self-identification processes and the prominence officially given to ethnicity and religion in prisons helped to forge distinctive patterns of sociability and solidarity among many – but not all – Muslim inmates. The range of practices extends from simple gestures of mutual recognition and greeting to more considered strategies for common protection. The opportunities that Muslim prisoners have for practising and celebrating their solidarity are equally varied, ranging from Friday prayers, through 'padding up' with fellow-Muslims in shared cells, to celebrations of Eid festivals. Not all our informants agreed, but there was clear evidence to support the frequent claim that 'Muslims tend to stick together' – subject to some of the complications that will be examined next and to the division between the 'main' prisoners and the 'vulnerable prisoners' (VPs) who need special protection.

Again, the intersection between ethnicity and religion is the main complicating factor. Leaving aside small groups of, say, Bosnian, Kosovan or Turkish Muslims, the two main groups of Muslims in prison are Asians and African-Caribbeans. On some occasions ethnic categories have primacy, while the religious marker generates a broader basis for social interaction. This can lead to confusion. For example, 'All Muslims stick together. Blacks are in one section, whites in another. But Blacks do tend to stick with Blacks; but they do socialise with Muslims' (Prison 1, Prisoner 3). In other cases the ethnic marker almost makes it difficult for an individual or a group to be accepted by other dominant groups of Muslims: 'With us Blacks, we are not easily identified as being Muslim by Asians' (Prison 3, Prisoner 9). There are also cases in which ethnic identification clearly takes precedence over any religious belonging. For example: 'All Asians hang together' (Prison 1, Prisoner 11). 'Yes, on the exercise yard you get Pakistanis, Blacks and whites. You won't see them on their own, they stay in groups, South Asian group rather than Muslim group' (Prison 1, Prisoner 12). 'Black and Asian cricket teams, based on nationality. It's not racism. You have a good laugh, no problem' (Prison 1, Prisoner 4).

Asian prisoners, amounting to 3 per cent of the prison population in 2002, interacted most intensely among themselves in spite of the fact that they were associated with religions that were hostile to each other in some parts of the Indian subcontinent. In one of the prisons studied, where Asian Muslims were the largest minority group, most Muslims were of Asian origins; and most Asians were Muslims. It might be thought, therefore, that Muslims did not need to incorporate non-Muslim Asians in their social networks, but one inmate suggested the opposite, 'On our wings all the Asians stick together, even Sikhs' (Prison 1, Prisoner 6). An Asian inmate who said that his roots lay with his father's religion, Islam, thought that the Asian correlation was a positive one for historical reasons. He explained his position in terms of his hostility to British imperialism: 'Yes, we are all mixed here, Hindu and Muslims, Asians, Hindus and Sikhs. I hate all association with British Imperialism' (Prison 1, Prisoner 7).

The salience of ethnicity in the prisons of England and Wales affects not only Asian prisoners but also Black inmates, the majority of whom are of African-Caribbean origin. Black prisoners constituted 15 per cent of the total prison population in 2002.[1] Approximately 16 per cent of Black prisoners are registered as Muslims. Nevertheless, our evidence shows that the tendency is for Black prisoners to identify themselves primarily in terms of their ethnicity. For example, a Black prisoner, born in Britain of African-Caribbean origins, was clear that 'ethnic groups are stronger than religious groups. Most Muslims are Asian, but Blacks stick together regardless of religion' (Prison 1, Prisoner 15). This perception may be related to the fact that some Asian Muslims are prejudiced against Black prisoners – especially those who convert to Islam in prison. Certainly, our informants gave the impression that interaction in the exercise yards was structured more by ethnicity than by religion.

Language is another factor that cuts across ethnic and religious categories – in prisons no less than in wider society. South Asian Muslim informants, for example, often used Urdu terms to refer to their in-group as '*apna*' (our people) and to white outsiders as '*gorahs*' and Black outsiders as '*khaleh*'. Linguistic differences place limits on possibilities for interaction, and this means that some Muslim prisoners feel isolated, as this African-Caribbean convert to Islam explained: 'Muslims, yes there are groups, but because I don't speak Arabic, Urdu or Punjabi, it's easy to be isolated' (Prison 3,

Prisoner 1). In addition to linguistic differentiations, a Muslim Palestinian did not find much in common between him and the Asian group in his prison on cultural grounds. He felt that there were simply too many 'different customs' between him and them. This feeling was reciprocal, since Asian Muslims also perceived him 'as different, as white' (Prison 3, Prisoner 12). This is a typical reflection of the British race relations paradigm which is intrinsically based on skin colour. It means that this unfortunate 'white' Muslim must suffer the consequences of a situation structured mainly by crude considerations of skin colour: both the other Muslims (mostly Asians) and the prison structures exclude him:

> I am also subject to racism and prejudice from Muslims, based on ethnicity. There's a group for racial minorities that the Imam chairs. I can't attend because I'm white. I want a group for Muslims only. I'm ostracised as white Muslim (Prison 1, Prisoner 6).

The interplay of ethnic and religious bases for interaction and solidarity is influenced by the composition of the population in each of the prisons that we studied. For instance, the prisoners in one of them had such a wide diversity of national origins that a 'miscellaneous' collection of Muslims who were neither African-Caribbean nor Asian nor white tended to congregate together. One of them, a black inmate from Eritrea, also mixed with African-Caribbeans:

> It's like most of the Indians stick together, most of the white boys stick together, and most of the black boys stick together. Do you know what I mean?... Yeah, African-Caribbean, I mix with them, me, because I'm black as well; but Asians they've got their own groups, you know what I mean? We speak to them, say 'hello', you know what I mean? But they stick with their own Asians, you know what I mean? (Prison 2, Prisoner 2).

When the interviewer asked him whether language was also a factor, his reply confirmed the point that solidarity can emerge from the sheer diversity of national origins and languages represented in a single prison:

> Yeah, I speak a different language as well, but in here there are a few Turkish Muslims, a Somalian, a Moroccan or Algerian. Us lot stick together. If I'm not with them I'm with the blacks [Interviewer: but is this because they are on your wing? Are there other Muslims on the wing who you don't hang out with, and why not?] They have got their own group; up here it's different, only one of our friends is downstairs... We do our own thing, and they do their own thing really. We speak to them and that but we don't really hang about together.

It must be added, however, that the tendency to form more or less exclusive networks varies from prison to prison, reflecting such things as the number of prisoners, their security classification, and the density of Muslims. Prison 1, for example, is a local prison with a sizeable Muslim population, most of whom are Pakistanis. To be more precise, many of them have their origins in the region of Azad Kashmir and live in specific areas of the nearest large city. Consequently, several of our informants had known each other before they entered prison. In this case there was a close correspondence between ethnic and religious identification; there was no ambiguity about the identity of *apnas* and *goras*. The position in our Prison 2, by comparison, was quite different because the Muslim inmates there had a greater variety of national origins and displayed differing ethnic characteristics. As a result, the Muslim prisoners were diverse and occasionally divided along these lines of difference. Differences of language reinforced ethnic divisions in this situation, particularly because some of the inmates did not speak English. In other words, the lack of a critical mass of prisoners from a similar background – in an establishment or on a particular wing – renders identification on an ethnic or religious basis much more difficult. This was clearly the case in one of our female prisons where most of the 15 inmates who attended Friday prayers were foreigners from at least ten different countries. The level of their common self-identification as Muslims was correspondingly low.

In addition, some of the prisoners convicted of the most serious crimes identified themselves partly on the basis of their association with others serving long sentences for similar offences. In fact, as Prisoner 20 in Prison 3 suggested, they may give the impression of shunning the company of prisoners who do not share their particular criminal profile: 'Lifers stick together. Twenty or so are in for importing drugs so they get on with each other. Lifers are lifers, they are good friends but you can never get close to them'. This view was echoed by Prisoner 10 in Prison 2:

> Those who have done drugs offences move with drugs offenders; and people who have done fraud like me, I did fraud, we move with fraud people; and people who do GBH [Grievous Bodily Harm] and ABH [Actual Bodily Harm] they move with other people.

This process of self-selection is not doubted by Prisoner 5 in Prison 3, but his explanation for it stresses its accidental character, 'It happens by accident. Someone is talking, and you realise that suddenly we are only gun-men in the room; drugs-man is with drugs-man; fraud-man hangs with fraud-man'.

There was nothing accidental, however, about the incidents of – sometimes violent – mutual protection that a number of our Muslim informants recounted. They were mostly occasions on which a prisoner had gone to the defence of a fellow-inmate allegedly out of a sense of Muslim solidarity. For example, 'When you find the odd racist, I have stood up for other Muslims' (Prisoner 15 in Prison 1) or 'You have unity if something happens. We stick together' (Prisoner 13 in Prison 1). More explicitly:

> There were two Serbian brothers, and I was the Muslim liaison for them. I stuck up for them because they were sex offenders and they were assaulted. My reputation was I'd batter anyone who battered a Muslim. I was assaulted with a knife; I was given two months in the block (Prison 3, Prisoner 6).

These incidents were only a few of those reported to us. They all indicate the situational character of Muslim identification. Depending on circumstances, being a Muslim may be of little significance or may be grounds for extraordinary conduct. Few prisoners in the British prisons where our research took place seemed to be continuously and strenuously asserting their Muslim identity. 'Extremists' or 'ideologues' were rarely a topic of discussion among Muslims – unlike the situation in French prisons, as we shall show in the next section.

Despite all the evidence of identification processes, self-identification practices and expressions of social solidarity, some Muslim prisoners noted that individualism was prevalent and that distrust of others was common. Their life experience undoubtedly combined with their experience of prison to make them suspicious of other people. This can work to the advantage of those members of the prison staff who seek to 'divide and rule' in their interaction with inmates, thereby ignoring the inmates' own loyalties and attachments. According to our informants, it is not difficult for prison officers to frustrate prisoners' desires to mix with their would-be associates by denying permission, re-arranging schedules, feigning ignorance of agreed arrangements, inventing emergencies, and so on. This was the experience of Prisoner 12 in Prison 1:

> When we were received, they asked for my religion. We weren't told anything. I came on C-wing (induction wing), I nearly had a fight, the screw didn't let me on the Muslim service. I made applications, and it took me three and a half weeks to get on. I used to complete applications and they come and collect them; but if a screw doesn't like you he just rips them up.

The suspicion that systematic discrimination was operating against Muslims or Islam in prison might lead some prisoners to experiment with radical or extremist currents of thought. There is certainly evidence of this in French prisons.

'Extremism', September 11th

Our interviews with prisoners, governors and staff sought evidence of extremism among Muslim inmates. Admittedly, the term 'extremism' is vague, but we focused its meaning on indications that prisoners were actively cultivating ideas and practices that sought to impose the most rigorous standards of Islamic law and morality on the whole of society. We were particularly keen to know whether the attacks on the USA on 11 September 2001 had boosted the expression of extremist views among Muslim prisoners and whether the attacks had provoked a hostile response from others.

Prison officers reported that most Muslim prisoners reacted calmly and without showing support for the hijackers, for the Al-Qaeda network or for Osama Bin Laden. Some officers had expected to encounter difficulties; and managers encouraged staff to be especially vigilant. In the event, however, 'September 11th never caused a problem' (Prison 3, Prison Officer 4), 'September 11th was no problem' (Officer 8 in Prison 3) or 'There was very little backlash following September 11th' (Prison 3, Prisoner Officer 11). A few incidents that might have jeopardised order occurred in places, but officers were quick to downplay their significance. Thus, 'I think there was a little bit of tension between prisoners' (Prison 2, Prison Officer 6) or 'There were a couple of incidents last year post September 11th. Some Muslims became vociferous and caused a bit of a problem. It has calmed down now' (Prison 3, Prison Officer 5). These incidents amounted to, for example, the use of 'inciting words regarding Bin Laden' (Prison 1, Prison Officer 6) and 'One [Muslim prisoner] had a Bin Laden poster up on his cell door' (Prison 3, Prison Officer 9). The only account of possibly more threatening responses, from Muslims and others alike, came from Prison 2 where Officer 4 reported,

> I felt that a lot of the younger Muslims became a little bit zealous in what they perceived to be the response of the non-Muslim world, and, er, there was some of the younger Muslims talking about going to Afghanistan, fighting the holy war etc., etc... And from a non-Muslim point of view there were a lot of people saying 'Let's beat the shit out of the Muslims'.

A similar incident was reported in Prison 1 by the RRLO, who had to warn two Muslim prisoners against shouting pro-Bin Laden slogans from their cell windows. The governing Governor was aware of only 'one silly prisoner' who shouted support for the attacks on the USA 'but staff very quickly put him out of the way, moved him on to another wing. That has gone away'. According to the Residential Manager of Prison 2, 'there were American flags being put up and pictures of, erm, I've forgotten his name – the most wanted man in the world'. In his opinion, 'There were more problems operationally when the World Cup was on, I mean racial tensions when the World Cup was on'. The RRLO in this prison explained that the Imam had played a central role in helping to defuse tension:

> When we've had an operational issue, [the Imam] has helped us out. He's very keen, and any issues are sorted out before they get too bad. For example, following September 11th we received several complaints from C-wing that a Muslim prisoner was shouting anti-American statements. I got hold of the Imam, and we interviewed the prisoner together. The prisoner accepted he was wrong. Then Bin Laden pictures were put up on notice boards and in cells; and then we had situations where staff were ripping them down. And I got wing managers to tell staff that if they've got a picture up, 'leave it and I will interview the prisoner'. I would explain, with the help of the Imam, that, 'yes, pictures are in the public domain; but morally is it right? And put them in drawers if you want'.

The Governing Governor did not regard these incidents as 'serious'. The Head of Security in Prison 3 considered that problems had actually been more severe in the aftermath of the assassination of Lord Mountbatten when hostility was intense towards the IRA prisoners who celebrated his death.

None of the Muslim prisoners to whom we spoke expressed support for the September 11th attacks or for any form of terrorism, although some of them were aware that the attitude of other prisoners and staff towards them had become harsher afterwards. Prisoner 21 in Prison 2, for example, said that he 'had a lot of arguments with a lot of people' on his landing because they started calling all Muslims 'terrorists' and 'suicide people'. Other prisoners apparently made jokes about 'killer Muslims', and discussion was heated on some wings. Prisoner 2 in Prison 3, for example, claimed that non-Muslim inmates:

> ... were trying to implicate that I was trying to make Muslim fanatics and they took the piss, calling me Bin Laden. I would go out of my cell and when I came back the newspaper would be open at a page with coverage of the Afghan war.

Another prisoner in the same establishment was mocked because of his physical resemblance to Richard Reid, the 'shoe bomber'. In addition to being saddened and annoyed by the anger and ridicule directed towards Muslims, these inmates also expressed their concern about the suspension of an Imam in a London prison for allegedly showing sympathy for Muslim extremists. Muslim prisoners made no criticisms of the response shown by the Imams in our three prisons to the events of September 11th and their aftermath.

Finally, in order to reinforce the point that solidarity on the basis of religion can produce worthwhile benefits other than physical protection, the two Muslims in our samples who had been appointed as 'Listeners' within the Prison Service's official scheme for informal self-help and counselling among prisoners, also reported that the common bond of Islam had helped them to achieve rapport with Muslim inmates who were vulnerable, anxious or withdrawn.

France

While the national Census in the UK and the Prison Service of England and Wales collect extensive statistics on ethnicity and religion, the collection of comparable statistics is strictly prohibited in France. As a consequence, official statistics on ethnicity and Islam in French prisons are non-existent. Nevertheless, there are estimates that between 50 per cent and 60 per cent of inmates have a Muslim background. Researchers in France generally agree that the number of Muslims in the whole of France is between four and five million – or between six and seven per cent of the total population. This suggests that Muslims outnumber non-Muslims in prison by about seven to one. Moreover, in two of the prisons under study, the rate is even higher with Muslims amounting to 70 or 80 per cent on some wings. In any case, the fact that more than half of the prison population is Muslim (or of Muslim background) and that the vast majority of prison officers in France seem to know little about Islam is, as such, an indication of the failure of the French prison service to adjust to this new population.

Categorisation by white prison officers

Given that France has few official agencies or mechanisms for monitoring ethnic and/or religious identities, the categorisation of Muslim prisoners is not institutionally grounded; instead, it is largely a function of prison officers' attitudes, which are themselves informed by prevalent views in wider society. Their own awareness of Islam is limited, and this means that they are primarily influenced by prejudices disseminated through the mass media. Admittedly, some prison officers have a better understanding of Islam because of their North African or Black African background but they remain a tiny minority: the figure of four out of 120 in Prison A seems to be representative.

As the position of these non-white prison officers is ambiguous in relation to ethnic and religious categorisation and self-identification, it is useful to take a closer look at their position in the prison system. On the one hand they are on the receiving end of racism and discrimination in wider society. The reason that they tended to give for their choice of employment was that they had found it difficult to obtain work in the private sector. One mentioned his Master's degree in law and the implicit racism that he encountered in the business world: he was rejected, whereas his white fellow students were hired.

> I have a Master's degree in business law [*droit des affaires*], but the financial milieu is conservative and they rejected me for a job for which I was qualified. This is why I chose public administration. I say to myself that I have succeeded in life without having really been successful. My French friends who got the same degrees have high positions in the private sector and are much better paid and have a high social status compared to mine which is looked down on in public opinion. We are called '*matons*' [screws].

Competition for most jobs in the French public sector is by competitive examinations in which the candidates' identity is not revealed. This is why these prison officers from ethnic and religious minorities had opted to take this particular route into the prison officers' profession. Some of them had even reached high levels in the prison service and had obtained positions of authority *vis-à-vis* prison officers of French descent who reacted with a touch of suspicion. Apparently, the latter did not express their suspicion explicitly but indirectly through bad moods.

On the other hand, Muslim prison officers played a much needed role in the prison system. First, they found better ways of coping with Muslim inmates than their French counterparts thanks to their cultural awareness. Second, they could convey their insights into the peculiarities of Islam to their non-Muslim colleagues. For example, during their daily prayer, prisoners can grow aggressive towards those prison officers who enter their cell without respecting their wish for privacy. Some prison officers interpret this as an obstructive attitude towards the regular inspection of cells. On many occasions, Muslim prison officers operated as go-betweens who were able to calm down prisoners who had accused prison officers of racism or of contempt for Islam. Muslim officers may also be called upon to play a mediating role between the institution and families that visit inmates. Female Muslim prison officers in particular can often communicate well with inmates' mothers. On the negative side they suffer from a double suspicion in a way that echoes the situation in British prisons. Other prison officers presume that their Muslim colleagues are too 'soft' towards ethnic minority prisoners and are likely to show favouritism. At the same time Muslim officers fall foul of Muslim inmates who often accuse them of having 'sold out'.

Moreover, ethnic tensions and racism have multiple dimensions in prison. Many black or brown Frenchmen from the DOM-TOM (French administrative departments and territories overseas, such as Guadeloupe in the Caribbean or La Réunion in the Pacific) choose work as prison officers because of high rates of unemployment in their places of birth. But this exposes them to two kinds of problem that can degenerate into racism: first, other French prison officers can give them problems; and second, North African inmates sometimes treat them as 'niggers' in the service of the 'whites'. The officers themselves can feel the temptation to be patronising towards North Africans, thus heightening tensions.

History

Non-Muslim prison officers consider 'the problem' of Islam in a historical perspective. In their view, there was no such problem as Islam in the prison service a decade earlier, but it has since become a major concern. For them, the problem of Islam is related to the imprisonment of second- or third-generation North Africans whom they refer to interchangeably as '*Arabes*', '*beurs*' or '*Maghrébins*'. They identify several problems that have followed from these changes in the prison regime and its population. On the one hand, prisons have opened up to the outside world during the last two decades. Many prisoners now move constantly between cell, workshop, clinic, sports room, classroom or open spaces during breaks. TVs in the cells have given prisoners even more independence. Prison officers considered all this as a partial loss of their capacity to control inmates and to apply pressure to them. In addition, prison officers feel that they have lost the respect that they used to enjoy among inmates. Their explanation for this new situation is that the prison intake has changed for the worse. They describe a golden past in which criminals observed the rule of honour that was accepted in their milieu so that relations between inmates and prison officers were based on mutual respect. Now, many of those in jail are *Banlieusards* [young men from poor suburbs] who do not belong to any specific cultural underground and who reject institutions, showing respect for nothing. One of the oldest prison officers who had been working in prisons for 27 years noted that 'previously, an inmate would never call a prison officer by his first name. They do it now'.

Prison officers contrast the past to the current situation whereby young men from the poor suburbs [*les jeunes des Banlieues*] are disrespectful of rules and norms in two ways: through their lack of discipline (they refuse to keep to the schedule for showers or for recreation) and through their language of abuse and insult (they call prison officers 'son of a bitch' [*fils de pute*] or 'mother-fucker' [*nique ta mère*]). This has become, according to one prison officer, a regular feature of prison life. Another officer attributed their behaviour to their lack of proper socialisation and the basic capacity to respect norms.

Furthermore, a major change has occurred in the last two generations of prison officers. Previously, they tended to come from an urban or rural working class milieu and they shared its culture. Many of the inmates came from the same milieu, and there was a kind of mutual understanding among them. The new generation of prison officers share their parents' working class culture but they do not share the cultural features of the *banlieues*. They face a prison population characterised by social and economic exclusion whose culture is alien to them. The reciprocal understanding between the old generation of prison officers and criminals no longer exists and has been replaced by a deeply entrenched mutual suspicion. Each side suspects the other of rejection or disrespect.

> Some 13 years ago [late 1980s], we had many more heavy criminals. But we didn't have lots of problems. They were heavily armed criminals [*gros braqueurs*] who accepted their long sentences. Now, we have to deal with prisoners from the *cités* [another word for the *banlieues* or deprived suburbs] who are doing one-year sentences or so. They cause problems. The '*gros braqueurs*' served their long sentences, and no one had problems with them. They were respected and feared by the other inmates. Now the 'young men' ['*les jeunes*', meaning young men from the *cités*] show no respect for anyone. They gang up and attack the others during exercise time.

What is thought to make matters worse is the outlook of the people from the *banlieues* who have not internalised as much as others any respect for institutions; they generally ignore legal sanctions, lack any long-term project for the future, cherish no positive hopes for their future (Khosrokhavar, 1997) and display a defiant attitude towards the law.

Young men from the *banlieues*

Islam is becoming another bone of contention for prisons and is not simply considered by many prison officers as just another religion to be coped with objectively. Prison officers generally cannot dissociate Islam from the young men from the *Banlieues*. The problem of Islam is primarily associated, in the prison officers' view, with young men from poor suburbs and with the Algerian problem which has exported radical believers and the threat of terrorism into France. This is, in turn, related to the issue of the *banlieues* through French people of Algerian descent.[2] It follows that prison officers blame this religion for the upsurge of unruliness in prison. They identify Islam mainly as the religion of the turbulent '*banlieusards*' who show no respect for other citizens.[3] This is a constant *Leitmotiv* with many prison officers. One claims:

> They insult us. It has become so frequent, they call us 'fucker' [*enculé*], 'I am going to fuck your mother', 'I fuck your wife'... They spit in our faces, with all the dangers of catching their illnesses. During the night, we hear those rude words in their cells. Sometimes they threaten us and swear 'on the head of their mother' [*sur la tête de leur mère*] that they will take their revenge.

The male *banlieusard* is perceived as the epitome of aggressive, de-socialised and disrespectful youth who is not afraid of the consequences of his acts and behaves in an unpredictable way. Local police officers in the poor suburbs share the prison officers' views:

> As individuals, there is no problem with them, but as a group, they become wild and devoid of any moral sense. All the disciplinary cases (16 this week in this building) were from these 'youths'. On their own, they are normal; but once four or five get together in a group, they start to shout: 'Son of a bitch'...

The unruliness of these young men is confirmed by another prison officer:

> There are many cases of verbal aggression. You tell them something, but you get the impression that you're talking to the wind. There are [prison] rules to observe, but many of them don't understand this. The respect between the prison officer and the prisoner has changed for the worse. The violence of the *banlieues* is brought here, into the prison.

Many prison officers do not regard these features as characteristic of Muslims in general – only of the violent *banlieuesards*. The young men from these *banlieues* are considered to be synonymous with violent young Arabs. In addition, prison officers accuse these young men of abusing the facilities at their disposal and voice a litany of complaints about them: for example, that they use the clinic to escape or to kill time; that many are on a detoxification programme and are aggressive and unpredictable; and others refuse to enter their cells because they do not like their cell mates:

> It is the young men from the *banlieues* who cause problems here. They deliberately irritate prison officers. They categorically refuse to do what they are told to do. They systematically look for confrontation. Every-one gets a quarter of an hour for a shower, but *they* stay in for half an hour. Just to wind us up. After exercise time, they refuse to go back to their cells. These are our daily problems with them.

The level of aggressiveness is out of all proportion, according to prison officers: 'They'll stab you in the back with a fork just for a cigarette. For a packet of cigarettes, they can cut you with a knife or with a razor blade'. The prison usually responds with disciplinary measures as described by one officer:

> We have a constant struggle for power with the young men from the *banlieues*. Sometimes, the prison officer gives up, and the problem comes to me as a Senior Officer. I try to reason with them. Most of the time, they don't understand, and I send them to the punishment cells.

One major problem identified by the prison authorities is the rampant presence of drugs, which exacerbates violence among young inmates. Drug trafficking within prison is recognised by the authorities,[4] but they are powerless to root it out for fear that controls might become too stringent and cause the inmates to rebel.

A final pejorative trait that prison officers attribute to young men from the *banlieues* is that they are considered as intrinsically lazy. The officers blame their families for failing to support them properly:

> But on the third floor, these people are being unduly helped by their families. They send them money; and these people get up at noon, don't work, and refuse to work. They receive their money order from the family. They spend lots of time in their cells, and this makes fights easier.

In a nutshell, the negative image that prison officers harbour of young Muslim inmates is primarily linked to their ethnicity and exclusion rather than to their religion.

Women

The preoccupation of prison authorities with young people from poor suburbs is also noticeable but less acute in the women's prison. Young women from the *banlieues* display similar patterns of behaviour and are labelled in a comparable fashion. One Director portrayed them as follows:

> Among the women under 21 years old from the *banlieues*, there is a rejection of authority at the level of language as well as in their attitude: they refuse to make their bed, to clean up their cell and to respect prison officers. Officers feel that their authority is being challenged.

These young women are perceived by prison officers as distinctly more aggressive than others: 'The *banlieusard* girls become aggressive. The others tend to abide by the rules or, when told to do so, they obey without grumbling'.

This phenomenon does not appear to have existed a few years ago and is on the increase. As in the case of young men, prison officers from the same background prove helpful; they amount to 10 out of 130 in one of our prisons. Its Director acknowledged that, 'We are happy to have prison officers of North African descent who can manage this problem better than the others'.

One feature differentiates the women's from the men's prison: according to prison officers, attempts at organising 'unofficial' collective prayers do not seem to occur in the women's section of Prison B, and proselytising is absent. On the whole, the attitude of female prison officers (there were relatively few male officers in the women's prison) towards the young women from the *cités* was not as negative as the male officers' attitude tended to be towards young men from the *banlieues*. This may be accounted for in the first place by their limited numbers: the proportion of young women of North African origin is less than 15 per cent of all female prisoners, whereas the rate for men is four times higher than the female rate. Second, the presence of female inmates from the poor suburbs is a relatively recent phenomenon.

Categories

Prison officers divide Muslims in the prison population into several categories: they conceptually separate out Black Africans, older North Africans and finally young North Africans from the *banlieues*. Neither Black Africans nor first-generation migrants from North Africa are identified as a source of problems, but the *banlieusard* young people are invariably perceived as trouble-makers.

> The tension is constantly high on the third floor where you find these young men from the *cités*. On the second floor, they all work: they are Black Africans or people from the Maghreb, a bit older than the third floor, and we have no problem with them.

Indeed, we were able to confirm that the inmates' group behaviour does not differ much from the prison officers' classification: it follows the lines of national origin, immigration status, and group identification based on ethnic cultural markers. In the words of one prison officer:

> During exercise time in prison, there are very few Frenchmen with the Muslims [most of whom are young men from the *banlieues*]. The '*Beurs*' [slang for French Arabs], the clandestine [who were arrested for entering France illegally], the Africans and the French do not mix.

The way in which inmates are distributed between prisons makes it easy for young men from the *banlieues* to gather together. They are held in their local prison [*départementalisation*] and therefore able to meet up and rebuild their gangs. This clearly demonstrates the existence of groups outside prison which are reconstituted inside on the basis of a cultural marker, especially being young men from the *banlieues* who share North African origins. Another indicator of their group identification is that they refuse to share with a cellmate who is not a Muslim.

Prison officers were happy to acknowledge that these arrangements had one redeeming feature, namely, the low representation of sex offenders among Muslims:

> Many of the Catholics are here for sexual offences [*affaires de mœurs*]. Very few [French] Muslims are here for this reason. They are drug dealers, thieves; they're on the look-out for easy money.

Islam

On the whole, the image of Islam among non-Muslim prison officers is either confused or heavily influenced by the media. It is less their experience with Muslims than stereotypes broadcast on television which provide them with their categories. This is usually (but not always) more pronounced in the higher echelons of the prison service. The main distinctions that are widely held are those between 'Muslim' (neutral), '*Intégriste*' (fundamentalist) and '*Islamiste*' (radical Muslim). Decision-makers in the prison generally regard Islam as a source of problems and adopt an *ad hoc* policy of, at best, ignoring it but of more often trying to contain it. There are exceptions to this generalisation, and one director was ready to take Islam into account by providing the Imam in his establishment with the necessary facilities to act as a spiritual guide in the daily concerns of prisoners. The problem with the prevailing distinctions (private Muslim/ fundamentalist/ Islamist) is that they tend to classify 'fundamentalism' (or '*intégrisme*') as a kind of waiting-room or preliminary for radical Islam (Islamism). This is compounded by implementing the sacrosanct policy of *laïcité* in such a way that no allowance can be made for fundamentalist, orthodox Muslims. For instance, the request for such things as a prayer rug gives rise to mistrust among prison authorities. As a result, they are forbidden on the grounds that they could be just a preliminary to potentially excessive claims that might end up in some kind of extremist arrogance. In the opinion of many prison officers, requests from Muslims are intended purely and simply to make their life difficult. They claim that inmates are not genuine believers but merely make use of Islam as a pretext for being unruly and disrespectful:

> They don't do the prayers, they don't meet the Imam, and they bother us at Ramadan (eating at different times, taking a rest or showering at the wrong time or more often than the usual three times a week). They do it to annoy us [*nous emmerder*].

The fact that many of the inmates who practise Islam in prison did not previously do so on the outside is enough to convince some prison officers, in Britain as well as France, that they are not sincere and that they are merely using religion for their own purposes. In addition, the frame of mind of many prison officers, imbued with a non-religious culture and a *laïque* outlook that is hostile to any institutional recognition of religion, makes it all the more difficult for them to grasp the religious needs of Muslims who want to meet their religious obligations as well as be recognised as Muslims. The only non-Muslim prison officer in our sample who had some understanding of Muslims' religious demands was a black Catholic from Africa who was himself a practising Christian. Most prison officers assume that young men become Muslim in order to talk to Muslim chaplains and to pass the time rather than because they are genuinely interested in the religion. They are reluctant to believe that inmates are driven by religious feelings but consider that Islam is merely an expedient for making demands. Others think that being a Muslim automatically means becoming an '*intégriste*', a 'fundamentalist', ready to be radicalised and prone to intolerance. A third group of prison officers is so deeply secular ('*laïc*' in the French sense) that they cannot understand the behaviour of people who make a public display of their religion instead of simply honouring it solely in their private life.

Converts

The lack of understanding of Islam – and the negative view of the religion – that is characteristic of prison officers also extends to their attitudes towards converts. According to Muslim chaplains, a growing number of inmates from Christian backgrounds want to convert to Islam, and each week some prisoners ask for conversion. This fact, and the absence (or rarity) of Muslims asking for conversion to other religious faiths, bothers some prison officers. This is because new converts to Islam begin to ask for the same kind of facilities as other Muslims, and this is interpreted as a sign of a deliberate attempt to annoy prison officers and to defy the authority of the institution. Indeed, officers think of converts as vulnerable people influenced, and taken advantage of, by Islamists:

> Now, the Islamists mingle with the normal prisoners and some of them, French and Catholic, convert to Islam. These new converts become disruptive [*font du tapage*]. They are supported by the Islamists.

Muslim prison officers

The views expressed above are those of white prison officers who seem to peddle prejudice based on two main grounds: the influence of the media and their insufficient knowledge both of the *banlieue* predicament and of Islam. This is confirmed by the fact that prison officers from Muslim backgrounds have a very different 'take' on these issues. Muslim officers adopt a contrasting approach in their dealings with young men from the *banlieues* because a cultural understanding exists between them and the prison officers of North African origin. Thus, they are able to intervene usefully when tension mounts in the prison. However, this does not protect them from suspicion of treachery by both sides. The experience of one particular Muslim prison officer is instructive:

> I do not share the same view as that of native French people [*Français de souche*]. My relations are somehow privileged with the Arabs [French people with Arab roots]. When I was the Director of the section holding sentenced prisoners, the prisoners of North African origin came to see me very easily. I solved their problems without taking any special

account of their origins. Sometimes, I asked for a change of cellmates for North African prisoners. I am a Senior Officer [*gradé*] and the young prison officers have to obey me. By asking to change an Arab's cellmate, I give them some extra work and they may think that I am giving some undue privilege to North African inmates. They let me know it sometimes indirectly.

Prison officers of North African origin do not share the prevalent view in France about young people from the *banlieues*; they are capable of analysing the causes of the *banlieusards'* failure and aggressiveness, attributing them to their spatial segregation in the *cités* and to their economic exclusion. One of them explains:

Young people are not all hooligans [*voyous*]. They find themselves hanging around the buildings [in the *cités*] with nothing to do and they form gangs. They look for easy money, they steal, and they sell drugs. Most of our prisoners are from the *cités* of the region. Within prison, the same gangs are re-formed. Just like the other prison [where I worked before]. There were people in it from the *banlieues* of Lille, Roubaix and Tourcoing. The recidivists know the prison inside out.

These officers also have a much better understanding of North African families. Their comments clearly demonstrated their empathy with the plight of inmates' families:

The mothers are in the forefront trying to defend their sons against fathers [their husbands] and the outside world. At first, they are aggressive towards us. The father refuses to come. The mothers are there but they don't understand administrative rules. In their view, these are gibberish ['*charabia*'], but when we begin to speak Arabic to them, they calm down. Sometimes, they call us traitors; they say we have been 'Frenchified' ['*francisés*'] too much, but we don't respond; and bit by bit, they calm down and at the end, they apologise. The others [French prison officers] would behave in an aggressive way towards them, but we understand their problems. For us, the new generation of North Africans are 'mutants': they are neither French nor Arab. The immigration project has failed. Mothers have a strong sense of failure. They feel ashamed to see their sons in prison; they feel '*hashma*' [shame], as they call it.

One Muslim female officer went further:

Mothers cry in front of us. I was touched. I had to learn how to set aside my feelings in order to help them. North African families have their own prejudices. We, as members of the police, the justice system and so on, we are unjustly criticised. Deep down, mothers do not understand why their sons are in prison. If there is any violence, they think that the other party is guilty of it. Some mothers are mystified by their sons: 'Walla, this is not my son; he hasn't done any harm', they say.

There is a major difference between the approach of the officers of North African origin and of their French counterparts. The former have an understanding of this new prison population that is caught between two worlds and that feels that it does not belong either here or in the country of its parents. The compassion of Muslim prison officers for these inmates eases communication problems. They are much closer to the mental world of these young people from the *banlieues* than are their French colleagues. North African officers are more open to these young inmates' problems, because they themselves have often experienced racism and stigmas. One male officer describes the discrimination he himself suffered:

> I joined the prison service because at that time the French extreme right [the Front National] was getting good results in the election, and there was no other place than the service for us.

The same experience of racism, the same kind of frustrations, the feeling of being unwelcome in society, all these facts equip prison officers with North African roots with the ability to reduce tension within the prison system. What they understand very well is the sensitive pride felt by these young people and how to best tackle it. They do not respond head-on, but in a cool manner that is very difficult for their non-Arab colleagues to accept: 'The young men are aggressive. I try not to become furious and I control my nerves. It's not so often that I get upset by their aggressive attitude'.

One key factor influencing the communication between these prison officers and young people from the *banlieues* is their common experience of racism. It is for this reason that prison officers who may not be Muslim but are of immigrant origin sometimes also have a privileged relation with young inmates. For example, 'I am of Cameroonian origin, and the Arab or black prisoners who have problems with the prison officers come and talk to me'.

Regarding Islam, North African prison officers have a diametrically opposed stance to that of their white colleagues: they view Islam rather favourably, as a resource which helps young people to acquire a longer term view of things:

> For the past four or five years we have seen parents bringing the Qur'an to their sons. Before that, we did not see it at all. Religion is their last hope. Perhaps, by reading the Qur'an, they'll become more balanced. I have also seen one or two examples of the Muslim scarf among the

girls who come here on visits. Religion is an investment for the future, perhaps after death. Usually, these people live in the short term; they have no projects. Religion opens up their mind to something that goes beyond their immediate life.[5]

This interpretation contrasts with that of their white French counterparts who perceive Islam as a threat, as a move towards fundamentalism or perhaps extremism. For North African prison officers, Islam is not automatically equated with obscurantism or fanaticism; on the contrary they see in it a way of answering the existential problems of people from certain backgrounds with whom they share many things in common. Non-Muslim officers have no notion of the strictly religious problems of Muslims and they attribute them to their '*banlieusard*' origins, to their making use of religion for non-religious purposes or simply to their attempt to stir things up, out of disrespect. North African officers have a sharper insight into religious issues. This is not necessarily the case because they are religiously-minded themselves. One prison officer interviewed was known among his colleagues for consuming too much alcohol, and the others did not seem particularly partial to any religion. But they had an 'ethnic' sense of Islam that allowed them to understand the demands that Muslim inmates made without attributing them solely to a confrontational attitude. The long exposition of Muslim demands which follows testifies to the prison officer's sensitive grasp of the issues at stake:

There are lots of problems for Muslims here. Many have problems with sharing a cell with non-Muslims. The others eat pork which is 'impure' for Muslims. The problem of *halal* meat is very important as well. There is no such meat here in prison. Many refuse to eat meat for that reason. The authorities refuse to serve *halal* meat. They offer a different menu whenever there is pork. But otherwise, they don't take this claim into account. They reject it in the name of *laïcité*. They have this idea that any practising Muslim is an Islamist. Another problem is the meat. Some meals are presented with round slices of meat that look like pork. The kitchen authorities certify that it is not pork, but prisoners do not believe them. Yet, the canteen tries to have a larger variety of food during Ramadan. Another problem is the ablutions. Some of them would like to have access to a shower every day for their ablutions instead of three times a week as scheduled by the authorities in this old prison. There is the Ramadan problem and its practice as well. During Ramadan, the tension escalates between the fasting Muslims and the prison officers. In our prison, there is the problem of refrigerators. Inmates could use them from May to September, and then they were removed (by the Administration). This happened only three days before Ramadan this year [December 2001]. We also have problems with the prayer room. It cannot hold more than 25 people, and so we restrict access to it as soon as we reach this number. The Catholics have a full-time chaplain here who can meet the prisoners freely. He carries a key to the cells. There are three other part-time Catholic priests as well. The Muslim chaplain is the only one for many more people here. We also have the problem of the 'bearded Muslim' [*le musulman barbu*] here. Muslims have no right to move around the prison dressed in a *djellaba* or otherwise.

Muslim radicals

There is a special category for inmates who are in prison either because they have been convicted for taking part in an 'association of criminals for the purpose of engaging in terrorist activities' (*association de malfaiteurs en vue d'action terroriste*) or because they are on remand awaiting trial or sentence under the same charge.[6] A few facts single them out from the rest of the prisoners. To begin with, the first Muslims were imprisoned under this charge in the 1990s when terrorist activities in France began to flow from networks related to the Groupe Islamique Armé (GIA). The problem had its roots in Algeria where the regime refused to recognise an electoral victory by a Muslim party. The Front Islamique du Salut (FIS) won the Algerian elections in 1992 but was barred from governing by the military establishment; as a consequence, the GIA, a radical guerrilla group, radicalised the FIS after its prohibition by the Algerian army in the 1990s. At the time, the FIS suspected the French state of active connivance with the Algerian armed forces so that radical networks transferred part of their activities to France with the aim of influencing French politics towards Algeria. In 1995 they recruited a small number of young men such as Kelkal, a Franco-Algerian, who felt alienated from French society because of what he called 'stigmatisation and racism' and had turned to Islam in order to demonstrate his rejection of society (Loch, 1995). Thus, while Islamic radicals only became a threat in most European countries after 11 September 2001, measures had been introduced in France against Islamic radicalism as early as the first half of the 1990s. By 1995, more than 200 people were imprisoned for 'terrorism'. Many were released after their trials, but some were sentenced to prison terms. After 11 September, the number of people accused of terrorism in France increased. The 11 September terrorist attacks also introduced the category of 'Islamist[7] prisoners' to the rest of Europe, whereas it had previously been specific to France.

Fifteen of the 21 inmates imprisoned on grounds of terrorism in one of the prisons that we studied agreed to be interviewed after lengthy discussions. One of their common features is their rejection of the category 'terrorist'. Some proclaimed their innocence, admitting that they had had relations with suspected activists but denying their own involvement. Others contended that Muslims were being repressed because of their faith.

The mere suspicion of terrorist activities can readily lead to an arrest. France has judges specialised in dealing with terrorist cases (five of these judges are dedicated to investigating radical Islamic activities at the time of writing) who are in a position to send someone to prison on the mere suspicion of terrorist activities. Being a foreigner usually speeds up incarceration. Given the large number of those imprisoned under this heading in the 1990s and a good proportion of those who were cleared and released, it is reasonable to surmise that this type of activity is, for social and political reasons, treated in a rather different way from ordinary crimes. Prompt imprisonment is a more likely outcome than for most other types of criminal charges.

Another distinguishing feature of Islamic radicals in French prisons is that they are in competition with Imams regarding the 'true' teachings of Islam. They undoubtedly exert an influence over Muslim prisoners, either because Imams are absent or because they are not numerous enough. But in any case, there is a feeling among Imams that radical Muslims represent a threat to their legitimacy. Since the Imams themselves are looked upon with suspicion by prison authorities (or, at least, are not treated on a par with Catholic or Protestant chaplains), this renders their position within the prison even more fragile. Imams have to show enough strength not to be treated by inmates as a mere tool of prisons and at the same time they have to be flexible enough not to be seen as 'fundamentalist' by prison officials. In this situation, some 'Islamists' (Muslim radicals) exert an undeniable influence, undermining the moral position of Imams in the eyes of some prisoners. Nevertheless, inmates display a wide range of attitudes towards Islamists.

Some prisoners reject 'Islamists' because of their inflexibility and bellicose interpretation of Islam. The latter are called '*barbus*' [the Bearded ones] by those inmates who do not accept that they are representative of true Islam but consider them as warmongers who are mistaken about the place of religion in society. Some others support Islamists in their opposition to the West because of the deterioration of the Palestinian situation; they may also cite events in Chechnya and Iraq. In their view, the enmity of the West towards Islam provides Muslims with sufficient justification to wage war, Jihad, against the Occident. Some inmates declared that they were ready to join the Palestinian and Chechen struggle against the West as soon as they had left prison. The Islamists themselves developed an idea of Western society as antagonistic to Islamic values not only in political terms but also in cultural terms. Their analysis of Western society emphasises its allegedly bestial promiscuity between men, women and sexually deviant people (mainly male and female homosexuals) compounded by the disappearance of masculine and feminine roles within the family and in wider society (Khosrokhavar, 2002). Notwithstanding this, relations between prison officers and Islamists are far from exclusively hostile. Some prison officers appreciated the ability of these prisoners to calm down others who might have become over-excited. Islamists played an arbitration role when there were tensions within prisons. They had a certain moral legitimacy in the eyes of prisoners which enabled them to intervene and pacify quarrels. In return, they were granted concessions by prison officers such as tolerance towards their 'collective prayers' in the prison courtyard.

While most Muslim radicals in French prisons in the 1990s were from Algeria (in addition to some from Morocco), they now include a wider variety of national origins including people of Lebanese or French backgrounds. The Islamists who are currently in prison also differ from those in the 1990s by virtue of their 'multicultural' universe: many of them speak between three and six languages and have spent long periods of time in other European countries. Another of their characteristics is their capacity to relativise the different cultures to which they have been exposed. Their position does not derive from traditionalism or from non-integration in Western societies. The issue is much more complex: on the one hand it is underpinned by the symbolic feeling of humiliation that Muslims experience in Western societies and on the other hand by the lack of norms in those societies. This problem may have been prevalent long before they became politically involved. Finally, Islamists usually have a higher level of intellectual and educational achievement than is common among prisoners.

On the whole, the feeling of other Muslim inmates towards Islamists is ambivalent. Many avoid them either because they condemn their attitude in the name of Islam or because they are afraid of being identified as one of them by the authorities. Other inmates, on the contrary, seek them out for answers about the Islamic way of doing things (such as prayers or Ramadan). Islamists generally play a role in prison which is not merely a function of their ideology. Many inmates admire the courage of the Islamists' efforts to shake off the yoke of Western imperialism. Muslim inmates are motivated by events in France and in other countries. The TV amply documents for them the repression of Palestinian youth by the Israeli army and of Chechens by the Russian army. For young North Africans there is a direct parallel between their own treatment at the hands of the French and that of Palestinians in Israel. This double identification makes them better disposed towards the acts of radical Muslims. Many resent being in prison as a sign of the injustice of the prison system which, to their mind, does not handle their cases impartially but punishes them, at least in part, because they are of North African descent. Racism, stigmatisation and the feeling of humiliation are counterbalanced by the Islamists who dare to do what many other Muslim prisoners are not brave enough to do themselves. This raises the radicals in their esteem.

At the same time, some inmates deplore the Islamists' failure to distinguish between innocent people and others. In other words, Islamists are esteemed because they challenge the double standards of the Western world but they are sometimes shunned or even condemned for their blind approach towards innocent people. This attitude is most evident in regard to the September 11th attacks. Many Muslim inmates deplore them. Yet, even those who refuse to accord these attacks the faintest Islamic credentials empathise with the sufferings of Palestinians, Bosnians, Chechens, Iraqis and many other Muslims. Some reject outright the idea that acts of terrorism are perpetrated by Al-Qaeda activists and are convinced that they are orchestrated, in their view, by the American secret services and the Israeli Mossad. Others accept that these attacks were directed by radical Muslim groups but consider that the Americans were simply reaping the harvest that they had sown. They do not therefore regard the attacks as morally reprehensible. Only a small minority of Muslim inmates do not feel concerned about the fate of the Palestinians or other Muslim groups in the world; they are generally older (over 40) and belong to the first generation of immigrants to the West.

A new type of 'Muslim consciousness' is developing in France. It is a process of Muslim identification which is visible in some *banlieues* and is accentuated in the closed world of prisons where the power of television is greater and where there are closer contacts with Islamists. As we observed earlier, the prison officers' categorisation of inmates straddles two main themes: the *'banlieues'* and Islam. These interweave and overlap in a way which is often replicated among the inmates themselves in the sense that their relationship with Islam is linked to their consciousness of discrimination and exclusion. This is how they define themselves.

Muslim inmates

The population of prisoners in France with a Muslim background consists mainly of young men from the *banlieues*. With the exception of radical Islamists whose group identification pertains to a certain interpretation of Islam, most of the *banlieusards* share a clear group identification based on their experience of exclusion and discrimination which runs deep in the cultures of the *banlieues*. Paradoxically, although most French prisons fail to provide institutionalised facilities for the practice of Islam, they unwittingly foster a stronger Muslim identification among inmates (as mentioned above). Such self-identification can take a variety of forms, depending on situations and individuals. We shall examine only the main tendencies among young men's self-definitions as Muslims.

The lack of institutional structures means that Islam does not constitute a standardised frame of reference. It also means that Muslim inmates do not give first priority to rituals and rules. Only a few insist on the primary importance of norms. For example, Chérif, a 20-year-old Frenchman of North African origin would like to be 'someone who does the five daily prayers, who is respectful, who has the love of others, the creatures, and who respects the rules [of religion]. Here, there are some good Muslims in prison who are correct'.

Ethical, spiritual, moderate leanings

Chérif is the exception rather than the rule. Indeed, it is more common for inmates to conceive of Islam as a guide to conduct in daily life. This is the viewpoint of Lakhdar, a 20-year-old Frenchman of Algerian descent, who associates the following characteristics with a good Muslim:

> Someone who doesn't drink [alcohol], who doesn't smoke, particularly pot, possibly cigarettes, who is a bit generous, who has a good heart with everybody. The best quality is first of all knowledge. For that, one should know the Qur'anic verses [*sourates*], history and share them with the others.

Similarly, Abdelhafid, a 23-year-old Moroccan, does not hesitate to argue that good behaviour takes precedence over the observance of religious duties. He considers that it is necessary for a good Muslim to show 'respect towards all God's creatures; and this is more important than the five pillars of Islam. One has to deal with one's own bad conduct'.

It is evident that many young North African inmates have internalised a secular conception of religion which marginalises Islamic rituals in favour of ethical considerations. Since most of them either do not know how to pray or do not practise, a moral perspective is perfectly suited to them. Some may even reduce Islam to a purely private, spiritual principle. Their religious identity stands in sharp contrast to that of radical Muslims. They are imbued with the *laïc* tenets of French culture, which has deeply influenced them. This is manifestly the case of Habib, a 34-year-old Tunisian, who declares that 'Islam is a philosophy for me and a lifestyle. I don't know if I'll keep on praying, but all of it is the result of my personal reflections'.

Morals and sprirituality are frequently presented as the hallmarks of the religion espoused by inmates from Muslim backgrounds. A kind of ecumenism characterises this tendency such as Hussein's understanding of 'the good Muslim', which brings him strangely close to the ten commandments:

> He should not kill, lie, he must respect his parents, his family, he shouldn't steal, he has to be neat. In my family, there are many good Muslims like that, like my brothers, for instance; they are not involved in politics. I have cousins who are Imams; my brothers have learned the religion well.

The definition of a good Muslim is slightly different for Aït Faska, a 28-year-old Moroccan:

A good Muslim is a preacher. We should all be preachers. You have to bring your children up well, overcome the ordeals [*surmonter les épreuves*], be respectful towards the family, the neighbours, do the five daily prayers, give without counting: in a word – be generous. Religion is peace in oneself and towards your brother and your neighbour, who is a brother as well. *Al Rasul* [the Prophet] prayed with Christians like brothers, while Muslims denounce them [today]. A neighbour is a brother as well. You should not do to others what you don't want others to do to you. God is the one who judges.

Young inmates like Aït Faska offer an interpretation of their Muslimhood which could apply to most religions and almost to humanists. In this case, religious ethics are defined in a general way, without any consideration of politics or specific contemporary Islamic problems in the world. On other occasions, morals are counterpoised to politics, particularly when they denounce terrorist violence. In the words of Habib, a 34-year-old from Tunisia:

A good Muslim is someone who does his prayers, who does good things [*qui fait du bien*], pays the *zakat* [an Islamic tax], who is not a hypocrite and is sincere, really sincere. He is someone who lives his religion in harmony with the religion of others, in an atmosphere of tolerance and not by giving it a political meaning. Politics and Islam do not go together even though, in a way, Islam is political! For instance, Islam is political in the sense that it provides a heritage for women but not in the sense of political parties like the FIS [Front Islamique du Salut] or the GIA [Groupe Islamique Armé], not politics in this sense; religion should be personal.

In a world of intolerance where Islamic extremism strives to radicalise Muslims, some, like Habib, preach the separation of religion and politics. This separation is based on an old (and perhaps unconscious in the case of the interviewee) Islamic idea in which Islam is to have a say in juridical matters but not in politics. The September 11 events in particular often provide a benchmark for Muslim ethics in the eyes of this group of inmates. For instance, Ali, a young Frenchman of North African background, not only stresses 'the right path: the faith, the qualities, not to lie, to be honest with oneself and others' but also adds as a condition of correct practice 'not to do harm to oneself and others'. Thus for a minority, the September 11 events could not be justified in the name of Islam. Younes, a 24-year-old Moroccan, is explicit about this:

It is deadly serious for me to kill innocent people like that; Islam is against it. I was shocked like the others and now I think that there are no limits to violence, and the TV has exaggerated all of this.

This opinion is confirmed by Karim, a 22-year-old French-Algerian, who despite his sympathies for Palestinians and Afghanis unreservedly condemns the terrorist attacks on the Twin Towers:

This [September 11 terrorist attacks] should not have happened [*ça se fait pas*]. There are many innocent people. The USA exaggerates [*en rajoutent*] too, but Bin Laden is a killer. The Palestinians, they are right and the Americans, as well, in this case. Bin Laden is a Muslim and he knows that killing an [innocent] person is *haram*. A good Muslim helps the poor; it is symbolic. If it is Bin Laden who has done this, for me he is not a Muslim. On the other hand, the Americans are making too much of it [*en font trop*], with the bombing of Afghanistan. If they catch Bin Laden, it won't change anything; his colleagues will carry on.

For a few inmates like Hamid, Islam is understood in an open manner. He rejects *intégrisme* and does not accept a closed conception of religion. This option is not necessarily followed by others who opt for an *intégriste* form of religion that could help them to overcome social anomie by reinforcing ties with a closed group such as the Tabligh. For Hamid, Islam opens up to others, independently of their creed. He is not looking so much for a meaningful and closed community as for opening up to the others without any restrictions, religious or other.

Although there are numerous inmates who stress morals rather than rituals in Islam, only a few unreservedly denounce violence. The general tendency among young people from the *banlieues* favours a more positive stance *vis-à-vis* radical Islam and Jihad.

Radical sympathies

The social and ethnic discrimination suffered by young inmates of North African origin provides the bedrock for their self-identification with radical Islam. A broken life, the perception of disappointment in a Western country which has not given Muslims a chance, the feeling that the powerful of the world have conspired against Muslims, compassion for those Muslims who have to endure a desperate situation in a ruthless world – all this feeds their sympathies for Bin Laden. In their eyes, Bin Laden has symbolically inverted things to show that the 'wretched of the earth' are oppressed by the Americans. This makes him a hero. In their view, Bin Laden has shaken the Arabs awake and has dared to do what others dreamed of doing without having the guts to do it.

The 'hatred' derived from their plight in the poor suburbs, the mixture of a TV-induced culture and the impunity enjoyed by seemingly corrupt politicians are at the root of this Jihad that inflames some young men against the USA. Others are more or less radicalised and preach a Holy War against all Western countries. They draw a parallel between their own situation and that of Muslims oppressed in other parts of the world. They feel that Muslims are mistreated all over the world; Afghanis by the Americans, Chechens by the Russians, and Palestinians by the Israelis in the same way as they themselves are mistreated by the white majority. The role of television is paramount; it acts as an 'amplifier' showing spectacular images of how Muslims are mistreated by an arrogant America all over the world. In this respect, the attitude of young Muslim men from poor suburbs in France is no different from that of discontented young men in Muslim countries; and this unites them in their rejection of America which symbolises the arrogance of affluence towards Muslims.

Watching television images of Palestinians in Israel reminds these young Muslims only too well of the humiliation suffered by the marginalised or the excluded in France. The Israeli soldier becomes the model of the French (or European) citizen who despises Arabs in France. The only dignified option they can envisage is to become violent and to humiliate their despisers in return. Violence becomes a legitimate means for them to defend the religion of Allah against 'Infidels' who abuse it. They are rediscovering the path identified by Fanon (1975) and Memmi (1972) for the colonised peoples of North Africa and for the violence that sprang from their oppression. Hassan perfectly illustrates this response:

> France does not respect Islam. Therefore, we need a Jihad against it. A good Muslim prays, believes in God, does good things [*fait le bien*], in a neat way. There are many people like that. But the USA and Europe make us dirty! [*nous salissent*].

Some Muslim inmates in French prisons emotionally swear that they will readily volunteer to fight on the fronts where Muslims are under assault when they are released. Others, like Dalmani, a 25-year-old Franco-Algerian, adopt a more analytical stance and attempt to explain the reasons for the young inmates' attitude; he notes that one should not kill innocent people but he attributes the burden of guilt to the USA first and foremost:

> You shouldn't kill innocent people, and the Americans do it to the people of the OLP [*Organisation de Libération de la Palestine*] or in Afghanistan. They sell their tanks to the Israelis to kill the Palestinians. Bin Laden does not do it for money, he is already rich. With their politics, the Americans create 'hatred' [*la haine*]; what Bin Laden has done is not good, but he has paid for it as well. It is better to attack the State. The USA does serious things everywhere, on the sly. One should alert people to it so that they know all these truths. Perhaps the nice guys (or those who appear to be nice) are the bad guys, even worse than that. Afterwards, I find it normal that there are people of North African origin who go to Afghanistan [to fight against Americans]. Young people

don't have any plans, they have nothing... Some people come to recruit them, they talk well, promise them many things, and so they sacrifice themselves. This is religion. If you're attacked, you'll attack. They kill us gently [*à petit feu*]. There is religion in it, but it's mainly the hatred they have in them which pushes them to go to Afghanistan. The hatred is born on TV: they show the injustices every day: politicians don't ever go to prison...

Dalmani thinks that the real issues have been deliberately muddled and need to be clarified: the Americans are not the good guys they purport to be; the young men's eagerness to fight in Afghanistan is born out of their frustration and hatred [*la haine*]. 'They kill us gently' says Dalmani about the routine treatment of Muslims in their everyday life. Thus, in his opinion, Muslim violence is induced by the daily violence wrought on them.

Aït Faska adds more substance to this analysis by identifying the undeclared material interests at stake for the Americans. He attempts to hold a balanced view of the US versus Bin Laden but in the last analysis sides with the poor and the oppressed. In this he is representative of young inmates of North African origin who emotionally identify with the plight of Muslims worldwide. This is how he puts it:

Are [terrorist attacks] right or wrong? I would say both. The USA hold Bin Ladin for a *Sheytan* [Devil]... They attack Bin Laden because he is one of the princes of Saudi Arabia, and the US have sullied this Holy Land with their military bases. The story is much broader: the US support the Jews. God only knows what really happens. There is a question of oil in all of this as well, the diamond mines. It's a story of dough [*pognon*]. Bin Laden, I envy him because he is with the poor and Palestine. In this respect, yes [I support him]. The Israelis shoot at Palestinians. When I see this on TV, my heart bleeds as if it were me who was hit. They prevent them from praying where the Prophet David prayed [in Jerusalem]. It is a war of tanks against stones. As the Qur'an says, they are afraid of dying. The Jews are wrong, they want to slander us. This, I don't accept.

Two themes run through the accounts given by North African inmates in French prisons: injustice and humiliation. They deplore the injustices suffered by Muslims and they approve of the just punishment incurred by the USA. In the last analysis they deem the USA responsible for the innocent casualties in the Twin Towers. The following comments accurately depict these widespread views:

For the Palestinians, the situation is grave. It is injustice that calls for the attacks. I can understand the Kamikaze Palestinians. I wouldn't do this but I understand them; and the guilty people are those who have pushed them into this situation. As for the attacks on America, I regret the innocent loss of life, but it is good for the humiliation of the Americans... The injustices that exist in Palestine, Iraq, Pakistan and Afghanistan won't last for ever. God will prevail.

But the Americans deserve it. They think they are the Lord of the world. They have been humiliated. Nobody is subordinated to anyone else.

Hocine sums up the events of September 11th with the phrase: 'They [the USA] have reaped what they sowed'.

The humiliation of the USA is repeatedly cited as retribution for the humiliation constantly suffered by Muslims. Omar, a 40-year-old Frenchman of North African descent, vents his resentment with:

I feel abandoned, cheated. They made me believe in [wonderful] things. I was told that I could be successful in France. But all this is false, all of it. In fact, there is fierce competition. You need a social title [diploma] to succeed. Me, I have learned only a bit of English and I use it to talk to my Muslim brothers. Islam is my second family. Faith is in the heart and it gives enough light to see things clearly. As young people of Arab origin, we have always been mistreated in every respect; there was nothing for us, and it's even worse now for the young generations. This is why, with all the injustices that happen to us everywhere and which are getting even worse, it is good to have people like Bin Laden awakening the masses. The Arabs are asleep. Bin Laden is a model for me. When I think of the miseries of the Chechens among others... I see how Bush's commitment to combat so-called terrorism is exploited by Israel and Putin's Russia. Muslims are given no chance... I feel abandoned by everybody. Nothing holds me in this world. It is injustice everywhere. People should be woken up. Bin Laden woke them up with what he did on September 11th. Israel, *wallah*, they deserve what happens to them. I feel hatred towards the Jews [*j'ai la haine contre les Juifs*]. Sharon looks for pretexts to raze Palestine to the ground; he has a good strategy, he first of all wants to destroy all the Palestinian infrastructures and then to take advantage of the moment.

Even Benamar, who holds a more sober view of the terrorist attacks on the USA, recognises that Bin Laden is considered as a hero by many:

It was a shock; you get scared. It was like the end of the world! The media exaggerate, particularly here. The TV says that the Islamists did it, without any evidence, with no evidence at all. Bin Laden is an idol, a star at this moment for the young men from the suburbs, because of the media. But it's not good for the innocent people who are dead. It would have been much better if the attacks had been directed against the state.

And all this has its roots in Israel and Palestine. The Jews control the media and the law; and they do what they want.

Bin Laden has created the opportunity for young people of North African origin to experience some dignity, thereby counterbalancing the humiliations to which they feel that they are regularly subjected. These young men demonstrate a transnational group identification with Muslims worldwide whom they perceive as poor and oppressed like themselves. The Palestinian question figures most prominently in their consciousness. It is not merely a matter of rational or intellectual identification; in fact, this process also entails strong emotional involvements. As one of the inmates who was quoted above puts it: 'When I see this on the TV, my heart bleeds as if it were me who was hit'.

The general malaise experienced by young Muslim inmates in French prisons is exacerbated in the case of a specific group whose fathers fought alongside the French during the Algerian war of independence [*les Harkis*]. Disappointment and marginalisation are compounded for them by the shame of belonging to a traitor's family.

The worst thing is that my father was an *Harki*; it hurts me that my father was that. The French exploited him down to his last drop of blood and then they threw him away like old socks; and for that I have a deep hatred of them that will never disappear. I am the son of an *Harki*. I have suffered from this, and when I think that I am the son of an *Harki*, shit, I am disgusted. My friends said to me: 'Your mother has slept with the French'. They made dirty remarks like that. I have never been understood; the doors closed in front of me. I have always been put on the wrong side of the barrier. I think now that life is nothing but hypocrisy. They made me believe in those illusions like equal rights, those stupid things; none of it is true, it is a paper decorum. In addition to that, there is a deep malaise in many young men like me, sons of *Harkis* or not. They talk about their problems, their misery [*mal être*]. There is a *hashma* [an Arabic word for shame], a shame that France has forced on us.

Finally, Islam can also help to overcome anomy and frustration through its community networks and group identification. Even before he was sent to prison, Younes, for instance, had grown closer to a Muslim group, the Tabligh, and had come to appreciate its beneficial influence:

The *da'wa* [invitation to religion, preaching] is therefore something good, and I need it; it allows me to fight against the *Sheytan* [Devil]. Outside, in the *cité* I frequently met with groups of young men who carried out the *da'wa* for other youngsters; they came from the Tablighi

Jamaat; they did the *da'wa* in the overheated suburbs [*les quartiers chauds*, where there is violence]. This is important, no one else does it.

Tabligh is particularly active in the poor suburbs where it calls upon young disaffected people to join with proselytising Muslims and to gain in dignity and self-respect. This attitude is also found in prisons, and the sense of belonging to a community of believers becomes vital to some of the inmates because it enables them to alleviate their feelings of anomie and lack of belonging. They gain in self-confidence once their loneliness and delinquent identity give way to a new missionary feeling that transforms empty time into time filled with daily prayers; they find meaning in the active calls upon other Muslims to join the lively faith community in which born-again Muslims feel deeply engaged.

Conclusion

The prisons of England and Wales categorise inmates in terms of ethnicity and religion. An explicit anti-discrimination policy – which covers religion – is implemented by means of various measures such as: the appointment of Race Relations Liaison Officers and Race Relations Management Teams; the enactment of specific policies on racism and on Islam; opportunities for training prison officers about these issues; the appointment of full-time Muslim chaplains; the establishment of ethnic monitoring and provisions for the practice of Islam; and, in some places, practices that permit Muslim prisoners to choose to share a cell with a fellow-Muslim. The Prison Service of England and Wales undoubtedly promotes the recognition of ethnic and religious diversity. On the other hand, prisons are not isolated from the culture of wider British society which is steeped in prejudice favouring the reproduction of stereotypes such as the image of aggressive Blacks and docile Asians. It is not surprising, then, that one of the main criticisms levelled at Islam by prison officers is that it creates additional work and complications, but the strongest resistance to Islam is the widespread scepticism about the sincerity of Muslim inmates' faith. Prison officers suspect them of using religion to gain advantages. As a result, officers are keen to 'police' Ramadan without showing the same inclination to police any Christian practices.

From the point of view of Muslim inmates, processes of identification in British prisons are multi-layered, combining ethnic and religious markers, although no combination includes 'British' (that is, British Muslim) as a group identifier. Inmates have various ways of expressing the solidarity of Muslims, and their practice of Islam is usually enhanced in prison. Nonetheless, Muslim prisoners often have to contend with divisions or hostility on the basis of ethnic markers such as Asians versus Blacks, or Kashmiris (from Azad Kashmir in Pakistan) versus other Pakistanis. The most common form of identification includes all South Asians independently of their religion. Occasionally, skin colour itself may actually play a role in situations where, for example, an Arab Muslim considered as white finds it hard to be accepted in the Black or Asian groups. Altogether, the self-identification of Muslim inmates is related to the numbers and density of national/ethnic populations in each prison. The significance and salience of being a Muslim vary from one context to another.

The contrast with French prisons is sharp. They have no framework for recognising or promoting ethnic and religious diversity. On the contrary, the paradigms of universalism and *laïcité* make it unlawful to recognise any minorities – be they regional, ethnic or religious – in the public domain and in public institutions. And, as in Britain, prisons reproduce a strong cultural framework of prejudices informed by popular television programmes and reflecting the prejudices prevalent in wider society. A particularly strong stigma is attached to young Muslims of North African origin who come from the *banlieues* and who constitute the majority of inmates in some prisons. They are perceived as rude, aggressive, unruly and lazy by white prison officers and more generally by prison authorities. Islam tends to be identified with these characteristics, except that Muslim radicals are regarded differently as 'organised terrorists'. Thus, prison authorities and prison officers indict Islam on three counts. First, it is equated with difficult young people from the *banlieues*, and prison officers tend to perceive it as a means of obtaining undue advantages or as an excuse for fomenting trouble. Second, 'fundamentalist' Islam is unacceptable in prisons because its practice takes public forms that seem to make it incompatible with the principles of *laïcité*. At best, French prison officers fail to understand it and, at worst, they lump the whole of Islam together under the blanket label of Radical Islam. Finally, Islam, in its radical forms, is equated with terrorism, with all the strong emotions that this term generates. However, prison officers enjoy an ambiguous relationship with Radical Islamists on whom they rely to restore order among Muslim inmates when trouble breaks out. Muslim officers from ethnic minorities adopt a totally different attitude towards Muslim inmates. Their shared experience of exclusion and racism renders them more sympathetic to the plight of inmates. All of them, including officers who are secular, tend to perceive Islam as a positive factor helping the rehabilitation of inmates.

The sense of group-identification is strong among young Muslim inmates in France thanks to the culture of their *banlieues* which is itself steeped in the plight of social exclusion and racism best formulated as '*la haine*' or hatred. Sub-Saharan Africans and older North Africans ('first generation immigrants') do not share this culture but find other ways of getting together in separate groups. Young Muslim inmates turn to Islam in a big way in prison. The lack of institutional structures for Islam in French prisons leads young Muslim inmates to their own '*bricolage*' of Islam; they pay little attention to rituals and they formulate, instead, a kind of individualised secular version of Islam, in which they find an escape from the pain of living [*mal de vivre*] through an ethical and spiritual code. However, young people from the *banlieues* are more often drawn to Radical Islamists for guidance on Islamic practices and for inspiration on dignity because they represent the reversal of the humiliation and stigma that young Muslims normally suffer. Young Muslims in French prisons also express a transnational identification with the poor and the oppressed (in Palestine, Iraq, Afghanistan and so on). Radical Islamists constitute a group *à part*. They organise themselves to make demands for collective religious practice against the rules. In addition to articulating a clear ideology, they claim authority on Islamic matters in *de facto* competition with the very few Imams working in prison. Altogether a new type of Muslim consciousness is developing – in prisons rather than outside – among young people from the *banlieues*.

The experience of being a Muslim prisoner differs considerably between France and England and Wales. This is not to deny any similarities: it is merely to argue that they are heavily outweighed by the differences. And, as the next chapter will show, many of the differences revolve around the roles that Imams play in their capacity as prison chaplains. These differences are not just a question of how individual Muslim chaplains choose to play this role but they are also – and much more importantly – a question of how each prison system structures the opportunities that Imams have to do their work.

7
Prison Imams

Introduction

Just as Muslim inmates in French and British prisons are diverse in terms of
their background, their paths to prison and their attitudes towards the
practice of Islam, so it is important to recognise that their spiritual and
religious teachers, Imams, also conform to no single pattern. As Beckford
and Gilliat (1998) showed, there were many different routes into the job of
providing pastoral and religious care for Muslim prisoners. Many Imams in
France and the UK are products of the numerous seminaries and colleges in
Europe, South Asia, North Africa and the Middle East that train boys
and men to become Imams. Some also train women to teach Arabic and
Islamic values in a variety of settings. Their training aims to give them a
sound understanding of the sacred texts of Islam, of Islamic law and of
approved forms of religious devotions and moral life.

Many of the institutions that prepare men for the Imamate are connected with one another by transnational networks of communication
and ideological affinities. For example, the *Institut européen des sciences
humaines* (IESH)[1] in rural France and its affiliate in Wales, the European
Institute of Human Sciences (EIHS),[2] are associated with Islamic universities in Saudi Arabia, Qatar, Kuwait, Pakistan and Malaysia as well
as with some secular institutions of higher education. The initiative
for establishing the IESR and EIHR came from the *Union des Organisations Islamiques d'Europe* (UOIE) and was implemented by the *Union
des Organisations Islamiques de France* (UOIF) in 1990. Some Islamic
seminaries have distinguished histories and are revered for the authority that they exercise in interpreting points of law and theology. Others
are associated with lineages of revered theologians and legal specialists.
Most can be identified with one of the four major schools of theology
and law that structure Islamic thought. The relative standing of these
institutions has an important bearing on the weight that is attached to
the legal judgements rendered by their scholar jurists.

In the absence of any centralised organisations in Islam that resemble Christian Churches, certification of Imams carries no implication of 'ordination' into a 'priesthood' or 'ministry'. It merely signifies competence to understand – and to teach – the sacred texts as well as to conduct prayers and other ceremonies in an appropriate manner. Men who have satisfactorily completed courses of training at Islamic institutions[3] can legitimately claim the title of 'Imam', but the title is also accorded to those who lack the formal training but who can still demonstrate their competence. It is possible that the Imams working in Europe who trained in seminaries and colleges elsewhere in the world will eventually be outnumbered by those whose qualification was obtained in Europe. At present, however, it seems as if the Imams trained in Europe represent a minority, although it must be admitted that estimates of the size of this minority are based mainly on hearsay evidence. In both Britain and France, there is a determination to train more 'home grown' Imams who speak English or French fluently. Indeed, the governments of both countries regard such training as an essential aspect of their resistance to Islamic extremism as well as of schemes for integrating Muslims more effectively with mainstream society.

The arrangements that exist in each country for recruiting and deploying Imams in prisons were outlined in Chapters 3 and 4. The focus of this particular chapter will be on the ways in which Imams (or 'Muslim chaplains', as the Prison Service of England and Wales now designates them) carry out their duties in prisons and how prisoners and prison staff respond to them. In view of the greater degree of integration of Muslim chaplains in the day-to-day running of prisons in England and Wales, the first half of the chapter will focus on issues that arise mainly from the chaplains' attempts to deliver a wide range of services. Comparison between Muslim and Christian chaplains will necessarily form part of the analysis. But in the second half of the chapter the focus of analysis on the role of Imams in French prisons will take a different form. Given the exclusion of most Imams from many prison routines, our attention will centre on each of the three prisons in turn where our fieldwork took place and on the Imams' own reflections on the place of Islam in these establishments.

Imams working in the prisons of England and Wales

Since the late 1990s the National Council for the Welfare of Muslim Prisoners (NCWMP) has helped to organise seminars and training courses about the care of Muslim inmates. It has also become routine for Muslim chaplains (who were called 'Visiting Ministers' until 2003) to be invited to participate in training courses organised by the Prison Service Chaplaincy. But there are still numerous Muslim chaplains who were recruited at a time when no training was available and when they were largely dependent on Christian chaplains for basic information about how to do their work.

Similarly, the selection of Muslim chaplains used to depend heavily on the discretion and the goodwill of the senior Christian chaplain in each establishment. Nowadays, the Muslim Adviser at Prison Chaplaincy headquarters is involved in considering the suitability of individuals for appointment; and governors have taken over some of the work that Christian chaplains used to do in facilitating appointments. There is now considerably more standardisation and oversight of the selection process and of the specification of Muslim chaplains' responsibilities. Governors have found it particularly helpful to have access to information and guidance from the Muslim Adviser.

The Imams working in our sample of three male prisons in England and Wales all came to their positions in different and largely adventitious ways. The first, who had already obtained high level academic qualifications before moving to the UK, was simply asked by his predecessor in the prison whether he would like to succeed him. There was no training for his tasks. He 'learned on the job' but he eventually undertook, at his own expense, training in counselling in a college of further education. The second Imam had had an even more adventitious entry into prison chaplaincy. Having had a long association with a particular prison in a voluntary capacity, he agreed to act as its Imam on a temporary basis after the prison had failed to fill a vacancy. It was the Anglican chaplain who approached him with a request to occupy the position that had been vacant for about a year. Again, no training was provided. The third Imam also entered prison chaplaincy by accident in the first instance. He had trained for the Imamate in the UK and had been asked by a friend to deputise for him temporarily in a prison near his home. This experience encouraged him to think of prison chaplaincy as an area in which he would like to work on a regular basis. He received no special preparation or training for his work in prisons. He described it as 'hands-on initially', although he subsequently followed numerous Prison Service training courses including the initial development course for chaplains. By his own admission, 'This I should have done in the first year but I did it in the eighth year' (Imam in Prison 3).

As for the extent of their integration into the life of prisons, our Imams' experiences were varied. The longest serving Imam acknowledged that prison staff knew him quite well 'but otherwise I remain as an intruder, or Visiting Minister, and visiting person rather than part of this establishment' (Imam in Prison 1). He had waited 14 years for permission to carry keys that would enable him to move around the prison unaccompanied. It took 15 years for him to be appointed to the Race Relations Management Team, and his involvement in writing reports in connection with sentence planning and parole applications had been patchy. If a prisoner specifically requested the Imam's involvement, then he would be invited to submit a report, but prison staff made no assumption that the Imam was normally consulted about report writing. Nor did this particular Imam feel that the

Christian chaplains had tried to co-operate with him. In fact, he claimed that 'sometimes there may be hostility, sometimes co-operation'. His explanation for this state of affairs was that

> Actually, the Church of England chaplains consider themselves as the most powerful and they now feel this power is drifting away from them. They try to keep their fist very tight. It may vary, but my experience is that they have at the back of their minds that by law and statute they are here etc., etc., and they try to, because there is a clash of interests as well, you know.

The Imam in Prison 2 conducted Friday prayers each week but was unable to find more time to spend in the prison. In any case, he said 'I've never been invited by the Chaplain for anything', adding:

> I feel that, as the acting Imam and the Muslim inmates here, we are always at a disadvantage; we are always kept in the cold because, as I said, the Anglican Church is a well established organisation. They see Islam as a threat to them because every week there are at least one or two people converting to Islam... They see us as a threat, and more and more people are coming to Islam within the Prison Service, and the attendance of the Muslims on a Friday is very large indeed. In terms of when you compare that with the attendance on a Sunday, whether it's to do with the Catholics or the Church of England, attendance is very, very poor... I am very, very sad that the Chaplaincy service has never consulted me, has never made any approach to me.

By contrast, the Imam who visited Prison 3 twice a week, felt that for the previous five years he had been fully involved in the chaplaincy's work and had never been excluded from meetings of the Chaplaincy Committee. In his words, 'The chaplaincy team work very closely, share work, seek advice and are very integrated. They are very understanding and flexible'. He credited the former Anglican chaplain with helping him to integrate in the prison and to learn what was expected of him. He was permitted to carry keys after his first two months in post, and he regularly wrote reports about prisoners.

At the time of our interviews, Imams received hourly payment for their work, but there were no provisions for paying them during sick leave or holidays. More contentiously, arrangements were uneven for appointing deputies or substitutes who could replace Imams when they were absent. *Ad hoc* arrangements had to be made in two cases, whereas a Substitute Muslim Visiting Minister had been appointed in Prison 1. Indeed, when the female Muslim teacher took extended maternity leave from one of the female establishments that we visited, no deputy or replacement visitor had been appointed for many months. The female teacher in another women's prison had not been paid for the previous six months at the time of our interview with her. Some of these issues were addressed by the Prison Service Chaplaincy headquarters in 2003 when the decision was taken to designate all Muslim Visiting Ministers as 'Muslim chaplains'.

Lack of transparency and consultation about chaplaincy budgets was an issue in two of our prisons. According to the Imam in Prison 1, resources to meet the religious needs of a large number of Muslim inmates 'should be provided by the Chaplain and the budget. But we don't know how much is the budget, and it's very difficult to get anything out of this budget or to get your fair share of the field'. For example, he resented the fact that he had to rely on charitable sources outside the prison for the purchase of prayer mats. Similarly, the Imam in Prison 2 regretted that the chaplain 'had never made any approach to me and said, "Look, this is the amount of money we are getting every year, and I think we ought to give you some towards the cost of, you know, the books that you bring, the materials that you bring"'. His predecessor allegedly had no resources whatsoever: 'The only thing that he was getting, he was getting all the resources from Iqra Press, Iqra Trust. He was getting it from Saudi Arabia, he was getting it from the Islamic Cultural Centre, and he was getting it from individual donations, like myself'. He could only express the hope that, if a full-time Imam was appointed he would have his own budget specifically for meeting the needs of Muslim inmates.

The opportunities and facilities for Imams to conduct prayers and to offer other services to Muslim inmates varied widely between prisons. Muslims in Prison 1 used a multi-faith area that had been carved out of space within the precincts of the former Christian chapel. The space could accommodate about 35 people, but the number of inmates regularly attending Friday prayers exceeded 50. The facilities that had been installed nearby for ritual ablutions were far from perfect. The difficulties of transporting a large number of prisoners to and from the multi-faith area for congregational prayers created further problems for the Imam. He described the conditions in which he worked as unsatisfactory 'because the number of the inmates and the allocation of time is not compatible. So, you don't have an opportunity to see a number of them except for those who come to congregation. There is no pastoral care you can provide and see them in the cells' (Imam in Prison 1).

Similar dissatisfaction was voiced by the acting Imam in Prison 2 who was highly critical of the design of his prison's relatively new, purpose-built multi-faith centre for failing to provide proper facilities for *wudhu* or ritual ablutions:

Had I been consulted I would have said to them that we have to make provision for *wudhu* area, in other words you have to have a seat when you are doing your *wudhu*. Where you're going to design the area as a prayer place then you must make sure that nobody walks about with their shoes on... We have a room there with a few taps, you know, a long stretch of tap so that they can wash. So, when you open the tap, everything gets completely soaked.

This particular Imam added that Muslim prisoners from overseas required much more intensive pastoral support than he or his predecessor, as part-time Visiting Ministers, had been able to provide in the time available to them. Facilities in Prison 3, however, met with the Imam's approval. He reported no difficulties in obtaining religious artefacts or in sharing the multi-faith centre with other faith groups. Yet, the use of multi-faith rooms does still give rise to problems for Muslims in some establishments. The General Secretary of the NCWMP cited the case of a prison with such a room

which is used by the Sikhs. And, as it happens, I think the Sikh minister visits on a Thursday, and then Friday prayers on the Friday. The first thing Muslims do when they come in, they have to make sure the food smell is out of the room. The room stinks. I actually went into it and I realised what the problem is. And then you cannot actually get fresh air into that room. It's quite a problem with multi-faith things (interview 26th June, 2003).

The Imams gave the strong impression that arrangements for ensuring that *halal* food was available had improved in each of our three male prisons. They all acknowledged that some prisoners were reluctant to accept their assurances that the food was *halal*, as in Prison 3 where the Imam reported:

There are good arrangements in place currently for *halal* food, including certification. Eid food has been prepared in-house for two years. Provisions are good for Ramadan. In the past it was difficult. Donations were made from the community, and it was difficult to get hold of enough *halal* meat. On occasions, prisoners still doubt whether the meat is *halal*. Presently, the meat is *halal*, but there is some concern about labels on meat being written by hand rather than being printed.

According to the NCWMP, however, there is evidence of deception and malpractice in some prison kitchens where Catering Managers make false declarations about the provenance of so-called *halal* products. When spot-checks by the Council's agents revealed a lack of invoices for some items, the complaints reached the highest echelons of the Prison Service.

The response of Imams was relatively relaxed to the fact that, as we reported in Chapter 4, some prison officers displayed moral zeal in policing the strict observance of Ramadan. The Imam in Prison 2, for example, took a pragmatic view of the situation. When an officer sent him a letter listing the names of prisoners who had been seen illicitly breaking their fast before sunset, the Imam 'explained to the officer that, if that person has committed that offence, he has broken his fast today. It doesn't prevent him from fasting tomorrow'. He was very conscious of the fact that prisoners varied in the strength of their religious faith and in the magnitude of the problems that they faced. Consequently, he argued, some of them 'fall on the wayside'. He added that, if he was working full-time as a Muslim chaplain, he would visit inmates on the wings and give them moral encouragement and counselling by saying 'Look, these rules have to be obeyed; and if you're going to break it, that doesn't mean you're going to get away with it because you have to replace that fasting day'. He was convinced that the presence of a full-time Imam in the prison chaplaincy would help to improve relations between Muslim inmates and prison officers. His recipe for success was as follows:

> What we have to do is we have to say to the officer that, once the prisoner realises that he is not going to get away with [breaking the Ramadan rules] he has to replace it; and after the month of Ramadan I, the Imam will go back to the officer and say, 'Right, we're going to make special provision for that particular day, for that particular prison, to fast' – you know, so that there is a way that we can approach this matter in a more flexible way – in a sensible way where everyone will be happy, and there are ways we can deal with that. That's the role of the full-time Imam.

He also detected inflexibility in some prison officers who used bureaucratic excuses for preventing inmates from attending Friday prayers or for deterring inmates from registering a change of religion. In his view, the obstructiveness of some officers was a tactic for 'stamping their authority' on prisoners.

The views that prison officers expressed about Imams were quite mixed. Relations between them were clearly considered to be very good in Prison 3, but officers in Prison 2 knew very little about the Imam – no doubt partly because of the year-long failure to replace an Imam who had left the prison. Opinions of the Imam in Prison 1 were divided. Officer 4 said that 'he's not very sociable; seems to think he is above everyone else. And I think there are a lot who think that', whereas Officer 5 described the Imam as 'very approachable and very respectful'. Nevertheless, prison officers in all three of our male establishments were mostly supportive of the idea that Muslim prisoners benefited from the time that they spent with Imams. As Officer 5 in Prison 2 put it, an Imam who could visit the prison three times a week would be helpful:

I can sit and listen to you and I can go as far as I can go, but there's nobody who knows the ins and outs better than perhaps the Imam that perhaps can give religious advice or, er, get in contact perhaps with somebody else or have a chat with [a prisoner's] family. Those things, I think, yes, do need looking at.

His colleague, Officer 6, went even further: 'We have a great number of Muslims throughout the establishment. And maybe those who are not so strong or active a Muslim, maybe their faith would be renewed if the Imam was more regularly available'. Indeed, few prison officers objected to the idea that it might be useful to appoint some Imams on a full-time basis.

An earlier study (Spalek and Wilson, 2001: 4) of nine Imams working in English prisons claimed that 'the problems encountered by the Imams amount to a form of "institutional racism"' as defined by the Macpherson (1999) report as 'unwitting prejudice, ignorance, thoughtlessness and racist stereotyping which disadvantages minority ethnic people'. Only one of our Imams, in Prison 2, interpreted his experiences in terms comparable to Macpherson's. He also alleged that prison officers had sometimes treated him with disrespect:

[A] number of officers here see my position here as a threat. I don't know why, and they put all kinds of obstacle... They try to sort of demean my position by their body language, by their attitude... I have walked into the wing where officers see me arriving with another colleague, they put their feet on the table, setting out to polish their shoes... Where you ask them questions, they are always very dismissive, very cynical... Some of them totally ignore you by the body language.

He stopped short of saying that he had been the target of explicit racism, however, because officers supposedly knew that this would have been unwise: 'They do it, they've got their own way of doing it... There's a boundary, they don't pass that boundary because they know the consequence will be very severe, because they know that the Governor will act upon it immediately' (Imam in Prison 2).

But there was no doubt that two of our Imams were well aware of their relatively disadvantaged and marginal position in prisons compared with that of Christian chaplains. They had also taken various initiatives to circumvent their disadvantages in order to provide artefacts, facilities and services that were essential to their work with prisoners.

Full-time Muslim chaplains

The appointment of the first cohort of full-time Muslim chaplains in England and Wales, beginning slowly at the end of 2001, occurred too late to be a focus of our research. By the Spring of 2004, however, it was becoming clear that their particular experiences of working in prisons were sufficiently different from those of the sessional or part-time chaplains in our three establishments to warrant separate analysis. Lengthy telephone interviews were therefore conducted with six of the 12 full-time Muslim chaplains who were in post at that time and who were all males; a visit to three of the prisons where one of them worked afforded the opportunity to observe his interaction with prisoners and prison staff. It is important to add, however, that none of the opinions that we collected from the inmates and staff of the three prisons where the bulk of our fieldwork took place related to any full-time Muslim chaplains.

The principal reason for our interest in full-time Muslim chaplains was to discover how far their work and experiences differed, if at all, from those of the much greater number of Muslim Visiting Ministers or sessional chaplains working part-time in the prisons of England and Wales. In particular, we wanted to establish whether, as a result of their full-time involvement in chaplaincy, the full-time chaplains took a distinctive view of the treatment of Muslim prisoners. It was a way of asking to what extent full-time Muslim chaplains believed that they could overcome the well documented difficulties facing their part-time counterparts (Spalek and Wilson, 2001). Given the relatively well established position of chaplaincies in British prisons, we expected that the work of full-time Muslim chaplains would probably benefit from being fully integrated into the structures and routines previously accessible only to full-time Christian chaplains. But we also wondered whether full-time Muslim chaplains would be at risk of being co-opted into basically Christian ways of formulating and delivering religious and pastoral services to prisoners. This is not to raise the question of whether a Christian model of chaplaincy was imposed on them: it is merely to ask how far the experience of working in structures impregnated with Christian ideals might affect the Muslim chaplains' approach to their work. Awareness of this issue is sufficiently developed in the Prison Service Chaplaincy for a Consultation Day to have been set aside in October 2003 for reflection on understandings of prison ministry.

Five of our sample of six full-time Muslim chaplains had received formal training in the UK or abroad that had prepared them for acting as Imams. The sixth chaplain had been brought up in a devout family and had gained experience of voluntary work in Muslim communities. They all spoke virtually perfect English and had spent most, if not all, of their life in the UK. The range of their previous occupational experiences was wide: health service manager, engineer, small business owner, university teacher and health care chaplain. Two of them had always intended to work as Imams, but none of the six had begun their working life as a prison chaplain. In fact, their 'routes' into prison chaplaincy were quite varied and, in some cases, adventitious. Four of them had served as Visiting Ministers in prison on a part-time basis before applying for full-time positions. All of them had applied formally for publicly advertised positions and had been selected by panels including staff drawn from the prison where they were to work and the Muslim Adviser to the Prison Service.

Although all of the full-time Muslim chaplains described their first experiences of chaplaincy work as variations on the themes of 'being thrown in at the deep end' and 'pick it up as you go', most of them had eventually completed the generic Chaplaincy Induction Course.[4] Instruction had also been provided in such things as security issues and suicide awareness. A few had also volunteered to undergo further Prison Service training in, for example, World Faiths, Race Relations, and Counselling. But the prevailing attitude was that their training and induction had been brief and inadequate. One Muslim chaplain even suspected that his local chaplaincy co-ordinator's reason for telling him to start slowly and not to take many training courses was to marginalise him. No other Muslim chaplain reported any reason for suspecting that their progress had been deliberately obstructed.

There was a strong feeling among the full-time Muslim chaplains that the Prison Service should provide more extensive training for Muslim chaplains, but this was tempered by an insistence that the training should be, in part, specific to Muslim issues and should draw on the expertise of Muslim chaplains. As one of them put it, 'Sadly we're becoming too generic... Everyone's being painted with the same brush'. This chaplain's suggestion was that, since the most experienced full-time Muslim chaplains were well placed to devise programmes of training related to the treatment of Muslim prisoners, they should deliver such programmes both to Muslim sessional chaplains and to prison staff. He had already devised ways of explaining the importance of prayer schedules to prison officers and of fostering community chaplaincy in the vicinity of the prison where he worked; another full-time Muslim chaplain had instituted a scheme for appointing a 'nominated co-ordinating prisoner' on each wing of the prison who was responsible for maintaining the list of Muslim prisoners registered for Friday prayers; a third had invented a menu card that explained the content of meals in pictures for the benefit of illiterate prisoners and those who could not read English; and a fourth had offered courses on 'victim awareness' and 'justice awareness'. These examples of the innovative and constructive role played by full-time Muslim chaplains are only a small selection of their many efforts to improve the effectiveness of chaplaincy. They indicate a much higher degree of 'ownership' of Muslim chaplaincy than was previously conceivable among part-time Visiting Ministers (Beckford and Gilliat, 1998; Spalek and Wilson, 2001). These examples also reflect the fact that full-time Muslim chaplains are in a much stronger structural position than their part-time counterparts to influence the treatment of Muslim prisoners.

Indeed, the full-time Muslim chaplains whom we interviewed were unanimous in reporting that their work was usually well received by prison staff. They said that prison officers – with a few exceptions – tended to show them respect and to realise that 'getting the Imam involved creates greater harmony'. The attendance of full-time Muslim chaplains at daily or weekly meetings of senior staff also raised their profile and authority in some establishments. Moreover, participation in meetings of the Race Relations Management Team enabled some full-time Muslim chaplains to challenge any racist procedures and behaviour.

The relations of full-time Muslim chaplains with Christian chaplains were generally said to be satisfactory but still dependent on the latter's attitudes. In establishments with effective chaplaincy teams, Muslim chaplains felt fully integrated and trusted. They still felt resentment, however, if they were excluded from the full round of statutory duties or from decision-making processes, especially regarding budgets. For example, a highly experienced chaplain reported that he obtained very little help from his chaplaincy team and that 'there was still a barrier there' because he was perceived as a threat to the common resources. One of our informants had also encountered obstructions from his co-ordinating chaplain to plans for attending training courses and seminars. But those with previous experience of work as part-time chaplains agreed that their new status had led to a much stronger sense of having a stake in the work of chaplaincy. Some also looked forward to the opportunity of being appointed as a local or an area co-ordinating chaplain, although several Muslim chaplains doubted whether Anglican chaplains would willingly release their grip on these positions in the near future. It was allegedly still the case in some establishments that Anglican chaplains could use their 'insider' relations with governors to bypass chaplaincy committees and thereby frustrate plans for a wider re-distribution of responsibility and resources. Nevertheless, vacancies for the post of Area Chaplain are all advertised and open to chaplains of all faiths.

As for their relations with fellow Muslims, the full-time Muslim chaplains did not believe that their appointments had created problems for part-time chaplains. On the contrary, their view was that the work of full-time chaplains could only strengthen the position of *all* Muslim chaplains by lending them confidence and by generating good advice. Not only did there appear to be no friction with part-time chaplains, but it was also becoming more common for full-time Muslim chaplains to offer formal and informal training to their part-time colleagues. Moreover, most Muslim prisoners reportedly appreciated having more opportunities to spend time with their full-time chaplains than had previously been possible with only part-time chaplains. The fact that full-time Muslim chaplains were more visible than their part-time predecessors was also said to reduce the prisoners' feeling of being a marginalised or devalued minority in prisons.

Full-time Muslim chaplains all had positive opinions of the role played by successive Muslim Advisers to the Prison Service. Although communication between them was not intense, they clearly shared the same ideals for the development of Muslim chaplaincy. Some of our informants had also co-operated with the Muslim Adviser in the production of official documents such as the PSO 4500 on Religion. Their expectation was that, if the number of full-time Muslim chaplains continued to increase, the work of the Muslim Adviser would become easier in the sense that he would be able to draw on a growing body of professional experience and expertise. It was also suggested that the cause of Muslim chaplaincy would be advanced by the appointment of, on the one hand, Assistant Muslim Advisers with special responsibility for visiting prisons containing only few Muslim prisoners and, on the other, 'Area Co-ordinating Imams'. Such developments would be essential, it was argued, to the continuing enhancement of professional standards among Muslim chaplains.

Opinion was sharply divided among our informants about the work of the National Council for the Welfare of Muslim Prisoners (NCWMP). Only one of them was actively involved in its operations, and several others were quite dismissive. Three full-time Muslim chaplains described it as, for example, 'a waste of space', 'not really effective, I must say', and 'a nothing'. There were also allusions to the in-fighting among Muslim organisations that had the effect of limiting the NCWMP's potential to be helpful. On the other hand, it seemed that full-time Muslim chaplains obtained only occasional advice and support from any other Muslim organisations in the UK. They certainly did not give the impression that they enjoyed the kind of relationship with Muslim organisations that full-time Anglican chaplains had with the Church of England. Consequently, it would not be surprising if full-time Muslim chaplains did not eventually form their own organisation.

All of the full-time Muslim chaplains to whom we spoke were agreed on the need for them to monitor prisoners' expressions of 'extremist' views and to try to cultivate an appreciation of Islam's non-violent aspects. They did not favour discussion of geo-political conflicts during question and answer sessions following Friday prayers, and their inclination seemed to be to direct prisoners' attention towards their own offending behaviour and the need to be 'better' Muslims. For example, the range of questions arising in one question and answer session in a Young Offender Institution (YOI) included the risks of smoking cigarettes and taking drugs, the acceptability of marrying a non-Muslim, the value of arranged marriages, the need to shower after a wet dream, the meaning of death, the permissibility of tattoos, and the meaning of '*jihad*'. With regard to the last question, the Muslim chaplain went to considerable lengths to stress that the term referred primarily to the struggle of Muslims for control over their own thoughts and actions. In fact, none of our informants had encountered more than sporadic expressions of 'extremist' views among Muslim prison-ers. And they tended to interpret the taunts of 'Osama', 'Saddam' or 'terror-ist' that non-Muslim prisoners occasionally directed at them as joking behaviour rather than as deep-seated anti-Muslim sentiment. They were inured to low-level racist prejudice among prisoners and prison officers alike, and their response was to try even harder to demonstrate Islam's capacity to inculcate peaceful and law-abiding conduct. 'I defuse the situation' is how one chaplain described his strategy for responding to Muslim prisoners with extremist demands. Another took the initiative to issue a statement condemning the attacks on the US on the anniversary of 11 September 2001.

The full-time Muslim chaplains had no doubt that conditions had improved for the practice of Islam in the prisons of England and Wales and that the presence of full-time chaplains had boosted the number of prison-ers regularly involved in Friday prayers and other activities for Muslims. Nevertheless, they were also keenly aware that the situation could, and should, be even better for themselves and for Muslim prisoners. Three areas in particular called for further improvement or, at least, clarification. First, they claimed that arrangements for replacing them during periods of leave or illness were unsatisfactory and that the conditions of their own employment were inferior to those of full-time Christian chaplains in so far as they could only move to another prison by applying for an advertised post rather than being re-assigned. In fact, a senior member of the Prison Service Chaplaincy headquarters team refuted this claim. He insisted that the Muslim chaplains' conditions of service were identical to those of their Christian counterparts. Second, there was concern about the Prison Service Chaplaincy's emphasis on generic training at the expense of faith-specific training programmes. Some of the full-time Muslim chaplains wanted to take more responsibility for providing training for part-time chaplains and prison staff on matters relating to the practice of Islam. They also wanted to create a communication network among themselves so that Muslim chaplains could have information about prisoners being transferred to their particular prisons. Moreover, there was strong interest in joining forces with probation officers to inquire into the resettlement and rehabilitation of released Muslim prisoners within the framework of the National Offender Management Service (NOMS) that came into operation in 2004. Third, long-standing problems associated with the authentication of *halal* food, with racism, with the provision of adequate facilities for ritual ablutions and prayer space, and with the difficulties of ensuring that all eligible prisoners had the opportunity of joining Friday prayers continued to exercise the full-time Muslim chaplains just as much as their part-time predecessors. But what is particularly noteworthy is that the problems have become more subtle. For example, it is no longer simply a matter of ensur-ing that *halal* food is available: it is also a question of ensuring that the storage of *halal* food and the use of containers and temperature probes do not contaminate it.

In general, then, full-time Muslim chaplains have fitted into the structure of prison chaplaincy in England and Wales with few problems. Their levels of satisfaction with their conditions of work and with their relations with other prison staff seem to be higher than among part-time Muslim chaplains. They feel that they are in a relatively strong position when it comes to influencing policy and practice regarding the treatment of Muslim prisoners, although shortage of resources remains a problem. The expertise that they have acquired is being shared with other Muslim chaplains, and their awareness of forming an influential group of specialist chaplains is increasing. Given the continuing growth of the Muslim population in British prisons, there will probably be pressure to make more full-time appointments. This development might give rise to tensions between them, the Muslim Adviser, part-time Muslim chaplains and Muslim organisations if their long-term career goals prove to be incompatible with the others' interests. At this time, however, the work of full-time Muslim chaplains meets with widespread approval and a sense of satisfaction that the boundaries of prison chaplaincy have been expanded in a way that is consistent with the Prison Service's commitment to respect for diversity.

Finally, the full-time Muslim chaplains are well aware of the risk that they might be swallowed up in – or co-opted by – a predominantly Christian chaplaincy service. Their response is partly to call for additional resources to develop the specifically Islamic aspects of their training, thereby supplementing the generic forms of training that are currently available. Another aspect of their response to the risk of being co-opted is to form closer relations of co-operation among themselves and with part-time Muslim chaplains. In other words, they are awake to the charge that their work might be excessively influenced by Christian models of chaplaincy; and they are confident of being able to preserve the distinctively Islamic nature of their way of working. Indeed, some of them aspire to introduce their own good practices into the generic, multi-faith practices of the Prison Service Chaplaincy.

Muslim prisoners' views of Imams

Estimates of the proportion of Muslim prisoners who regularly attend Friday prayers vary between establishments, but it would safe to say that the percentage does not normally fall below 60 per cent of inmates registered as Muslims. On special occasions the proportion is closer to 80 per cent. This indicates that most Muslim inmates are willing to take part in activities led by an Imam. Indeed, in prisons where the Imam also runs Arabic classes or Islamic study groups, there is sometimes a waiting list for admission. Furthermore, inmates' opinions about the services that their

Imams provide in prison are overwhelmingly positive. With some exceptions, the Muslim prisoners whom we interviewed were not only appreciative of the work of Imams but also enthusiastic about the idea of having
them in their prison for longer periods of time. The reasons that prisoners
gave for wanting to spend more time with an Imam included the desire to
study Islam or the Arabic language in greater depth, the need to provide
constant support for recent converts to Islam, the request for more pastoral
support and the hope that a full-time Imam would be in a position to
defend the interests of Muslims and to push for better access to such things
as more frequent showers or better quality food. For example, 'I want him
on a full-time basis. He should do more work, like, with probation. We
would have more luck with probation. I think if we had a full-time Imam
all our problems would be sorted instead of being fobbed off' (Prison 1,
Prisoner 7). This also indicates an underlying awareness of inequality of
provision between faiths:

> I want a full-time Imam. The Church has a lot of power. I have seen it in
> other jails as well. Muslim friends have lost family and they have not
> been allowed to attend the funeral, but Christians, every single one they
> got to go (Prison 3, Prisoner 17).

At the same time, some prisoners made it clear that they only wanted
Imams who could communicate with them in good English.

A few prisoners were content for the Imam to offer limited services such
as 'the basic five pillars, prayers, not counselling' (Prison 1, Prisoner 1),
whereas others appreciated the fact that the Imam talked about such things
as 'praying and reading the Qur'an, trying to be a good Muslim, learn
about Islam' (Prison 1, Prisoner 12) or 'about family, talk about offences,
about how I lost my faith when I was younger and how I am trying to get
back into it now' (Prison 1, Prisoner 14). The level at which Imams
discussed Islam was a problem, however, for prisoners who were already
knowledgeable about the religion. Imams were expected to retain their
interest as well as to introduce recent converts to the most basic elements
of Islam.

Another difficult issue facing Imams concerned politics. Prisoner 16 in
Prison 2, for example, complained that the Imam's predecessor 'was mostly
talking about people and their countries, what they are suffering, what
country does what, you understand? That's politics: that's not religion.
Religion, you have to show people, like,... how our religion came, what we
had to do. Those are the things what change people'. By contrast, Prisoner
2 in Prison 3 regretted that 'there are certain things he won't talk about.
When we talk about politics, he won't speak about this... A lot of Muslims
don't come because they think the Imam is not good'. By contrast, Prisoner
15 in Prison 2 alleged that 'When I was in [a notorious London] prison...

everyone was complaining about the Imam there, everyone, every single person going to the mosque was complaining about the Imam – that he doesn't know what he's doing, he wasn't praying properly, and everything. So, we are lucky to have got this Imam here'. In fact, our informants were evenly balanced in their opinions about the superiority or inferiority of Imams in prisons where they had lived prior to the establishments where we interviewed them.

In other words, it is virtually impossible for Imams to satisfy all the expectations of Muslim prisoners, some of whom want to discuss politics within an Islamic framework of thought while others want to keep religion and politics separate. The Imams to whom we spoke all agreed that it was not good practice for them to introduce politics into their sermons or classes. Moreover, none of the Muslim prisoners reported that Imams currently working in our three male prisons talked about politics, even in the wake of the attacks on the USA on 11 September, 2001.

Outright criticism of Imams was not frequent among prisoners, and it usually had a personal – rather than an ideological – basis. For example, 'He doesn't care. Two or three times I explained that I am doing a life sentence and I wished to see him. He said, "Make an application". I did, and he never came; and when I made an application for the Board of Visitors, then he came' (Prison 2, Prisoner 19). A much more comprehensive dispute between a prisoner and an Imam was reported by Prisoner 16 in Prison 3 as follows:

I'm not happy. He's not a proper Imam. I felt the Imam is like a screw. Once I got up to punch him, but I felt bad. Once he said to another prisoner, who was Black and wanted to go on Ramadan, that he could not. I had to intervene. I felt the Imam didn't respect me. The Imam, he doesn't know what it means to be an Imam. I've been off Friday prayers for nine weeks and he never came to see me to ask why I didn't come.

It transpired later in the interview that the dispute had originated in a particular incident:

I fell out with the Imam over Ramadan, over taking fruit down to the workshop. An officer stopped me from bringing food into the workshop and I was nicked and adjudicated. The Imam said you could take the food down, no problem after 13/14 Ramadan. The Imam did not take any action on my behalf, so I stopped going to Friday prayers. The Imam doesn't know what it means to be an Imam. Other prisoners call him by name and I call him 'Imam', and he tells me to 'fuck off!'. I once asked the Imam to pray for a bereavement during Friday prayers and he said, 'Pray for them yourself'.

This type of breakdown in the relationship between a Muslim prisoner and his Imam is not common, but the prisoner's grievance is interesting because it illustrates the difficulty that can arise in a closed community where the prisoner does not have the option of visiting a different mosque and where he is bound to meet the Imam from time to time. Thus, 'Once I met the Imam in the exercise yard and I said "Salaam", and he asked why I was not coming to prayers, and I replied "you"' (Prisoner 16 in Prison 3). When another prisoner, who accused the Imam of visiting the prison only to pick up his fees, tried to complain about the situation, the Imam supposedly said, "You find another Imam". I said, "How can I find one"? (Prison 2, Prisoner 12).

Prisoners and Imams alike framed such disputes as personal: not ideological, philosophical or theological. In fact, the prisoners' understanding of differences between schools of Islamic thought and jurisprudence was weak. Most of them did not even recognise the names of the main schools of thought. Only a handful of Muslim prisoners mentioned Sh'ias; and although literature about the Ahmadiyas had been placed in the multi-faith area of one establishment, none of the prisoners shared the Imam's consternation about it. Two inmates had been in contact with the Nation of Islam, and one had migrated from the Tabligh *via* Hizb-ut-Tahrir to a Salafi group. In short, Imams rarely had to contend with deep-rooted theological differences among inmates – unlike the situation in many American prisons where the Nation of Islam has a large following and where, as a result, the authority of Sunni Imams to speak on behalf of all Muslims is sometimes contested. The only case that we encountered of basic theological or ideological tension concerned the inmate who had been active in Hizb-ut-Tahrir (HT), who admitted,

> I had a few run-ins with the Imams when I was with HT. We managed to get a lot of youngsters in the mosque. HT may not be teaching them the right way, but it was a step in the right direction. HT wanted Islamic law to be imposed (Prison 1, Prisoner 7).

We also heard an uncorroborated allegation that a foreign Imam who was being held in Category-A conditions on a long sentence for inciting racial hatred had taken advantage of the regular Imam's absence in order to lead Friday prayers himself and to make inappropriate, fiery comments. As a result, the prison authorities banned him from Friday prayers.

A few prisoners from South Asian backgrounds who were knowledgeable about Islam suggested that Imams could do more to teach recent converts, especially Black converts, about the 'proper' ways to perform ablutions, to pray and to show respect for other people at prayer. One Imam was also criticised for not disciplining inmates who allegedly took advantage of congregational prayers in order to chat with friends and to deal in drugs.

Again, the Imam found himself in a difficult position not because of any theological disagreements but because of 'racial' and cultural tensions between Asian and African or African-Caribbean inmates (who constituted a large proportion of recent converts). For example, Prisoner 19 in Prison 2 said, with some exasperation, 'It is the job of the Imam to explain... how to pray. Out of these 100 Muslims only 25 are proper Muslims. And the Black Muslims, they have converted to Islam because of the food'. A similar frustration was expressed by Prisoner 8 in Prison 3:

> The Imam should be able to bring someone to a wing and talk to him one-to-one. Either he doesn't have the authority or he isn't exercising it. I mean, there are four or five Blacks and they don't know how to pray. Nobody has taught them how to pray.

The presence of so many converts to Islam in at least two of our male prisons also complicated the Imam's role because it required him to work with, and retain the interest of, Muslims with vastly different degrees of knowledge and experience of Islam. Dissatisfaction with the Imam's performance is virtually inevitable among some prisoners.

Arrangements for the celebration of Ramadan and its associated festivals are a potential source of difficulties for Imams because they do not have control over all aspects of the events. Complex co-ordination is required between the RRLO, the catering staff, security officers, wing officers, relevant governors and the Imam – to say nothing of Christian chaplains in prisons without a full-time Imam. And, despite general agreement that Ramadan arrangements usually work much better nowadays than in the past, problems still arise on occasion. If, for example, the part-time Imam arrives late, decisions have to be made about who is to lead the prayers in his absence. If officers allege that particular prisoners have broken the fasting rules, the Imam has to decide whether to intervene on their behalf. In another case, Prisoner 16 in Prison 3 claimed that:

> On Eid, the Imam said he wanted to go home at 3 pm. I said to the Imam, 'Don't tell the screws, because the Governor has given us permission until 4.30 pm'. But the Imam did not honour this; and at 3 pm the screws moved us, and I decided the Imam was not worth praying behind.

A much more common challenge facing Imams is to convince Muslim inmates that the *halal* food is authentic. The appointment of a Muslim Adviser at chaplaincy headquarters, the monitoring work of the NCWMP and the publication of PSO 5000 on catering have all helped to take the pressure off Imams at local level, but not all prisoners have faith in the system of authentication or the method of food preparation. For example, a Muslim prisoner made an allegation in one establishment that some of the inmates who worked in the kitchens were classified as 'Vulnerable Prisoners' (VPs) and were, therefore, unfit to prepare food for Muslims.

Imams working as chaplains in French prisons

In contrast to the English system where the provision of part-time Muslim chaplains in prisons has been extensive for many years (Beckford and Gilliat, 1998), there is a real problem in France about the appointment of Imams in prisons. There are, according to different statistics, between 39 and 69 Muslim chaplains in French prisons.[5] This number is derisory compared to the 437 Catholic, 236 Protestant and 67 Jewish chaplains,[6] all the more so as, in many prisons, the proportion of Muslim inmates is as high as 70 per cent of the population. Informal estimates place the percentage of Muslim prisoners as high as 50 or 60 per cent of the country's entire prison population. The problem is institutional as well as cultural, for the appointment of a Muslim chaplain requires approval both from the Ministry of the Interior and from the prison in question. Moreover, there are numerous stumbling blocks along the path of appointment.

In the first place, fear of Islamic radicalism or fundamentalism [*intégrisme*] paralyses many prison officials when it comes to the appointment of Muslim chaplains – not to mention difficulties in obtaining approval from the Ministry of the Interior. This fear is much more in evidence in France than in England and Wales. It has its roots in the late 1980s and 1990s when groups affiliated to the *Groupe Islamique Armé* (GIA), a radical group which split from the mainstream *Front Islamique du Salut* (FIS), opted for the strategy of armed struggle against the military government in Algeria and the French state, which they accused of supporting the Algerian government.

The second obstacle to the appointment of Muslim chaplains in French prisons is the suspicion that they might not be imbued with the culture of *laïcité*. Even if they are not radical Islamists, they might not be considered sufficiently secular or '*laïc*'. Since the criteria of *laïcité* are not very clear, the decision about whether someone is *laïcité*-friendly is left to the subjective opinion of each prison director – within the framework of a few formal principles.[7] This ambiguity makes it difficult to express clear-cut opinions about whether a candidate for the position of Muslim chaplain should be allowed to hold an official post in the French prison system. An example from another sphere may help to clarify this situation. If female Muslim students wear a headscarf in state-funded national schools [*écoles publiques*], this is taken as opposition to the principle of *laïcité*. However, the *Conseil d'Etat* ruled in 1989 that girls wearing the headscarf should not be excluded from school on condition that they attend all classes, do not disturb good order in school and do not proselytise. Nevertheless, this judgement ran contrary to the subjective attachment to the ideals of *laïcité* felt by many teachers and others in the French educational system. In fact, assessing the 'degrees of *laïcité*' is as much a cultural process as a judicial decision. When conflicts arise, people's attitudes towards *laïcité* reflect not only their personal views and their position in institutional hierarchies but also the general atmosphere in French society at the time. A new law enacted early in 2004, with the support of about two thirds of French people, prohibits the display of 'ostensible' or ostentatious religious symbols in state schools.

The situation in a women's prison in Paris illustrates the prevailing ambiguity and confusion about *laïcité*. Muslim inmates have no right to wear headscarves outside their cells, whereas the Catholic nuns who work in the prison as volunteers are allowed to wear their own kind of head covering. Muslim women who wear the Islamic headscarf are regarded as a challenge to *laïcité*, but the nuns' form of head covering is perceived very differently – as an expression of 'tradition'. There are many comparable situations in France: how far does the principle of *laïcité* allow for tolerance towards Islamic ways of life and how does it determine when Islamic dress and rituals are deemed incompatible with the principle? The only general guide provided by *laïcité* is that there should be no proselytising in public institutions and that a strict separation of the private and public sphere must be maintained. But many social and cultural movements, most notably the women's movement, call this distinction into question and publicly denounce both the confinement of women to the sphere of private life and the domination exercised by men when they exclude women from the public sphere.

The dividing line between religion and the public sphere has also suffered some setbacks owing to the decline of vigilance on the part of Republicans who lost their main opponents when compromises were made with the Catholic Church. In any case, the principle of *laïcité* is becoming more and more a 'frame of mind' as well as a formal and objective principle. Nevertheless, its vagueness allows for wide diversity of interpretations, many of which are opposed to each other (and this is likely to continue despite the law introduced in 2004).

Laïcité becomes increasingly elusive as it varies with the outlook of managers in prisons, the traditions of the prisons themselves and the capacity of inmates to mobilise themselves. This makes it a tall order to find a common denominator between all the different interpretations, leaving aside agreement on the exclusion of proselytising and on the need to protect the integrity of the public sphere. This ambiguity adversely affects the recruitment of Muslim chaplains. The main reason put forward for being cautious about recruiting them is that they are not sufficiently imbued with the culture of *laïcité* and might, therefore, jeopardise the fragile balance that exists in prisons between different faith communities.

Another obstacle to the recruitment of Muslim chaplains is the ambiva-lence of rules within prison itself. Since the director of each prison has to agree to the appointment of Muslim chaplains after they have been approved by the Ministry of the Interior and Religions, he becomes respon-sible for their good behaviour. His responsibility is at stake in the appoint-ment. Many directors find it more convenient not to take risks at this stage, preferring to run their prison as it is rather than taking initiatives that might jeopardise their reputation. The internalised notion of *laïcité* and prejudices against Islam, which is often perceived as intrinsically antagonistic to *laïcité*, make this process even more difficult.

The resulting scarcity of Muslim chaplains creates a situation in which most Muslim prisoners have no access to any authority telling them what Islam is and is not. This means that they can be influenced all the more easily by those who hold a puritanical or extremist view of Islam, thereby setting a self-fulfilling prophecy in motion. French prisons, as we shall see, become a breeding ground for activists and extremists at least partly because of the lack of Muslim chaplains who could tell Muslim inmates what is religiously permitted and what is prohibited. The widely debated 'radicalisation' of Muslims in prison – a notion that contains some truth – has to do with the scarcity of Muslim chaplains in prisons. And this is at least partly owing to the refusal of authorities to appoint them.

The case of one prison where there is an Imam, working as a Muslim chaplain, shows that he can be a moderating factor within the prison and that his presence can forestall many problems that might otherwise arise from the lack of an Islamic mediator between the prison management and Muslim inmates. This creates a strange paradox. The inadequate number of Muslim chaplains in prison is one of the factors that jeopardises the very neutrality towards religion in prison. This paradox is apparent but not real. Neutrality towards religion implies the recognition of religions as such, in so far as they agree to show mutual respect among faiths and do not adversely affect human rights issues. In French prisons, the tense atmos-phere surrounding Islam, the fear of Islamic radicals, the prison officers' feelings of insecurity *vis-à-vis* young people from the *banlieues* where Muslim radicals have emerged, all of this makes it impossible for the authorities to be neutral towards Islam. As far as Muslim inmates are con-cerned, what prevails is a feeling of being stigmatised, rejected and not being treated on a par with members of other religious faiths (mainly Christianity and Judaism). This exacerbates tensions and leads a sizeable proportion of inmates to believe that the French are against Islam. This, in turn, helps some radical Muslims in prison to recruit inmates who are deeply shocked by the way Islam in general and Muslims in particular are mistreated in prison. On the whole, the atmosphere surrounding Islam is tense in the prisons that we studied and is shot through with a generalised suspicion that is shared by prison officers, managers and Muslim inmates alike. Prison officers and managers suspect Muslims of not abiding by the rules set by *laïcité*, while Muslims suspect the authorities of being biased and of having a racist attitude towards them.

One of the three prisons that we studied had no Muslim chaplain of its own, although a chaplain occasionally visited from another prison. The second prison had a part-time Muslim chaplain, and the third had one Muslim chaplain for more than 2,000 Muslim inmates. It makes sense, therefore, to examine the situation in each prison in turn because they represent such different cases.

Prison A: the missing Imam

No Imam had been appointed to work in Prison A, and the one who volunteered to visit from time to time came from a prison in a neighbouring town. The absence of an Imam attached to the prison was justified by the authorities on the grounds that prisoners had not asked for his services. This argument is, at best, circular. Because he is not present, inmates think that he is not available. Because he is not available, they do not ask for him. This does not mean that they do not need him as such but that they just accept a reality which is not in their interests but is presented to them as a plain fact. Having assumed that Muslim inmates are not interested in having an Imam based in their prison, management attempts to explain this situation in their own way. One reason given is that the occasional Imam had allegedly put pressure on Muslim inmates to be more disciplined; in the words of one Assistant Director,

> We don't have a Muslim minister here. There is one who comes from the neighbouring town for religious festivities but not very often. The prisoners do not like him too much either. This is natural since he talks to them about discipline, for instance not throwing rubbish out of the window. They don't like that.

Another manager from Prison A suggested that prisoners did not ask for Muslim ministers because they were somehow secularised. Our research shows that these explanations are wide of the mark. As a matter of fact, many prisoners had internalised the lack of an Imam, and this made them more suspicious towards prison authorities. The more this supposedly secular frame of mind among prisoners was put forward as a reason for postponing the hiring of a Muslim chaplain, the more inmates found fault with the institution. For them, the lack of an Imam was a further sign of the contempt in which the institution held them. This increased their suspicion *vis-à-vis* the prison. This complete misunderstanding is all the more surprising as the prison managers seemed to think quite highly of the Imam from the neighbouring prison, and their reluctance to appoint one probably derives from their fear of making a 'bad' appointment, as revealed by an Assistant Director:

> But I would say that this minister is a good one; he conforms to the rules of our establishment. This is important for us. It's difficult to find a Muslim minister like him... We don't know how to find [ministers] for Islam. Obviously, we cannot accept someone from the GIA [*Groupe Islamique Armé*] or other extremists. We cannot control their teachings.

The judge attached to this prison confirmed, in his interview with us, that the prison authorities had approached an Imam who had been found to be a 'fundamentalist', that is, one who they assumed might not exert a moderating influence on the prisoners. They had to discard him, and this fear of '*intégriste*' Imams prevented them from looking for another one.

Prison B: the welcome Imam

The Imam in Prison B has a part-time contract for 25 hours a week. He is in the enviable position of working in a prison where the director supports his ministry to Muslim prisoners. Moreover, the director also supported the appointment of the Imam's wife as a part-time Muslim teacher for the women's section of the prison. On the whole, this Imam's role is highly valued by the prison authorities, and he enjoys the trust of the director. He plays an important role *vis-à-vis* both inmates and prison managers. It is an indication of his favourable position that he is the only Muslim chaplain in the French prisons under study who is able to go around the prison collecting the Muslim faithful for the celebration of Friday collective prayers. He was initially reluctant to meet our researchers in anything other than a purely formal setting in spite of the fact that the director supported our research. He was suspicious towards academics who, he thought, might have been linked to the French intelligence services.

Long after the research had begun, the Imam agreed, still rather reluctantly, to talk to the researchers in his own home. He did not dwell on his conditions of work or the facilities available – which he found satisfactory on the whole. He did refer, however, to the lack of ritual washing facilities, explaining that this prison was built at the beginning of the twentieth century and was incapable of satisfying the Muslims' requirements. For example, since showers cannot be used more than three times a week, Muslims feel 'polluted' by such things as involuntary ejaculations because they cannot perform the appropriate purification ritual [*Ghusl*] before undertaking their religious obligations. This makes them especially anxious.

In talking about the various dimensions of his role within the prison, the Imam stressed that deterring Muslim inmates from becoming radicalised in the name of religion was one of his most important contributions. A second important aspect of his work was helping prisoners in many ways, one of them being to provide them with the basics of Islam which had previously been unknown to most of them. Thirdly, he felt that his contribution included offering meaning and advice to prisoners and becoming a 'significant other' for them.

Radical or fundamentalist Islam

According to the Imam of Prison B, many inmates thought that they should participate in a *jihad* [holy war] against the Israelis, the Americans or the Western world. He tried to show them that this whole issue was much more complex. But, as he emphasised, he refused to talk about holy war in specific terms. On political questions, he usually gave the prisoners elusive answers. His argument was that they knew those problems much better than he did, so he deliberately abstained from intervening in cases where the prisoners had become radicalised. Instead, he preferred to try to deter others from getting involved in radical Islam. This is why some inmates considered that he had 'sold out' to French institutions. His neutral stance on problems such as the Palestinian conflict and his refusal to take sides on these problems made him uncongenial to prisoners who thought that Islam was in danger and needed their help. His contribution was to ward off radicalisation rather than to reshape the mental world of those who were already radicalised.

The policy of this Imam, who was also a secondary school teacher trained in France, was to work in close co-operation with prison officials by dissociating politics from religion. His unwavering response to any question about *jihad*, the news about Muslim societies such as those in Chechnya or Bosnia, or the Palestinian question was twofold: on the one hand, those who asked him the question knew more about these matters than he did and, on the other, there is no 'Islamic' solution to a problem unless it is fully and totally understood in all its details. Consequently, he argued, since the issues concerning those Muslim societies were, at best, only partially understood, no definitive Islamic answer could be provided for the time being. Thus:

In general, I avoid speaking about the news. I always talk about general things. I say to them, 'You are better informed than me on these topics. On Afghanistan, we don't have all the data; there are many things at stake beneath the visible state of affairs; and we can only see the tip of the iceberg. Therefore, it's impossible to talk about them in an exhaustive way'.

One of his main objectives is undoubtedly to prevent any disturbances in the name of Islam within prison. A good illustration of this approach is his way of dealing with the topic of Afghanistan:

You have Afghanistan over there; here you are in France. We do not have enough data to judge the matter satisfactorily. When they [the

Americans] bomb women and children, no one approves of it, but we should not throw fuel on the flames.

When prisoners questioned him about Holy War, he refused to allow a debate but offered an answer that was inspired by his mystical interpretation of Islam:

> When they begin to talk about *jihad*, I don't let them finish their questions. I refuse to give any answers about the news and politics. I keep them out of any discussion. I tell them you have to have all the facts in order to defend a case. Besides, *jihad* is primordially a *'jihad al nafs'*, a holy war against the selfish part of ourselves. Above all, we have to control ourselves. The holy war is against vice. Even in a military context, *jihad* is a defensive war [and not an offensive one]. I tell them, 'It's the holy war against the Self [*jihad al nafs*] that is principally mentioned in the Qur'an'.

The Imam's strategy was to prevent any discussion of 'oversensitive' topics and to stress the mystical side of Islam against its warrior aspect. In doing so he was elaborating on two divergent interpretations of Islam that have varied with prevailing religious traditions throughout its history. According to the Imam, 'One should not encourage rebellion or revolt. Or else, this ends up in criminal acts'. What about martyrdom related to *jihad*, as promoted by recent events and by those radical Muslims who want to fight for religion? His response to inmates was again in keeping with the spiritual tenets of his faith:

> The theory of sudden death in the service of religion is meaningless. You have to live a long life in order to adore God in the best way. The issue of martyrdom [*shahada*] is in itself fuzzy. For me, the most important thing is to live in the best way and to do the best things according to religion.

The Imam denounced the radical versions of Islam not only for the sake of prison authorities but also in line with his own religious convictions which insisted on a spiritualised representation of religion. He had himself been influenced by Sufism in Morocco where he was born and where a *sheikh* had inspired him. Consequently, his profound belief about radical Islam stands in perfect conformity to the views of prison authorities.

The basics of Islam: mentoring

The Imam of Prison B refused to talk politics; he simply did not want to get involved in any kind of discussion with prisoners that might lead him to take sides about policies. In his view, his duty was to inform them about the elementary rules of Islam such as the correct way of performing ritual ablutions, daily prayers, the kind of charity that is obligatory, what kind of earnings are licit and so on. In this respect, he was quite successful. Many prisoners wanted to talk to him in order to get practical solutions for their concrete problems (such as talking to relatives or reading the Qur'an). His Friday prayers were meant to make the life of prisoners meaningful, and up to a maximum of 50 of them attended prayers every week out of a population of about 600 Muslims, many of whom were non-practising. The upper limit was imposed by the prison authorities because of concerns about safety and security. The area set aside for prayers, at the end of a corridor, was not big enough to accommodate more than this number. There was a lengthy waiting list of prisoners who had requested permission to attend Friday prayers.

The kind of Islam that this Muslim chaplain promoted is based on rituals, intense personal concern with life and death and the teaching of religious knowledge to prisoners, many of whom are lacking in any Islamic culture, according to him. He placed special emphasis on patience [*sabr*] and constantly referred to the 67 occurrences of this term in the Qur'an during his Friday sermons [*khutbah*]. He also spoke about the Qur'an's statements on Islamic law and imprisonment [*fiqh* and *sujun*] in order to reveal Islamic models of their situation in prison.

According to this particular Imam, Islam was expanding in prisons as a consequence of the quest for identity. He was in no doubt that his mission was to reject the warrior or political side of Islam in order to promote its spiritual one:

> Most of the prisoners (that is, the *banlieusards*) want to know more about Islam: to perform prayers, invocations. My mission is very clearly demarcated: politics is the role of TV; I am here for prayers and fasting.

He suggested that prisoners were characterised by 'something inside them that pushes them towards questions about Islam. Most of the time, they experience a vacuum that they want to fill'. The Imam had discovered that the prisoners' ignorance about Islam left the young ones susceptible to the influence of radical Muslims from Algeria or elsewhere who could read the Qur'an in Arabic and had at least a basic knowledge of Islam.

He was worried that young Muslims who were exposed to the influence of radicals in prison were an easy prey because what characterised these young people from the *cités* above all was the 'hatred' that they felt (Dubet, 1987; Tietze and Khosrokhavar, 1999). This expression gained currency in the 1980s in the *banlieues* and came to mean hating the wider society that stigmatised the people from these poor suburbs. The Imam used strong terms to describe this phenomenon:

> This hatred is gangrene, an illness. These youngsters sometimes meet extremist people who tell them anything about Islam and quote some Qur'anic verses that suit their purposes; they are easily indoctrinated by

them. They don't really know the meaning of *Shahid* [martyrdom or witness, according to context], daily prayer [*salat*], the Testimony to God's existence and unity [*Shahada*] and so on. The vast majority of them don't know anything about that.

He did not believe that it was possible to prevent the radicalisation of young Muslims by denying them their religious culture. On the contrary, he argued that by providing them with healthy religious information, the influence of radicals could be blocked. In this respect, the Imam of Prison B is in agreement with the Imam in Prison C. Both would like to promote knowledge of Islam, particularly its basics, among French Muslims in prison as well as the teaching of Arabic so that prisoners could read the Qur'an more easily and become rooted in Islamic culture. But he concluded that it had been impossible to accomplish this second part of his mission.

The Imam explained that sheer ignorance about Islam derived from the breakdown of religious transmission between parents and their children:

Muslims born in France have never seen their parents practise their religion. They say to me, 'My father has never talked to me about Islam'. The majority of them know nothing about it. On the whole, less than 20 per cent of them know how to do the daily prayers.

Nonetheless, the Imam reported that many prisoners were concerned about what was allowed and what was prohibited in religion. They displayed an interest in learning about the daily prayers, the basic rituals, the distinctions between what is licit and what is not:

For instance, they say, 'I have made this mistake. How can I put it right? Can someone who has committed a murder be forgiven?'. Or, 'I have done something wrong [*j'ai fait des bêtises*] to someone. What can I do?'. They ask questions about the sins they've committed. This is, in turn, related to the problem of death in their mind.

According to the Imam, these prisoners were rootless: they had no way of accessing either the culture in which their parents had grown up or mainstream French culture. They felt somehow caught in between, unable to master the codes of one side or the other. Above all, they had lost the hope of becoming normal citizens like others. This is how he described them:

They are in a desperate situation. I try to give them some hope. Without hope, life is meaningless. These people are violent because they have no hope. They develop a negative reaction towards society. They want to do harm to those whom they accuse of being at the root of their own misery. They have hatred towards society.

The Imam did not consider that parents could help; in his view, young people sought an escape in religion:

> The parents are ignorant. At school, their children fail exams, they are not aware of their children's failure. Then the children feel that their parents can't defend them and that they have to do it themselves. This is at the root of their violence at an early age. Most of the young offenders are ours, they are Muslims. The teachers, on the other hand, are ignorant about Islam. The mosques, too, don't know how to straighten things up. This generation is aggressive towards society. They look for some escape through religion.

This is why he had adopted the role of a spiritual mentor for young Muslim prisoners. He saw them as fatherless in the symbolic sense of the word (and even, in many cases, in the literal sense, since many of them come from broken families) and in search of someone who could show them the way: 'They need a reference point and they come to see me. If I fulfil that need, they come back and see me again. If not, they stop coming'.

Prison officers and the institution

Prison officers in Prison B described the Imam as a very shy and discreet person who did his work without fuss and avoided any action that might cause a disturbance in the prison. They were aware that the Muslim chaplain co-operated with prison authorities in order to ward off any kind of religious radicalisation that might upset the fragile balance within the prison. The Prison Director perceived the Imam's role as positive especially when he intervened if tension developed between Muslims or between them and prison staff. In the Imam's own words:

> One Friday just before the bombing of Afghanistan by the Americans, a prison officer told me that a group of prisoners had decided to take prison officers hostage if the Americans attacked Afghanistan. In the Friday prayer, the same day, I said, 'As Muslims you shouldn't set a bad example to others'.

One problem that the Imam identified was the extent of misunderstanding between Muslim prisoners and prison officers. The officers had no knowledge of Islam in a jail where more than half of the inmates were Muslims; and they misinterpreted as threats what were, most of the time, nothing but examples of religious practice. The Imam reasoned that:

> In the prison, prison officers should have special training in Islam. Their only sources of information are the media and the prisoners.

They internalise the negative stereotypes about Islam. They need good information about this religion. An example: a woman was using a magnet in her cell to look for the *Kaabah* [the direction of Mecca for the celebration of the daily prayer]. The prison officer got the impression that she was trying to escape by using this piece of metal. Another misunderstanding concerns prayer time and the intrusion of prison officers into the cells during prayers. They do not realise how much they upset some prisoners by doing this. The prisoners feel it is a profanation, not only showing disrespect towards them but also desecrating a religious act, an attempt to destroy Islam.

He acknowledged that things were beginning to change slowly since some prison officers with North African origins, who introduced some understanding of Muslim prisoners, had been employed in the prison. He found that the employment of female officers, too, had changed the atmosphere for the better because male inmates tended not to behave in the same way towards them as towards male officers. Inmates were thus less aggressive, and the female prison officers themselves usually tackled situations in a more accommodating way.

The Imam considered that there were two kinds of prison officers. Where older officers were concerned, the Algerian war of independence was still a factor that influenced their behaviour towards North Africans. The younger generation of officers seemed much more resistant to this prejudice but had problems coping with the young generation from the *banlieues*. These officers held the view that, since young Muslims harboured such deep hatred towards society, they refused to obey the rules, they had no respect for others and blamed society for their misery.

The Imam also assisted prison officers in their dealings with prisoners suffering from mental problems. He described one incident as follows:

> One prisoner claimed to be the Messiah. The prison officers told me that he was dangerous and unpredictable. I talked to him and said that there were warning signs before the Messiah would appear and that they had not appeared. In the end, I succeeded in calming him temporarily. There are lots of pathological cases like this one.

The Imam identified two general kinds of problems related to Islam within prison: on the one hand, the fascination with radical Islam and, on the other, the fear of sorcery [*sehr*] or of being ritually poisoned by food. This was more common among women who apparently 'come and ask me for a cure for sorcery. I give them some Qur'anic verses to read. For each specific case, I have a particular treatment to hand'.

Prison C: Imam against the odds

The differences between the conditions in which the Imams in Prisons B and C have to work are so great that we need to analyse their accounts separately. As we have just seen, Prison B does not make life particularly easy for its Muslim chaplain, but the Imam in Prison C faces insuperable difficulties in the exercise of his ministry. Prison C in reality consists of seven semi-autonomous sub-prisons, each with its own Sub-Director: five are for men, one is a women's prison, and the last one is a prison for young offenders. A single Director has overall responsibility for all of them. The sheer number of prisoners coupled with the administrative and physical separation between the different prisons conspire to make the Imam's conditions of work virtually unmanageable. This is compounded by the fact that the prison's management appears to be, at best, indifferent to, and, at worst, obstructive *vis-à-vis* the needs of Muslims. The Imam described the Director's attitude towards him as 'reserved'. Although the Imam occupies a full-time post, there are so many prisoners that they generally cannot meet him. Many are not even aware of his existence. Although he is unable to meet the prisoners' demands due to their sheer number and to the limitations of his timetable, the prison authorities are not making any move to hire an additional Imam.[8] This particular Imam is of Algerian origin and belongs to an orthodox or mainstream school of Islam. In the prison where he officiates, 65 per cent of inmates are Muslims, and more than 50 per cent of the prisoners are young people of North African origin.

Difficult conditions

These circumstances account for many of the difficulties encountered by the Imam in delivering his services. Since prisoners cannot move in groups from one building to another because of administrative restrictions, he cannot celebrate Friday prayers. This leads to frustration among some prisoners who consider that it is completely unjust to see so many Christian ministers in the prison – and even a rabbi for about 40 Jewish inmates – but only one Imam. Since the Imam serves more than 2,000 Muslims he can neither visit them personally nor celebrate collective prayers with them, particularly on Fridays. His description leaves no doubt about his plight:

> We have an insoluble problem – the insufficient number of Muslim ministers. I am the only one entitled to help some 2,000 Muslims in this prison. There are eight Christian ministers – Catholic and Protestant – and two nuns, all in all ten for the Christian prisoners and only one Muslim minister! This is not fair. There are five buildings here and, for security reasons, the inmates cannot go from one to the other. If you

include the young offenders' prison and the women's prison, we have seven. We need seven Imams to cope with their religious problems. How can I organise Friday prayers on my own? I can't even meet them one by one. Sometimes, they write to me three months in advance and I don't find time to see them. The only solution I have found is to meet them collectively, in groups of five or six, but some of them would like to talk to me alone, and I cannot help them.

The Imam is overworked and frustrated, while inmates are sometimes reproachful towards him and the prison because they are unable to talk to him directly. The religious needs of inmates are very far from being satisfied. For women, there is a female Muslim teacher who comes to see them occasionally, but the issue of collective prayers remains unresolved for them as well.

Because he cannot meet inmates individually, the Imam devised a makeshift solution, gathering them into groups of five or six in order to discuss religious matters. But this strategy had its own flaws: many had jobs in the prison and could not attend, while others would have liked to talk to him alone about their private problems. Moreover, the organisation of meetings was problematic for many prisoners. They had to write to the Imam and give their letters to prison officers who were supposed to forward them to the Imam. According to many inmates, they never received a reply, even after two or three months. They suspected that the prison officers had destroyed their letters instead of sending them to the Imam. The Imam, himself, realised that he could not deal with all the letters sent by prisoners, owing to a shortage of time. The suspicious attitude of the prisoners towards prison staff was thus heightened because the Imam himself could not reply to their letters. Prisoners sometimes argued that the prison officers did not send their letters, be it to the Imam or to doctors, because they wanted to punish them for supposedly being difficult during the day. An atmosphere of mutual suspicion was created in which everyone played a role, albeit unwittingly at times.

Many prisoners were not even aware that there was an Imam in the prison. Because no collective Islamic events took place, and because inmates did not receive information about the presence of an Imam, they were unaware that they could write to him. Consequently, they simply thought that there was no Muslim chaplain in the prison and complained that the Christians and the Jews had their own chaplains.

One of the Imam's tasks was to provide religious literature for inmates. He could not afford to purchase it, however, and there was no budget for this in the prison. He obtained donations of books in French and Arabic from Saudi Arabia, so that he could distribute them in the prison free of charge. Despite the French authorities' suspicions about Saudi ideological influence over Muslim prisoners, the Imam was grateful to Saudi Arabia for its support:

> I am glad that Saudi Arabia helps us to have free copies of the Qur'an and other religious books. For Ramadan, they sent us a ton of dates. I asked the Paris Mosque for help – they didn't do anything. On the contrary, the Saudis are generous and give us the Qur'an and other religious books in French and Arabic.

Copies of the Qur'an in French and Arabic were thus available as well as other books by Saudi religious authorities. The Imam put his seal on the books so that they could be identified as coming from him and he gave them away to the inmates, although the vast majority could not read Arabic. The French version of the Qur'an was much more useful than the Arabic one.

One of the tasks of the Imam was to teach inmates about prayer rituals. Since he had no time to do it personally, he gave them books where the ablution rituals [*wudhu*] and the prayer itself [*salat*] were explained in simple words and pictures. Whereas he would have liked to accompany Muslim inmates in their observance of fasting at Ramadan, he struggled to find a way of obtaining the necessary provisions. He nevertheless succeeded in extracting a promise from the prison authorities that *halal* food would be put on sale in the prison canteen alongside kosher food:

> 80 per cent of [prisoners] fast during Ramadan. But the food does not meet the requirements for *halal* meat. They complain about these problems, and I cannot solve them. It is contrary to the norms of *laïcité*. I try to devise solutions. They have promised to sell *halal* meat in the canteen. The same holds true for the Feasts of Eid al-Kabir.

His main achievement is the organisation of an Eid celebration in the women's prison, for which he had to overcome a large number of obstacles:

> Last year, we organised [an Eid al-Kabir feast] in the women's prison on the 27th day of Ramadan, and everybody, Muslim or not, took part. When the Qur'an was quoted everybody cried. They thought it was a marvellous day. But we had lots of problems organising it. And we couldn't have done it for the men. The number of women is much smaller.

However, he could not help Muslim women who wanted to wear a headscarf because, 'Women have no right to put a scarf on in the prison. It is allowed only in the cells. But in religious terms, the scarf is for the public sphere!'.

The one area which complied with Islamic requirements was the availability of showers: 'To be able to practise their religion, the prisoners should have access to showers. On the whole, this condition is satisfied here'.

Radical or fundamentalist Islam

Like the Imam in Prison B, the Imam in Prison C disapproved of radical Islam but differed in his approach to the Islamists, whom he was prepared to challenge about their interpretation of Islam. One reason for this is that this particular Imam is much more attracted by orthodox Islam and its legalist tradition rather than by Sufism. He was willing to discuss the burning issues of the day and the question of *jihad* with radical Islamists. What he did in the case of Islamic radical inmates was to show them the merciful and forgiving side of Islam. As he said, many of those who had been radicalised had never heard anything about the leniency of Islam, and their picture of it was distorted by the violent interpretation of *jihad*. By accepting the challenge of exchanging arguments with Islamic radicals he was able to make them more sensitive to the non-violent aspects of Islam:

> Islamists are active here in prison and they have a prestige of their own. One of them has been condemned to 30 years' imprisonment, and the others admire him. At the beginning of his sentence, he transformed his cell into a mosque and attracted many 'Arabs'. He enjoys some prestige among them. He sent me a letter accusing us of being traitors to Islam. He is someone who has deviated from religion. Still, I have been able to mellow him bit by bit.

The Imam confirmed that the basics of Islam were an unknown quantity to most inmates. In his view, this made it easy for those who were against society and the public interest to cultivate inappropriate interpretations of Islam. Since very few Muslim inmates came equipped with basic Islamic culture, some were pushed into radical interpretations by other inmates who lacked any critical sense. The lack of knowledge about primary religious tenets encouraged radicalisation through the influence of those who, in the absence of a Muslim with institutional authority, filled the vacuum and offered their radical view as the only legitimately Islamic one. Imams are either non-existent in prisons or available in only derisory numbers. Consequently, they cannot tackle the spiritual (and sometimes material) problems of their people, so the prisoners themselves do it independently. They help each other and constitute groups with various sensitivities, divided into two main tendencies: the orthodox (who teach how to conform more or less strictly to religious observance of what is allowed and what is forbidden) and the radical (who preach *jihad* or some form of denunciation of the Western world). There is a hidden struggle between radical Islamists and Imams in prison. Radical Islamists object to the Imam siding with French institutions against the Muslims in the world; they sometimes accuse Imams of being police agents in prisons. The prisoners are happy to see these inmates, either from the radical school or the orthodox school, preaching in prison; and many prefer them to the remote Imam whom they cannot meet because he is too busy or simply absent. One prisoner who had not even tried to get in touch with the Imam expressed his admiration for the Islamists who acted in the name of the Islamic *da'wa*, the call to Muslims to come back to Islam and acknowledge the rule of God. Hussein, a 23-year-old Pakistani, said:

> I haven't written to the Imam to see him but I read Arabic. I was in a *madrassa* from the age of five to ten and I learned Arabic and the Qur'an there. What is marvellous here is that we have *da'wa* in prison. Four or five brothers [in religion] make *da'wa*. They are bearded. I love it when they talk about God, Allah. I am a Muslim and I love Muslims. I love all the Muslims and I don't give a damn [*je m'en fous*] if the authorities regard them as terrorists.

In his attempt to counteract those influences, the Imam strove to promote a form of Islam that was an alternative to that of the radicals. He recognised that 'My aim is to develop a tolerant and peaceful Islam here. But the people are dazzled by the Islamists'.

Mentoring

The Imam defined his role as partially that of a mentor who attended to the multiple needs expressed by young Muslims in prison. He considered them as a lost generation who needed guidance not only in religious matters but also in their personal life:

> Young people are exposed to the hardships of life. They are exposed to the empty life of modern society and its urge to become rich and well off. Since they cannot achieve it normally they do it illegally, through drug trafficking or violence.

His analysis closely paralleled the diagnosis given by the Imam in Prison B, that is, young inmates needed his help with the general conduct of their life in order to make up for absent or powerless parents:

> Parents leave young people at a loose end. They give up on their education. As a minister I have many different tasks: to teach them religion, but also to educate them. In many cases, they have problems with their parents and I try to repair their broken relationships. I do it gently.

He also detected great eagerness among Muslim inmates to practise their religion:

> They are eager to rediscover themselves. They are traumatised, isolated, a long way from their family, sometimes abandoned by them. When I meet them, their first reaction is to cry. They find solace in returning to God. Prison officers sometimes say to me, 'How is it that they are so peaceful after prayers?'.

The Imam explained the attraction to Islam in terms of the conditions of life facing the second and third generations of North African immigrants in poor suburbs as well as their particular conditions in the prison. He considered Islam in this context as a catharsis: it released emotions and brought solace to the prisoners. It thus helped them to cope with a life of confinement in prison. He described how religion gave an outlet for emotions by freeing individuals from oppression and the restrictions of daily life in confinement:

> By performing the rituals, the individual moves away from the world and gets closer to God. For instance, by making ablutions Muslims communicate with Allah. A week later, they tell me, 'Sheikh, I have performed my ablutions properly, I am practising the daily prayers, and I have rediscovered the joy of life'.

In the Imam's view, religion was there to soothe the pains and the injuries of these people; they asked for religion and they wanted to conform to it in order to achieve peace of mind. The Imam's tasks thus included helping them to gain this peace. The fact is that many people from the poor suburbs are tempted to embrace Islam as a way of solving their existential and even practical problems; this in turn may place them in a difficult position *vis-à-vis* French society and its non-religious norms, including its refusal to consider religious symbols as acceptable in the public sphere.

Prison officers

The Imam's view of prison officers in Prison C was ambivalent. He surmised that they did not appreciate him and that they were much less co-operative with him than with Catholic or Protestant ministers. He even felt that they despised him as a Muslim and an Algerian. On the whole, he was forthright about the disadvantaged position of Islam in France and thought that nothing was done to give comfort to Muslims, particularly in prisons.

Although the Imam had gained all the necessary security clearances, prison officers allegedly treated him with suspicion. He had done his best to alleviate their concern:

At the beginning, I did not have the right to go into cells. During my talks with inmates, a prison officer kept watch on me. To reassure them, I left the door open during the talks, so that they could hear what I said. I did the same with the groups. Since then, it's OK.

In addition, prison officers' suspicions tended to be heightened by would-be converts to Islam. The Imam mentioned that not a single week passed by without some Christian prisoners asking to convert to Islam. It appears that prison officers did not pass on their requests for a meeting with the Imam:

Each week my appointments list contains the name of Europeans who are asking to be converted. I am very careful to see whether they are really motivated or whether it is just a whim. Even a Protestant minister wanted to convert to Islam. He asked me for the Qur'an, and I gave him a copy. Few Muslims ask to be converted to Christianity. The prison officers are suspicious towards converts and they don't always give me the names of the would-be converts. Sometimes, they don't allow them to come to the meetings with me – or they hide their names and don't give them to me. When Christians ask to meet the Muslim minister, prison officers become inflexible and suspicious towards them.

On the other hand, the very prison officers who suspected the Imam of proselytising and spied on him came to him for help when there were troubles with young prisoners from the *cités*: 'When there are troubles with the 'Arabs', they don't call the Christian or Jewish minister, but me. The role of the Muslim minister is very important here'.

There are major differences between Prison B and Prison C in terms of how they accommodate and incorporate their respective Muslim chaplains. The Imam in Prison C faces much greater difficulties in the exercise of his ministry. This is related to two factors. On the one hand the sheer size and structure of the prison – which is subdivided into separate sections, all of which hold vast numbers of Muslim inmates – creates difficulties. On the other hand, difficulties for the Imam flow from the prison authorities' suspicious attitude towards him. In Prison B, by contrast, the number of Muslim inmates is much more manageable and the prison consists of one single unit for male prisoners. In addition, the director is tolerant towards Islam and extends his trust to the Imam. As explained above, the theological differences between the two Imams also place the Imam in Prison C at a disadvantage because he is a follower of orthodox or mainstream Islam, whereas the Imam in Prison B is a practitioner of a more mystical strand of the religion – Sufism.

In spite of these differences, both Imams share the same views on their responsibilities and the role of Islam in prison. They both oppose radical

Islam – albeit in different ways: the Imam in Prison C gets involved in debates with the adepts of radical Islam, but the Imam in Prison B refuses to discuss it. However, both of them preach a tolerant and peaceful Islam in opposition to the tenets of '*jihadism*' with a view to protecting young inmates from its influence. They also analyse the background of young Muslim inmates in the same terms, that is, as a lost generation in need of guidance and support. The two Imams consider their ministry as the only way forward which might contribute to meeting the needs of these young people. According to the Imam in Prison C:

> Being appointed as an Imam in a French prison is like running an obstacle race. To obtain the approval of the French Ministry of Justice and then, the Ministry of the Interior as well as that of the Prison System, Imams must satisfy many contradictory requirements: those of security, of a 'quiet Islam' and of *laïcité* by means of a ministry based on an inconspicuous form of religious practice which avoids offending against '*laïque*' norms. This places an enormous limitation on the number of applicants to become prison Imams who could satisfy these criteria. In turn, the lack of Imams in prisons throws young people into the hands of the Islamists who are much better informed about Islam. The Islamists master Arabic and can claim to know the meaning of religion, and this grants them some kind of legitimacy.

Conclusion

Historically, the position of Imams or Muslim chaplains in the prisons of England and Wales was rather precarious. It raised an employment issue since they only did sessional work and did not enjoy the same holiday, sick leave and pension rights as chaplains. Moreover, they remained dependent on the goodwill of Christian chaplains for their integration into the chaplaincy team. Another contentious question has been the control of the chaplaincy budget and the distribution of resources. However, in prisons where Imams have been appointed to full-time posts (15 of them by mid-2004), their position has been strengthened. The views of the Imams whom we interviewed about prison staff (prison officers and chaplains) and *vice versa* are mixed and mostly dependent on the situation in the prisons studied: the attitudes of the senior Christian chaplain and the governor seem to be a determining factor. Muslim chaplains play an important role in authenticating *halal* food, organising Ramadan and Eid, leading Friday collective prayers and counselling prisoners. Inmates generally welcome the presence of Muslim chaplains and most inmates would like them to be available for longer periods of time. Few areas of dissatisfaction arise with regard to Muslim chaplains, but one problem that faces them is how to pitch their teaching at a level that will satisfy inmates with such varied standards of Islamic knowledge. Another problem is whether to engage in debates around political issues that some inmates want to place on the agenda but to which others object. Finally, Muslim chaplains in England and Wales often find themselves caught up in disputes about the authenticity of *halal* food.

One of the dilemmas facing Imams working in prisons all over Europe is how to distance themselves from radical Muslims, or 'Islamists', without arousing suspicion among Muslim prisoners that they are 'selling out' to the powers that be. It is probably easier to strike a workable balance between these cross-pressures in other European countries (and particularly in Britain), than in France. The reason is that Imams in the UK can try to win over the sympathisers with mainstream Islam whilst keeping radical Islam at arm's length. In France, however, that particular option is not available. Orthodoxy, for Muslims in France, means such things as accepting the legitimacy of the veil (*hijab*) and other religious attitudes which are widely regarded in France as '*intégriste*' or 'fundamentalist', and thus incompatible with *laïcité*. Whereas the orthodox option is open to Muslim prison chaplains in other European countries, it is much more problematic in France. Imams in French prisons have to strike a delicate balance between the Islamists who have their sympathisers among Muslim inmates, and the Prison Service which is suspicious of any expression of '*intégrisme*'.

Another problem is that *laïcité*, as it is usually implemented with strictness in French prisons, fails to distinguish between 'orthodox' and 'radical' Muslims. Both kinds of Muslim call into question the entirely private character of religion and demand some form of public recognition of their cultural specificity (for instance, the right to perform their daily prayers in a collective fashion in prison or to have *halal* food in their diet, and so on). In many other European countries, 'orthodox' or mainstream Muslims are tolerated, and many of their requirements are met (such as *halal* food, wearing a headscarf or collective prayer). 'Orthodox' Muslims have every interest in keeping the radical Muslims at arm's length in order not to jeopardise their privileges as 'recognised' Muslims. But since the *laïcité* principle in France is usually interpreted in an inflexible way by managers in, for example, public sector schools, in the Civil Service in general and in prisons in particular, the distinction between radical Muslims and mainstream Muslims tends to be blurred. As a result, orthodox Muslims tend to find it difficult to reject their mainstream brethren outright because of the uncompromising treatment that they receive themselves from public institutions and public opinion.

Only Muslims with an 'individualist' or 'privatised' style of religiosity openly state their divergences from radicalised Muslims in France. In fact, 'individualised' Muslims, unlike radical and orthodox Muslims, are the only ones to feel 'satisfied' with their situation in French society.

Mainstream or 'orthodox' Muslims denounce their predicament and the tenacious social prejudices which identify them with radical Muslims, in the eyes of the public. Some Muslim inmates draw attention to this phenomenon in order to criticise the way in which prison officers and prison authorities look askance at every Muslim with a beard or anyone who asks for the right to collective prayer.

When *laïcité* is interpreted and applied rigidly, it precludes social dialogue and increases suspicion and rejection of cultural differences in the name of universality. It also pushes many 'orthodox' Muslims either towards some form of radicalisation or towards a vindictive and resentful attitude towards society.

On the whole, all French prisons are in dire need of Muslim ministers because they have none or too few. This problem is critical, not only because inmates regard the scarcity of Imams as further evidence of the French bias against Islam but also because, having no one to talk to and seek counsel from on religious issues, many prisoners are virtually forced to associate with inmates who appear to have a deeper knowledge of Islam. In this way, some of these 'devout' Muslims give them a radical version of Islam that contributes to the heightening of tensions within prison. A short-sighted view of *laïcité*, based on a refusal to recognise the religious needs of Muslim inmates and a fear among prison authorities of getting involved in a process of officially recognising Islam, produce consequences that run counter to what prisons purport to achieve, namely, good order, security, the rejection of radical Islam and the acceptance of a 'religious-blind' social system.

Conclusions

The issue of Muslims in prison was not high on the public agenda when we began to plan the research on which this book is based. Neither in France nor in Britain were politicians, journalists or academics asking questions about the treatment of Muslims in prison. There was certainly concern about the issue among prison chaplains in England and Wales, but its significance for the rest of British society was low in most people's opinion. Even among Muslim organisations and in the Muslim press in the UK, only a small group of campaigners was actively seeking to raise awareness about Muslim prisoners. The situation in France was even clearer: public concern with Muslims being held in French prisons was virtually non-existent.

Al-Qaeda's attacks on the USA in September 2001 changed the situation in France and Britain in two important respects. The attacks drew attention to the possibility that French and British prisons might eventually house 'Islamic terrorists' or 'Muslim extremists'; and they paved the way for emergency legislation that increased the likelihood that the number of Muslims held on suspicion of involvement in terrorism would grow. In addition, conditions at the American Camp Delta at Guantánamo Bay in Cuba, where the predominantly Muslim suspects of hostilities against Americans in Afghanistan are detained in harsh conditions, focused world-wide attention on Muslims as prisoners. It is not at all surprising, therefore, that questions about Muslims in the prisons of France and Britain rapidly began to attract massive public interest at the end of 2001 – and continue to do so at the time of writing in 2004.

Nevertheless, the main focus of our research was not on the aftermath of tragic and spectacular events in Afghanistan, in the USA on 11 September 2001 or in Cuba. In any case, French prisons had been holding people identified as Islamic terrorists for many years prior to these events. Moreover, the number of Muslims serving prison sentences for offences completely unrelated to terrorism had been growing steadily in France and Britain since the 1980s. In other words, there were good reasons for investigating the imprisonment of Muslims well before the fighting against the

Taliban in Afghanistan and 9/11. It is important to bear this in mind and to avoid the trap of thinking that questions about Muslims in prison are only about terrorists and pro-Taliban fighters. Public attention is currently riveted to the spectacular and occasionally apocalyptic scenario of the so-called clash between Muslim and Western civilisations, but social scientists and cool-headed observers can see that France and Britain have other reasons for trying to understand the place of Muslims in their prisons. There are two major considerations.

The first is that France and Britain have the largest and longest established populations of Muslims in Western Europe. The fact that the Muslim population of French and British prisons has been growing more rapidly than any other ethnic or religious category of prisoner since the 1980s should not be a surprise. What is more noteworthy is the fact that young Muslim men are over-represented in British and French prisons and that there is so much diversity among Muslim inmates. Muslims in France come predominantly from North Africa, whereas Muslims in Britain originate mainly from South Asia. Nevertheless, the number of Muslim inmates from Central and Eastern Europe, from Sub-Saharan Africa and – mainly in the person of converts – from Western Europe, is increasing. What is more, the category of 'Muslim' masks extensive diversity in the economic, cultural, social and spiritual backgrounds and interests of people coming to Western Europe from the same regions of the world. Muslims born in France or Britain also display wide variations in wealth, status, educational attainment and attitudes towards Islam. Our research takes these variations into account whilst recognising that prisons, nonetheless, have a tendency to categorise their inmates in a fairly rigid fashion. Our findings highlight the tension between the diversity of Muslim prisoners and the forces at work in prisons to standardise the category of 'Muslim' in England and Wales or 'Arab' in France.

The second reason for examining the situation of Muslim prisoners in France and Britain is that these two countries have had sharply different religious and political histories in modern times. One of the implications of the two countries' different paths to modernity is that religious institutions occupy a completely different place in the public life of each one. In particular, the legal status of religious organisations, relations between religions and the state, and the role of religion in politics are not only different between France and Britain but also contradictory in some respects. For, whereas British governments have sought to involve faith communities in many areas of public life, the principle of *laïcité* in France has had the effect of excluding religion from public life. The contrast could hardly be sharper between, on the one hand, the current policy in Britain of forging closer links between government departments and faith communities (O'Beirne, 2004)[1] and, on the other, the French government's determination to strengthen the legal framework of *laïcité*, especially in state schools and hospitals (Stasi, 2003) as reflected in the law of 2004 that prohibits the wearing of '*ostensible*' symbols of religion in the Republic's institutions.

Running in parallel with the different places occupied by religion in the public spheres of Britain and France is a pattern of differences relating to ethnic minorities. This second point of contrast between the two countries turns on their respective notions of citizenship, societal solidarity and the status of minorities. As other commentators have observed (Lapeyronnie, 1993; Wieviorka, 2001; Benbassa, 2003), the universalist idea that the French Republic is one and indivisible tends to mean that the law and public institutions in France take very little account of ethnic differences. The equality of all citizens before the law takes precedence over all differences between minorities, thereby favouring policies of assimilation that relegate ethnic and other collective differences to the private sphere. The United Kingdom, by contrast, has never been a highly centralised, indivisible entity and currently operates with relatively high levels of national and regional devolution of power. More importantly, societal integration rests at least as much on cross-cutting communal identities as on ideas of a single nation. Many social policies therefore favour the cultivation of sub-national communities based on geography, ethnicity or religion.

The treatment of Muslims in French and British prisons must be seen in context against this background of national differences in the policies and practices relating to the accommodation of religious and ethnic minorities. In fact, these national differences are thrown into unusually sharp relief in connection with prisons because they are institutions that force people from widely varying backgrounds and cultures into close proximity with one another – in some cases over long periods of time. Indeed, living conditions in most prisons enforce much more intensive interaction between inmates than would be normal among people in such other public institutions as schools, health care facilities or military institutions.[2] In this respect, prisons afford an exceptionally clear view of state policies regarding the social and cultural diversity of the people for whom they are responsible. In particular, prisons demonstrate the extent to which agencies of the state are prepared to go in recognising, and responding to, diversity. There must be rules that apply to all prisoners without regard to their background, but some prison systems also permit practices and entitlements that reflect certain differences between categories of prisoners. For example, most prison systems regard differences of age, sex, health care status and 'vulnerability' as relevant grounds for the differential categorisation and treatment of prisoners. The question of how – and how far – religion and ethnicity are also institutionally recognised as valid grounds for differential treatment of inmates lies at the heart of our research.

We investigated the extent to which prisons in France and England and Wales treat Muslim inmates differently from other prisoners. In addition to examining the broad cross-national differences and similarities, this involved consideration of the distinction between policies and practices. It also required the analytical separation of official and unofficial practices.

The views of prisoners, prison officers, governors, chaplains and other staff as well as prison service officials and representatives of Muslim organisations, all had to be compared. Moreover, we looked for changes over time in the implementation of these distinctions and views. In short, the comparison between French and British prisons involved many different dimensions and analytical distinctions. The findings are varied and complex, but we shall summarise them here for each country.

England and Wales

The long and important history of Christian chaplaincy in British prisons created a set of opportunities that Muslims have been able to turn to their advantage – with or without the assistance of Christian chaplains. The Prison Service of England and Wales has gradually put in place policies, provisions and practices that enable Muslim inmates to feel that they are able to honour many of their religious obligations. Improvements in the opportunities and facilities for the practice of Islam have been remarkable since the late 1990s, including the appointment of a full-time Muslim Adviser to the Prison Service and at least 15 full-time Muslim chaplains. Levels of self-identification as Muslims and participation in Islamic activities are probably higher in British prisons than outside, although cross-cutting identities based on nationality, skin colour, language and ethnicity can also erode the sense of Muslim solidarity. At the same time, levels of explicit racism directed at Muslim inmates seem to have declined, although incidents of racist violence as well as more subtle acts of anti-Muslim discrimination remain common.

The increasing attention given to Islam in British public life and the relatively rapid growth in the number of Muslim inmates have lent weight to formal and informal attempts to improve the religious and pastoral provision for them. This has occurred against a background of continuing concern with 'race' relations, injustice, discrimination, inequality and Islamophobia.[3] The mobilisation of Muslim organisations, voluntary associations and pressure groups has helped to keep these problems on the public agenda at a time when electoral support for candidates representing extreme right-wing political parties in the UK has been increasing. In some respects, the Prison Service of England and Wales has shown itself more willing than other parts of the public sector to tackle these issues by implementing policies that outlaw discrimination on the grounds of religion, by training staff in matters of religious sensitivity, and by including respect for religious diversity among the values that it tries to promote.

Admittedly, the situation in individual prisons does not always reflect these ambitious policies. We showed that the attitudes of individual prison officers, governors, chaplains and prisoners all have an important impact on the extent to which respect is actually shown to Muslims and their religious requirements. And, given the continuing ascendancy of Church of England chaplains over prison chaplaincies, their particular attitudes towards the introduction of multi-faith principles of chaplaincy and inclusive forms of organisation have often been crucial to the success of schemes for treating Islam no less favourably than Christianity. The presence of full-time Muslim chaplains in a growing number of prisons, however, is already helping to make respect for Islam less dependent on the attitudes of Christian chaplains. Indeed, the process of integrating Muslims and their requirements into the normal, daily routines of prison life has made significant advances in prisons served by full-time Muslim chaplains. These chaplains are confident that levels of Islamic extremism or militancy are very low in British prisons and that even Muslim prisoners being detained in connection with 'Islamic terrorism' are not in a position to exert significant influence on their fellow inmates.[4]

Nevertheless, the situation for Muslims in the prisons of England and Wales is far from ideal. The problems that persist for Muslim prisoners in Britain have three main sources. They are partly a function of the mostly low level discrimination and racism to which many prisoners continue to be subjected; partly a function of the failure of Muslim organisations to provide better support for prisoners, chaplains and released prisoners; and – ironically – partly a function of the progress that has already been made in improving their opportunities for religious practice and pastoral care.

Solutions to the problem of discrimination against Muslim prisoners lie in the aggressive promotion and defence of the values enshrined in the race relations policy of the Prison Service of England and Wales. This implies not only methodical programmes of education, training and monitoring but also effective disciplinary procedures and penalties. Nonetheless, it must be recognised that the Prison Service cannot solve problems that have their origins in the inequalities, injustices and resentments that fuel hostility to Muslims in British society. Moreover, since roughly 11 per cent of all prisoners are foreign nationals, it would be reasonable to assume – in the absence of published statistics – that the proportion of foreign nationals among Muslim prisoners must be even higher. Consequently, the problems facing Muslim prisoners are not confined to those with causes in British society.

Muslim organisations such as the Islamic Cultural Centre in London, the Iqra Trust and the National Association for the Welfare of Muslim Prisoners have worked hard to raise awareness of the plight of Muslims in prison. They have received encouragement and support from leading representatives of Muslim communities such as Lord Ahmed of Rotherham. But the cause of prisoners' welfare is not popular among British Muslims and is not well resourced. It is possible that the development of 'community chaplaincy' will elicit stronger support in the future from Muslim communities for prisoners being held in their locality.[5] But the need is probably even greater – and more urgent – for Muslim initiatives in the field of after-care, rehabilitation and resettlement. The challenge facing Muslim organisations is to support this work at a time when there are many competing calls on their time and resources – and when they are preoccupied with more pressing issues in Afghanistan, Palestine, Iraq, Chechnya and so on, to say nothing of Islamophobia and the threat of urban disorder in some British cities.

A particularly difficult challenge concerns the provision of religious and pastoral support for *female* Muslim prisoners. The current provision is widely acknowledged to be patchy and, in some places, non-existent. At least three of the 18 establishments for female prisoners have no female Muslim chaplain. Much depends on the goodwill of individual women who volunteer to visit Muslim women in prison as teachers, counsellors or friends. But organisations representing Muslims acknowledge that they still have some way to go to meet the particular requirements of Muslim women prisoners, many of whom are foreign nationals and/or converts to Islam.

The improvements that the Prison Service of England and Wales has already made in satisfying many of the requirements of male Muslim prisoners have, however, raised prisoners' standards and expectations. Now that full-time and sessional Muslim chaplains have helped to improve the level of facilities and opportunities for the practice of Islam in prison, questions of comparability with the provision made for Christians, still the largest faith group, are assuming greater importance. Muslims no longer see themselves as just a tolerated minority: they want parity of treatment and respect with the Christian majority as a matter of right.[6] Tolerance and concessions may have been the watchwords when Muslim Visiting Ministers first gained a toehold in British prisons in the 1980s, but the discourse is now more about rights and entitlements – and pride in the accomplishments already achieved. Demands are insistent for, among other things, convincing authentication of *halal* food, more frequent access to showers, the removal of obstacles to the conduct of Friday prayers at the proper times, the provision of 'modesty screens' in shared cells and communal showers, and more time to be spent with Muslim chaplains. The fact that these demands are all for the extension or enhancement of existing provision for Muslims confirms our point that their reported 'deprivations' are relative to raised expectations. It will be for other researchers to discover whether any improved provision for Muslims will give rise to resentment on the part of prisoners from other faith communities. There is certainly evidence that some representatives of Christian and Buddhist prisoners are already unhappy with what they regard as the channelling of disproportionate resources towards the religious and pastoral requirements of Muslim inmates.

Furthermore, our findings raise the question of whether the Prison Service of England and Wales has provided so many opportunities, facilities and services for Muslim prisoners that Islam is somehow at risk of becoming not only institutionalised but also co-opted in British prisons. This question arises partly because the legislation governing prisons remains The Prison Act 1952, which attributed most responsibility for overseeing religion in prisons to the Church of England and prison governors. Subsequent amendments to Prison Rules, Standing Orders and circulars to governors have re-distributed much of this responsibility, but the fact remains that Muslim chaplains work in a system over which they exercise, by right, very little control. Significantly, the Muslim Adviser to the Prison Service is definitely not an Assistant Chaplain General, although his post is graded at the same level as that of the existing Assistant Chaplains General. And, although it is in principle possible for a Muslim chaplain to acquire the status of a Co-ordinating Chaplain, this is still rare. Moreover, we have seen no indication that a post at the rank of Assistant Chaplain General, to say nothing of Chaplain General, is likely to be made available to Muslim applicants in the foreseeable future. The question of being co-opted is not, therefore, idle.

Finally, it seems to us that the way forward for policy makers and other parties involved in questions about the treatment of Muslims in the prisons of England and Wales is to grapple with the following three challenges. The challenges are inter-related, of course, but for the sake of analysis we have kept them separate here.

The first is to continue working on a broad front to combat all the varied forms of social exclusion, anti-Muslim discrimination and racism to which Muslims inside and outside prisons are subjected. This work must involve much more than implementing programmes of respect for ethnic or religious diversity. Such programmes have their place, but the urgent priority is for action that will help to eliminate the conditions of deprivation, discrimination and misunderstanding that explain in part the increasing rate at which Muslims are being incarcerated. The plight of foreign nationals and women calls for particularly careful attention.

The second is to keep under review the improvements that have undoubtedly occurred in the facilities available for Muslim activities in the prisons of England and Wales since the late 1990s and to press for further changes that will ensure the full integration of Muslim chaplains and other leading representatives of Islam in the administration of prison chaplaincies. This may eventually require fresh legislation, but the record of recent years clearly shows that considerable improvements can be achieved within the existing framework of law. In particular, policies have been put in place for enhancing the opportunities for Muslim chaplains to receive all the training available to chaplains from other faith traditions and to become eligible for appointment to all co-ordinating, area and headquarters posts. If it eventually proved impossible to appoint a Muslim – or a member of any other non-Christian faith community – as the Chaplain General, then a more radical overhaul of the Prison Service Chaplaincy might be necessary. This is one of the issues that should certainly be at stake in any serious re-consideration of the current relations between the Church of England and the British state.

The third challenge concerns Muslim organisations. It is clear from the results of the 2001 Home Office Citizenship Survey (O'Beirne, 2004) that Muslims are disproportionately unlikely to participate in voluntary associations – for reasons that probably have much to do with social deprivation and exclusion. There is also a common perception that some Muslim organisations find it difficult to co-operate with each other and to agree on appropriate forms of representation in the public sphere. We certainly found evidence of mutual suspicion and recrimination among some of the leading Muslim agencies and individuals in the field of prison welfare. These difficulties do not help to advance the cause of Muslim prisoners. They also obstruct the process of raising awareness among Muslims of the problems facing Muslim prisoners. The challenge is therefore to find ways of overcoming some of these rivalries or obstructions and of presenting a united front to Muslim communities and to the Prison Service. The current experiments with community chaplaincy in some prisons may herald the dawn of a new era of co-operation between local Muslim groups and the Muslim chaplains serving in prisons in their locality. It would be particularly rewarding if Muslim groups took some responsibility for the rehabilitation or resettlement of released prisoners.

France

Although nobody knows the precise number of Muslims in French prisons, there are clear indications that the proportion of Muslims is probably higher than in the prisons of England and Wales. Estimates of their presence in sections of urban prisons go as high as 80 per cent. Despite their numerical strength, however, Muslim inmates in France have never come even close to obtaining the kind of consideration that British prisons show towards the religious and pastoral care of Muslims. This is primarily because the French prison service, like all other agencies of the French Republic, regards religion as an essentially private matter that has no official place in public institutions. The principles of *laïcité* are observed with just as much rigour in prisons as in schools, health care institutions and military establishments. Moreover, the fact that chaplaincy has never been a prominent feature of French prisons in modern times means that Muslims have been unable to take much advantage of the facilities and opportunities provided – mainly on a voluntary basis – for Christian prisoners.

To make matters more difficult for Muslims, the French prison service is ambiguous and inconsistent in its treatment of inmates' religion, supposedly in accordance with the principles of *laïcité*. For example, some prisons stock kosher – but not *halal* – meat in their shops, although Jewish prisoners are much less numerous than Muslims. On the other hand, prison kitchens acknowledge the requirements of Muslims when they supply alternatives if pork is on the menu. Similarly, female Muslim prisoners are not allowed to wear veils or headscarves outside their cells, whereas Catholic nuns working in prisons have usually enjoyed permission to wear their traditional forms of head covering. Moreover, prisons in the Alsace-Moselle region, where a Concordat is still in operation between the French state and 'recognised' religions, are not bound by the principles of *laïcité*. It is not easy to reconcile these inconsistencies with the confident assertion of the Stasi report (2003) that *laïcité*, as one of the cornerstones and founding values of the French Republic, rests on three inseparable values, the second of which is equality before the law of spiritual and religious choices. The report also insists on re-affirming strict rules governing *laïcité* for the sake of assuring collective life in a plural society. One of these rules requires public institutions to abolish public practices that discriminate. There are certainly good grounds for thinking that French prisons discriminate against Muslims, and the new law enacted in 2004 seems to be aimed mainly against the wearing of 'Muslim' headscarves in state schools.

Thus, although control of the French state is exceptionally centralised and standardised, the treatment of Muslim prisoners is surprisingly inconsistent and variable. Directors of prisons enjoy considerable freedom to decide how far to accommodate the demands of Muslims, resulting in considerable variations in practice. The difference between 'liberal' and 'conservative' directors can have major implications for the treatment of Muslim inmates. In the absence of clear instructions and criteria governing the employment of Imams as sessional prison chaplains, much depends on the attitudes of individual directors and Imams. The overriding concern of directors, which seems to be to avoid unnecessary bureaucratic complications and security risks, often militates against engaging Imams as chaplains. In some cases, it also means a preference for Imams who espouse mystical, rather than orthodox, currents of Islamic thought. This preference is based on the belief that Sufis, for example, are unlikely to encourage or to tolerate the activities of Radical Islamists.

These ambiguities in the meaning and operationalisation of *laïcité* are also reflected in the preference expressed by the then French Minister of the Interior, Dominique de Villepin, for a scheme to 'begin training Muslim clerics in a moderate Islam that respects human rights and the republican code' (*Guardian*, 23 April 2004). One wonders how such sentiments can be reconciled with the principles of *laïcité* reflected in the new law of 2004 regarding the notion of the French state's neutrality in matters of religion. In fact, there is a long history of government initiatives to create a 'French Islam'. *Le Nouvel Observateur* reported on 1 March, 2004 for example, that the Garde des Sceaux had approved a plan to train prison officers to look for the warning signs of 'islamist proselytism' and 'religious fundamentalism' among prisoners.

The reluctance of prison directors to appoint Imams – and the consequent lack of Muslim chaplains in many French prisons – has produced an ironic outcome. The shortage of Imams creates an ideological vacuum that some radically minded prisoners are all too willing to fill. The result is that the directors' attempts to prevent the development of radical or extremist ideas among Muslim inmates actually increase the probability that radical Muslim prisoners will not only attract the attention of their fellow religionists but will also have cogent grounds for arguing that French prisons are hostile to Islam because they fail – or refuse – to appoint Imams. Moreover, some prisons then find that they have to 'turn a blind eye' to the activities of radical Muslim prisoners in return for their co-operation in maintaining order among Muslim inmates. This 'deal' may be convenient for both parties, but it seems like a fragile basis for orderly prisons in the long term, especially if the proportion of Muslim inmates continues to rise at its current rate of growth.

One looks in vain for the effective intervention of organisations representing Muslims in France in debates about prison conditions and in pressure group activities to demand better opportunities for religious practice. Neither the state-supported French Council of the Muslim Religion [*le conseil français du culte musulman*] nor Muslim voluntary associations have successfully taken up the issue of the treatment of Muslim prisoners. Moreover, the relatively few Imams who visit prisons on a full-time or a part-time basis lack any form of co-ordination or representative authority in the eyes of the prison service. As a result, the prisoners' complaints about the lack of Imams, their inability to hold collective prayers, the anti-Islamic racism of some prison officers, and the scarcity of *halal* food can find no voice in public life. It is as if French prisons reproduce – and possibly amplify – the sense of exclusion and powerlessness that is so characteristic of the young, disaffected Muslims from the poor *banlieues*. The image of a vicious circle is not far from the truth.

As far as public policies are concerned, the over-riding challenge for the French prison service and for organisations representing Muslim interests is to find a point of balance between respect for the principle of *laïcité* and recognition that the freedom to practise Islam in prisons calls in question the distinction that has prevailed since the late eighteenth century in many Western societies between the public and the private. As long as the practice of religion is relegated by prison authorities to the private sphere alone, Muslim prisoners will feel that their religion is not only disrespected but also rejected.

A second challenge is to institute a more equitable and transparent scheme for attracting and recruiting suitably qualified Imams to work as Muslim chaplains. This may require a nationally co-ordinated initiative but at the very least it will require a procedure that reduces the element of arbitrariness and places limits on the discretion of individual directors to decide whether the appointment of a Muslim chaplain is desirable. Such a scheme would also have implications for the method of allocating funds for the remuneration of chaplains.

The third challenge is to ensure that all chaplains of all faith traditions meet clear criteria of suitability and receive adequate training and supervision for their work. This will require political will and proper resourcing. There should also be training for prison officers and prison administrators in the specificities of Muslim beliefs and practices. This would present obvious advantages to officials who are concerned about the security threats often attributed to Muslims, but we recommend such training because it is an essential pre-condition for harmonious relations between Muslim prisoners and prison staff.

Wider issues

The way in which national prison systems treat Muslim inmates in member states of the EU is subject to all relevant treaties and international agreements on human rights. In particular, the protection of religious freedom is an obligation that is accepted by all European states, but the interpretation of 'religious freedom' and the implementation of measures designed to protect it display bewildering variety. It is also common for constitutions to guarantee the freedom of religion but to make it conditional on the maintenance of public order and security. Another common – but far from universal – feature of constitutions is to assert the state's neutrality in regard to religion. At the same time, of course, Concordats still exist between the Catholic Church and the state in some southern European countries. In addition, the UK, Greece and some Scandinavian states have retained 'established' or 'national' churches, while other states maintain special relationships with one or more particular religions. In short, there is no single benchmark for the legal protection of religious freedom, but Muslims and others will no doubt eventually bring pressure to bear on legislatures and courts of law to clarify its meaning. The European Court of Human Rights has already resolved a small number of cases concerning the actions of states in relation to members of Christian minority groups, and it is to be expected that the treatment of Muslims in prison will eventually give rise to other cases. The findings of our research indicate that Muslim prisoners feel particularly deprived of their rights if they are denied access to collective prayers, *halal* food, protection of modesty, and the spiritual support of suitably qualified Imams.

There is a school of thought that is resistant to the idea of catering fo the needs of faith communities, as expressed by their leading representa tives. According to this approach, questions about rights to religiou freedom should make no reference to the alleged needs of any particula community. Rather, the issue is said to be framed more appropriately a one of individual rights and of equality of rights – regardless of the faith community concerned. This line of reasoning has much to recommend it but, as we argued in Chapter 2, it tends to ignore the fact that definition of what is required for religious freedom vary substantially between different religions. Equally important is the tendency for arguments about individual rights to focus exclusively on what is permissible in the private sphere – with no consideration of the fact that some religions also have implications for conduct in the public sphere. Indeed, the very boundary between public and private is itself subject to different definitions in differ- ent faith traditions. There is a risk, therefore, that the defence of religious freedom solely on grounds of individual rights may exclude the protection of collective practices if they involve the public sphere. Yet, some religious traditions require individuals to participate in collective activities or to interact with other people in particular forms of dress, head covering or language as a religious obligation. In short, the defence of individual freedom to practise religion is necessary but not sufficient by itself to protect all religious freedoms.

This rationale for treating religious freedom as an issue that necessarily involves – but transcends – individual rights to belief and practice in the private sphere applies with special cogency to prisons. For, given that prisons are by definition part of the public sphere, they contain no spaces that are really private. It is therefore potentially open to administrators to decide that no religious practices will be permitted because the entire institution is public and must therefore be free of all religious activity. This is an unlikely scenario, but it serves to highlight the problematic nature of the public/private distinction and the potentially arbitrary character of decisions about prisoners' individual rights to practise religion. Admittedly, there is no guarantee that decisions about the permissibility of collective worship and other rituals will not be equally arbitrary, but at least the prospects of collective pressure or protest are probably better if group rights and comparisons are seen to be at stake.

Another contentious issue with a direct bearing on our research is the question of whether it was advisable for us to devote so much attention to the imprisonment and, by implication, the criminality of Muslims. Has the very topic of our research only served to reinforce public perceptions of young Muslim men in particular as a problem for Britain and France? Should we not have expended our energies and other resources on studying the underlying causes and conditions of the apparently high rate of imprisonment among Muslims? Well, there is no question about the importance of understanding the broader picture, and two of us have made our own contributions (Khosrokhavar, 1997; Joly, 1995). Other researchers have also explored these issues at length (Lewis, 1994; Boyer, 1998; Cesari, 1998). Moreover, there is widespread agreement on the urgent need for agencies of the British state 'to seriously tackle the issues of poverty, exclusion and discrimination that have made British Muslims the most impoverished group in the country' (Nahdi, 2004). Moreover, the largest proportion of respondents to the 2001 Home Office Citizenship Survey reporting that the government was doing too little to protect the rights of people belonging to religions came from the Muslim and Sikh communities (O'Beirne, 2004: 24). The same survey also showed that Muslim respondents had the lowest levels of outright home ownership and the highest levels of residence in areas of deprivation. It is not surprising, therefore, that the Director of the Minority Rights Group has claimed that 'The situation of Muslims is one of the most pressing issues facing British society today' (Ansari, 2002: 3). In fact, a steadily growing number of young Muslims find themselves in British and French prisons where huge disparities are evident in the extent to which the religious needs, demands and interests of Muslim inmates are satisfied. One possibility is simply to ignore these experiences while waiting for Muslims' social conditions to improve to the point where the likelihood of their imprisonment will decline. Since there is no certainty that this decline will occur even in the long term, however, it would be unwise to refrain from conducting research on Islam in prison out of a fear of possibly reinforcing unfavourable public perceptions of Muslims.

More importantly, the treatment of Muslim prisoners can serve as an indicator of their position outside prisons. It could also inform Muslims about the extent to which they are excluded or included in social processes and rewards. In short, the treatment of prisoners is precisely one of the social conditions that need careful investigation. We were aware of the risk that our research might reinforce stereotypes about Muslims as criminals or victims of their circumstances, but we were also confident that we could minimise this risk by explaining our objectives clearly and by showing how the study of Muslims in prison can throw light on some of the difficult social conditions affecting the overwhelming majority of law-abiding Muslim citizens in Britain and France.

Ideally, our research will lead to studies of the place that Islam occupies in the lives of Muslims *after* their release from prison. We know that many Muslims come to a significant understanding of Islam for the first time in British prisons. Men and women who were born into Muslim families do not always become familiar with Islamic teachings and practices during their most formative years, but the experience of life in the prisons of England and Wales provides them with the opportunity and encouragement to practise their religion more thoroughly and knowledgeably.

However, no research has investigated the long-term consequences of an engagement with Islam in prison. The same is also true for prisoners who convert to Islam before, during or after imprisonment. Again, careful research is needed to ascertain how far these converts are able to maintain their Islamic faith outside the clearly structured environment of prisons.

In the case of Muslims released from French prisons, it would be particularly interesting to discover whether the experience of prison produces any long-term effects on their religious beliefs, practices and engagement with Muslim organisations. It seems unlikely, in the virtual absence of collective prayers and Qur'anic study in many French prisons, that released prisoners would find it easy to start or to resume relations with mosques and Muslim organisations. But an alternative hypothesis would suggest that the exclusion – or, at best, the marginalisation – of Islam in French prisons could provoke some prisoners and ex-prisoners into embracing Islam out of a sense of hostility and resentment towards the society that had apparently rejected them. What is needed is a programme of research that could examine these hypotheses methodically and, thereby, produce findings that would replace the sensationalist and ill-founded accounts of Islam in prison that are all too common in the mass media (Open Society Institute, 2002: 379–81). This is not to deny that some Muslim prisoners cultivate extremist views that may be associated with terrorism: it is merely to call for research that would place extremist elements in the context of all the other views expressed by Muslims in prison.

Notes

Chapter 1   Introduction: Aims, Access and Analysis

1. Beckford acknowledges with gratitude the generous support of the Leverhulme Trust for the earlier project.
2. We are grateful to the Economic and Social Research Council for funding for our project entitled 'Muslims in prison: a European challenge'.
3. The four major components of the UK are Scotland, Northern Ireland, Wales and England. For some legal and administrative purposes, Wales is combined with England. This is the case as far as prisons are concerned. The Prison Service of England and Wales is separate from the Northern Ireland Prison Service and the Scottish Prison Service. For reasons of style we occasionally use the term 'Britain' as an alternative to 'England and Wales'.
4. See Le Caisne 2000 for further insights into the methodological and ethical difficulties of conducting research in French prisons.
5. In 2000, a French doctor, Dominique Vasseur (2000) working in the Parisian prison of La Santé wrote a hypercritical book about the health conditions and the hygiene of the prisoners. The book had caused uproar among prison authorities who found it too one-sided and not sufficiently distant from prisoners' statements and attitudes. They also accused the book of ignoring the progress made in previous years in terms of inmates' conditions in this very old jail. This made some Directors reluctant to give access to researchers who might also be highly critical or one-sided.
6. This term has no equivalent in the English language. It refers to the form of republican secularism that requires the French state to be neutral towards religions and excludes religion from the public sphere in France. The moral ethos of *laïcité* is particularly pervasive in state schools. See Chapter 3: 16–19.
7. See Combessie 2001 on the general problems of prison and the general trends of research on prisons.
8. In its relation to the French State, Islam was partially institutionalised through the creation of a Consistory-like institution, 'le Conseil Français du Culte Musulman', in December 2002 under the aegis of the Minister of the Interior, Nicolas Sarkozy. But this newborn Muslim institution has not convincingly shown that it is capable of effectively tackling the concrete problems of French Muslims.
9. §14(2) Prison Act 1952 requires that prisoner accommodation be 'certified' by an inspector as being suitable for the purpose. The CNA is the ideal maximum number of prisoners to be held in any particular establishment.
10. The Research Fellow received official permission to use a tape recorder in Prison 1 only in the final week of his three months' fieldwork. The request had taken nearly three months to work its way through the local bureaucracy.
11. See: http://www.homeoffice.gov.uk/justice/prisons/inspprisons/index.html.
12. Home Office. *Prison Population Brief*. November 2003. Online at: http://www.homeoffice.gov.uk/rds/pdfs2/prisnov03.pdf [accessed 30.3.04].
13. *Les Chiffres Clés de l'Administration Pénitentiaire*, Paris: Ministère de la Justice, novembre 2003: 30.

14. *Prison Statistics, England and Wales 2002*. National Statistics, Cm 5996, Table 2.2
15. It is worth adding for the sake of historical comparison that women represented as much as 17.1 per cent of all inmates in 1900.
16. See Table 1.03 of *Les Chiffres Clés de l'Administration Pénitentiaire*, Paris: Ministère de la Justice, November 2001, which shows that the 'class factor' plays an impor tant part in all age groups, but particularly so between the age of 18 and 24 when the rate of imprisonment is higher than in other age groups.
17. The main categories of ethnicity were broken down into sub-categories such a 'Pakistani' in editions of *Prison Statistics* prior to 2002.

Chapter 3   Research Contexts

1. The survey was commissioned by BBC Radio 4 (http:www.bbc.co.uk/radio4, today/reports/archive/features/muslimpoll.shtm) [accessed 19/3/03].
2. http://www.icmresearch.co.uk/reviews/2004/guardian-muslims-march-2004.htm [accessed 30/5/04].
3. 'Attitudes towards British Muslims: a survey commissioned by the Islamic Society of Britain and conducted by YouGov, November 2002' (online at: http://www.isb.org.uk/iaw/docs/SurveyIAW2002.pdf) [accessed 19/3/03].
4. Census, 2001, England and Wales.
5. Representatives of faith communities – other than mainstream Christian churches – who conducted religious services, teaching, study groups and pastoral support in prison were called 'Visiting Ministers' until the Prison Service Chaplaincy decided in 2002 to refer to them all by the more inclusive title of 'sessional chaplains'.
6. In addition, the Al-Khoei Foundation began looking after the religious interests of the small number of Shi'a Muslim inmates in 1994.
7. Online document at:
http://www.angulimala.org.uk/Religion%20in%20Prisons%20(Disc%20Paper).pdf [accessed 3/9/2003].
8. According to the *'Administration pénitentiaire: rapport annuel d'activité 2000'* online at: http://www.ladocumentationfrancaise.fr/BRP/024000162/0000.pdf [accessed 10/9/03]
9. Boyer 1998 estimates the number of Muslims in France to be around 4,155,000. He categorises them as follows: 2.9 million of North African descent, among whom 1.55 million from Algeria, 1 million from Morocco and 350,000 from Tunisia. In addition, there are 315,000 from Turkey and 250,000 from Black Africa. A further 100,000 are from the Middle East and about 350,000 are political asylum seekers. See also Frégosi, 1998.
10. One of German's *Länder* has also banned the wearing of scarves in state schools.
11. Most of them have not had the kind of employment that would have given them entitlement to benefits; and those below the age of 25 are not entitled to the minimum monthly unemployment benefit.

Chapter 4   The Practice of Islam in Prison

1. *The Prison Rules* 1999 (as amended in 2000) available online at: http://www.hmprisonservice.gov.uk/filestore/1027_1412.pdf [accessed 11/09/03].
2. HM Prison Service Order on *Religion*, PSO 4550, 2002, 1.10.

3. HM Prison Service Order on *Race Relations*, PSO 2800, 1997, Chap. 3.13.2.
4. HM Prison Service 'Prison Service Race Relations Policy Statement' *Prison Service Order on Race Relations* PSO 2800, 1997.
5. HM Prison Service *Prison Service Order on Religion*, PSO 4550, 2000.
6. HM Prison Service *Prison Service Order on Race Relations*, PSO 2800, 1997, 5.6.4.
7. See, especially, the document entitled 'Religion in the prisons of England and Wales' that was presented to the Home Secretary on 27 March 1996. Online document available at:
   http://www.angulimala.org.uk/Religion%20in%20Prisons%20(Disc%20Paper).pdf.
8. In the Chaplain General's words, 'The whole of the religion bit should be done within the Chaplaincy' (interview at Prison Service Headquarters, 13 May 2003).
9. HM Prison Service *Prison Service Order on Religion*, PSO 4500, 2000, 3.5.
10. HM Prison Service *Prison Service Order on Catering*, PSO 5000, 2001.
11. In the past, the nuns did the work of prison officers in women's prisons.
12. In fact there were 59 Muslim chaplains in France in 2001, 31 of whom were salaried employees of the French Prison Service. The prisoner wants to stress the insufficient number of Muslim chaplains in comparison to other faiths.
13. '*Bricolage*' means 'do-it-yourself' activity, often with the connotation of 'tinkering'.
14. In a prison near Metz, *halal* meat is available to all prisoners. Christians have no objection to that, and the Jews are a very tiny minority. But this is a local decision, at best.
15. Theoretically, only those prisoners who work in the kitchen or in related areas or who have the kind of job that prevents them from eating at normal hours have the right to prepare their own food. In practice, many inmates prepare their food with rudimentary utensils, or eat canned fish.
16. This question seems to be on the agenda in Prison B, and, according to the Director of the Women's section of Prison C, there will be *halal* meat for Muslim women in the prison's canteen in the future.
17. In some prisons in the Alsace-Moselle region of France, that is still subject to a Concordat, prison authorities have decided to serve only *halal* meat: in this way, Catholics who have no religious restrictions can eat it as well as Muslims. But some people fear that this might be used by extreme-right wing political movements to denounce the Islamisation of France and the capitulation to Muslims' demands.
18. Better known in Britain as the festival of Eid al-Fitr.

Chapter 5   Islam, 'Race' Relations and Discrimination in Prison

1. Our analysis in this section relies heavily on the pioneering work of McDermott (1989) and Genders and Player (1989).
2. Incidentally, there are limits to the inclusiveness of the Prison Service's policy: it denies recognition to the Church of Scientology, Rastafarianism and the Nation of Islam.
3. See Solomos, 1986; Benyon and Solomos, 1987; Waddington, 1992; Keith 1993.
4. http//www.hmprisonservice.gov.uk/corporate/dynpage.asp?page=104.
5. http://www.hmprisonservice.gov.uk/corporate/dynpage.asp?page=260.
6. By comparison, the percentage of all Home Office staff in the minority ethnic category was 18.2 per cent in April 2002. Minority ethnic staff in the Prison Service at *senior* Civil Service level amounted to 26.4 per cent (http://

www.civil-service.gov.uk/statistics/documents/pdf/ethnic02.pdf. Available online
Accessed 26/9/03).

7. See, in particular, reports by Burnett and Farrell, 1994; and National Association
of Probation Officers & the Association of Black Probation Officers, 1996.

8. Available online at http://www.hmprisonservice.gov.uk/statistics/ dynpage.asp?Page=1
[accessed 26/9/03].

9. The statistics published on the Prison Service website record a total staffing level
of 45,328, but 10.33 per cent of prison staff fall into the categories of 'Mixed'
'Other', 'Not Stated' and 'Data Unavailable'. It is possible, therefore, that the
number of Muslims could be slightly higher than our estimate of 1 per cent.

10. Lord Falconer, Hansard, House of Lords, 6 November 2002.

11. The Chief Inspector's report on a visit to this particular prison shortly before our
project began also found that Black and minority ethnic prisoners had reported
racism that was 'mild' and 'under the surface'.

12. Muslim prisoners can *volunteer* to observe Ramadan. It is not an automatic
consequence of registering as a Muslim. We found no evidence that prisoners
were put under pressure to join the list.

13. Burnett and Farrell's (1994: 53) finding that 'nearly three-quarters of the
officers described officer-inmate relations as "generally good"' is echoed in our
research.

14. This accords with the finding of Edgar and Martin, 2004: 20–3 about the
importance of prisoners' perceptions of the 'informal partiality' that prison
officers can exercise in allocating or permitting access to facilities, resources
and activities.

15. Not a single one of the 20 inmates with whom we held discussions in female
establishments reported that she knew the identity of her Race Relations Officer

16. After the completion of our interviews Boards of Visitors were re-named
'Independent Monitoring Groups'.

17. President Chirac commissioned a report on *laïcité* in July 2003 from a 20-person
committee that included well-known intellectuals and politicians but not a
single representative of a religious group. Under the chairmanship of Bernard
Stasi, Ombudsman and former politician, the committee considered the history
of *laïcité*, its current status and its likely future.

18. In 1989 and in 1995 many girls who wore a Muslim headscarf were excluded
from government schools (*écoles publiques*) because they were wearing an 'ostentatious' religious symbol. The problem with Muslim girls continued for some
years but with much less acrimony. See Gaspard and Khosrokhavar, 1995.

19. See Loch, 1995; Khosrokhavar, 1997.

20. A piece of twig used for cleaning teeth and gums.

Chapter 6 Categorisation and Self-definition among Muslim Prisoners

1. Black women amounted to 24 per cent of all female prisoners in the Black category.

2. Algerians are the most numerous immigrants in France. They number about
1.5 million, more than one million of whom are French citizens.

3. The sociology of the '*Banlieues*' was extensively developed in the 1990s in France.
See among others Dubet and Lapeyronnie, 1992; Castel, 1995.

4. The Directors of two of our prisons admitted that drug dealing took place within
their prisons.

5. This is on the whole what the young men who had returned to religion told us a few years previously: in a world where there is no hope for the future, by embracing Islam they opened up a future in the very long term, for eternity, beyond the uncertainties of this world where they had no place. See Khosrokhavar, 1997.

6. The majority of them are Muslim radicals, but some others, like the Basques or the Corsicans, fall into the same legal category.

7. We use the word 'Islamist', instead of 'Islamicist', to mean Islamic radical.

Chapter 7   Prison Imams

1. http://www.iesh.org/sommaire.htm.

2. http://www.eihs.org.uk/index.php. The Institute has an accreditation partnership with the University of Wales, Lampeter.

3. One such institution, the Markfield Institute in Leicester, operates in conjunction with the English system of state funded higher education but is based on Islamic principles. Its awards, validated by the University of Loughborough, include a two-semester Certificate in Muslim Chaplaincy. This course, which provides for a placement lasting 60 hours in a prison, is designed in collaboration with the Muslim Adviser and the Chaplaincy Training Officer. The Institute is sponsored by the Islamic Foundation. See http://www.mihe.org.uk/aboutus.html.

4. Since March 2003 a new Chaplaincy Starting Out course has been available to full-time and sessional chaplains of all faiths.

5. The number of Muslim ministers is 44 according to Ternissien (2002); 59 according to Colette and Letourneux (2002); 41 according to the Director of Prison A in April 2002; and 39 according to Thiébaud (2000). The '*Rapport annuel d'activité 2000*' for French prisons shows that there were 42 Muslim chaplains in post, of whom 19 were salaried. By 2003 the number had increased to 69 Muslim chaplains, of whom 30 were salaried.

6. '*Administration pénitentiaire: rapport annuel d'activité 2000*' online at: http://lesrapports.ladocumentationfrancaise.fr/BRP/024000162/0000.pdf [accessed 17.03.04].

7. They include the state's neutrality towards religion; the recognition that France is a religiously diverse country; and the exclusion of religion from the public sphere.

8. While we were conducting our research, there was discussion of appointing a part-time female Muslim teacher.

Chapter 8   Conclusions

1. According to the Head of the Faith Communities Unit in the Home Office 'policies for building community cohesion, promoting civic renewal and building active citizenship cannot be fully effective unless they take account of the particular needs and perspectives of faith communities' O'Beirne, 2004: i.

2. This is not to deny, of course, that many prisoners eventually learn how to restrict their interactions as far as possible to those with whom they feel some sympathy or shared interests.

3. Commission on British Muslims and Islamophobia, 1997, 2001, 2004; Cantle, 2001; Weller, Feldman and Purdam, 2001; Hepple and Chaudhury, 2001; Open Society Institute, 2002; Ansari, 2002.

4. This does not mean that Muslim chaplains are necessarily content with the practice of detaining prisoners without charge for indefinite periods of time.

5. At this time of writing, Muslims are particularly active in community chaplaincy at HMP Leeds and HMP YOI Feltham.
6. According to Ansari (2002: 31), 'Space in public life has been "stretched" to include Islam, and facilities now exist in Britain enabling Islam to be practised in diverse ways', but the Commission on British Muslims and Islamophobia (2001: 23) still insists that 'Legislation needs to be altered in order to give members of non-Christian religions the same recognition as is provided for Christians' in prisons and hospitals.

References

Adil, A. (1998) 'Muslim Advisor for Prison Service'. *Muslim News* 25th December: 1.

Al-Khoei, Y. (2001) 'UK: Muslims in prisons and the NCWMP'. *Dialogue* (November): 3.

Amiraux, V. (2002) 'The situation of Muslims in France' in *Monitoring the EU Accession Process: Minority Protection*, vol. 2, Open Society Institute.

Ansari, H. (2002) *Muslims in Britain*. London: Human Rights International.

Anwar, M. and Q. Bakhsh (2003) *British Muslims and State Policies*. University of Warwick, Centre for Research in Ethnic Relations.

Archer, M. (1995) *Realist Social Theory: A Morphogenetic Approach*. Cambridge: Cambridge University Press.

Banton, M. (1967) *Race relations*. London: Tavistock.

Barth, F. (1969) *Ethnic groups and boundaries*. London: Allen & Unwin.

Baubérot, J. (1997) *La morale laïque contre l'ordre moral*. Paris: Seuil.

Baubérot, J. (2000) *Histoire de la Laïcité*. Paris: PUF.

Baumann, G. (1999) *The Multicultural Riddle. Rethinking National, Ethnic, and Religious Identities*. London: Routledge.

Beckford, J. A. (1999) 'Social justice and religion in prison: the case of England and Wales'. *Social Justice Research* 12 (4): 315–22.

Beckford, J. A. and S. Gilliat (1996) *The Church of England and other faiths in a multi-faith society*. University of Warwick.

Beckford, J. A. and S. Gilliat (1998) *Religion in Prison. Equal Rites in a Multi-Faith Society*. Cambridge: Cambridge University Press.

Benbassa, E. (2003) *La France face à ses Immigrés*. Paris: Mille et Une Nuits.

Benyon, J. and J. Solomos (eds) (1987) *The Roots of Urban Unrest*. Oxford: Pergamon.

Boepflug, F., Dunand, F. and Willaime, J-P. (1996) *Pour une Mémoire des Religions*. Paris: La Découverte/Essais.

Botterhill, D. and M. Gora (2000) *Guidelines for the Preparation of Food for Muslim Prisoners and Procedures for Ramadan*. London: Iqra Trust.

Boyer, A. (1998) *L'islam de France*. Paris: Presses Universitaires de France.

Bradney, A. (1993) *Religions, Rights and Laws*. Leicester: University of Leicester Press.

Brown, C. (1984) *Black and White Britain: the third PSI Surrey*. London: Heinemann.

Burlet, S. and H. Reid (1998) 'A gendered uprising: political representation and minority ethnic communities'. *Ethnic and Racial Studies* 21(2): 271–287.

Burnett, R. and G. Farrell (1994) 'Reported and Unreported Racial Incidents in Prisons'. Oxford: University of Oxford Centre for Criminological Research.

Burnley Task Force (2001) 'Report of an inquiry into disturbances in Burnley in June 2001'.

Candappa, M. and D. Joly (1994) *Local authorities, ethnic minorities and pluralist integration*. University of Warwick, Centre for Research in Ethnic Relations.

Cantle, T. (2001). 'Community cohesion: a report of the independent review team'. London: Home Office.

Carter, R. (2000), *Realism and Racism: Concepts of Race in Sociological Research*. London: Routledge.

Castel, R. (1995) *Les métamorphoses de la question sociale*. Paris: Fayard.

Cesari, J. (1998) *Musulmans et Républicains. Les Jeunes, l'Islam et la France.* Bruxelles Complexe.

Colette, E. and F. Letourneau (2002) 'L'Islam derrière les barreaux'. *L'Intelligent*, 2186 2nd December.

Combessie, P. (2001) *Sociologie de prison.* Paris: La Découverte.

Commission on British Muslims and Islamophobia (1997) *Islamophobia: A Challenge for Us All.* London: Runnymede Trust.

Commission on British Muslims and Islamophobia (2001) *Addressing the Challenge of Islamophobia. Progress Report, 1999–2001.* London: CBMI.

Commission on British Muslims and Islamophobia (2004) *Islamophobia: issues challenges and action.* Stoke on Trent: Trentham Books.

Commission for Racial Equality (nd) 'The management of Race Relations within prison establishments'. London: CRE.

Commission for Racial Equality (2003a) 'The murder of Zahid Mubarek. A formal investigation by the Commission for Racial Equality into HM Prison Service of England and Wales', Part 1. London: CRE.

Commission for Racial Equality (2003b) 'Racial equality in prisons. A formal investigation by the Commission for Racial Equality into HM Prison Service of England and Wales', Part 2.

Coyle, A. (2002) *A Human Rights Approach to Prison Management.* London International Centre for Prison Studies.

Daniel, W. W. (1968) *Racial Discrimination in England.* London: PEP/Penguin.

Dubet, F. (1987) *La Galère: jeunes en survie.* Paris: Fayard.

Dubet, F. and D. Lapeyronnie (1992) *Les Quartiers de l'Exil.* Paris: Seuil.

Edgar, K. and C. Martin (2004) 'Perceptions of race and conflict: perspectives of minority ethnic prisoners and of prison officers'. Home Office Online Report, no. 11/04. London: Home Office. Online at: http://www.homeoffice.gov.uk/rds/pdfs2/rdsolr1104.pdf [accessed 01.04.04].

El Hassan S. (1999) *Practising Islam in Prison.* London: Iqra Trust.

Ellis, T., C. Tedstone, *et al.* (2004) 'Improving race relations in prisons: what works?' Home Office Online Report 12/04. London: Home Office. Online at: http://www.homeoffice.gov.uk/rds/pdfs2/rdsolr1204.pdf. [Accessed 02.04.04].

Fanon, F. (1975) *Pour la Révolution africaine.* Paris: Maspéro.

FitzGerald, M. and P. Marshall (1996) 'Ethnic minorities in British prisons: some research implications' in *Prisons 2000.* R. Matthews and P. Francis (eds). London: Macmillan: 139–62.

Foucault Michel (1975) *Surveiller et punir, naissance de la prison.* Paris: Gallimard.

Frégosi, F. (ed.) (1998) *La Formation des Cadres musulmans de France.* Paris: L'Harmattan.

Gaspard, F. and F. Khosrokhavar (1995) *Le foulard et la République.* Paris: La Découverte.

Gauchet, M. (1998) *La Religion dans la démocratie, parcours de la laïcité.* Paris: Gallimard.

Genders E. and E. Player (1989) *Race Relations in Prisons.* Oxford: Clarendon Press.

Gilliat-Ray, S. (2001) 'Sociological perspectives on the pastoral care of minority faiths in hospital' in *Spirituality in Health Care Contexts.* H. Orchard (ed.). London: Jessica Kingsley Publishers: 135–46.

Goffman, E. (1990) *Asiles, Etudes sur la condition sociale des malades mentaux.* Paris: Minuit [published in English as *Asylums.* Harmondsworth: Pelican in 1968].

Guessous, F., N. Hopper and U. Moorthy (2000) 'Religion in Prisons 1999 and 2000'. *National Statistics Bulletin*, 15/01. London: National Statistics.

Hargreaves, J. (nd) 'Caring about other faiths'. London: Prison Service Chaplaincy, 2 pp.

Hepple, B., and Choudhury, T. (2001) 'Tackling religious discrimination: practical implications for policy-makers and legislators'. Home Office Research Study 221. London: Home Office.

Hewer, C. (1994) 'Recent developments amongst Muslims in Britain'. Birmingham: CSIC, No. 13. December.

HM Chief Inspector of Prisons (2000) *Annual Report*. London: Stationery Office.

HM Chief Inspector of Prisons (2002) *Annual Report*. London: Stationery Office.

HM Prison Service (nd) *Race Relations and Religion, A pocket guide for prison staff*. London: HM Prison Service.

HM Prison Service (1991) *Race Relations Manual*. London: HM Prison Service.

HM Prison Service (1997) *Prison Service Order on Race Relations*. PSO 2800. London: HM Prison Service [revised 2002].

HM Prison Service (1999) *Prison Rules*. Online at: http://www.penlex.org.uk/pages/rules99.htm.

HM Prison Service (2000) *Prison Service Order on Religion*. PSO 4550. London: HM Prison Service.

HM Prison Service (2001) *Prison Service Catering Manual*. PSO 5000. London: HM Prison Service.

Home Office (1999) *Inside Faith. The Prison Service Chaplaincy*. London: HMSO.

Home Office (2001) 'Building Cohesive Communities: a report of the ministerial group on public order and community cohesion'. London: Home Office.

Home Office (2004) 'Religion in England and Wales: Findings from the 2001 Home Office Citizenship Survey'. Home Office Research Study 274. London: Home Office.

Hyest, J-J. and G-P. Cabanel (2001) 'La lutte contre le racisme et la xénophobie', rapport présenté à Monsieur le Premier Ministre, Commission nationale consultative des droits de l'homme, Paris.

Jacobson, J. (1997) 'Religion and ethnicity: dual and alternative sources of identity among young Pakistanis'. *Ethnic and Racial Studies* (20) 2: 238–56.

Jenkins, R. (1997) *Rethinking ethnicity*. London: Sage.

Joly, D. (1995) *Britannia's Crescent: Making a place for Muslims in British Society*. Aldershot: Avebury.

Joly, D. (1996) *Haven or Hell: Asylum policies and refugees in Europe*. Oxford: Macmillan.

Joly, D. (2001) *Blacks and Britannity*. Aldershot: Avebury.

Joly, D. and K. Imtiaz (2002) 'Muslims and citizenship in the United Kingdom' in R. Leveau, K. Mohsen-Finan and C. de Wenden (eds), *New European Identity and Citizenship*. Aldershot: Ashgate: 117–33.

Joly, D. and J. Nielsen (1985) *Muslims in Britain: an annotated bibliography, 1960/1984*. University of Warwick, Centre for Research in Ethnic Relations.

Jupp, V. (1989) *Methods of Criminological Research*. London: Allen & Unwin.

Jupp, V., P. Davies and P. Francis (eds) (2000) *Doing Criminological Research*. London: Sage.

Kahani-Hopkins, V. and N. Hopkins (2002) '"Representing" British Muslims: the strategic dimension to identity construction'. *Ethnic and Racial Studies* (25) 2: 288–309.

Keith, M. (1993) *Race, Riots and Policing. Lore and Disorder in a Multi-Racist Society*. London: UCL Press.

Kelly, L. (2001) 'Programme, policies, people: the interaction between Bosnia refugees and British society'. Unpublished PhD thesis, University of Warwick.

Kelly, L. and D. Joly (1999) 'Refugees' reception and Settlement in Britain'. Coventry A report for the Joseph Rowntree Foundation.

Kepel, G. (1993) *À L'ouest d'Allah*. Paris: Seuil.

Khosrokhavar, F. (1996) 'L'universel abstrait, le politique et la construction d l'islamisme comme forme d'altérité' pp. 113–51 in M. Wieviorka (ed.), *Une sociéé fragmentée?* Paris: La Découverte.

Khosrokhavar, F. (1997) *L'Islam des Jeunes*. Paris: Flammarion.

Khosrokhavar, F. (2000) 'L'Islam des jeunes Musulmans', *Comprendre* 1: 81–97.

Khosrokhavar, F. (2002) *Les nouveaux Martyrs d'Allah*. Paris: Flammarion.

Khosrokhavar, F. (2004) *L'Islam dans les Prisons*. Paris: Balland.

Knott, K. and Khokher, S. (1993) 'Religious and ethnic identity among youn Muslim women in Bradford'. *New Community* 19 (4): 593–610.

Kymlicka, W. (ed.) (1995) *The Rights of Minority Cultures*. New York: OUP.

Lapeyronnie, D. (1993) *L'individu et les minorités*. Paris: Presses Universitaires d France.

Law, I. (1996) *Racism, ethnicity and social policy*. Hemel Hempstead: Prentice Hall.

Law, I. (1999) 'Modernity, anti-racism and ethnic managerialism', in P. Bagguley an J. Hearn (eds) *Transforming Politics*. Houndsmill: Macmillan: 206–26.

Layton-Henry, Z. (1984) *The politics of immigration*. Oxford: Blackwell.

Le Caisne, L. (2000) *Prison: une ethnologue en Centrale*. Paris: Odile Jacob.

Leech, M. and D. Cheney (2001) *The Prisons Handbook*. Winchester: Waterside Press.

Levi-Strauss, C. (1997) *Race et histoire*. Paris: Gallimard.

Lewis, P. (1994) *Muslim Britain*. London: I. B. Tauris.

Lindley, J. (2002) 'Race or religion? The impact of religion on the employment an earnings of Britain's ethnic communities'. *Journal of Ethnic and Migration Studie* 28 (3): 427–42.

Lloyd, C. (1998) *Discourses of antiracism in France*. Aldershot: Ashgate.

Loch, D. (1995) 'Moi, Khaled Kelkal'. *Le Monde*, October 7th (the interview wa conducted October 3rd, 1992).

Macey, M. (1999) 'Class, gender and religious influences on changing patterns o Pakistani Muslim male violence in Bradford'. *Ethnic and Racial Studies*, 22 (5) 845–66.

Macpherson, Sir W. (1999) *The Stephen Lawrence Inquiry: Report of an Inquiry b Sir William Macpherson of Cluny*. London: The Stationery Office.

Marpsat, M. and R. Laurent (1997) 'Le chômage des jeunes est aggravé par l'apparte nance à un quartier en difficulté?', in *En Marge de la Ville, au Coeur de la Société, ces Quartiers dont on parle*. Paris: Editions l'Aube.

McDermott, K. (1989) '"We have no problem": the experience of racism in prison' in *International Migration Review* 23: 213–28.

Memmi, A. (1972) *Portrait du colonisé*. Montréal: L'Etincelle.

Miles, R. (1989) *Racism*. London: Routledge.

Miles, R. and A. Phizacklea (1984) *White man's country*. London: Pluto Press.

Modood, T. (1990) 'Muslims, race and equality in Britain'. Birmingham: CSIC, No. 1, June.

Modood, T. (1992) *Not easy being British. Colour, culture and citizenship*. Stoke-on-Trent: Runnymede Trust and Trentham Books.

Modood, T. (1994) 'Muslim identity: social reality or political project?' in J. Rex and Tariq Modood (eds) *Muslim identity real or imagined?*. Birmingham: CSIC Papers 12, November: pp. 7–12.

Modood, T. (2000) 'Anti-Essentialism, Multiculturalism and the "Recognition" of Religious Groups', in W. Kymlicka and W. Norman (eds), *Citizenship in Diverse Societies*. Oxford: Oxford University Press.

Modood, T. and P. Werbner (eds) (1997) *The politics of multiculturalism in the new Europe*. London: Zed.

Mohammed, J. (1992) *Race Relations and Muslims in Great Britain*. London: Muslim Parliament of Great Britain.

Morén-Alegret, R. (2002) *Integration and resistance*. Aldershot: Ashgate.

NACRO (2000) *Race and prisons. A Snapshot Survey*. London: NACRO.

Nahdi, F. (2004) 'Bring back real Islam to our shores'. *The Guardian* 7 April.

National Association of Probation Officers and the Association of Black Probation Officers (1996) 'Race discrimination and the criminal justice system', online document at: http://www.blink.org.uk/abpoa.htm [accessed 21/5/02].

Nielsen, J. (1992) 'Islams, Muslims and British local and central government'. Birmingham: CSIC Papers, May.

Nielsen, J. (1997) 'Muslims in Europe: history revisited as a way forward?' *Islam and Christian Muslim Relations* (8) 2: 135–287.

Nielsen, J. (1999) *Towards a European Islam*. Basingstoke: Macmillan.

O'Beirne, M. (2004) 'Religion in England and Wales: Findings from the 2001 Home Office Citizenship Survey'. Home Office Research Study 274. London: Home Office.

Oldham (2001) 'Oldham Independent Review Panel Report', 11 December.

Open Society Institute (2002) 'The Situation of Muslims in the UK', pp. 361–444 in *Monitoring the EU Accession Process: Minority Protection*. Budapest: Open Society Institute.

Potter, H. (1991) 'Speaking from the heart'. *New Life* 8: 67.

Poulat, E. (1987) *Liberté, laïcité, la guerre des deux France et le principe de la modernité*. Paris: Cerf/Cujas.

Race Equality Advisor (2000) 'Assessment of race relations at HMP Brixton'. London: RESPOND. Online at www.hmprisonservice.gov.uk/filestore/202_206.pdf. [accessed 25/9/03].

Recht, S. (2002) 'Anti-discrimination legislation in EU member states. France', report prepared under the guidance of the Migration Policy Group. Vienna: The European Monitoring Centre on Racism and Xenophobia.

Rex, J. (1988) *The Ghetto and the underclass*. Aldershot: Avebury.

Rex, J. and B. Drury (1994) *Ethnic Mobilisation in a Multi-Cultural Europe*. Aldershot: Avebury.

Rex, J., D. Joly and C. Wilpert (eds) (1987) *Immigrant associations in Europe*. Aldershot: Avebury.

Rex, J. and R. Moore (1967) *Race, Community and Conflict: a study of Sparkbrook*. Oxford: Oxford University Press.

Rex, J. and S. Tomlinson (1979) *Colonial immigrants in a British city: a class analysis*. London: Routledge.

Sacranie, I. (1998) 'Feeling of alienation due to marginalisation'. *Muslim News*, 25 December: 7 .

Sacranie, I. (1998) 'Recognising Muslims as a religious group'. *Muslim News*, 25 December: 7.

Saifullah Khan, V. (1977) 'The Pakistanis: Mirpuri villagers at home and in Bradford', in *Between two cultures*, J. L. Watson (ed.). London: Blackwell: 57–89.

Samad, Y. (1997) 'The plural guises of multiculturalism: Conceptualising a fragmented paradigm' in *The Politics of Multiculturalism in the New Europe*. T. Modood and P. Werbner (eds). London: Zed Books: 240–60.

Scarman, Lord (1981) *The Brixton Disorders 10–12 April 1981*. London: HMSO.

Schiffauer, W. (1998) 'The civil society and the outsider. Drawing the boundaries in four political cultures'. Online at http://viadrina.euv-frankfurt-o.de/~anthro veronli_s.html, accessed 25/07/2001, 11 pp.

Smith, A. D. (1981) *The Ethnic Revival*. Cambridge: Cambridge University Press.

Smith, D. (1974) *Racial Discrimination in Employment*. London: PEP.

Smith, G. (2004) 'Faith in community and communities of faith? Government rhetoric and religious identity in urban Britain'. *Journal of Contemporary Religion* 19 (2): 185–204.

Solomos, J. (1986) 'Riots, urban protest and social policy: the interplay of reform and social control'. *Policy Papers in Ethnic Relations*, no. 7, University of Warwick Centre for Research in Ethnic Relations.

Spalek, B. and D. Wilson (2001) 'Not just "visitors" to prison: the experiences of Imams who work inside the penal system'. *The Howard Journal* 40 (1): 3–13.

Stasi, B. (2003) 'Rapport de la commission de réflexion sur l'application du principe de laïcité dans la République'. Paris: la Documentation Française.

Ternissien, X. (2002) *La France des Mosquées*. Paris: Albin Michel.

Thiébaud, J-M. (2000) *Prison et Justice: Mode d'Emploi pour les Détenus et leurs Familles* Paris: L'Harmattan.

Tietze, N. and F. Khosrokhavar (1999) 'Violences, médias et intégration' in *Violence en France*. M. Wieviorka (ed.). Paris: Seuil.

Tournier, P. (2000) 'Apports de la démographie à l'étude du changement dans l'univers carcéral (1978–1998)' in *La Prison en Changement*. C. Veil and D. Lhuilier (eds). Paris: Erès: 103–26.

Vagg, J. (1991) 'Correcting manifest wrongs? Prison grievance and inspection procedures in England and Wales, France, Germany and the Netherlands' in *Imprisonment: European Perspectives*. J. Muncie and R. Sparks (eds). London: Harvester Wheatsheaf: 146–65.

Vagg, J. (1994) *Prison Systems: A Comparative Study of Accountability in England, France, Germany and the Netherlands*. Oxford: Clarendon Press.

Vasseur, V. (2000) *Médecin-Chef à la Prison de la Santé*. Paris: Le Cherche Midi.

Waddington, D. (1992) *Contemporary Issues in Public Disorder*. London: Routledge.

Wahlbeck, O. (1999) *Kurdish diasporas: a comparative study of Kurdish refugee communities*. Basingstoke: Macmillan.

Walman, S. (1986) 'Ethnicity and the boundary process in context' in J. Rex and D. Mason (eds) *Theories of Race and Ethnic Relations*. Cambridge: Cambridge University Press: 226–65.

Walmsley, R., L. Howard and S. White (1992) 'The National Prison Survey: Main Findings'. London: HMSO.

Weber, Max (1978) *Economy and Society*. Berkeley: University of California Press.

Weller, P., Feldman, A. and K. Purdam (2001) 'Religious discrimination in England and Wales'. Home Office Research Study 220. London: Home Office.

Wieviorka, M. (2001) *La Différence*. Paris: Balland.

Willaime, J-P. (2004) *Europe et Religions. Les Enjeux du XXIᵉ Siècle*. Paris: Fayard.

Wilson, B. R. (1995) 'Religious toleration, pluralism and privatization'. *Kirchliche Zeitgeschichte* 8 (1): 99–116.

Wilson, D. (2000) *Prison Imams. An Ethno-Graphic Study*. London: Iqra Trust.

Wilson, D. and D. Sharp (1998) *Visiting prisons; a handbook for imams*. London: Iqra Trust.

Glossary

Ahmadis. Followers of Mirza Ghulam Ahmad of Qadiyan in India (1839–1908), properly divided into *Lahori Ahmadi*s and *Qadiyani Ahmadi*s. The *Lahori* following recognise Ahmad as a 'renewer' of the faith (*mujadid*) whereas the *Qadiyani*s claim he was a prophet (*nabi*); the latter is rather problematic as the orthodox Muslim belief is that there is no prophet after Muhammad.

Alhamdulillah. Arabic. Linguistically it means 'All praise be to God'; an expression of gratitude to God.

Apna. Urdu. Linguistically it means 'our own'; a term of self-identification as 'ourselves'.

Arabe. Second (or even third) generation of French citizens with North African backgrounds. The word also applies to Arabs in general, but in the specific context of contemporary France it applies mainly to people of North African backgrounds who live in poor suburbs.

Arabe de service. Token Arab.

As-salamu 'alaykum. Arabic. Linguistically 'Peace be upon you'; the usual greeting offered by Muslims.

Banlieue. Poor suburb, with roughly the same meaning as *Cité*. The word originally meant simply a 'suburb' but it now refers largely to disadvantaged suburbs with high rates of unemployment and deprivation, high density of residents with backgrounds in North Africa, Sub-Saharan Africa or South East Asia, high rates of crime and strong feelings of insecurity.

Banlieusard. A resident of the Banlieues, especially young men with a bad reputation for their supposedly aggressive attitude and their anti-social behaviour.

Beur. An inverted and modified slang word for 'Arab'. It refers to the second generation of French citizens with North African backgrounds. The word can carry a derogatory connotation that is resented by many people, including Arabs.

Braquage. Armed robbery.

Circular Instructions. Instructions issued by the Prison Service of England and Wales to prison Governors.

Cité. A poor suburb where levels of poverty and exclusion are high. '*Cités*' are usually part of municipal authorities, but the word can also apply to districts of a city where poor or deprived people live such as Neuhof in Strasbourg, North East France. The same is true for Marseille and its northern district.

Commission d'Application des Peines. A small Committee in each prison that offers advice to the Juge d'Application des Peines.

Conseil d'Etat. France's highest administrative court.

Da'wa. Arabic. Its linguistic meaning is 'Invitation' or 'Summons'; in Muslim terminology, it usually refers to the invitation to Islam through propagation by word or example.

Du'a. Arabic. 'Supplication', i.e. to God.

Eid al-Adha. Arabic. Linguistically, 'The Feast of Sacrifice'; in Muslim terminology, it refers to the festival on the 10th day of the 12th month in the Muslim calendar, commemorating the story of the Prophet Abraham and his son. Also known as *Eid al-Kabir*

Eid al-Fitr. Arabic. Linguistically, 'the Feast of Fast-Breaking'; in Muslim terminology, it refers to the festival marking the end of Ramadan, the 9th month in the Muslim calendar in which Muslims fast from dawn till dusk. [Hence it is on the 1st day of *Shawal*, the 10th month.]

Eid al-Kabir. Arabic. Linguistically, 'the Great Feast'. See *Eid al-Adha*.

Fiqh. Arabic. Linguistically, 'understanding'; in Muslim terminology it refers to understanding specific details of practice in Muslim jurisprudence.

Fundamentalist. A theological term that originates in late nineteenth century Protestantism in the USA but which has come to mean 'radically extreme'. Journalists use it interchangeably with '*intégriste*' in French. Muslims often take exception to being called 'fundamentalist', since it implies that one should not follow the fundamentals, which would then lead to heresy.

Galère. Hell on earth.

Gamelle. French prison slang for a meal.

Ghusl. Arabic. Linguistically it means 'Bath'; in Muslim terminology it refers to a bath that removes major ritual impurities from the individual. (A Muslim must be free of such ritual purities in order to offer his/her ritual prayers.)

Gora. Urdu. Linguistically it means 'fair'; colloquial term for a Caucasian.

Gradé. A Senior or Principal Officer in French prisons.

Greffe. Prison records office or registry.

Gris. Arabs who live in the Banlieues and who are not socially or economically integrated in mainstream French society. The literal meaning of the word is 'grey'.

Gros braqueurs. Heavily armed criminals.

Hadith. Arabic. Linguistically, 'Report'; in Muslim terminology it usually refers to a report of what the Prophet Muhammad said.

Halal. Arabic. Linguistically, 'Licit' or 'Permissible'; i.e. in accordance with Muslim jurisprudence. It often refers to food ['*halal* food'], which would mean food that was licit or permissible to eat (since certain types of foods are not permissible under Muslim jurisprudence).

Haram. Arabic. Linguistically, 'Illicit' or 'Forbidden', according to Muslim jurisprudence.

Harkis. North African troops who remained loyal to France during the struggles for Algerian independence.

Hashma. Arabic. 'Shame'.

Haut Conseil à l'Intégration. High Council on Integration, an agency of the state for overseeing the integration of minorities into French society.

Hijab. Arabic. Linguistically, 'a concealment' or 'a barrier'; in Muslim terminology, it may refer to the name of a garment that covers the head, excluding the face, which many Muslim women wear as a religious or cultural obligation.

Hizb-ut-Tahrir. Arabic. Linguistically, 'Party of Liberation'. A political movement that originated in Jerusalem in the 1950s, dedicated to creating an Islamic revolutionary state in the Arab world.

Inspection des Services Pénitentiaires. French prison service's internal inspection department.

Inspection Générale des Affaires Sociales. French government inspectorate of social services.

Intégriste. A person whose religious outlook is not compatible with the French expectation that religious feelings should not be expressed in public and who is suspected of being mildly intolerant. The term is ambiguous enough to include all outlooks that call *laïcité* into question. The word is becoming synonymous with 'fundamentalist'.

Islamiste. This term has yet to be adequately defined; in popular parlance, it may refer to a Muslim who is 'radical' and 'extreme', particularly in political matters, although not exclusively.

Jeunes. Young men who live in the Banlieues. It is a vague term, including men as old as 30, that usually refers specifically to 'Arab' Frenchmen. It is a euphemistic way of avoiding direct talk of ethnicity.

Jihad. Arabic. Linguistically, 'struggle' or 'striving': it can take a number of different forms, whether it be a martial form in defence of Islam, or the eradication of poverty, and the like. Commonly translated as 'Holy War', which is rather misleading.

Juges d'Application des Peines. Judges attached to prisons who advise Directors on the treatment of inmates and who make decisions about home leave and parole.

Jumu'a or **Jummah**. Arabic. Linguistically 'congregation'; often referring to the prayer at midday on Friday (*Salat-al-Jumu'a*) that is compulsory for all able sane male Muslim mature residents to attend; alternatively, it may refer simply to the day of Friday.

Ka'aba. Arabic. 'Cube'. It commonly refers to the cube-like stone structure in Mecc that according to Muslim tradition (and also pre-Islamic tradition) was built as 'House of God' in the time of Adam. Muslims around the world face the direction o the *Ka'aba* in their ritual prayers.

Kalb. Arabic. 'Dog'.

Kaleh. Urdu. Linguistically 'blacks' (plural of *kalah* [black]); referring to dark-skinnee individuals.

Kalima. Arabic. Linguistically, 'word' or 'phrase'; in Muslim terminology, ofter referring to the words an individual says in the *shahada* (testification of faith).

Khutba. Arabic. 'Sermon'. A *khutba* would be obligatory to perform in a number o Muslim observances, including the weekly congregational sermon and prayer or Friday midday.

Klebs. The plural of *'kalb'* (i.e. 'dog') in Maghrebi Arabic is *kleb*. In Maghrebi French colloquial, the plural form is given as *kleb*s (i.e. *kleb* made plural).

Laïcité. A legal, moral and political principle of State neutrality in matters of religior which excludes them from the public sphere.

Maghrébin. A person from the former French colonies of Algeria, Morocco or Tunisia – or a descendant of immigrants to France from North Africa.

Maton. French slang for Prison Officer or 'screw'.

Najas. Arabic. Linguistically, 'filthy'. For Muslims, it means the kind of impurity that is associated with touching or eating pork.

Namaz. Urdu, originally Farsi/Persian. 'Ritual prayer'; the equivalent word in Arabic and Muslim terminology is *'salat'*.

Naze. Bad or dirty in Maghrebi French colloquial (*najas* possibly the original word which would be Arabic for 'unclean').

Rak'a. Arabic. Linguistically, 'cycle'; in Muslim terminology, it would usually refer to a cycle in the ritual prayer, which would include standing and reciting the Qur'an, bowing and prostrating twice.

Robeux. Inverted French slang for 'Arabs'.

Salafi. Arabic. Adjective, derived from *salaf*, which literally means 'predecessors'. In modern parlance, it refers to a movement amongst Muslims who claim to follow the practice of the companions of the Prophet Muhammad, and the two generations after them. The assertion is, implicitly and explicitly, that Muslims not of this move- ment have strayed from that practice; something that the overwhelming majority of the Muslim world community does not accept.

Salat. Arabic. Linguistically, 'prayer': referring to ritual prayers that Muslims offer. One of the five pillars of Islam is the requirement to offer the five obligatory ritual prayers every day.

Sapara. Urdu. A term for 1/30th of the Qur'an (in teaching, the Qur'an is often split up into 30 sections, each of which is called a *juz* in Arabic, and a *sapara* in Urdu).

Shahada. Arabic. Linguistically 'testimony'; in Muslim terminology, this refers most often to testifying, or bearing witness to, faith in the words 'There is no god but God, and Muhammad is his messenger'.

Shahid. Arabic. Literally, 'witness'; in Muslim terminology, this may refer to one who has borne witness to faith through death (i.e. martyrdom), but the meaning of the word is more wide-ranging.

Shaytan. Arabic for 'Satan', the Devil.

Shaykh. Arabic. Linguistically, 'old man'; in Muslim terminology it usually refers to a male (the female would be called '*shaykha*') well versed in some way, particularly in a sacred science such as law or mysticism. In some parts of the Arab world, it has also taken on the meaning of 'leader'.

Sihr. Arabic. 'Magic'.

Siwak. Arabic. 'Toothstick'. A piece of twig used for cleaning teeth and gums; a practice of the Prophet Muhammad.

Subh. Arabic. 'Dawn'. It often refers to *salat-al-subh*, i.e. the ritual prayer offered at dawn.

Sujun. Arabic. 'Imprisonment'.

Surveillant. Prison officer in a French prison.

Tablighi Jama'. Urdu. 'The congregation that conveys'. A spiritual movement originating in India in the early twentieth century that seeks to convey the message of Islam. In Arabic, the same group is referred to as ' *jam'at al-da'wa*'. It is probably the most important transnational Islamic organisation in the world, with headquarters in Pakistan and a European centre in England.

Téléphone arabe. Bush telephone.

Vajib. Urdu. See *wajib*.

Wajib. Arabic. 'Necessary'; in Muslim terminology it refers to those actions that are considered legally necessary. In Urdu, it is sometimes pronounced as *vajib*.

Wudu' or *Wudhu*. Arabic. Linguistically, 'ablution'; in Muslim terminology it refers to a ritual washing that removes minor ritual impurities from the individual. (A Muslim must have full purity before offering his/her ritual prayers.)

Index

Printed in the United States
71134LV00001B/46